Western Film
Highlights

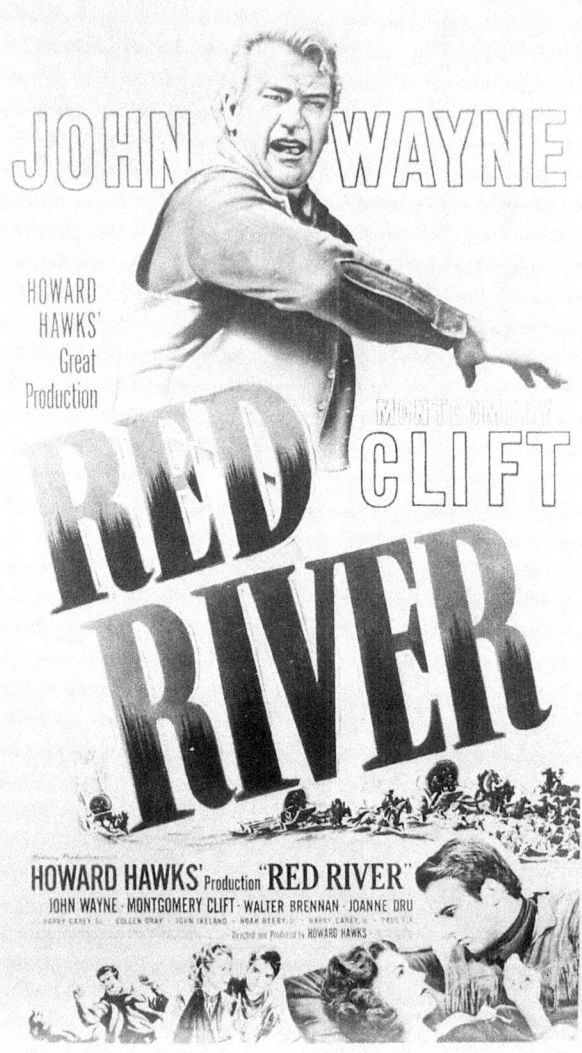

WESTERN FILM HIGHLIGHTS

The Best of the West, 1914–2001

Henryk Hoffmann

McFarland & Company, Inc., Publishers
Jefferson, North Carolina, and London

ALSO BY HENRYK HOFFMANN

"A" Western Filmmakers: A Biographical Dictionary of Writers, Directors, Cinematographers, Composers, Actors and Actresses (McFarland, 2000; paperback 2008)

FRONTISPIECE: American poster for *Red River* (UA, 1948)

The present work is a reprint of the illustrated case bound edition of Western Film Highlights: The Best of the West, 1914–2001, *first published in 2003 by McFarland.*

LIBRARY OF CONGRESS CATALOGUING-IN-PUBLICATION DATA

Hoffmann, Henryk, 1949–
Western film highlights : the best of the West, 1914–2001 / by Henryk Hoffmann.
p. cm.
Includes bibliographical references and index.

ISBN 978-0-7864-4501-1
softcover : 50# alkaline paper ∞

1. Western films—United States—History and criticism. I. Title.
PN1995.9.W4H54   2009   791.43'6278—dc21   2003006887

British Library cataloguing data are available

©2003 Henryk Hoffmann. All rights reserved

No part of this book may be reproduced or transmitted in any form or by any means, electronic or mechanical, including photocopying or recording, or by any information storage and retrieval system, without permission in writing from the publisher.

Front cover image ©2009 Comstock

Manufactured in the United States of America

*McFarland & Company, Inc., Publishers
Box 611, Jefferson, North Carolina 28640
www.mcfarlandpub.com*

To the two generations of the Hoffmann clan—in particular,
Barbara, Jerzy & Danuta,
and
Beata & Katarzyna—
always ready to talk film.

Acknowledgments

While my thanks are due to several people who helped me with this project in many different ways, at least two of them deserve special recognition in writing. Thus, I would like to express my sincere gratitude to my wife Betsy, my linguistic adviser as well as my faithful companion and guide during the endless search for obscure titles in hundreds of used book stores all over the eastern part of the United States. I am also grateful to her for her extensive support during both the conceptual and executive stages of the project. Moreover, I wish to acknowledge my manifold indebtedness to Jacek Jaroszyk, a friend of mine and president of the film society "Kinematograf '75" (Poznań, Poland) during those dozen years (1980s and early 1990s) when, together, we tried to revive the dying interest in the artistic cinema with numerous commemorative events.

Table of Contents

Acknowledgments vii
Preface 1

ANNUAL ENTRIES 1914 THROUGH 2001 3

Appendix A
Top 100 Films 145

Appendix B
Top 100 Novels Filmed 164

Appendix C
Top 10 Nonfiction Books Filmed 168

Appendix D
Top 25 Short Stories/Novellas Filmed 169

Appendix E
Top 50 Songs Used 171

Appendix F
Top 20 Authors 173

Appendix G
Top 20 Screenwriters 174

Appendix H
Top 20 Directors 175

Appendix I
Top 20 Cinematographers 176

Appendix J
Top 20 Composers 177

Table of Contents

Appendix K
Top 20 Leading Men   178

Appendix L
Top 20 Leading Ladies   179

Appendix M
Top 20 Supporting Actors   180

Appendix N
Top 20 Supporting Actresses   181

Select Bibliography   183

Index   185

Preface

While writing my first book, *"A" Western Filmmakers: A Biographical Dictionary of Writers, Directors, Cinematographers, Composers, Actors and Actresses*, I recognized the need to provide readers with instant information about the greatest western films of all time, as well as the significant achievements in each year of the genre's history. As this became impossible due to the scope of that project, the gap is filled now by *Western Film Highlights*, which thus emerges as a complement to *"A" Western Filmmakers*. The new book not only evaluates the genre in the 14 appendices composed of lists of the top western films, books, authors, directors, actors, and so on, but also evaluates the western film by listing the best achievements in multiple categories of the genre from 1914 through 2001.

The entries include the nine evaluated categories found in *"A" Western Filmmakers* (authors, screenwriters, directors, cinematographers, composers, leading men, leading ladies, supporting actors and supporting actresses), plus a few additional ones, such as best picture, best novel filmed, best nonfiction book filmed, best short story/novella filmed, and best song. The inclusion of some categories may depend upon a given year. For example, music and songs are obviously not evaluated until the sound era; cinematography, on the other hand, is sometimes represented by one category—either black-and-white only (in the old days) or color only (after 1964)—and sometimes by two categories for color and monochrome (1936–1964). At the same time, any category can be excluded in any year if there is no relevant achievement deserving recognition.

In *"A" Western Filmmakers*, I came up with the notion "quasi-western" to distinguish standard westerns from those that either do not meet the criteria set forth in the definition of a western (because of the time setting or location) or feature explicit and dominant elements of different genres. Since quasi-westerns are a matter of controversy, being included in the genre by some and excluded by others, I decided to include them in *"A" Western Filmmakers*, though with the indication "(q-w)." In this book, however, because of their aesthetic and thematic differences, quasi-westerns are excluded. (Consequently, for example, only songs from non-musical westerns are considered here.) Television productions are not taken into account either, but foreign western films are. Both quasi-westerns and television productions, however, do receive some consideration in the analytical parts of some entries, especially when they were nominated for or won major awards.

Preface

Each annual entry consists of three parts—Outstanding Achievements, the Academy Awards and Nominations (starting with 1929), and Deaths and/or Births of western-related celebrities—followed by a discussion and analysis of the year's achievements.

It needs to be made clear that all the appendices focus exclusively on people and achievements related to the western film (theatrical productions). Thus, no one should be surprised to find out that the list of top original authors lacks a number of outstanding western writers (e.g. Willa Cather, Elmer Kelton or Larry McMurtry), who have been excluded only because their work has not been sufficiently represented on the big screen.

In addition to some obvious abbreviations, two will be used quite often that may need to be explained: AA, standing for Academy Award, and AAN, meaning Academy Award nomination. The term "filmed as" is used extensively both in the annual entries and in the appendices, but it can mean a few different things: that a movie was based, inspired or suggested by a given literary work, or that a part of the work was used in the script.

While there is no limit to the number of pictures, novels, nonfiction books or short stories/novellas listed among the outstanding achievements in each annual entry, only three items per year were allowed in the remaining categories to keep the lists manageable and interesting.

Annual Entries 1914 through 2001

1914

Outstanding Achievements

PICTURE: *The Squaw Man; The Virginian; Salomy Jane; The Spoilers; Rose of the Rancho; Chip of the Flying U*
NOVEL FILMED: *The Virginian: A Horseman of the Plains* by Owen Wister, filmed as *The Virginian*; *The Spoilers* by Rex Beach; *Chip of the Flying U* by B.M. Bower
PLAY FILMED: *The Squaw Man* by Edwin Milton Royle; *The Rose of the Rancho* by David Belasco and Richard Walton Tully
SHORT STORY FILMED: "Salomy Jane's Kiss" by Bret Harte, filmed as *Salomy Jane*
SCREENPLAY (ADAPTATION): Cecil B. De Mille, *The Virginian*; Cecil B. De Mille, Oscar Apfel, *The Squaw Man*; Colin Campbell, *The Spoilers*
DIRECTION: Cecil B. De Mille, Oscar Apfel, *The Squaw Man*; Cecil B. De Mille, *The Virginian*; Colin Campbell, *The Spoilers*
CINEMATOGRAPHY: Alvin Wyckoff, *The Virginian*; Alfred Gandolfi, *The Squaw Man*; Alvin Wyckoff, *Rose of the Rancho*
MALE LEADING ROLE: Dustin Farnum, *The Virginian*; Dustin Farnum, *The Squaw Man*; William Farnum, *The Spoilers*
FEMALE LEADING ROLE: Beatriz Michelena, *Salomy Jane*; Winifred Kingston, *The Squaw Man*; Winifred Kingston, *The Virginian*
MALE SUPPORTING ROLE: J.W. Johnston, *The Virginian*; Frank Clark, *The Spoilers*; Billy Elmer, *The Virginian*
FEMALE SUPPORTING ROLE: Jane Darwell, *Rose of the Rancho*; Bessie Eyton, *The Spoilers*

Births. Writer Gordon D. Shirreffs; screenwriters Carl Foreman, Roland Kibbee; directors William Castle, Martin Ritt, Robert Wise; songwriter Stan Jones; actors Richard Basehart, David Brian, Richard Conte, Jeff Corey, Wendell Corey, Richard Denning, Charles Drake, Robert Emhardt, John Hodiak, John Ireland, Arthur Kennedy, Ian MacDonald, Charles McGraw, Frank Silvera, Woody Strode, Richard Widmark; actress Julie Bishop.

Just like Edwin S. Porter's *The Great Train Robbery* (1903) — a picture generally regarded as the first western—the other early western films were also shot on the East Coast. It was only because of the threat from the Trust, Edison's Patents Company trying to monopolize filmmaking in the United States, that several small and independent companies eventually went west. Thus, in the first, and at the beginning of the second decade of the twentieth century, more and more companies were producing western motion pictures in the area of Los Angeles, enjoying the more suitable scenery, cheap labor and the nearness to the Mexican border. Despite the emergence of the first western screen idol, Gilbert M. 'Broncho Billy' Anderson, as soon as 1910, and the artistic aspirations of some early western filmmakers (e.g. David Wark Griffith and Thomas H. Ince), the quality feature western (five reels or longer) was not born until 1914, which coincided with the arrival in California of Cecil B. De Mille.

De Mille broke into the motion picture industry in a spectacular way. First, together with Oscar Apfel, he wrote the script for and directed *The Squaw Man*, an impressive adaptation of Edwin Milton Royle's 1906 play telling a captivating story of an English exile marrying an Indian girl. Then, by himself, he undertook the first screen rendition of Owen Wister's quintessential 1902 western book *The Virginian*, (which was eventually selected as one the best 12 western novels by the Western Writers of America in their 1995 survey). Dustin Farnum and Winifred Kingston delivered memorable performances in both pictures.

Dustin Farnum's younger brother, William, played the leading role in Colin Campbell's *The Spoilers* (co-starring Thomas Santschi and Kathlyn Williams), the first screen version of the popular 1906 Alaska novel by Rex Beach. Thus, for a short time, the two brothers would be the dominant screen cowboys—at least until William S. Hart would take over.

In addition to *The Virginian* and *The Spoilers*, another major western novel found its way to the big screen. B.M. Bower's *Chip of the Flying U* (1904) became a minor four-reeler, with Tom Mix being the first (of several) Chip Bennett and Kathlyn Williams playing the Little Doctor. The film was directed by Colin Campbell.

To complete the 1914 scenario, the first great year for the western genre also offered one superior film based upon a story by Bret Harte, the master of the western short form. Searle Dawley and Alex E. Beyfuss's *Salomy Jane* (featuring Beatriz Michelena and House Peters) was inspired by Harte's short story "Salomy Jane's Kiss," as well as its stage adaptation by Paul Armstrong.

1915

Outstanding Achievements

PICTURE: *The Girl of the Golden West; Captain Courtesy; On the Night Stage; The Long Chance*

NOVEL FILMED: *The Long Chance* by Peter B. Kyne

PLAY FILMED: *The Girl of the Golden West* by David Belasco

SHORT STORY FILMED: "M'liss" by Bret Harte

SCREENPLAY (ORIGINAL): Edward Childs Carpenter, *Captain Courtesy*

SCREENPLAY (ADAPTATION): Cecil B. De Mille, *The Girl of the Golden West*

DIRECTION: Cecil B. De Mille, *The Girl of the Golden West*; Hobart Bosworth, *Captain Courtesy*

CINEMATOGRAPHY: Alvin Wyckoff, *The Girl of the Golden West*

MALE LEADING ROLE: House Peters, *The Girl of the Golden West;* Dustin Farnum, *Captain Courtesy;* William S. Hart, *On the Night Stage*

FEMALE LEADING ROLE: Mabel Van Buren, *The Girl of the Golden West;* Barbara Tenant, *M'liss;* Winifred Kingston, *Captain Courtesy*

MALE SUPPORTING ROLE: Billy Elmer, *The Girl of the Golden West;* Raymond Hatton, *The Girl of the Golden West*

FEMALE SUPPORTING ROLE: Winona Brown, *Captain Courtesy;* Anita King, *The Girl of the Golden West*

Births. Writers John M. Cunningham, Charles Neider, Lewis B. Patten; screenwriter Leigh Brackett; director William Witney; songwriters Ray Evans, Jay Livingston; actors Lyle Bettger, Yul Brynner, Jim Davis, John Dehner, Lorne Greene, Douglas Kennedy, Victor Mature, Gary Merrill, Henry (Harry) Morgan, Edmond O'Brien, Anthony Quinn, Fernando Rey, Dan Seymour, Frank Sinatra, Eli Wallach, Richard Webb, Cornel Wilde; actresses Helen Brown, Ellen Drew, Ann Sheridan.

Much less impressive than 1914, the year 1915 brought but a few major westerns, only one of which was a masterpiece of the genre. *The Girl of the Golden West*, based on the 1905 play by David Belasco, was brilliantly directed by Cecil B. De Mille, while the trio consisting of Mabel Van Buren, House Peters and Theodore Roberts delivered magnetic performances. Anita King, Billy Elmer and Raymond Hatton provided strong sup-port in smaller parts, while Alvin Wyckoff (who had photographed last year's *The Virginian* and *Rose of the Rancho*) once again did a great job behind the camera.

Dustin Farnum continued his career as a cowboy in Hobart Bosworth's superior *Captain Courtesy* (co-starring Winifred Kingston, again, and Herbert Standing), whereas William S. Hart—now a rising star—appeared in Reginald Barker's somewhat disappointing *On the Night Stage* (featuring Rhea Mitchell and Robert Edeson).

1916

Outstanding Achievements

PICTURE: *Hell's Hinges; The Apostle of Vengeance; A Knight of the Range; The Aryan; The Good Bad Man; The Parson of Panamint; Ramona; Tennessee's Partner; The Patriot*

NOVEL FILMED: *Ramona* by Helen Hunt Jackson; *Whispering Smith* by Frank H. Spearman; *The Three Godfathers* by Peter B. Kyne

SHORT STORY FILMED: "Tennessee's Partner" by Bret Harte; "The Parson of Panamint" by Peter B. Kyne; "In the Carquinez Woods" by Bret Harte, filmed as *The Half Breed*

SCREENPLAY (ORIGINAL): C. Gardner Sullivan, *Hell's Hinges;* Monte M. Katterjohn, *The Apostle of Vengeance;* C. Gardner Sullivan, *The Aryan*

SCREENPLAY (ADAPTATION): Julia Crawford Ivers, *The Parson of Panamint;* Marion Fairfax, *Tennessee's Partner*

DIRECTION: William S. Hart, Charles Swickard, *Hell's Hinges;* William S. Hart, Clifford Smith, *The Apostle of Vengeance;* Allan Dwan, *The Good Bad Man*

CINEMATOGRAPHY: Joseph August, *Hell's Hinges;* Joseph August, *The Apostle of Vengeance;* Victor Fleming, *The Good Bad Man*

MALE LEADING ROLE: William S. Hart, *Hell's Hinges;* Douglas Fairbanks, *The Good Bad Man;* Harry Carey, *A Knight of the Range*

FEMALE LEADING ROLE: Adda Gleason, *Ramona;* Bessie Love, *The Aryan;* Winifred Kingston, *The Parson of Panamint*

MALE SUPPORTING ROLE: Jack Standing, *Hell's Hinges;* Hoot Gibson, *A Knight of the Range;* Raymond Hatton, *Tennessee's Partner*

FEMALE SUPPORTING ROLE: Mabel Van Buren, *Ramona*

Births. Writers Bill Gulick, Donald Hamilton, Frank O'Rourke; screenwriters William Bowers, Charles Schnee, Irving Wallace, George Zuckerman; directors Jack Arnold, Budd Boetticher, Ralph Nelson, Robert Parrish; cinematographer Philip H. Lathrop; composer Lionel Newman; songwriter Terry Gilkyson; actors Richard Boone, Jack Buetel, Ken Curtis, Kirk Douglas, Jack Elam, Glenn Ford, Sterling Hayden, George Montgomery, Gregory Peck, Keenan Wynn; actresses Olivia de Havilland, Virginia Gregg, Arleen Whelan.

Deaths. Writer Jack London (b. 1876).

After a few minor pictures in 1915, William S. Hart conquered the screen in 1916 with a number of excellent achievements. While *Hell's Hinges* (co-starring Clara Williams and Jack Standing), which Hart co-directed with Charles Swickard, remains an unquestioned masterpiece and the quintessential example of the actor's screen image and recurrent theme (a bad man reformed by love), there were also other outstanding Hart films—*The Apostle of Vengeance* (co-starring Nona Thomas and Joseph J. Dowling), *The Aryan* (featuring Bessie Love and Louise Glaum), and *The Patriot* (with George Stone and Joe Goodboy)—all directed by Hart, the first two in collaboration with Clifford Smith. C. Gardner Sullivan scripted both *Hell's Hinges* and *The Aryan*, while Joseph August, one of the most brilliant cinematographers in Hollywood's history, was in charge of the camerawork in all of the above (as well as many future pictures of Hart's).

In 1916, two other leading men appeared in their first major westerns: Douglas Fairbanks—an actor more successful outside the genre, especially in swashbuckling films—in Allan Dwan's *The Good Bad Man* (co-starring Sam de Grasse), and Harry Carey—an actor associated mostly with westerns—in Jacques Jaccard's *A Knight of the Range* (featuring Olive Golden and Hoot Gibson), with both films scripted by their male stars.

As the tendency to use literary material was quite obvious at that time, a number of westerns were based on either recognized short stories—e.g. George Melford's *Tennessee's Partner* (starring Fannie Ward and Jack Dean) and Allan Dwan's *The Half Breed* (featuring Douglas Fairbanks and Alma Rubens) from Bret Harte's prose—or classic novels—Donald Crisp's *Ramona* (with Adda Gleason and Monroe Salisbury) from the 1884 book by Helen Hunt Jackson, or J.P. McGowan's *Whispering Smith* (starring Helen Holmes and McGowan), based on the 1906 novel by Frank H. Spearman.

1917

Outstanding Achievements

PICTURE: *Truthful Tulliver; The Man from Painted Post; Nan of Music Mountain; The Desire of the Moth*

NOVEL FILMED: *Nan of Music Mountain* by Frank H. Spearman; *The Desire of the Moth* by Eugene Manlove Rhodes

SCREENPLAY (ORIGINAL): J.G. Hawks, *Truthful Tulliver;* Douglas Fairbanks, *The Man from Painted Post*

SCREENPLAY (ADAPTATION): Beulah Marie Dix, *Nan of Music Mountain*

DIRECTION: William S. Hart, *Truthful Tulliver;* Joseph Henabery, *The Man from Painted Post;* George H. Melford, *Nan of Music Mountain*

CINEMATOGRAPHY: Joseph August, *Truthful Tulliver;* Paul Perry, *Nan of Music Mountain;* Victor Fleming, Harry Thorpe, *The Man from Painted Post*

MALE LEADING ROLE: Douglas Fairbanks, *The Man from Painted Post;* William S. Hart, *Truthful Tulliver;* Wallace Reid, *Nan of Music Mountain*

FEMALE LEADING ROLE: Ann Little, *Nan of Music Mountain;* Alma Rubens, *Truthful Tulliver;* Eileen Percy, *The Man from Painted Post*

MALE SUPPORTING ROLE: Frank Campeau, *The Man from Painted Post;* Charles Ogle, *Nan of Music Mountain;* Walter Perry, *Truthful Tulliver*

Births. Writers Harry Brown, William Dale Jennings; director Earl Bellamy; actors R.G. Armstrong, William Bishop, Ernest Borgnine, Raymond Burr, Steve Cochran, Howard Keel, Lash La Rue, Dean Martin, Robert Mitchum; actress Virginia Grey.

Among the few major westerns of 1917, there was another superior picture starring William S. Hart—*Truthful Tulliver* (co-starring Alma Rubens), directed by Hart himself; and another major film with Douglas Fairbanks—*The Man from Painted Post* (featuring Eileen Percy and Frank Campeau), directed by Joseph Henabery.

George Melford's *Nan of Music Mountain* (starring Wallace Reid and Ann Little), from the 1916 novel by Frank H. Spearman, and Rupert Julian's *The Desire of the Moth* (featuring Ruth Clifford and Rupert Julian), based on the 1917 book by Eugene Manlove Rhodes, turned out to be the most successful screen western adaptations of the year.

1918

Outstanding Achievements

PICTURE: *M'liss; Headin' South; Blue Blazes Rawden; Riders of the Purple Sage; A Woman's Fool; The Rainbow Trail*

NOVEL FILMED: *Riders of the Purple Sage* by Zane Grey; *The Rainbow Trail* by Zane Grey; *Lin McLean* by Owen Wister, filmed as *A Woman's Fool; The Border Legion* by Zane Grey; *The Light of Western Stars* by Zane Grey

PLAY FILMED: *The Squaw Man* by Edwin Milton Royle

SHORT STORY FILMED: "M'liss" by Bret Harte

SCREENPLAY (ORIGINAL): Allan Dwan, *Headin' South*

SCREENPLAY (ADAPTATION): Frances Marion, *M'liss;* George Hivey, *A Woman's Fool*

DIRECTION: Marshall Neilan, *M'liss;* Arthur Rosson, *Headin' South;* William S. Hart, *Blue Blazes Rawden*

CINEMATOGRAPHY: Joseph August, *Blue Blazes Rawden;* Walter Stradling, *M'liss;* Ben Reynolds, *A Woman's Fool*

MALE LEADING ROLE: William S. Hart, *Blue Blazes Rawden;* Harry Carey, *A Woman's Fool;* Douglas Fairbanks, *Headin' South*

FEMALE LEADING ROLE: Mary Pickford, *M'liss;* Maude George, *A Woman's Fool;* Katherine MacDonald, *Headin' South*

MALE SUPPORTING ROLE: Thomas Meighan, *M'liss;* Frank Campeau, *Headin' South;* Charles Ogle, *M'liss*

FEMALE SUPPORTING ROLE: Marjorie Daw, *Headin' South;* Helen Kelly, *M'liss*

1919

Births. Writer Glendon Swarthout; screenwriter Martin Rackin; director Robert Aldrich; composer Herschel Burke Gilbert; actors Claude Akins, Jeff Chandler, Alan Hale, Jr., William Holden, Ben Johnson, Cameron Mitchell, Robert Preston, Joseph Wiseman; actresses Susan Hayward, Ida Lupino, Mercedes McCambridge, Teresa Wright.

Although Marshall Neilan's *M'liss* (with Mary Pickford and Theodore Roberts), based on Bret Harte's short story (previously filmed in 1915), and Arthur Rosson's *Headin' South* (starring Douglas Fairbanks and Katherine MacDonald) remain the top western achievements of 1918, the year would be primarily remembered for the introduction of Zane Grey's fiction to the big screen. Out of four relatively unremarkable 1918 films based on Grey's books, *Riders of the Purple Sage* and its sequel, *The Rainbow Trail* (from the books written in 1912 and 1915, respectively), clearly stand out. While William Farnum played the leading role in both films under the guidance of Frank Lloyd, his brother Dustin and Winifred Kingston co-starred in another Grey adaptation, Charles Swickard's *The Light of Western Stars*, based upon the 1914 book of the same name.

It needs to be noted that Grey's *Riders of the Purple Sage* would be selected as one of the best 12 western novels in the Western Writers of America's 1995 survey.

At the same time, *Blue Blazes Rawden* (featuring Maude George and Gertrude Claire) emerged as another major western with William S. Hart as actor and director; and Harry Carey, after a series of shorts made with Jack (John) Ford, finally appeared in the director's first remarkable feature, *A Woman's Fool* (co-starring Molly Malone), based on Owen Wister's 1898 (prior to *The Virginian*) novel *Lin McLean*.

1919

Outstanding Achievements

PICTURE: *The Outcasts of Poker Flat; Breed of Men; Riders of Vengeance; A Man in the Open; The Money Corral; Marked Men; The Valley of the Giants*

NOVEL FILMED: *The Three Godfathers* by Peter B. Kyne, filmed as *Marked Men; The Valley of the Giants* by Peter B. Kyne; *Desert Gold* by Zane Grey

SHORT STORY FILMED: "The Outcasts of Poker Flat"; "The Luck of Roaring Camp" by Bret Harte, filmed as *The Outcasts of Poker Flat*; "Cressy" by Bret Harte, filmed as *Fighting Cressy*

SCREENPLAY (ORIGINAL): Harry Carey, Eugene B. Lewis, *Riders of Vengeance*; J.G. Hawks, *Breed of Men*

SCREENPLAY (ADAPTATION): H. Tipton Steck, *The Outcasts of Poker Flat*; H. Tipton Steck, *Marked Men*

DIRECTION: Jack (John) Ford, *The Outcasts of Poker Flat*; William S. Hart, Lambert Hillyer, *Breed of Men*; Jack (John) Ford, *Riders of Vengeance*

MALE LEADING ROLE: Harry Carey, *The Outcasts of Poker Flat*; William S. Hart, *Breed of Men*; Dustin Farnum, *A Man in the Open*

FEMALE LEADING ROLE: Cullen Landis, *The Outcasts of Poker Flat*; Seena Owen, *Riders of Vengeance*; Jane Novak, *The Money Corral*

MALE SUPPORTING ROLE: J. Farrell MacDonald, *The Outcasts of Poker Flat*; Bert Sprotte, *Breed of Men*; Vester Pegg, *Riders of Vengeance*

FEMALE SUPPORTING ROLE: Gloria Hope, *The Outcasts of Poker Flat*; Claire DuBrey, *A Man in the Open*; Irene Rich, *A Man in the Open*

Births. Writer Milton Lott; screen-

1920

Outstanding Achievements

PICTURE: *The Toll Gate; The Testing Block; Overland Red; Sand; The Westerners; The River's End*

NOVEL FILMED: *The Shepherd of the Hills* by Harold Bell Wright; *The Westerners* by Stewart Edward White; *Chip of the Flying U* by B.M. Bower, filmed as *The Galloping Devil*; *The River's End* by James Oliver Curwood

SCREENPLAY (ORIGINAL): William S. Hart, Lambert Hillyer, *The Toll Gate*; William S. Hart, Lambert Hillyer, *The Testing Block*

DIRECTION: Lambert Hillyer, William S. Hart, *The Toll Gate*; Lynn Reynolds, *Overland Red*

CINEMATOGRAPHY: Joseph August, *The Toll Gate*; Joseph August, *The Testing Block*; Hugh McClung, *Overland Red*

MALE LEADING ROLE: William S. Hart, *The Toll Gate*; Harry Carey, *Overland Red*; Lewis Stone, *The River's End*

FEMALE LEADING LADY: Anna Q. Nilsson, *The Toll Gate*; Eva Novak, *The Testing Block*; Vola Vale, *Overland Red*

MALE SUPPORTING ROLE: Richard Headrick, *The Testing Block*; Joe Harris, *Overland Red*; Jack Richardson, *The Toll Gate*

FEMALE SUPPORTING ROLE: Florence Carpenter, *The Testing Block*; Patricia Palmer, *Sand*

Births. Screenwriters Irving Ravetch, Daniel B. Ullman; directors Andrew V. McLaglen, Joseph Pevney; actors Rodolfo Acosta, James Brown, William Conrad, Richard Farnsworth, DeForest Kelley, Jack Lambert, Walter Matthau, Michael Pate, Denver Pyle, Mickey Rooney, Mickey Shaughnessy, Jack War-

writer Wendell Mayes; composers Paul Dunlap, Sol Kaplan; actors Martin Balsam, Lex Barker, Steve Brodie, Jock Mahoney, Strother Martin, John Mitchum, Jack Palance, Slim Pickens, Jay Silverheels, Robert Stack, Kenneth Tobey, Forrest Tucker: actresses Karin Booth, Barbara Britton, Kathleen Freeman, Mary Beth Hughes, Evelyn Keyes, Eve McVeagh.

The peak of the Jack Ford/Harry Carey collaboration took place in 1919. In addition to several minor films, they made together *The Outcasts of Poker Flat* (featuring Cullen Landis, Gloria Hope, Joseph Harris and J. Farrell MacDonald), an outstanding adaptation of two short stories by Bret Harte, "The Outcasts of Poker Flat" and "The Luck of Roaring Camp" (both to be selected by the Western Writers of America, in their 1995 poll, among the best 12 western short stories of all time); *Riders of Vengeance* (co-starring J. Farrell MacDonald, Seena Owen and Joseph Harris), which was co-written by Carey himself; and *Marked Men* (with J. Farrell MacDonald), the second feature version of Peter B. Kyne's 1912 novel *The Three Godfathers*.

The other major westerns of the year include two William S. Hart movies, *Breed of Men* (co-starring Seena Owen) and *The Money Corral* (featuring Jane Novak), both co-directed by Hart and Lambert Hillyer, and both photographed by Joseph August. Also released this year was one Dustin Farnum picture, *A Man in the Open* (with Hershall Mayall and Lamar Johnstone), which was directed by Ernest C. Warde; and one Wallace Reid film, *The Valley of the Giants* (co-starring Grace Darmond), James Cruze's adaptation of Peter B. Kyne's 1916 novel.

den; actresses Virginia Christine, Virginia Mayo, Maureen O'Hara, Gene Tierney.

Even though several major western novels were adapted for the screen in 1920, including Harold Bell Wright's *The Shepherd of the Hills* (1907), Stewart Edward White's *The Westerners* (1901), James Oliver Curwood's *The River's End* (1919) and B.M. Bower's *Chip of the Flying U*, the overall quality of the year's western films was considerably lower than of those from the previous year. Moreover, the most remarkable westerns of the year were made from original screenplays—three William S. Hart films, *The Toll Gate* (co-starring Anna Q. Nilsson), *The Testing Block* (featuring Eva Novak) and *Sand* (with Mary Thurman), all directed by Lambert Hillyer and all scripted by Hart either alone (the last one) or in collaboration with Hillyer (the first two); and one Harry Carey picture, *Overland Red* (co-starring Vola Vale), directed by Lynn Reynolds.

1921

Outstanding Achievements

PICTURE: *The Killer; The Sky Pilot; White Oak; The Night Horseman; The Wallop; O'Malley of the Mounted; Where Men Are Men; Bar Nothin'*
NOVEL FILMED: *The Night Horseman* by Max Brand; *The Sky Pilot: A Tale of the Foothills* by Ralph Connor; *The Man of the Forest* by Zane Grey; *The Killer* by Stewart Edward White; *The Last Trail* by Zane Grey; *The Mysterious Rider* by Zane Grey
SCREENPLAY (ORIGINAL): William S. Hart, Bennet Musson, *White Oak;* William S. Hart, *O'Malley of the Mounted*
SCREENPLAY (ADAPTATION): John McDermott, Faith Green, *The Sky Pilot;* E. Richard Schayer, *The Killer;* George C. Hull, *The Wallop*
DIRECTION: Howard Hickman, *The Killer;* King Vidor, *The Sky Pilot;* Jack (John) Ford, *The Wallop*
CINEMATOGRAPHY: Joseph August, *O'Malley of the Mounted;* Harry Vallejo, *The Killer;* Harry Fowler, *The Wallop*
MALE LEADING ROLE: Jack Conway, *The Killer;* Tom Mix, *The Night Horseman;* John Bowers, *The Sky Pilot*
FEMALE LEADING ROLE: Claire Adams, *The Killer;* Colleen Moore, *The Sky Pilot;* Eva Novak, *O'Malley of the Mounted*
MALE SUPPORTING ROLE: Frank Campeau, *The Killer;* David Butler, *The Sky Pilot;* Bert Sprotte, *White Oak*
FEMALE SUPPORTING ROLE: Gertrude Wilson, *Where Men Are Men;* Helen Holly, *White Oak*

Births. Director Sergio Leone; composers Ernest Gold, Nelson Riddle; songwriter Hal David; actors John Agar, James Anderson, Neville Brand, Charles Bronson, Harry Carey, Jr., Chuck Connors, John Doucette, Richard Egan, Brian Keith, John Russell, James Whitmore, Sheb Wooley; actresses Linda Darnell, Barbara Hale, Nancy Kulp, Ella Raines, Donna Reed, Jane Russell, Alexis Smith, Phyllis Thaxter.

The major westerns of 1921 included three adaptations of remarkable novels: Howard Hickman's *The Killer* (starring Claire Adams, Jack Conway and Frank Campeau), from Stewart Edward White's book of the same title; King Vidor's *The Sky Pilot* (featuring John Bowers, Colleen Moore and David Butler), based on the 1899 novel by Ralph Connor; and Lynn Reynolds's *The Night Horseman* (with Tom Mix, May Hopkins and Harry Lonsdale), inspired by Max Brand's novel of 1920.

As Tom Mix joined the group of the top screen cowboys, offering unusual garb along with plenty of action and stunt work, the other significant western leading men successfully stayed in the saddle. William S. Hart appeared in two superior Lambert Hillyer pictures, *White Oak* (co-starring Vola Vale) and *O'Malley of the Mounted* (with Eva Novak), the latter scripted and the former co-scripted by Hart; and Harry Carey made another fine western under the guidance of Jack Ford, playing John Wesley Pringle, a Eugene Manlove Rhodes character, in *The Wallop* (featuring Mignonne Golden, William Gettinger, Joe Harris and J. Farrell MacDonald).

1922

Outstanding Achievements

PICTURE: *The Crimson Challenge; The Long Chance; North of the Rio Grande; While Satan Sleeps; Man to Man; Step on It!; Just Tony*

NOVEL FILMED: *The Long Chance* by Peter B. Kyne; *The Gray Dawn* by Stewart Edward White; *Good Men and True* by Eugene Manlove Rhodes; *Alcatraz* by Max Brand

SHORT STORY FILMED: "The Parson of Panamint" by Peter B. Kyne, filmed as *While Satan Sleeps*; "M'liss" by Bret Harte, filmed as *The Girl Who Ran Wild*

SCREENPLAY (ADAPTATION): Beulah Marie Dix, *The Crimson Challenge*; William M. Ritchie, *North of the Rio Grande*; Raymond Schrock, *The Long Chance*

DIRECTION: Jack Conway, *The Long Chance*; Paul Powell, *The Crimson Challenge*; Joseph Henabery, *North of the Rio Grande*

CINEMATOGRAPHY: Faxon M. Dean, *North of the Rio Grande*; Ben Reynolds, *The Long Chance*; Harry Perry, *The Crimson Challenge*

MALE LEADING ROLE: Jack Holt, *While Satan Sleeps*; Harry Carey, *Man to Man*; Henry B. Walthall, *The Long Chance*

FEMALE LEADING ROLE: Dorothy Dalton, *The Crimson Challenge*; Marjorie Daw, *The Long Chance*; Bebe Daniels, *North of the Rio Grande*

MALE SUPPORTING ROLE: Frank Campeau, *The Crimson Challenge*; Charles Ogle, *North of the Rio Grande*; Harold Goodwin, *Man to Man*

FEMALE SUPPORTING ROLE: Mabel Van Buren, *While Satan Sleeps*; Fritzi Brunette, *While Satan Sleeps*; Shannon Day, *North of the Rio Grande*

Births. Writers Will Cook, Les Savage, Jr.; screenwriter Blake Edwards; directors Burt Kennedy, Arnold Laven, Arthur Penn, Paul Wendkos; cinematographer Fred J. Koenekamp; composers Elmer Bernstein, Jerry Fielding; actors John Anderson, Michael Ansara, Rory Calhoun, Sunset Carson, Gene Evans, Leo Gordon, John Larch, Guy Madison, Leslie Nielsen, Paul Picerni, Jason Robards, Jr., William Schallert; actresses Yvonne De Carlo, Rhonda Fleming, Coleen Gray, Janis Paige, Eleanor Parker, Marie Windsor.

The most impressive western of 1922 was indisputably Paul Powell's *The Crimson Challenge* (featuring Dorothy Dalton, Jack Mower and Frank Campeau). Based upon the novel *Tharon of Lost Valley* by Vingie E. Roe, it may have been the first film centered on a female gunfighter.

The other major 1922 westerns include three pictures derived from remarkable prose: Jack Conway's *The Long Chance* (starring Henry B. Walthal and Marjorie Daw), from Peter B. Kyne's 1914 novel; Joseph Henabery's *While Satan Sleeps* (with Jack Holt, Wade Boteler and Mabel

Van Buren), based on Kyne's short story "The Parson of Panamint"; and Lynn Reynolds's *Just Tony* (featuring Tom Mix and Claire Adams), inspired by Max Brand's novel *Alcatraz*.

In addition to Tom Mix and Jack Holt—a new face among the screen cowboy heroes, whose other 1922 western with Henabery was *North of the Rio Grande* (co-starring Bebe Daniels and Charles Ogle), based upon Vingie E. Roe's novel *Val of Paradise*—the other western leading men also marked their presence in the genre: Harry Carey appeared in Stuart Paton's *Man to Man* (with Lillian Rich) and in Val Paul's unremarkable *Good Men and True* (opposite Vola Vale), based on Rhodes's 1910 novel of the same name; while William S. Hart starred in one of his lesser pictures, Lambert Hillyer's *Travelin' On* (featuring James Farley).

1923

Outstanding Achievements

PICTURE: *The Covered Wagon; Salomy Jane; The Girl of the Golden West; To the Last Man; The Virginian; The Mysterious Witness*
NOVEL FILMED: *The Virginian: A Horseman of the Plains* by Owen Wister, filmed as *The Virginian*; *The Covered Wagon* by Emerson Hough; *The Spoilers* by Rex Beach; *To the Last Man* by Zane Grey
PLAY FILMED: *The Girl of the Golden West* by David Belasco
SHORT STORY FILMED: "Salomy Jane's Kiss" by Bret Harte, filmed as *Salomy Jane*
SCREENPLAY (ADAPTATION): Jack Cunningham, *The Covered Wagon*; Adelaide Heilbron, *The Girl of the Golden West*; Waldemar Young, *Salomy Jane*
DIRECTION: James Cruze, *The Covered Wagon*; George Melford, *Salomy Jane*; Edwin Carewe, *The Girl of the Golden West*
CINEMATOGRAPHY: Karl Brown, *The Covered Wagon*; Bert Glennon, *Salomy Jane*; Sol Polito, *The Girl of the Golden West*
Male Leading Role: Richard Dix, *To the Last Man*; J. Warren Kerrigan, *The Covered Wagon*; Kenneth Harlan, *The Virginian*
FEMALE LEADING ROLE: Jacqueline Logan, *Salomy Jane*; Sylvia Breamer, *The Girl of the Golden West*; Lois Wilson, *The Covered Wagon*
MALE SUPPORTING ROLE: Russell Simpson, *The Girl of the Golden West*; Ernest Torrence, *The Covered Wagon*; Charles Ogle, *Salomy Jane*
FEMALE SUPPORTING ROLE: Ethel Wales, *The Covered Wagon*; Rosemary Theby, *The Girl of the Golden West*; Louise Dresser, *Salomy Jane*

Births. Screenwriter Barney Slater; cinematographer William A. Fraker; actors James Arness, Charlton Heston, Pat Hingle, Dale Roberston; actresses Anne Baxter, Helena Carter, Joanne Dru, Dorothy Hart, Jan Sterling, Jean Willes.

Deaths. Writer Emerson Hough (b. 1857); actor Wallace Reid (b. 1891).

The passing away of Emerson Hough, one of the pioneers of western fiction, coincided with the release of the first western epic, which was based upon his best novel, *The Covered Wagon*, published only the previous year. The screen version of the book, craftily scripted by Jack Cunningham, brilliantly directed by James Cruze and beautifully photographed by Karl Brown, is rightly considered to be a milestone in the genre's development. The competent cast included Lois Wilson (as Molly Wingate), J. Warren Kerrigan (Will Banion), Ernest Torrence (Jackson), Charles Ogle (Mr. Wingate), Ethel Wales

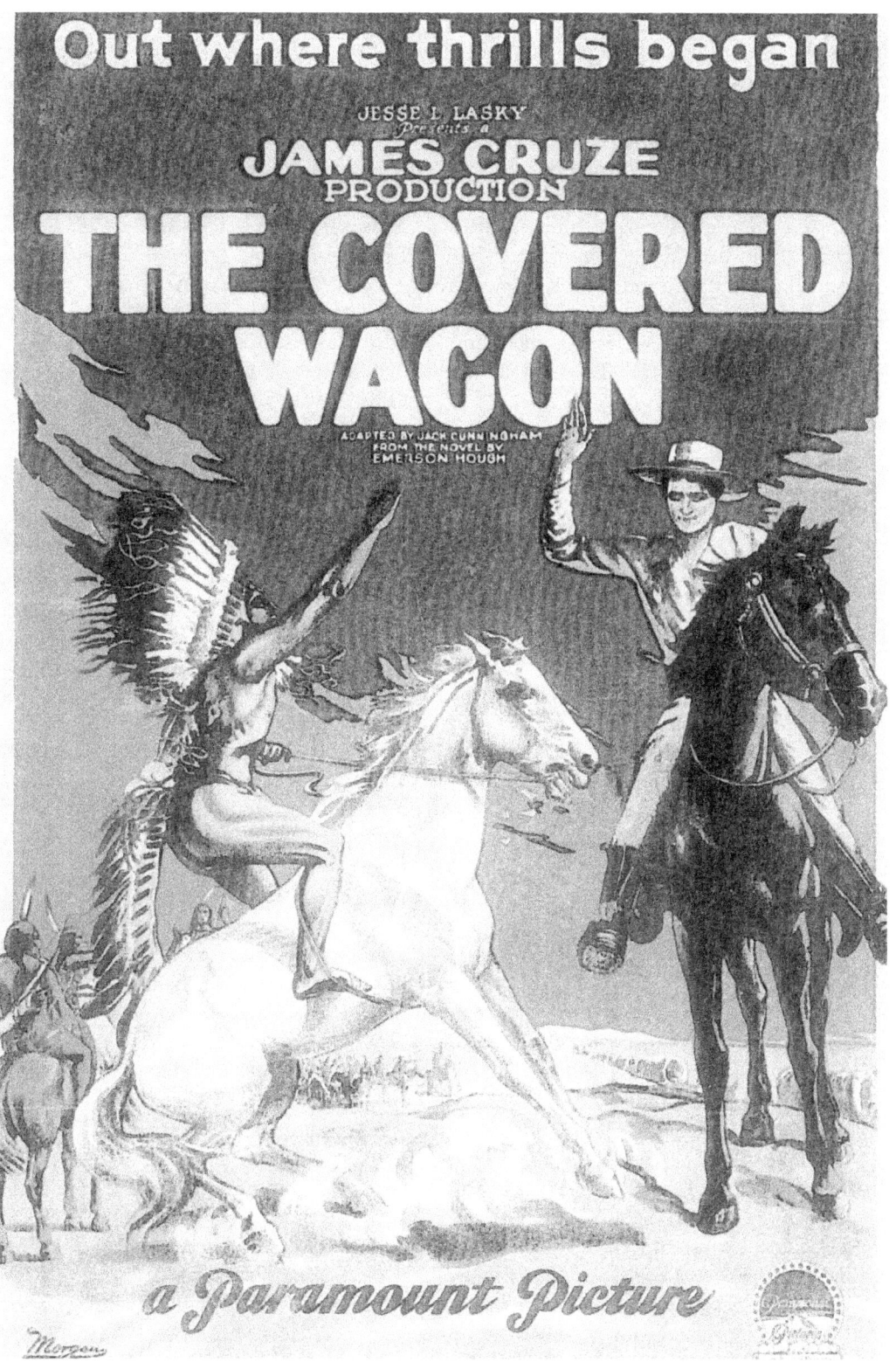

American poster for *The Covered Wagon* (FP/Par., 1923), one of two silent epics based on the novels of Emerson Hough.

(Mrs. Wingate) and Alan Hale (Sam Woodhull, the villain).

The other major 1923 westerns included two remarkable adaptations: George Melford's *Salomy Jane* (starring Jacqueline Logan, George Fawcett and Charles Ogle), from Bret Harte's short story "Salomy Jane 's Kiss"; and Edwin Carewe's *The Girl of the Golden West* (featuring Sylvia Breamer, J. Warren Kerrigan and Russell Simpson), from David Belasco's 1905 stage play.

Somewhat less successful were the renditions of three popular novels: Victor Fleming's *To the Last Man* (with Richard Dix and Lois Wilson), from Zane Grey's 1922 book; Tom Forman's *The Virginian* (starring Kenneth Harlan, Florence Vidor and Russell Simpson), from Owen Wister's 1902 classic; and Seymour Zeliff's *The Mysterious Witness* (featuring Robert Gordon and Elinor Fair), based on Eugene Manlove Rhoses' 1921 novel *The Stepsons of Light*.

1924

Outstanding Achievements

PICTURE: *The Iron Horse; North of 36; Against All Odds; The Man from Wyoming; Secrets; When a Man's Man; The Mine with the Iron Door*

NOVEL FILMED: *North of 36* by Emerson Hough; *The Heritage of the Desert* by Zane Grey; *When a Man's a Man* by Harold Bell Wright; *The Mine with the Iron Door* by Harold Bell Wright; *The Border Legion* by Zane Grey; *Wyoming* by William MacLeod Raine; *Wanderer of the Wasteland* by Zane Grey

PLAY FILMED: *Secrets* by Rudolf Besier and May Edington

SCREENPLAY (ORIGINAL): John Russell Kenyon, Charles Kenyon, *The Iron Horse*

SCREENPLAY (ADAPTATION): James Shelley Hamilton, *North of 36*

DIRECTION: John Ford, *The Iron Horse;* Irvin Willat, *North of 36;* Frank Borzage, *Secrets*

CINEMATOGRAPHY: George Schneiderman, Burnett Guffey, *The Iron Horse;* Alfred Gilks, *North of 36*

MALE LEADING ROLE: George O'Brien, *The Iron Horse;* Jack Holt, *North of 36*

FEMALE LEADING ROLE: Madge Bellamy, *The Iron Horse;* Norma Talmadge, *Secrets;* Lois Wilson, *North of 36*

MALE SUPPORTING ROLE: Fred Kohler, *The Iron Horse;* J. Farrell MacDonald, *The Iron Horse;* Noah Beery, *North of 36*

FEMALE SUPPORTING ROLE: Gladys Hulette, *The Iron Horse*

Births. Writers Marvin H. Albert, Thomas Berger; screenwriters Harold Jack Bloom, Gene L. Coon, John Gay; composer Maurice Jarre; actors Scott Brady, Marlon Barando, Steve Forrest, Russell Johnson, Lee Marvin, Audie Murphy, Telly Savalas, Dennis Weaver; actresses Arlene Dahl, Cathy Downs, Gloria Grahame, Martha Hyer, Geraldine Page, Ruth Roman, Gail Russell.

The silent western was at its prime in 1924 when two epic masterpieces were made: *The Iron Horse* and *North of 36*. While John Ford's *The Iron Horse* (starring George O'Brien, Madge Bellamy, Cyril Chadwick and Fred Kohler) dealt with the construction of the first transcontinental railroad, Irvin Willat's *North of 36* (featuring Jack Holt, Ernest Torrence, Lois Wilson and Noah Beery) followed the story of Emerson Hough's recently published novel and focused on a spectacular cattle drive from Texas to

Kansas after the Civil War. Both movies were superbly photographed by George Schneiderman and Burnett Guffey, and by Alfred Gilks, respectively.

Screen versions of Zane Grey's prose had been made every year since 1918, and there were four adaptations released in 1924—Irvin Willat's *The Heritage of the Desert* (with Bebe Daniels, Ernest Torrence and Noah Beery) and *The Wanderer of the Wasteland* (starring Jack Holt and Noah Beery), Lynn Reynolds's *The Last of the Duanes* (featuring Tom Mix and Marian Nixon) and William K. Howard's *The Border Legion* (with Antonio Moreno and Helene Chadwick)—albeit none of them ranking high.

More successful were the renditions of two novels (published in 1916 and 1923) by Harold Bell Wright—*When a Man's a Man* (starring John Bowers and Marguerite De La Motte, and directed by Edward F. Cline) and *The Mine with the Iron Door* (featuring Pat O'Malley, Dorothy Mackaill and Raymond Hatton, and directed by Sam Wood).

1925

Outstanding Achievements

PICTURE: *Tumbleweeds; The Lucky Horseshoe; The Vanishing American; Riders of the Purple Sage; The Rainbow Trail; Ridin' the Wind; The Pony Express*

NOVEL FILMED: *Riders of the Purple Sage* by Zane Grey; *The Rainbow Trail* by Zane Grey; *The Vanishing American* by Zane Grey; *Tumbleweeds* by Hal G. Evarts; *The Thundering Herd* by Zane Grey; *Wild Horse Mesa* by Zane Grey; *The Light of Western Stars* by Zane Grey

SCREENPLAY (ORIGINAL): Robert Lord, John Stone, *The Lucky Horseshoe*

SCREENPLAY (ADAPTATION): C. Gardner Sullivan, *Tumbleweeds;* Edfrid Bingham, *Riders of the Purple Sage;* Lynn Reynolds, *The Rainbow Trail*

DIRECTION: King Baggot, *Tumbleweeds;* J.G. Blystone, *The Lucky Horseshoe;* George B. Seitz, *The Vanishing American*

CINEMATOGRAPHY: Joseph August, *Tumbleweeds;* Dan Clark, *Riders of the Purple Sage;* Karl Brown, *The Pony Express*

MALE LEADING ROLE: William S. Hart, *Tumbleweeds;* Tom Mix, *The Lucky Horseshoe*

FEMALE LEADING ROLE: Barbara Bedford, *Tumbleweeds;* Billie Dove, *The Lucky Horseshoe*; Betty Compson, *The Pony Express*

MALE SUPPORTING ROLE: J. Gordon Russell, *Tumbleweeds;* J. Farrell MacDonald, *The Lucky Horseshoe;* George Bancroft, *The Pony Express*

FEMALE SUPPORTING ROLE: Clarissa Selwynne, *The Lucky Horseshoe;* Mabel Ballin, *Riders of the Purple Sage*

Births. Writer Elmore Leonard; director Sam Peckinpah; cinematographer Harry Stradling, Jr.; actors Tony Curtis, Richard Erdman, Peter Graves, Rock Hudson, Jeffrey Hunter, George Kennedy, Keith Larsen, Paul Newman, Hugh O'Brian, Fess Parker, Rod Steiger, Lee Van Cleef; actresses Lola Albright, Corinne Calvet, Jeanne Crain, Joan Leslie, Dorothy Malone, Patricia Owens.

The top western achievements of 1925 were *Tumbleweeds* and *The Lucky Horseshoe*, two excellent movies with the two most representative stars of the silent western—William S. Hart (an ambitious and versatile filmmaker oscillating towards the artistic and intellectual variety of westerns) and Tom Mix (whose westerns focused on action and the spectacular and were clearly aimed at the less demanding audience). However, while King Baggot's *Tumbleweeds* (featuring Barbara

Bedford and Lucien Littlefield, scripted by C. Gardner Sullivan from Hal G. Evarts's prose, and photographed by Joseph August) turned out to be a 'swan song' in Hart's outstanding career, J.G. Blystone's *The Lucky Horseshoe* (co-starring Billie Dove and J. Farrell MacDonald, scripted by John Stone and photographed by Dan Clark) was made when Mix was in his prime. Needless to say, in 1925 Mix appeared in two more remarkable westerns—*Riders of the Purple Sage* and *The Rainbow Trail*, both based on Zane Grey's superior novels, both directed by Lynn Reynolds, and both photographed by Dan Clark.

The other significant westerns of the year include one more Zane Grey adaptation, George B. Seitz's *The Vanishing American* (with Richard Dix, a rising star in the genre, Lois Wilson and Noah Beery), Del Andrews and Alfred Werker's *Ridin' the Wind* (starring Fred Thomson and Jacqueline Gadsdon), and James Cruze's *The Pony Express* (featuring Betty Compson, Ricardo Cortez and Ernest Torrence).

1926

Outstanding Achievements

PICTURE: *The Winning of Barbara Worth; The Great K & A Train Robbery; Whispering Smith; Three Bad Men; Tony Runs Wild; Arizona Wildcat; The Desert's Price; The Desert's Toll; The Yankee Senior; Hands Across the Border*

NOVEL FILMED: *Whispering Smith* by Frank H. Spearman; *The Winning of Barbara Worth* by Harold Bell Wright; *Chip of the Flying U* by B.M. Bower; *The Man of the Forest* by Zane Grey

SCREENPLAY (ORIGINAL): Henry Herbert Knibbs, Edfrid Bingham, Robert Lord, *Tony Runs Wild*

SCREENPLAY (ADAPTATION): John Stone, *The Great K & A Train Robbery*; Frances Marion, *The Winning of Barbara Worth*; Elliott J. Clawson, Will M. Ritchey, *Whispering Smith*

DIRECTION: Henry King, *The Winning of Barbara Worth*; Lewis Seiler, *The Great K & A Train Robbery*; John Ford, *Three Bad Men*

CINEMATOGRAPHY: Charles G. Clarke, Joe LaShelle, *Whispering Smith*; George Barnes, *The Winning of Barbara Worth*; George Schneiderman, *Three Bad Men*

MALE LEADING ROLE: Ronald Colman, *The Winning of Barbara Worth*; Tom Mix, *The Great K & A Train Robbery*; H.B. Warner, *Whispering Smith*

FEMALE LEADING ROLE: Vilma Banky, *The Winning of Barbara Worth*; Olive Borden, *The Yankee Senior*; Lillian Rich, *Whispering Smith*

MALE SUPPORTING ACTOR: Gary Cooper, *The Winning of Barbara Worth*; Eugene Pallette, *Whispering Smith*; Tom Santschi, *Three Bad Men*

FEMALE SUPPORTING ROLE: Lilyan Tashman, *Whispering Smith*; Vivian Oakland, *Tony Runs Wild*

Births. Writer Edmund Naughton; director Roger Corman; cinematographer Conrad Hall; composer Laurence Rosenthal; actors James Best, Richard Crenna, John Derek, John Ericson, Pedro Gonzalez-Gonzalez, Richard Jaeckel, Harry Dean Stanton, Stuart Whitman; actresses Julie Adams, Peggie Castle, Mona Freeman, Julie London, Marilyn Monroe, Jean Peters, Patrice Wymore.

Deaths. Director Tom Forman (b. 1893).

The last great year of the silent western was an interesting mixture of what was typical in the past and what was about

1926

Top: A star of many silent westerns and a few talkies, Tom Mix (1880–1940) was in his prime when he made Lewis Seiler's unforgettable *The Great K & A Train Robbery*. *Bottom:* Hoot Gibson (1892–1962) played Chip Bennett, opposite Virginia Browne Faire as the Little Doctor, in the third of four screen versions of B.M. Bower's popular novel *Chip of the Flying U.*

to come in the near future. On the one hand, Tom Mix, an actor whose career in the sound period would be reduced essentially to B productions, impressed the audience with a few more excellent and fast screen adventures—Lewis Seiler's *The Great K & A Train Robbery* (co-starring Dorothy Dwan), Clifford Smith's *Arizona Wildcat* (featuring Dorothy Sebastian), Thomas Buckingham's *Tony Runs Wild* (opposite Jacqueline Logan) and Emmett Flynn's *The Yankee Senior* (with Olive Borden). On the other hand, Henry King made a successful adaptation of Harold Bell Wright's spiritual 1911 novel *The Winning of Barbara Worth*, not only casting the gentlemanly Englishman Ronald Colman in the leading role, but also giving a supporting part to the sensitive Gary Cooper, an actor who would rule in and outside the genre for the next 35 years.

Furthermore, in addition to the release of Lynn Reynolds's screen version of *Chip of the Flying U* by B.M. Bower (an author whose popularity would almost vanish in the sound era), there were adaptations of Frank H. Spearman's *Whispering Smith* and Zane Grey's *The Man of the Forest*, two books that would be filmed, at least once again, as talkies. In this second rendition of Bower's popular novel, Hoot Gibson played the titular hero, Chip Bennett, a character who may seem to have been inspired by Charles M. Russell (who illustrated the 1906 edition of the book) or Gary Cooper (who, just like Chips, was a young and sensitive Montana cowboy with strong artistic inclinations). However, either similarity is accidental, as Cooper was only three at the time the book was first published, while Russell met the author after the character had been well developed.

It needs to be noted that in 1926 John Ford, already one of the major figures in the genre, made his last silent western, *Three Bad Men* (featuring George O'Brien,

Olive Borden, Lou Tellegen, Tom Santschi and J. Farrell MacDonald), and would not make another western until 1939.

1927

Outstanding Achievements

PICTURE: *The Last Trail; Outlaws of Red River; Nevada; Silver Valley; Jim the Conqueror; White Gold; Jesse James; Arizona Bound*

NOVEL FILMED: *Arizona Nights* by Stewart Edward White; *Nevada* by Zane Grey; *Flying U Ranch* by B.M. Bower; *The Valley of the Giants* by Peter B. Kyne; *Jim the Conqueror* by Peter B. Kyne; *The Last Trail* by Zane Grey; *The Mysterious Rider* by Zane Grey

SCREENPLAY (ORIGINAL): Gerald Beaumont, Harold Shumate, *Outlaws of Red River*; Harry Sinclair Drago, Harold B. Lipsitz, *Silver Valley*

SCREENPLAY (ADAPTATION): John Stone, *The Last Trail*; John Stone, L.G. Rigby, *Nevada*; Will M. Ritchey, *Jim the Conqueror*

DIRECTION: Lewis Seiler, *The Last Trail*; John Waters, *Nevada*; William K. Howard, *White Gold*

CINEMATOGRAPHY: Dan Clark, *The Last Trail*; Lucien Andriot, *White Gold*; Hal Rosson, *Jim the Conqueror*

MALE LEADING ROLE: Tom Mix, *The Last Trail*; Gary Cooper, *Nevada*; Fred Thomson, *Jesse James*

FEMALE LEADING ROLE: Jetta Goudal, *White Gold*; Marjorie Daw, *Outlaws of Red River*; Elinor Fair, *Jim the Conqueror*

MALE SUPPORTING ROLE: William Powell, *Nevada*; George Bancroft, *White Gold*; Tully Marshall, *Jim the Conqueror*

FEMALE SUPPORTING ROLE: Ellen Woonston, *Outlaws of Red River*; Mary Carr, *Jesse James*

Births. Actors L.Q. Jones, Clint Walker; actresses Mari Blanchard, Susan Cabot, Katy Jurado, Janet Leigh, Barbara Payton, Barbara Rush.

Deaths. Writer James Oliver Curwood (b. 1878); director Lynn Reynolds (b. 1891).

The major westerns of 1927, generally above average but not outstanding, included several adaptations of books by three of the most popular authors of the genre—Zane Grey, Peter B. Kyne and B.M. Bower—as well as several pictures with some minor western stars—William Boyd (*Jim the Conquerer*), Fred Thomson (*Jesse James*), Tom Tyler (*The Sonora Kid*) and others. On the other hand, Stewart Edward White's excellent book *Arizona Nights* (1907), commendable for both content (genuine and beautiful stories) and form (partially borrowed from *Canterbury Tales* and partially anticipating the unusual structure of *Monte Walsh*), turned out to be too much of a challenge for director Lloyd Ingraham, whose screen adaptation (starring Fred Thomson, Nora Lane and J.P. McGowan) emerged as a major disappointment.

What needs to be emphasized is the fact that Gary Cooper, when finally given the chance, proved to be an extremely promising western hero. In 1927 he starred in three westerns, two of which—*Nevada* (featuring Thelma Todd and William Powell), based on Zane Grey's 1926 novel, and *Arizona Bound* (with Betty Jewel and El Brendel)—both directed by John Waters, are clearly superior to Arthur Rosson's *The Last Outlaw* (featuring Jack Luden and Betty Jewel).

1928

Outstanding Achievements

PICTURE: *Avalanche; The Apache Raider; The Desert Pirate; The Pioneer Scout; Arizona Days; Ramona*

NOVEL FILMED: *Ramona* by Helen Hunt Jackson; *The Shepherd of the Hills* by Harold Bell Wright

SCREENPLAY (ORIGINAL): Ford J. Beebe, *The Apache Raider*; Frank M. Clifton, *The Pioneer Scout*

SCREENPLAY (ADAPTATION): Finis Fox, *Ramona*

DIRECTION: Otto Brower, *Avalanche*; Lloyd Ingraham, Alfred L. Werker, *The Pioneer Scout*

CINEMATOGRAPHY: Roy Clark, *Avalanche*

SONG: (m/ly) Mabel Wayne, L. Wolf Gilbert, "Ramona" from *Ramona*

MALE LEADING ROLE: Jack Holt, *Avalanche*; Warner Baxter, *Ramona*

FEMALE LEADING ROLE: Dolores Del Rio, *Ramona*; Nora Lane, *The Pioneer Scout*

MALE SUPPORTING ROLE: Tom London, *The Apache Raider*; William Courtright, *The Pioneer Scout*

FEMALE SUPPORTING ROLE: Vera Lewis, *Ramona*; Barclanova, *Avalanche*

Births. Writer Clair Huffaker; screenwriter William Norton; composer Ennio Morricone; actors Stephen Boyd, James Coburn, James Garner, Earl Holliman, Roddy McDowall, Warren Oates, George Peppard, Mitch Ryan, Henry Silva; actresses Dianne Foster, Rita Gam, Wanda Hendrix, Barbara Lawrence, Estelita Rodriguez, Shirley Temple, Helen Westcott.

Deaths. Director Colin Campbell (b. 1859).

Similar to the previous year, 1928 provided several unremarkable adaptations of some popular novels: Helen Hunt Jackson's *Ramona* (starring Dolores Del Rio and Warner Baxter, one more rising western star), directed by Edwin Carewe; Harold Bell Wright's *The Shepherd of the Hills* (featuring Alec B. Francis and Molly O'Day), directed by Albert Rogell; and a few renditions of Zane Grey's minor novels—Otto Brower's *Avalanche* (with Jack Holt and Richard Winslow), Herman C. Raymaker's *Under the Tonto Rim* (starring Richard Arlen and Mary Brian) and others.

1929

Outstanding Achievements

PICTURE: *The Virginian; In Old Arizona; Points West; Wolf Song; Stairs of Sand; Romance of the Rio Grande; Sunset Pass; Tide of Empire*

NOVEL FILMED: *The Virginian: A Horseman of the Plains* by Owen Wister, filmed as *The Virginian*; *Tide of Empire* by Peter B. Kyne; *Points West* by B.M. Bower; *Sunset Pass* by Zane Grey

SHORT STORY FILMED: "The Caballero's Way" by O. Henry, filmed as *In Old Arizona*

SCREENPLAY (ADAPTATION): Tom Barry, *In Old Arizona*; Howard Estabrook, Edward E. Paramore, Jr., Grover Jones, Keene Thompson, *The Virginian*; Marion Orth, *Romance of the Rio Grande*

DIRECTION: Irving Cummings (and Raoul Walsh), *In Old Arizona*; Victor Fleming, *The Virginian*; Alfred Santell, *Romance of the Rio Grande*

CINEMATOGRAPHY: Arthur Edeson, *In Old Arizona*; J. Roy Hunt, Edward Cronjager, *The Virginian*; Arthur Edeson, *Romance of the Rio Grande*

1929

SONG: Lew Brown, B.G. DeSylva, Ray Henderson, "My Tonia" from *In Old Arizona;* Richard Whiting, Alfred Bryan, "Mi Amado" from *Wolf Song;* Richard Whiting, Alfred Bryan, "Yo Te Amo Means I Love You" from *Wolf Song*

MALE LEADING ROLE: Warner Baxter, *In Old Arizona;* Gary Cooper, *The Virginian*

FEMALE LEADING ROLE: Mary Brian, *The Virginian;* Dorothy Burgess, *In Old Arizona*

MALE SUPPORTING ROLE: Walter Huston, *The Virginian;* Edmund Lowe, *In Old Arizona;* Antonio Moreno, *Romance of the Rio Grande*

FEMALE SUPPORTING ROLE: Martha Franklin, *Points West;* Helen Ware, *The Virginian*

1928–1929 Academy Awards/ Nominations

In Old Arizona—AA: actor Warner Baxter; AAN: production; direction (Irving Cummings); writing achievement; cinematography.

Births. Screenwriter James Lee Barrett; composers Jerry Goldsmith, André Previn; actors Christopher George, Skip Homeier, Don Murray, Max Von Sydow, Rod Taylor; actresses Amanda Blake, Carolyn Jones, Vera Miles, Joan Taylor.

Deaths. Director Charles Swickard (b. 1861); actor Dustin Farnum (b. 1874).

As 1929 was the year between the silent and the sound periods, the major westerns released in that year include silent pictures, talkies and "half-talkies."

One of the sound westerns, *In Old Arizona*, stands out in film history as the first western recognized by the Academy. As a recipient of one Oscar and four other nominations, *In Old Arizona*, depicting the adventures of O. Henry's Cisco Kid, was quite an enjoyable picture with a number of assets, particularly the flamboyant characterization by Warner Baxter, who, in the Academy Award competition, defeated such actors as Paul Muni, Lewis Stone, George Bancroft and Chester Morris.

However, a western film more important to the genre was Victor Fleming's *The Virginian*, an almost flawless (for that time) rendition of the classic novel, based—just like the other three screen versions—not only on Owen Wister's book but also on its dramatization by Kirk La Shelle. The first sound movie in Gary Cooper's career, it was also the best of all the film adaptations of the highly acclaimed novel. Impressively directed by the future maker of *Gone with the Wind*, the movie is memorable for the superb performances of the four key players—Cooper in the titular role, Walter Huston as Trampas, Mary Brian as Molly Wood and Richard Arlen as Steve. "The story is cleverly developed by the director, Victor Fleming, who deserves great credit for the production and especially for the effective but at the same time gentle humor that pops up periodically," praised the *New York Times*. "It is also a capitally timed picture, with characters going here and there with natural movement.... The sounds, whether footfalls, horses' hoofs, rumbling wheels or voices, are really remarkably recorded and reproduced. A good deal of this film was made in the open and it would seem that stories of Western life, if pictured in a rational fashion, would be

Opposite: Poster for *The Virginian*, the first sound version of the quintessential western novel by Owen Wister, featuring Gary Cooper as the hero, Mary Brian as the schoolmarm and Walter Huston (in his film debut) as villain Trampas.

"You don't think I want to do this Molly?
But you won't ask me to run away—"

The Virginian

GARY COOPER
WALTER HUSTON
RICHARD ARLEN
MARY BRIAN

A VICTOR FLEMING

a Paramount Picture

unusually successful, for they are aided immeasurably by the audibility of the screen."

Especially significant was the decision to cast Cooper in the role of the quintessential western hero. He gave a great performance, but—more importantly—he furnished the screen cowboy with a new, more modern image (clearly different from that of the Farnum brothers or William S. Hart), thus paving the way for such actors as John Wayne, Randolph Scott and Joel McCrea. At the same time, Cooper's performance in *The Virginian* made him one of the few primary figures in the genre. He would star in two major westerns in 1930 and one in 1931, and later on he would keep revisiting the genre on a more or less regular basis, in spite of the enormous recognition he was bound to gain in other types of movies.

Prior to *The Virginian*, Victor Fleming directed another western with Cooper, an adventure romance called *Wolf Song* (featuring Lupe Velez and Louis Wolheim), which was advertised as a "half-talkie" due to the two songs added to that otherwise silent picture.

Among the worthy silent westerns of 1929 were Arthur Rosson's *Points West* (starring Hoot Gibson, Alberta Vaughn and Frank Campeau), from a so-so 1927 mystery/adventure novel by B.M. Bower; two competent Zane Grey adaptations—*Stairs of Sand* (featuring Wallace Beery and Jean Arthur) and *Sunset Pass* (with Jack Holt and Nora Lane), both directed by Otto Brower; and Allan Dwan's *Tide of Empire* (featuring Renée Adorée, George Duryea and George Fawcett), based on a superior, 1927, California gold rush novel by Peter B. Kyne.

The 1929 obituaries announced the premature death of Dustin Farnum, an accomplished actor who—in addition to being the first screen impersonator of *The Virginian*—starred in such popular westerns as *The Squaw Man* (1914), *The Parson of Panamint* and *The Light of Western Stars*.

1930

Outstanding Achievements

PICTURE: *The Big Trail*; *Billy the Kid*; *Hell's Heroes*; *The Spoilers*; *The Texan*

NOVEL FILMED: *The Spoilers* by Rex Beach; *The Three Godfathers* by Peter B. Kyne, filmed as *Hell's Heroes*; *The Border Legion* by Zane Grey; *The Light of Western Stars* by Zane Grey

NONFICTION BOOK FILMED: *The Saga of Billy the Kid* by Walter Noble Burns, filmed as *Billy the Kid*

PLAY FILMED: *The Girl of the Golden West* by David Belasco; *The Bad Man* by Porter Emerson Browne

SHORT STORY FILMED: "A Double-Dyed Deceiver" by O. Henry, filmed as *The Texan*

SCREENPLAY (ADAPTATION): Wanda Tuchock, Laurence Stallings, Charles MacArthur, *Billy the Kid*; Bartlett Cormack, Agnes Brand Leahy, *The Spoilers*; Tom Reed, *Hell's Heroes*

DIRECTION: William Wyler, *Hell's Heroes*; Raoul Walsh, *The Big Trail*; King Vidor, *Billy the Kid*

CINEMATOGRAPHY: Lucien Andriot Arthur Edeson, *The Big Trail*; Gordon Avil, *Billy the Kid*; George Robinson, *Hell's Heroes*

MUSIC: David Broekman, *Hell's Heroes*

MALE LEADING ROLE: Gary Cooper, *The Texan*; Charles Bickford, *Hell's Heroes*

FEMALE LEADING ROLE: Kay Johnson, *Billy the Kid*; Fay Wray, *The Texan*; Marguerite Churchill, *The Big Trail*

MALE SUPPORTING ROLE: Tully Marshall, *The Big Trail*; Raymond Hatton, *Hell's Heroes*; Russell Simpson, *Billy the Kid*

FEMALE SUPPORTING ROLE: Emma Dunn, *The Texan;* Fritzi Ridgeway, *Hell's Heroes;* Blanche Frederici, *Billy the Kid*

Births. Cinematographer Vilmos Zsigmond; actors Pedro Armendariz, Jr., Clint Eastwood, Gene Hackman, Richard Harris, Steve McQueen, Robert Wagner; actresses Anne Francis, Dolores Michaels.

Deaths. Actor Milton Sills (b. 1882).

Raoul Walsh's *The Big Trail* (featuring John Wayne, Marguerite Churchill and Tully Marshall) was without a doubt the best western of 1930. Despite the reservations on critics' part and the failure at the box office, it is a solidly directed and beautifully photographed (in two different versions, standard and wide screen) epic, less dated than some of the more recognized pictures of that period. Though Wayne does not shine in the role as wagon train guide Breck Coleman, his performance is not as bad as was implied by a number of reviewers. Yet his relegation to "B" productions as a result of that critique turned out beneficial for the actor. After learning a great deal about filmmaking (and acting, in particular), he would receive a fresh start in "A" pictures, beginning with John Ford's *Stagecoach* in 1939.

In addition to Walsh, there were two other great directors, William Wyler and King Vidor, who came up with fine westerns in 1930, both based on superior literary material. Wyler's *Hell's Heroes* (featuring Charles Bickford, Fred Kohler and Raymond Hatton) was the first sound version of Peter B. Kyne's *The Three Godfathers* (1912), while Vidor's *Billy the Kid* (starring Johnny Mack Brown and Wallace Beery) was based on Walter Noble Burns' biographical book *The Saga of Billy the Kid* (1926). The films may seem rather dated today, but both stand out for their irresistibly fabulous cinematography—shot on location in the Mojave and Panamint Deserts (the former), and around the Grand Canyon and in the actual areas of Lincoln County, New Mexico (the latter).

More enjoyable, albeit artistically less significant, were the two westerns starring Gary Cooper—Edwin Carewe's *The Spoilers* (featuring Kay Johnson and William "Stage" Boyd) and John Cromwell's *The Texan* (co-starring Fay Wray and Russ Columbo). While in the former, which was the third screen adaptation of the popular 1906 novel by Rex Beach, the actor demonstrated mostly the physical part of his persona (particularly in the climactic fistfight), his role in the latter, based on O. Henry's short story, required a combination of charm and sensitivity that only Cooper could provide.

Raoul Walsh's classic epic *The Big Trail*, with John Wayne in his first starring role, undeservedly turned out to be a box office failure and caused the actor's relegation to "B" productions for nearly a decade.

A glimpse at the 1930 Births list reveals a strange coincidence. The names include three actors—Clint Eastwood, Gene Hackman and Richard Harris—that, 62 years later, would appear together in *Unforgiven*, the last masterful western film of the twentieth century.

1931

Outstanding Achievements

PICTURE: *Cimarron; Fighting Caravans; The Painted Desert; River's End*

NOVEL FILMED: *Cimarron* by Edna Ferber; *The River's End* by James Oliver Curwood; *Fighting Caravans* by Zane Grey

PLAY FILMED: *The Squaw Man* by Edwin Milton Royle

SCREENPLAY (ADAPTATION): Howard Estabrook, *Cimarron*; Edward E. Paramore, Jr., Keene Thompson, Agnes Brand Leahy, *Fighting Caravans*

DIRECTION: Wesley Ruggles, *Cimarron*; Otto Brower, David Burton, *Fighting Caravans*

CINEMATOGRAPHY: Edward Cronjager, *Cimarron*; Lee Garmes, *Fighting Caravans*; Harold Rosson, *The Squaw Man*

MUSIC: Max Steiner, *Cimarron*; John Leipold, Oscar Potoker, Emil Bierman, Max Bergunker, Emil Hilb, Herman Hand, Karl Hajos, Sigmund Krumgold, A. Cousminer, *Fighting Caravans*

MALE LEADING ROLE: Richard Dix, *Cimarron*; Gary Cooper, *Fighting Caravans*; Charles Bickford, *River's End*

FEMALE LEADING ROLE: Irene Dunne, *Cimarron*; Lily Damita, *Fighting Caravans*; Lupe Velez, *The Squaw Man*

MALE SUPPORTING ROLE: George E. Stone, *Cimarron*; J. Farrell MacDonald, *The Painted Desert*; Ernest Torrence, *Fighting Caravans*

FEMALE SUPPORTING ROLE: Edna May Oliver, *Cimarron*; Estelle Taylor, *Cimarron*; May Boley, *Fighting Caravans*

1930–31 Academy Awards/ Nominations

Cimarron—AA: picture; screen adaptation; art direction (Max Ree); AAN: direction; cinematography; actor Richard Dix; actress Irene Dunne.

Births. Screenwriter William Goldman; director/cinematographer Jan Troell; composer Dominic Frontiere; actors Ray Danton, Robert Duvall, Tab Hunter; actresses Carroll Baker, Anne Bancroft, Kathleen Crowley, Angie Dickinson, Valerie French, Rita Moreno, Mary Murphy, Janice Rule, Karen Steele, Gloria Talbott.

Deaths. Playwright David Belasco (b. 1859); actor Tom Santschi (b. 1878).

Two years after *In Old Arizona*, another western film played a significant role in the Academy Award competition. In fact, Wesley Ruggles' *Cimarron* was an even stronger contender and earned seven nominations, three of which turned out to be winners. One of the Oscars was granted in the category of best picture, an accomplishment which would happen among western films only two more times, but not until the 1990s. *Cimarron* is a remarkable epic, spanning in time from 1890 to 1930, and telling the story of the pioneer family of the Cravats in an unusually modern way. A true milestone in the genre's history, it fascinates with every detail and in every capacity, whether nominated for an Oscar or not. Among the assets unnoticed by the Academy was Max Steiner's music, which impresses even more when compared to the other scores of early talkies, which were usually quite primitive. *Cimarron* has a first-rate cast, starting with the Oscar-nominated leading couple—Richard Dix (whose suitably overacted characterization of Yancey Cravat eclipses even Gary Cooper's performance in *Fighting Caravans*) and Irene Dunne (as Sabra Cravat, in her rare western appearance)—and finishing with the key supporting players: Estelle Taylor (as Dixie Lee), George E. Stone (Sol Levy) and Edna May Oliver (Mrs. Tracy Wyatt).

The other major westerns of 1931—Otto Brower and David Burton's *Fighting Caravans* (featuring Cooper, Lily Damita, Tully Marshall and Ernest Torrence), Howard Higgin's *The Painted Desert* (starring William Boyd, Helen Twelvetrees and William Farnum) and Michael Curtiz's *River's End* (with Charles Bickford, Evalyn Knapp and ZaSu Pitts)—are by far less impressive, despite their authentic look. The one that can still captivate the viewer is *Fighting Caravans*, even though as an adaptation of Zane Grey's epic novel (1926) it has to be discredited because of numerous discrepancies. *The Painted Desert*, on the other hand, is significant for the appearance of Clark Gable (in the role of the villain named Brett, without a mustache), but his acting in this one is not very impressive.

The death of David Belasco in 1931 reminds us that some westerns, but not many, were inspired by stage plays. Belasco contributed to the genre with two western plays—*The Girl of the Golden West* (1905) and *The Rose of the Rancho* (1906, co-written with Richard Walton Tully)—which were filmed three and two times, respectively.

1932

Outstanding Achievements

PICTURE: *Law and Order; The Conquerors; Rider of Death Valley; Destry Rides Again*

NOVEL FILMED: *Destry Rides Again* by Max Brand; *The Heritage of the Desert* by Zane Grey; *Saint Johnson* by W.R. Burnett, filmed as *Law and Order; Wild Horse Mesa* by Zane Grey

SCREENPLAY (ORIGINAL): Howard Estabrook, Robert Lord, *The Conquerors;* Jack Cunningham, Stanley Bergerman, *Rider of Death Valley*

SCREENPLAY (ADAPTATION): John Huston, Tom Reed, *Law and Order;* Isadore Bernstein, Robert Keith, Richard Schayer, *Destry Rides Again*

DIRECTION: Edward L. Cahn. *Law and Order;* William A. Wellman, *The Conquerors*

CINEMATOGRAPHY: Jackson Rose, *Law and Order;* Edward Cronjager, *The Conquerors;* Archie Stout, *Heritage of the Desert*

MUSIC: Max Steiner, *The Conquerors*

MALE LEADING ROLE: Walter Huston, *Law and Order;* Richard Dix, *The Conquerors;* Tom Mix, *Rider of Death Valley*

FEMALE LEADING ROLE: Lois Wilson, *Rider of Death Valley;* Ann Harding, *The Conquerors*

MALE SUPPORTING ROLE: Raymond Hatton, *Law and Order;* Francis Ford, *Destry Rides Again;* Fred Kohler, *Rider of Death Valley*

FEMALE SUPPORTING ROLE: Edna May Oliver, *The Conquerors*

Births. Writer Theodore V. Olsen; composers Lalo Schifrin, John Williams; actor Anthony Perkins; actresses Mara Corday, Felicia Farr, Abbe Lane, Piper Laurie, Colleen Miller.

Deaths. Writer Walter Noble Burns (b. 1872).

The first three years of the sound era—characterized by a number of historically significant western films—were followed by several lean years in which the genre was dominated by B productions.

Especially disappointing was the period 1932–1935, which altogether brought about less than half a dozen artistically notable westerns.

The creator of *Little Caesar*, W.R. Burnet, surprised western fans with a superior western novel, *Saint Johnson* (1930), which Edward L. Cahn turned, in 1932, into a remarkable picture, *Law and Order*. Beautifully photographed by Jackson Rose, the movie tells a story of the conflict between the Earp brothers and the Clanton gang in Tombstone, Arizona. The main characters, under disguised names, are impressively portrayed by Walter Huston (as Frame Johnson, i.e. Wyatt Earp) and Harry Carey (Brandt, i.e. Doc Holliday).

As *Law and Order* was definitely the finest western of the year, 1932 is also notable for the commencement of the Zane Grey-Henry Hathaway-Randolph Scott series of movies (to blossom in the following year), and for the introduction to talkies of Tom Mix with three pictures, including two relatively successful standard westerns. While *Rider of Death Valley*, directed by Albert S. Rogell, is generally considered to be the actor's best sound movie, *Destry Rides Again*, directed by Ben Stoloff, is important for being Mix's first talkie and the first adaptation of the popular 1930 novel by Max Brand. Unlike the two later versions of Destry, both directed by George Marshall, which clearly strayed from the book's story line, Rogell's rendition was quite faithful and thus maintained the resemblance to Dumas' classic novel *The Count of Monte Cristo*.

1933

Outstanding Achievements

PICTURE: *Secrets; To the Last Man; The Thundering Herd; Robbers' Roost*

NOVEL FILMED: *To the Last Man* by Zane Grey; *The Thundering Herd* by Zane Grey; *The Man of the Forest* by Zane Grey; *Robbers' Roost* by Zane Grey

SCREENPLAY (ADAPTATION): Frances Marion, *Secrets*; Jack Cunningham, *To the Last Man*; Dudley Nichols, *Robbers' Roost*

DIRECTION: Henry Hathaway, *To the Last Man*; Frank Borzage, *Secrets*

CINEMATOGRAPHY: Ben Reynolds, *To the Last Man*; Ray June, *Secrets*; George Schneiderman, *Robbers' Roost*

MALE LEADING ROLE: Randolph Scott, *To the Last Man*; Leslie Howard, *Secrets*; George O'Brien, *Robbers' Roost*

FEMALE LEADING ROLE: Esther Ralston, *To the Last Man*; Maureen O'Sullivan, *Robbers' Roost*; Mary Pickford, *Secrets*

MALE SUPPORTING ROLE: Harry Carey, *The Thundering Herd*; C. Aubrey Smith, *Secrets*

FEMALE SUPPORTING ROLE: Mona Maris, *Secrets*; Blanche Frederici, *The Thundering Herd*

Births. Writer Charles Portis; cinematographer Laszlo Kovacs; composer John Barry; actors Robert (Bobby) Blake, Gian Maria Volonte; actresses Suzan Ball, Kathryn Grant, Lori Nelson, Sheree North, Debra Paget, Joan Weldon.

Deaths. Actors Roy Stewart (b. 1883), Ernest Torrence (b. 1878); actress Blance Frederici (b. 1878).

A major highlight in the lean period for the artistic western was the series of seven Zane Grey adaptations made by Henry Hathaway with Randolph Scott in the leading role. Released by Paramount (with some footage of the studio's previous silent versions of the same novels) between 1932 and 1934, the pictures stand out among the low- and middle-budget productions of that period for their relatively literate scripts (written usually by Harold Shumate, alone or in collaboration, or Jack Cunningham, alone or in collaboration), energetic direction, superior cinematography (by either Archie Stout or Ben Reynolds) and decent acting. In addition to Scott, the players that appeared in more than one entry in the series include Sally Blane, Harry Carey, Sr., Noah Beery, Sr., Barton MacLane, Larry "Buster" Crabbe, Fred Kohler, Monte Blue and Fuzzy Knight. The best examples of the series are *To the Last Man* (featuring Esther Ralston, Larry "Buster" Crabbe, Jack LaRue, Noah Beery, Sr., and—in a bit part—Shirley Temple), a westernized version of *Romeo and Juliet;* and *The Thundering Herd* (co-starring Judith Allen, Noah Beery, Sr., Raymond Hatton, Harry Carey and Larry "Buster" Crabbe), an ecological tale focused on buffalo hunting in Texas.

Robbers' Roost, another relatively successful rendition of a Zane Grey book, was directed by Louis King, while the leading roles were played by George O'Brien, Maureen O'Sullivan and Reginald Owen. However, a movie artistically more ambitious than any of the Grey adaptations was Frank Borzage's *Secrets* (featuring Mary Pickford, Leslie Howard and C. Aubrey Smith), one of a few examples of a western film inspired by a stage play (by Rudolf Besier and May Edington, previously filmed also by Borzage in 1924, with Norma Talmadge).

1934

Outstanding Achievements

PICTURE: *Frontier Marshal; The Last Round-Up; West of the Pecos*
NOVEL FILMED: *Fighting Caravans* by Zane Grey, filmed as *Wagon Wheels; The Border Legion* by Zane Grey, filmed as *The Last Round-Up; West of the Pecos* by Zane Grey
NONFICTION BOOK FILMED: *Wyatt Earp: Frontier Marshal* by Stuart N. Lake
SCREENPLAY (ADAPTATION): William Conselman, Stuart Anthony, *Frontier Marshal;* Milton Krims, John Twist, *West of the Pecos*
DIRECTION: Lew Seiler, *Frontier Marshal;* Henry Hathaway, *The Last Round-Up*
CINEMATOGRAPHY: James Van Trees, Russell Metty, *West of the Pecos;* Robert Planck, *Frontier Marshal;* Archie Stout, *The Last Round-Up*
MALE LEADING ROLE: George O'Brien, *Frontier Marshal;* Randolph Scott, *The Last Round-Up;* Richard Dix, *West of the Pecos*
FEMALE LEADING ROLE: Irene Bentley, *Frontier Marshal;* Martha Sleeper, *West of the Pecos*
MALE SUPPORTING ROLE: Ward Bond, *Frontier Marshal;* Samuel S. Hinds, *West of the Pecos;* Monte Blue, *The Last Round-Up*
FEMALE SUPPORTING ROLE: Louise Beavers, *West of the Pecos*

Births. Director Sydney Pollack; composer Dave Grusin; actors Glenn Corbett, Russ Tamblyn; actresses Brigitte Bardot, Joan Evans, Shirley Jones, Inger Stevens.

Deaths. Writers Hal G. Evarts (b. 1887), Eugene Manlove Rhodes (b. 1869).

As the Zane Grey adaptations continued to be made (mostly by Hathaway, but also by other directors, with or without Randolph Scott), the highlight of 1934 was the first (out of three) screen version of the popular biographical book *Wyatt Earp: Frontier Marshal* (1931) by Stuart N. Lake. Directed by Lewis Seiler and starring George O'Brien, Irene Bentley and

George E. Stone, the 1934 version received the title *Frontier Marshal*, just like the next, 1939, rendition directed by Allan Dwan. Seiler's *Frontier Marshal* was the first picture to mention the name of Wyatt Earp, as *Law and Order*, made two years before from another literary source, depicted the same figures and events in a disguised manner.

The 1934 obituaries announced the death of two early western writers. Especially Eugene Manlove Rhodes, best known for his outstanding novella "Paso por Aqui" (filmed as *Four Faces West*, 1948), deserves recognition as one of the most distinguished pioneers of the genre.

There were no Academy Awards granted to a standard western made in 1934. But Jack Conway's *Viva Villa!* (featuring Wallace Beery, Fay Wray and Leo Carrillo), the biography of the Mexican patriot-revolutionary, received one Oscar and three additional nominations (including one for best picture).

1935

Outstanding Achievements

PICTURE: *Annie Oakley; The Arizonian; Powdersmoke Range*

NOVEL FILMED: *When a Man's a Man* by Harold Bell Wright; *Thunder Mountain* by Zane Grey

SCREENPLAY (ORIGINAL): Dudley Nichols, *The Arizonian;* Joseph A. Fields, Stewart Adamson, Joel Sayre, John Twist, *Annie Oakley*

DIRECTION: George Stevens, *Annie Oakley;* Charles Vidor, *The Arizonian*

CINEMATOGRAPHY: J. Roy Hunt, *Annie Oakley;* Harold Wenstrom, *The Arizonian*

MALE LEADING ROLE: Richard Dix, *The Arizonian;* Harry Carey, *Powdersmoke Range*

FEMALE LEADING ROLE: Barbara Stanwyck, *Annie Oakley;* Margot Grahame, *The Arizonian*

MALE SUPPORTING ROLE: Moroni Olsen, *Annie Oakley;* Louis Calhern, *The Arizonian;* Guinn "Big Boy" Williams, *Powdersmoke Range*

Births. Actors Jim Brown, Michael Dante, Alain Delon, Roy Jenson, Geoffrey Lewis, Doug McClure, Elvis Presley, John Saxon.

One of the least impressive years for the genre, 1935 is notable for George Stevens' first western as a director. A curiosity among the biographical pictures on Western women, *Annie Oakley* (featuring Barbara Stanwyck, Preston Foster, Melvyn Douglas and Moroni Olsen), boasting a memorable performance by Stanwyck, is nevertheless a modest picture that hardly announces the grandeur of the director's future masterpieces, *Shane* and *Giant*. Charles Vidor's *The Arizonian* (with Richard Dix, Louis Calhern, Margot Grahame and Preston Foster), and *Powdersmoke Range*, directed by Wallace Fox, are routine movies, albeit clearly superior to the rest of the year's productions. *Powdersmoke Range* based on the fiction by William Colt MacDonald, stands out as the highlight of all B westerns, primarily for the impressive cast of A/B westerners, including Harry Carey, Hoot Gibson, Bob Steele, Tom Tyler, Guinn "Big Boy" Williams, William Farnum, Wally Wales and Buddy Roosevelt.

1936

Outstanding Achievements

PICTURE: *The Plainsman; The Texas Rangers; Robin Hood of El Dorado; Three Godfathers; Sutters's Gold; Ramona*

1936

NOVEL FILMED: *Ramona* by Helen Hunt Jackson; *The Three Godfathers* by Peter B. Kyne; *The Mine with the Iron Door* by Harold Bell Wright

NONFICTION BOOK FILMED: *The Texas Rangers: A Century of Frontier Defense* by Walter Prescott Webb; *The Robinhood of El Dorado* by Walter Noble Burns

SHORT STORY FILMED: "M'liss" by Bret Harte, filmed as *M'liss*

SCREENPLAY (ADAPTATION): King Vidor, Elizabeth Hill (Vidor), Louis Stevens, *The Texas Rangers*; Waldemar Young, Harold Lamb, Lynn Riggs, Jeanie MacPherson, *The Plainsman*; William A. Wellman, Melvin Levy, Joseph Calleia, *Robin Hood of El Dorado*

DIRECTION: King Vidor, *The Texas Rangers*; Cecil B. De Mille, *The Plainsman*; William A. Wellman, *Robinhood of El Dorado*

CINEMATOGRAPHY (B&W): Edward Cronjager, *The Texas Rangers*; Victor Milner, George Robinson, *The Plainsman*; Joseph Ruttenberg, *Three Godfathers*;

CINEMATOGRAPHY (COLOR): William Skall, Chester Lyons, *Ramona*

MUSIC: George Antheil, *The Plainsman*; William Axt, *Three Godfathers*; Alfred Newman, *Ramona*

MALE LEADING ROLE: Gary Cooper, *The Plainsman*; Fred MacMurray, *The Texas Rangers*; Warner Baxter, *Robin Hood of El Dorado*

FEMALE LEADING ROLE: Jean Arthur, *The Plainsman*; Jean Parker, *The Texas Rangers*

MALE SUPPORTING ROLE: Lloyd Nolan, *The Texas Rangers*; Porter Hall, *The Plainsman*; J. Carrol Naish, *Robin Hood of El Dorado*

FEMALE SUPPORTING ROLE: Helen Burgess, *The Plainsman*; Katherine Alexander, *Sutter's Gold*

Academy Award Nomination

The Texas Rangers—AAN: sound recording (Franklin Hansen).

Births. Writer Larry McMurtry; cinematographer Owen Roizman; composer Fred Karlin; actors Joe Don Baker, David Carradine, Matt Clark, Bruce Dern, Dennis Hopper, Kris Kristofferson, Burt Reynolds, Anthony Zerbe; actresses Linda Cristal, Jill Ireland.

Deaths. Actors John Bowers (b. 1899), Henry B. Walthall (b. 1878).

The series of lean years in the production of the artistic western was interrupted in 1936. The westerns released in that year include six major pictures, two of which—*The Plainsman* and *The Texas Rangers*—are definite classics, two—*Robin Hood of El Dorado* and *Three Godfathers*—are examples of modest artistic achievements, and two—*Sutter's Gold* and *Ramona*—are interesting failures of ambitious endeavors.

Cecil B. De Mille's *The Plainsman* is clearly one of the year's most memorable movies and by far its finest western. Due to *The Plainsman's* impressive production values and the leading players' charming performances—Gary Cooper as Wild Bill Hickok, Jean Arthur as Calamity Jane and James Ellison as Buffalo Bill Cody—it has held the entertaining merits till now. A critic in the London *Times* noted: "If the West in its pioneer days is to be opened up again, Mr. Cooper and Miss Arthur, with the lavish assistance of Mr. Cecil De Mille, are certainly the people to do it."

Almost on the same level is King Vidor's *The Texas Rangers*. Beautifully photographed by Edward Cronjager, it is a fascinating morality tale focused on the relationships between five characters—Jim

Gary Cooper as Wild Bill Hickok in Cecil B. De Mille's *The Plainsman*, the most successful western of the mid-1930s.

Hawkins (Fred MacMurray), Wahoo Jones (Jack Oakie), Amanda Bailey (Jean Parker), Sam McGee (Lloyd Nolan) and Major Bailey (Edward Ellis). Those characters, however, do not appear on the pages of Walter Prescott Webb's 1935 book (included among the 13 best nonfiction books in the Western Writers of America's 1995 survey), on which the movie was allegedly based.

Three of the remaining westerns were derived from superior literary material. William A. Wellman's *Robin Hood of El Dorado* (starring Warner Baxter, Margo, Bruce Cabot and Ann Loring) was based on a biographical 1932 book by Walter Noble Burns; Richard Boleslawski's *Three Godfathers* (featuring Chester Morris, Lewis Stone and Walter Brennan) was the fifth (second sound) version of the 1912 novel by Peter B. Kyne; and Henry King's *Ramona* (with Loretta Young and Don Ameche) was the fourth (and last, to date) adaptation of the classic novel (1884) by Helen Hunt Jackson.

The 1936 obituaries reported the premature death of John Bowers, a forgotten actor who appeared in a few silent westerns, including *The Sky Pilot* (1921), *When a Man's a Man* (1924) and *Whispering Smith* (1926). His tragic life and suicide became the inspiration for Robert Carson and William A. Wellman's Academy Award–winning screen story of *A Star Is Born*, to be filmed in 1937, and then remade in 1954 and 1976.

1937

Outstanding Achievements

PICTURE: *Wells Fargo; The Outcasts of Poker Flat*

SHORT STORY FILMED: "The Outcasts of Poker Flat" and "The Luck of Roaring Camp" by Bret Harte, filmed as *The Outcasts of Poker Flat*

SCREENPLAY (ORIGINAL): Stuart N. Lake, Paul Schoefield, Gerard Geraghty, Frederick Jackson, *Wells Fargo*

SCREENPLAY (ADAPTATION): John Twist, Harry Segall, *The Outcasts of Poker Flat*

DIRECTION: Frank Lloyd, *Wells Fargo*; Christy Cabanne, *The Outcasts of Poker Flat*

CINEMATOGRAPHY (B&W): Theodor Sparkuhl, *Wells Fargo*; Robert De Grasse, *The Outcasts of Poker Flat*

MUSIC: Victor Young, *Wells Fargo*

MALE LEADING ROLE: Joel McCrea, *Wells Fargo*; Preston Foster, *The Outcasts of Poker Flat*

FEMALE LEADING ROLE: Frances Dee, *Wells Fargo*; Jean Muir, *The Outcasts of Poker Flat*

MALE SUPPORTING ROLE: Van

Heflin, *The Outcasts of Poker Flat*; Bob Burns, *Wells Fargo*; Henry O'Neill, *Wells Fargo*

Female Supporting Role: Mary Nash, *Wells Fargo*

Academy Award Nomination

Wells Fargo—AAN: sound recording (L.L. Ryder).

Births. Cinematographer Bruce Surtees; actors John Davis Chandler, Jack Nicholson, Robert Redford, Timothy Scott; actresses Jane Fonda, Suzanne Pleshette.

Deaths. Writer Frank H. Spearman (b. 1859); screenwriter Keene Thompson (b. c. 1886); directors Emmett J. Flynn (b. 1892), Clifford Smith (b. 1894).

Even though both Frank Lloyd's *Wells Fargo* (featuring Joel McCrea, Frances Dee, Bob Burns and Robert Cunnings) and Christy Cabanne's *The Outcasts of Poker Flat* (with Preston Foster, Jean Muir, Van Heflin and Virginia Weidler) could impress the contemporary audiences with their merits, neither movie was a thoroughly successful endeavor, and neither belongs among the very top achievements of the genre. Consequently, 1937 can be summed up as a year with an unremarkable contribution to the western film.

While it is important to note the first appearance in a western picture of two major actors—Joel McCrea in the role of Ramsay MacKay in *Wells Fargo*, and Van Heflin as the preacher in *The Outcasts of Poker Flat*—the death of Frank H. Spearman this year is a good opportunity to recognize the assets of his western prose, which included the popular 1906 railroad novel *Whispering Smith*.

1938

Outstanding Achievements

Picture: *Gold Is Where You Find It; The Texans; The Bad Man of Brimstone*

Novel Filmed: *North of 36* by Emerson Hough, filmed as *The Texans*; *The Valley of the Giants* by Peter B. Kyne; *The Mysterious Rider* by Zane Grey

Screenplay (Adaptation): Bertram Millhauser, Paul Sloane, William Wister Haines, *The Texans*

Direction: Michael Curtiz, *Gold Is Where You Find It*; James Hogan, *The Texans*

Cinematography (B&W): Theodor Sparkuhl, *The Texans*; Clyde De Vinna, *The Bad Man of Brimstone* (originally in sepia, later in B&W)

Cinematography (Color): Sol Polito, *Gold Is Where You Find It*

Music: Max Stainer, *Gold Is Where You Find It*

Song: Leo Robin, Ralph Rainer, "Silver on the Sage" from *The Texans*

Male Leading Role: Randolph Scott, *The Texans*; George Brent, *Gold Is Where You Find It*

Female Leading Role: Olivia de Havilland, *Gold Is Where You Find It*; Joan Bennett, *The Texans*

Male Supporting Role: Walter Brennan, *The Texans*; Bruce Cabot, *The Bad Man of Brimstone*

Female Supporting Role: May Robson, *The Texans*; Margaret Lindsay, *Gold Is Where You Find It*

Births. Actor Christopher Lloyd.

Deaths. Writer Owen Wister (b. 1860); director John G. Blystone (b. 1892); actor Fred Kohler (b. 1889).

The last of the lean years for the genre brought about the second, only partially successful, adaptation of Emerson Hough's superior novel *North of 36* (1924); entitled *The Texans*, it was directed by James P. Hogan, who gathered a superior cast, including Randolph Scott, Joan Bennett, May Robson, Robert Cummings and Walter Brennan (in a role anticipating his trademark characterization in *Red River*). The year was also notable for the western debut of Olivia de Havilland in Michael Curtiz's somewhat disappointing *Gold Is Where You Find It* (co-starring George Brent and Claude Rains), and—above all—for the passing away of Owen Wister, the legendary author of the highly acclaimed and most influential western novel *The Virginian: A Horseman of the Plains* (which served as the basis of four movies and one television series).

1939

Outstanding Achievements

PICTURE: *Stagecoach; Destry Rides Again; Jesse James; Union Pacific; Dodge City; Frontier Marshal; The Oklahoma Kid; Man of Conquest; Stand Up and Fight*

NOVEL FILMED: *Destry Rides Again* by Max Brand; *The Heritage of the Desert* by Zane Grey; *Trouble Shooter* by Ernest Haycox, filmed as *Union Pacific*

NONFICTION BOOK FILMED: *Wyatt Earp: Frontier Marshal* by Stuart N. Lake, filmed as *Frontier Marshal*

SHORT STORY FILMED: "Stage to Lordsburg" by Ernest Haycox, filmed as *Stagecoach*

SCREENPLAY (ORIGINAL): Nunnally Johnson, *Jesse James* ; Robert Buckner, *Dodge City*

SCREENPLAY (ADAPTATION): Dudley Nichols, *Stagecoach;* Felix Jackson, Gertrude Purcell, Henry Myers, *Destry Rides Again;* Sam Hellman, *Frontier Marshal*

DIRECTION: John Ford, *Stagecoach;* George Marshall, *Destry Rides Again;* Henry King, *Jesse James*

CINEMATOGRAPHY (B&W): Bert Glennon, *Stagecoach;* Victor Milner, Dewey Wrigley, *Union Pacific;* Hal Mohr, *Destry Rides Again*

CINEMATOGRAPHY (COLOR): George Barnes, W. Howard Greene, *Jesse James*; Sol Polito, Ray Rennahan, *Dodge City*

MUSIC: Richard Hageman, W. Franke Harling, John Leipold, Leo Shuken, *Stagecoach;* Victor Young, *Man of Conquest;* Sigmund Krumgold, John Leipold, *Union Pacific*

SONG: Frederick Hollander, Frank Loesser, "The Boys in the Back Room" from *Destry Rides Again;* Frederick Hollander, Frank Loesser, "Little Joe the Wrangler" from *Destry Rides Again*

MALE LEADING ROLE: James Stewart, *Destry Rides Again;* John Wayne, *Stagecoach;* Errol Flynn, *Dodge City*

FEMALE LEADING ROLE: Claire Trevor, *Stagecoach;* Marlene Dietrich, *Destry Rides Again;* Barbara Stanwyck, *Union Pacific*

MALE SUPPORTING ROLE: Thomas Mitchell, *Stagecoach;* John Carradine, *Stagecoach;* Samuel S. Hinds, *Destry Rides Again*

FEMALE SUPPORTING ROLE: Louise Platt, *Stagecoach;* Ann Sheridan, *Dodge City;* Jane Darwell, *Jesse James*

Academy Awards/ Nominations

Stagecoach—AA: score; supporting actor Thomas Mitchell; AAN: picture; direction; B&W cinematography; editing (Otho Lovering, Dorothy Spencer); interior decoration (Alexander Toluboff).

Man of Conquest—AAN: original score (Victor Young); sound recording (C.L. Lootens); interior decoration (John Victor Mackay).

Union Pacific—AAN: special effects (photographic—Farciot Edouart, Gordon Jennings; sound—Loren Ryder).

Births. (Screen)writers Brian Garfield, Thomas McGuane; actors James Caan, Peter Fonda, George Hamilton, Sal Mineo, Patrick Wayne; actresses Claudia Cardinale, Liv Ullmann.

Deaths. Writer Zane Grey (b. 1872); actor Douglas Fairbanks (b. 1883).

While in Europe the year 1939 marked the beginning of World War II, for the American cinema it was a year of highest prosperity, rightly referred to as Hollywood's *annus mirabilis*. In addition to an impressive number of outstanding pictures outside the genre, 1939 brought about several remarkable westerns.

After being away from the genre for 13 years, John Ford made his first sound western in 1939. Superior to most of his previous endeavors in all genres, including his prestigious adaptations of some major literary works made in the 1930s, *Stagecoach* turned out to be a masterpiece and a milestone not only in the development of the genre, but also in the history of the cinema in general. The extremely modern language that Ford honed to perfection in his new movie, in addition to the unusually intellectual story brimming with social commentary and political innuendoes, would influence generations of filmmakers throughout the world, including Orson Welles, who admitted seeing it many times while working on *Citizen Kane*. The reviews were enthusiastic, and the Academy recognized it with two Oscars and

American poster for Lloyd Bacon's *The Oklahoma Kid* (WB, 1939), a popular western starring James Cagney.

five more nominations. In two of the nominated categories, best picture and director, the movie lost (rather undeservedly) to *Gone with the Wind* and its director, Victor Fleming. Ford, however, was honored with the New York Critics Best Director

A Powerful Story
of 9 Strange People
STAGECOACH
A
WALTER WANGER
PRODUCTION
Directed by
JOHN FORD
with
CLAIRE TREVOR · JOHN WAYNE · ANDY DEVINE
JOHN CARRADINE · THOMAS MITCHELL · LOUISE PLATT · GEORGE BANCROFT
DONALD MEEK · BERTON CHURCHILL · TIM HOLT
Released Thru
UNITED ARTISTS

Award. The irresistibly beautiful musical score, based on American folk songs, was granted one of the two Oscars, while the other one went to Thomas Mitchell, who gave a superb performance as the alcoholic Dr. Josiah Boone, defeating in the Oscar run such actors as Harry Carey and Claude Rains (both nominated for *Mr. Smith Goes to Washington*), Brian Aherne (*Juarez*) and Brian Donlevy (*Beau Geste*). In their 1995 poll, the Western Writers of America selected *Stagecoach* as one of the best 15 western films of all time, and Ernest Haycox's "Stage to Lordsburg" (1937) as number three (tied with two others) short story.

No westerns were nominated for an Academy Award in the categories of best actor and best actress, even though the year boasted a number of superior performances. The leading men that deserve special recognition include James Stewart, for his excellent portrayal of Tom Destry in *Destry Rides Again*, John Wayne, for making the character of the Ringo Kid in *Stagecoach* bigger than it was in the script, and Errol Flynn, for his charismatic portrayal of Wade Hatton, an Irish soldier of fortune turned sheriff in Michael Curtiz's *Dodge City*. Unforgettable were also Tyrone Power and Henry Fonda in their likable characterizations as

Above: George Bancroft, John Wayne and Louise Platt in John Ford's classic *Stagecoach*, a picture that began a new era for the western genre. *Opposite:* American poster for *Stagecoach* (UA, 1939), the first film (out of many) derived from Ernest Haycox's prose.

Henry Hull, Nancy Kelly, John Russell and Randolph Scott in the conclusive funeral scene from Henry King's hit *Jesse James*, starring Tyrone Power and Henry Fonda.

the outlaw brothers in *Jesse James*, and Joel McCrea as the incorruptible railroad troubleshooter Jeff Butler in Cecil B. De Mille's *Union Pacific*. Claire Trevor gave a fine, restrained performance as Dallas in *Stagecoach*, while Marlene Dietrich, as Frenchy (singing three songs, including "The Boys in the Back Room") in *Destry Rides Again*, and Barbara Stanwyck, as Mollie Monahan in *Union Pacific*, were perfect matches for Stewart and McCrea, respectively.

There is no doubt that 1939, the golden year of Hollywood, was also a turning point in the history of the genre. It stopped a series of "lean" years for the artistic western and began a new era, the golden period, which would last until the early 1960s. It has to be noted, however, that the year brought two painful losses. Among the celebrities that died were Zane Grey (*Riders of the Purple Sage*, *The Heritage of the Desert*, *To the Last Man*, *The Vanishing American*), the most popular western author of the first half of the century (and whose books would keep being filmed through the mid–1950s); and Douglas Fairbanks (*The Good Bad Man*, *The Half Breed*, *The Man from Painted Post*, *Headin' South*), an accomplished leading man of the adventure film, to whom the Academy granted a Special (Commemorative) Award—"recognizing the unique and outstanding contribution of Douglas

Fairbanks, first president of the Academy, to the international development of the motion picture."

1940

Outstanding Achievements

PICTURE: *The Westerner; Arizona; The Return of Frank James; Virginia City; Dark Command; When the Daltons Rode; North West Mounted Police; Santa Fe Trail*

NOVEL FILMED: *Arizona* by Clarence Budington Kelland; *Arouse and Beware* by MacKinlay Kantor, filmed as *The Man from Dakota*; *The Dark Command* by W.R. Burnett; *The River's End* by James Oliver Curwood; *The Light of Western Stars* by Zane Grey

SCREENPLAY (ORIGINAL): Stuart N. Lake, Niven Busch, Jo Swerling, *The Westerner;* Sam Hellman, *The Return of Frank James*

SCREENPLAY (ADAPTATION): Claude Binyon, *Arizona;* Grover Jones, Lionel Houser, F. Hugh Herbert, Jan Fortune, *Dark Command*

DIRECTION: William Wyler, *The Westerner;* Fritz Lang, *The Return of Frank James;* Wesley Ruggles, *Arizona*

CINEMATOGRAPHY (B&W): Gregg Toland, *The Westerner;* Joseph Walker, Harry Hollenberger, Fayte Brown, *Arizona;* Sol Polito, *Virginia City*

CINEMATOGRAPHY (COLOR): Victor Milner, W. Howard Greene, *North West Mounted Police;* George Barnes, William V. Skall, *The Return of Frank James*

MUSIC: Victor Young, *Arizona;* Victor Young, *Dark Command;* David Buttolph, *The Return of Frank James*

SONG: Victor Young, Frank Loesser, "Does the Moon Shine Through the Tall Pine? from *North West Mounted Police*

MALE LEADING ROLE: Gary Cooper, *The Westerner;* Henry Fonda, *The Return of Frank James;* William Holden, *Arizona*

FEMALE LEADING ROLE: Jean Arthur, *Arizona;* Gene Tierney, *The Return of Frank James;* Claire Trevor, *Dark Command*

MALE SUPPORTING ROLE: Walter Brennan, *The Westerner;* Henry Hull, *The Return of Frank James;* Paul Harvey, *Arizona*

FEMALE SUPPORTING ROLE: Lillian Bond, *The Westerner;* Marjorie Main, *Dark Command*

Academy Awards/Nominations

The Westerner—AA: supporting actor Walter Brennan; AAN: original story (Stuart N. Lake); B&W interior decoration (James Basevi).

Arizona—AAN: original score; B&W interior decoration (Lionel Banks, Robert Peterson).

Dark Command—AAN: original score; B&W interior decoration (John Victor Mackay).

North West Mounted Police—AA: editing (Anne Bauchens); AAN: color cinematography; original score (Victor Young); color interior decoration (Hans Dreier, Roland Anderson); sound recording (Loren Ryder).

Births. Actor Michael Sarrazin; actresses Luana Anders, Susan Clark, Raquel Welch.

Deaths. Writers B.M. Bower (b. 1871), Courtney Ryley Cooper (b. 1886); screenwriters J.G. Hawks (b. 1874), Grover Jones (1893); director Edwin Carewe (b. 1883); actors Tom Mix (b. 1880), Charles Ogle (b. 1865).

1940

As the tide of prosperity for the genre continued, eight major westerns were released in 1940, one of which—*The Westerner*—is a masterpiece, and at least two—*Arizona* and *The Return of Frank James*—are recognized classics. The grandeur of *The Westerner* consists of Niven Busch and Jo Swerling's original script from Stuart N. Lake's Oscar-nominated screen story, William Wyler's highly inspired direction, Gregg Toland's brilliant black-and-white cinematography, and two performances of a quality absolutely unique in the genre. While Walter Brennan's Academy Award–winning characterization of Judge Roy Bean is a definite scene-stealing job, its effectiveness was enhanced by Gary Cooper's suitably restrained acting in the role of the stalwart hero, Cole Hardin. Cooper and Brennan had been friends since the time they both were starting their Hollywood careers as extras in the mid–1920s, and they would have played together in six movies by 1950. Their on-screen chemistry, always commendable, is extraordinary in *The Westerner*.

The Return of Frank James, a sequel to Henry King's *Jesses James*, with several actors—including Henry Fonda as Frank James—repeating their roles, was also a fine movie, beautifully photographed in Technicolor by George Barnes and William V. Skall. Robert W. Dana wrote in *The New York Herald Tribune*: "Fritz Lang's methodical direction may exasperate those who look for a faster tempo in a drama of the outdoors, but its emphasis on small things like gestures and shadows and sounds of nature reveal the Western in a new and interesting light."

A faithful rendition of Clarence Budington Kelland's enjoyable 1939 novel of the same name, Wesley Ruggles' *Arizona* (starring Jean Arthur and William Holden) was summed up by a *Variety* critic in these words: "Partly because the approach seems to have been superficial, partly because the action is sporadic and frequently interrupted, *Arizona* lacks the sweep and dramatic impulse that would have made it a great picture. Even so, it is a romantic episode with fine camerawork, great scenery, interesting details and a sufficient amount of action to give it general popularity."

Among the remaining major westerns of the year, three were notable for their director-actor collaboration. *Virginia City* and *Santa Fe Trail* continued the fruitful association of Michael Curtiz and Errol Flynn, who had made together a series of successful swashbuckling movies, as well as the remarkable 1939 western *Dodge City*. *Dark Command*, on the other hand, marked the reunion of Raoul Walsh and John Wayne ten years after their collaboration on the underrated epic *The Big Trail*.

An unusual record was set by Victor Young, who won three Academy Award nominations in the category of best original score (for *Arizona*, *Dark Command* and *North West Mounted Police*). He lost the award to Leigh Harline, Paul J. Smith and Ned Washington, the winners of the Oscar for *Pinocchio*. In fact, the unlucky Young won altogether four Oscar nominations for 1940, losing the fourth one—in the category of best score (for *Arise, My Love*)—to Alfred Newman for *Tin Pan Alley*.

Tom Mix, one of the most important western heroes of the silent period, died in 1940 in a car crash in Arizona. His major credits include *The Night Horseman*, *The Lucky Horseshoe*, *The Great K & A Train Robbery* and *Outlaws of Red River*. Incidentally, Mix was the first Chip Bennett, the most memorable character in the prose of B.M. Bower (*Chip of the Flying U*, *Flying U Ranch*, *Points West*), who also passed away in 1940. Despite her waning popularity, Bower deserves to be recognized as one of the pioneer western writers, the

Gary Cooper in William Wyler's *The Westerner*, a picture that brought Walter Brennan (playing the role of Judge Roy Bean) his third Academy Award for best supporting actor.

1941

female counterpart of Owen Wister—both excelling in ranch romance in their own way.

1941

Outstanding Achievements

PICTURE: *Western Union; Texas; The Shepherd of the Hills; Billy the Kid; Honky Tonk; The Lady from Cheyenne*
NOVEL FILMED: *The Shepherd of the Hills* by Harold Bell Wright; *Western Union* by Zane Grey
NONFICTION BOOK FILMED: *The Saga of Billy the Kid* by Walter Noble Burns, filmed as *Billy the Kid*
SHORT STORY FILMED: "The Parson of Panamint" by Peter B. Kyne
SCREENPLAY (ORIGINAL): Horace McCoy, Lewis Meltzer, Michael Blankfort, *Texas*
SCREENPLAY (ADAPTATION): Robert Carson, *Western Union*; Harold Bell Wright, Grover Jones, Stuart Anthony, *The Shepherd of the Hills*
DIRECTION: George Marshall, *Texas*; Fritz Lang, *Western Union*; Henry Hathaway, *The Shepherd of the Hills*
CINEMATOGRAPHY (B&W): George Meehan, *Texas* (originally in sepia); Harold Rosson, *Honky Tonk*
CINEMATOGRAPHY (COLOR): William V. Skall, Leonard Smith, *Billy the Kid*; Edward Cronjager, *Western Union*; Charles Lang, Jr., W. Howard Greene, *The Shepherd of the Hills*
MUSIC: David Buttolph, *Western Union*; David Snell, *Billy the Kid*
SONG: Ormond B. Ruthven, Albert Mannheimer, "Viva La Vida" from *Billy the Kid*; Charles Previn, Sam Lerner, "Ladies from Paree" from *The Lady from Cheyenne*
MALE LEADING ROLE: Randolph Scott, *Western Union*; William Holden, *Texas*; Glenn Ford, *Texas*
FEMALE LEADING ROLE: Loretta Young, *The Lady from Cheyenne*; Claire Trevor, *Texas*; Betty Field, *The Shepherd of the Hills*
MALE SUPPORTING ROLE: Edgar Buchanan, *Texas*; Harry Carey, *The Shepherd of the Hills*; Dean Jagger, *Western Union*
FEMALE SUPPORTING ROLE: Beulah Bondi, *The Shepherd of the Hills*; Marjorie Main, *Honky Tonk*

Academy Award Nomination

Billy the Kid—AAN: color cinematography.

Births. Actors Stacy Keach, Tommy Rettig.

Deaths. Screenwriter Jack Cunningham (b. 1882).

The major westerns released in the year of *Citizen Kane*—although none a masterpiece—were each characterized by solid direction, remarkable camera work, an enjoyable story and several impressive characterizations. The ones that stand out in the group are *Western Union*, *Texas* and *The Shepherd of the Hills*.

Although *Western Union* was only the second western in Fritz Lang's filmography, the director managed to create a solid piece of entertainment with a fascinating story (which, however, except for the title and the general setting—the building of the telegraph—has little to do with Zane Grey's 1939 novel on which it was allegedly based). Randolph Scott heads the commendable cast (including Robert Young, Virginia Gilmore, Dean Jagger, Chill Wills and Barton MacLane) and gives possibly the best performance in the first half of his career.

Texas (featuring William Holden, Glenn Ford, Claire Trevor, Edgar Buchanan and George Bancroft), which is as vivid a picture as *Western Union*, was summed up by Henry T. Murdock in the *Philadelphia Evening Ledger* in the following words: "Whenever the circumstances warrant, Director Marshall jams vigorous comedy into the plot…. Oddly enough, while some of the action isn't far from slapstick, it never interferes with a really exciting tale of the cattle country. Both young men acquit themselves well. They are spirited, personable and resourceful."

The Shepherd of the Hills (arguably the best, albeit not very accurate, rendition of the popular 1907 spiritual book by Harold Bell Wright) was notable for being the first (out of five) movies of the Henry Hathaway-John Wayne association, and for the teaming up of Wayne with Harry Carey—the Duke's boyhood idol and now a close friend (they would play together again in *The Spoilers*, *Angel and the Badman* and *Red River*).

1942

Outstanding Achievements

PICTURE: *They Died with Their Boots On*; *The Spoilers*; *The Great Man's Lady*; *Tombstone*; *Valley of the Sun*

NOVEL FILMED: *The Spoilers* by Rex Beach; *Sundown Jim* by Ernest Haycox; *The Valley of the Rising Sun* by Clarence Budington Kelland, filmed as *Valley of the Sun*

NONFICTION BOOK FILMED: *Tombstone: An Iliad of the Southwest* by Walter Noble Burns, filmed as *Tombstone*

SHORT STORY FILMED: "Stage Station" by Ernest Haycox, filmed as *Apache Trail*

SCREENPLAY (ORIGINAL): Aeneas MacKenzie, Wally Kline, *They Died with Their Boots On*

SCREENPLAY (ADAPTATION): Lawrence Hazard, Tom Reed, *The Spoilers*; Horace McCoy, *Valley of the Sun*

DIRECTION: Raoul Walsh, *They Died with Their Boots On*; Ray Enright, *The Spoilers*; George Marshall, *Valley of the Sun*

CINEMATOGRAPHY (B&W): Russell Harlan, *Silver Queen*; William C. Mellor, *The Great Man's Lady*

MUSIC: Victor Young, *Silver Queen*; Max Steiner, *They Died with Their Boots On*; Victor Young, *The Great Man's Lady*

MALE LEADING ROLE: Errol Flynn, *They Died with Their Boots On*; John Wayne, *The Spoilers*; George Brent, *Silver Queen*

FEMALE LEADING ROLE: Barbara Stanwyck, *The Great Man's Lady*; Olivia de Havilland, *They Died with Their Boots On*; Marlene Dietrich, *The Spoilers*

MALE SUPPORTING ROLE: Sydney Greenstreet, *They Died with Their Boots On*; Harry Carey, *The Spoilers*; Brian Donlevy, *The Great Man's Lady*

FEMALE SUPPORTING ROLE: Margaret Lindsay, *The Spoilers*

Academy Award Nominations

The Spoilers—AAN: B&W interior decoration (John B. Goodman and Jack Otterson; Russell A. Gausman and Edward R. Robinson).

Silver Queen—AAN: scoring of a dramatic or comedy picture.

Births. Actors Harrison Ford, Brandon De Wilde, Bo Hopkins; actress Katharine Ross.

Deaths. Writers Will James (b. 1892), Edwin Milton Royle (b. 1862); director James Cruze (b. 1884); actor Buck Jones (b. 1889); actress Edna May Oliver (b. 1883).

1943

Randolph Scott, John Wayne and Marlene Dietrich in Ray Enright's *The Spoilers*, the fourth screen version of the popular novel by Rex Beach.

Even though most of the important westerns of 1942 were made by some major directors of the genre—Raoul Walsh (*They Died with Their Boots On*), William A. Wellman (*The Great Man's Lady*), George Marshall (*Valley of the Sun*) and Ray Enright (*The Spoilers*)—their artistic appeal was rather limited. A possible exception was *They Died with Their Boots On* (starring Errol Flynn and Olivia de Havilland), an impressively staged epic which, however, can be criticized for its overly glamorized, or even heroic, approach to the career of George Armstrong Custer.

While *The Spoilers* (the fourth screen version of the popular novel by Rex Beach) earned its reputation because of its great amount of action (especially the extensive fistfight between hero John Wayne and villain Randolph Scott, *The Great Man's Lady* lacks excitement but is laudable for its intellectual message (anticipating that of the 1962 movie *The Man Who Shot Liberty Valance*), as well as its original structure (to be used again almost 30 years later in *Little Big Man*).

1943

Outstanding Achievements

PICTURE: *The Ox-Bow Incident; The Outlaw; The Desperadoes; The Kansan*

NOVEL FILMED: *The Ox-Bow Incident* by Walter van Tilburg Clark; *Peace*

Marshal by Frank Gruber, filmed as *The Kansan*

SCREENPLAY (ORIGINAL): Jules Furthman, *The Outlaw;* Max Brand, Robert Carson, *The Desperadoes*

SCREENPLAY (ADAPTATION): Lamar Trotti, *The Ox-Bow Incident;* Harold Shumate, *The Kansan*

DIRECTION: William A. Wellman, *The Ox-Bow Incident;* Charles Vidor, *The Desperadoes;* Howard Hughes, *The Outlaw*

CINEMATOGRAPHY (B&W): Arthur C. Miller, *The Ox-Bow Incident;* Gregg Toland, *The Outlaw;* Russell Harlan, *The Kansan*

CINEMATOGRAPHY (COLOR): George Meehan, Allen M. Davey, *The Desperadoes*

MUSIC: Cyril J. Mockridge, *The Ox-Bow Incident;* Walter Scharf, *In Old Oklahoma;* Gerard Carbonara, *The Kansan*

MALE LEADING ROLE: Henry Fonda, *The Ox-Bow Incident;* Richard Dix, *The Kansan;* Walter Huston, *The Outlaw*

FEMALE LEADING ROLE: Claire Trevor, *The Desperadoes;* Jane Russell, *The Outlaw;* Jane Wyatt, *The Kansan*

MALE SUPPORTING ROLE: Dana Andrews, *The Ox-Bow Incident;* Frank Conroy, *The Ox-Bow Incident;* Edgar Buchanan, *The Desperadoes*

FEMALE SUPPORTING ROLE: Jane Darwell, *The Ox-Bow Incident;* Evelyn Keyes, *The Desperadoes;* Mary Beth Hughes, *The Ox-Bow Incident*

Academy Award Nominations

The Ox-Bow Incident—AAN: picture.

In Old Oklahoma—AAN: scoring of a dramatic or comedy picture; sound recording (Daniel J. Bloomberg).

The Kansan—AAN: scoring of a dramatic or comedy picture.

Births. Cinematographer Dean Semler; actors Michael Anderson, Jr., Christopher Mitchum; actress Beverly Washburn.

Deaths. Directors Hobart Bosworth (b. 1867), James P. Hogan (b. 1891), W.S. Van Dyke (b. 1889); actor Tully Marshall (b. 1864).

The notable westerns of 1943 included two superior actioners dealing with the struggle for law and order—George Archainbaud's *The Kansan* (starring Richard Dix and Jane Wyatt) and Charles Vidor's *The Desperadoes* (featuring Randolph Scott, Glenn Ford and Claire Trevor). Also released was one relatively successful psychoanalytical treatise on friendship, famous for its erotic scene— Howard Hughes's *The Outlaw* (with Jack Buetel, Jane Russell, Walter Huston and Thomas Mitchell), and one masterpiece focused on mob psychology—William A. Wellman's *The Ox-Bow Incident*.

Even though *The Ox-Bow Incident* lacks the major attributes of the standard western—action, hero and mythological elements—both Wellman and Walter Van Tilburg Clark, the author of the 1940 book (chosen as one of the best 12 western novels by the Western Writers of America in their 1995 survey) on which the film was based, deserve the highest praise for exposing the dark side of human nature through tackling the weighty issues of intolerance, violence and insensitivity. The message can be interpreted either literally as an anti-lynching statement or allegorically as a warning against any form of bigotry and violence, particularly in the context of the world's new threat: fascism. In addition to its intellectual values, the picture offers a number of aesthetical merits—meticulous direction, Arthur C. Miller's excellent camera work (despite the controversial decision to shoot most of it in the studio), Cyril J. Mockridge's low-key musical score using the "Red River Valley"

1944

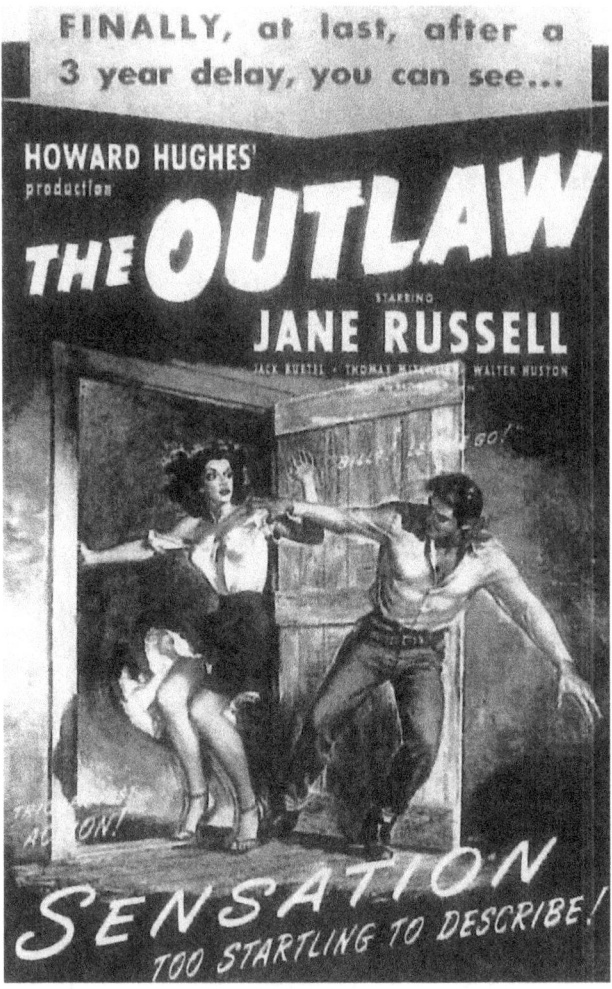

American poster for *The Outlaw* (UA, 1943), a scandalous and controversial western directed by Howard Hughes.

motif, and several first-rate performances (especially by Henry Fonda, Dana Andrews, Frank Conroy, Jane Darwell, Harry Davenport and Anthony Quinn).

1944

Outstanding Achievements

PICTURE: *Buffalo Bill*; *Tall in the Saddle*; *The Woman of the Town*

NOVEL FILMED: *Gentle Annie* by MacKinlay Kantor

SCREENPLAY (ORIGINAL): Aeneas MacKenzie, Clements Ripley, Cecile Kramer, *Buffalo Bill*; Paul Fix, Michael Hogan, *Tall in the Saddle*

DIRECTION: William A. Wellman, *Buffalo Bill*; Edwin L. Marin, *Tall in the Saddle*

CINEMATOGRAPHY (B&W): Robert De Grasse, *Tall in the Saddle*

CINEMATOGRAPHY (COLOR): Leon Shamroy, *Buffalo Bill*

MUSIC: Miklos Rozsa, *The Woman of the Town*; David Buttolph, *Buffalo Bill*; Roy Webb, *Tall in the Saddle*

MALE LEADING ROLE: Joel McCrea, *Buffalo Bill*; John Wayne, *Tall in the Saddle*

FEMALE LEADING ROLE: Maureen O'Hara, *Buffalo Bill*; Claire Trevor, *The Woman of the Town*; Ella Raines, *Tall in the Saddle*

MALE SUPPORTING ROLE: Thomas Mitchell, *Buffalo Bill*; Ward Bond, *Tall in the Saddle*; Edgar Buchanan, *Buffalo Bill*

FEMALE SUPPORTING ROLE: Linda Darnell, *Buffalo Bill*; Elizabeth Risdon, *Tall in the Saddle*

Academy Award Nomination

The Woman of the Town—AAN: best scoring of a dramatic or comedy picture.

Births. Screenwriter John Milius; actor Sam Elliott.

Deaths. Writers Frederick Schiller Faust (Max Brand/Evan Evans, b. 1892), Harold Bell Wright (b. 1872); director George B. Seitz (b. 1888).

In the filmography of the genre's greatest star, John Wayne, Edwin L. Marin's *Tall in the Saddle* (co-starring Ella Raines, George "Gabby" Hayes and Ward Bond) is possibly the most important western of the mid-1940s, even though it does not measure up to most of the actor's future films.

While its main assets are competent direction, swift pacing, and a lot of action, the appeal of William A. Wellman's *Buffalo Bill* (starring Joel McCrea, Maureen O'Hara and Linda Darnell) arises from the elegance of the staging and photography, as well as the charm of the major players. *Buffalo Bill*, which was the second (and last) western of the Wellman-McCrea partnership (after *The Great Man's Lady*), is definitely one of the most pleasing biographies of a Western figure.

The celebrities that passed away in 1944 include two extremely popular western writers—Max Brand/Evan Evans (*The Night Horseman*, *Destry Rides Again*, *Singing Guns*), who was killed in Italy during a German night attack, and Harold Bell Wright (*The Shepherd of the Hills*, *The Winning of Barbara Worth*, *When a Man's a Man*).

1945

Outstanding Achievements

PICTURE: *Along Came Jones*; *San Antonio*

NOVEL FILMED: *Useless Cowboy* by Alan LeMay, filmed as *Along Came Jones*; *West of the Pecos* by Zane Grey; *Wanderer of the Wasteland* by Zane Grey

SCREENPLAY (ORIGINAL): Alan LeMay, W.R. Burnett, *San Antonio*

SCREENPLAY (ADAPTATION): Nunnally Johnson, *Along Came Jones*

DIRECTION: David Butler, *San Antonio*; Stuart Heisler, *Along Came Jones*

CINEMATOGRAPHY (B&W): Milton Krasner, *Along Came Jones*; Jack Marta, *Dakota*

CINEMATOGRAPHY (COLOR): Bert Glennon, *San Antonio*; George Robinson, Charles P. Boyle, *Frontier Gal*

MUSIC: Max Steiner, *San Antonio*; Arthur Lange, Hugo Friedhofer, Charles Maxwell, *Along Came Jones*; Walter Scharf, *Dakota*

SONG: Ray Heindorf and M.K. Jerome, Ted Koehler, "Some Sunday Morning" from *San Antonio*

MALE LEADING ROLE: Gary Cooper, *Along Came Jones*; Errol Flynn, *San Antonio*

FEMALE LEADING ROLE: Loretta Young, *Along Came Jones*; Alexis Smith, *San Antonio*

MALE SUPPORTING ROLE: Dan Duryea, *Along Came Jones*; S.Z. Sakall, *San Antonio*; Andy Devine, *Frontier Gal*

FEMALE SUPPORTING ROLE: Florence Bates, *San Antonio*; Ona Munson, *Dakota*

Academy Award Nominations

San Antonio—AAN: song "Some Sunday Morning"; color interior decoration (Ted Smith, Jack McConaghy).

Births. Writer Michael Blake.

Stuart Heisler's *Along Came Jones* was Gary Cooper's first western since 1940, when the actor had appeared in two westerns—*The Westerner*, one of his best, and *North West Mounted Police*, notable primarily for being his first color picture. Based on a 1943 novel by Alan LeMay (the future author of *The Searchers*), *Along Came Jones* (featuring Loretta Young, Dan Duryea and William Demarest) is a relatively enjoyable movie with a few humorous situations and several likeable characters. A *Variety* critic noted, "Cooper plays

1946

American poster (painting by Norman Rockwell) for *Along Came Jones* (RKO, 1945), the first film (out of four) based on Alan LeMay's prose.

his usually languid self impressively, while Miss Young is decorative and photographed well. Demarest is in for some comedy relief, of which there is too little, while Dan Duryea is properly menacing as the killer."

San Antonio (starring Errol Flynn and Alexis Smith), directed by David Butler with an uncredited assistance from Raoul Walsh, is also a piece of solid entertainment, albeit rather unoriginal and clearly deprived of higher artistic pretensions.

1946

Outstanding Achievements

PICTURE: *My Darling Clementine; Canyon Passage; Duel in the Sun; Abilene Town; The Virginian ; California; Bad Bascomb*

NOVEL FILMED: *The Virginian: A Horseman of the Plains* by Owen Wister, filmed as *The Virginian; Canyon Passage* Ernest Haycox; *Duel in the Sun* by Niven Busch; *Trail Town* by Ernest Haycox, filmed as *Abilene Town*

NONFICTION BOOK FILMED: *Wyatt Earp: Frontier Marshal* by Stuart N. Lake, filmed as *My Darling Clementine*

SCREENPLAY (ORIGINAL): William Lipman, Grant Garrett, *Bad Bascomb*

SCREENPLAY (ADAPTATION): Sam Hellman, Samuel G. Engel, Winston Miller, *My Darling Clementine;* Ernest Pascal, *Canyon Passage*

DIRECTION: John Ford, *My Darling Clementine;* Jacques Tourneur, *Canyon Passage*

CINEMATOGRAPHY (B&W): Joseph MacDonald, *My Darling Clementine;* Archie Stout, *Abilene Town*

CINEMATOGRAPHY (COLOR): Edward Cronjager, *Canyon Passage;* Lee Garmes, Hal Rosson, Ray Rennahan, Charles Boyle, *Duel in the Sun*

MUSIC: Cyril Mockridge, *My Darling Clementine;* Dimitri Tiomkin, *Duel in the Sun;* Frank Skinner, *Canyon Passage*

SONG: Hoagy Carmichael, Jack Brooks, "Ole Buttermilk Sky" from *Canyon Passage*

MALE LEADING ROLE: Henry Fonda, *My Darling Clementine;* Dana Andrews, *Canyon Passage;* Randolph Scott, *Abilene Town*

FEMALE LEADING ROLE: Jennifer Jones, *Duel in the Sun;* Susan Hayward, *Canyon Passage;* Linda Darnell, *My Darling Clementine*

MALE SUPPORTING ROLE: Walter Brennan, *My Darling Clementine;* Charles Bickford, *Duel in the Sun;* Brian Donlevy, *Canyon Passage*

FEMALE SUPPORTING ROLE: Lillian Gish, *Duel in the Sun;* Jane Darwell, *My Darling Clementine*

Academy Award Nominations

Canyon Passage—AAN: song "Ole Buttermilk Sky."

Duel in the Sun—AAN: actress Jennifer Jones, supporting actress Lillian Gish.

Births. Actresses Candice Bergen, Susan Tyrrell.

Deaths. Writer Stewart Edward White (b. 1873); director Otto Brower (b. 1895); cinematographer Hugh McClung (b. 1874); actors Arthur Aylesworth (b. 1883), Noah Beery (Sr.) (b. 1884), William S. Hart (b. 1870), Donald Meek (b. 1880).

Once World War II ended on all fronts, the movie industry benefited from the increase in the number of good pictures, the quality western being a part of such a tendency. Especially commendable among the major western films of 1946 were three productions—*My Darling Clementine, Duel in the Sun* and *Canyon Passage.*

Stuart N. Lake's book *Wyatt Earp:*

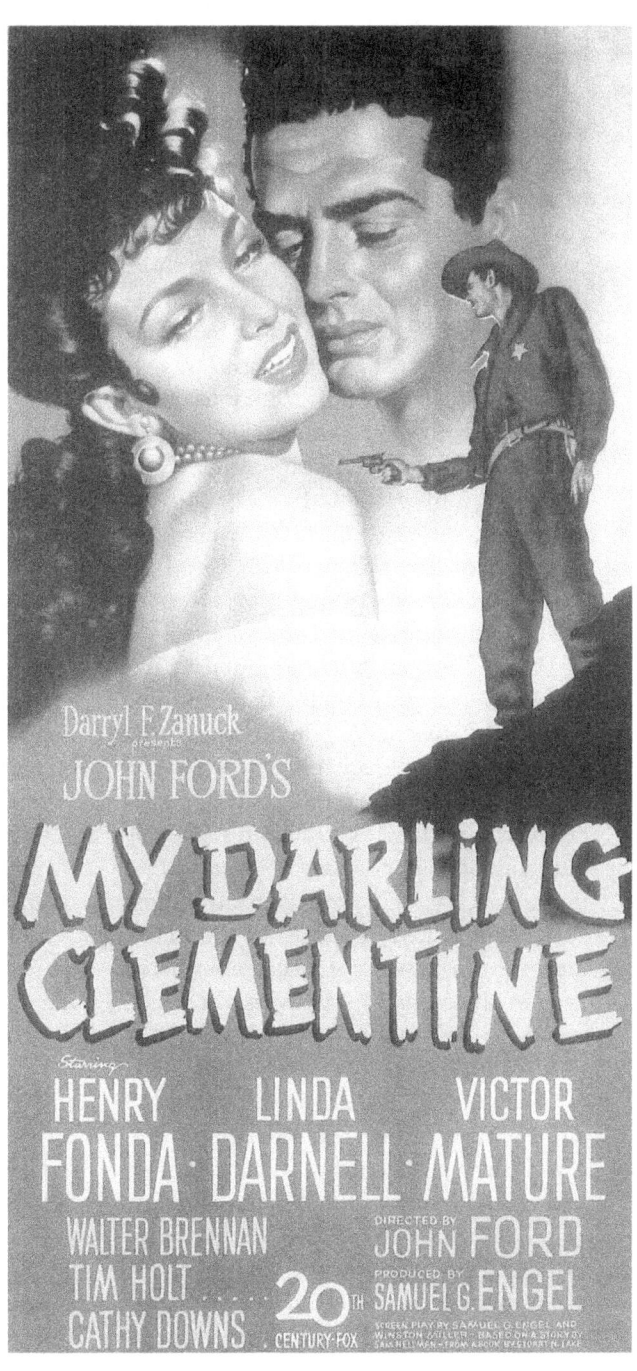

American poster for John Ford's *My Darling Clementine* (20th CF, 1946), one of the greatest westerns of all time.

Frontier Marshal was first made into a movie in 1934 by Lewis Seiler. Five years later, Sam Hellman used it again as the basis for his competent screenplay which Allan Dwan filmed as *Frontier Marshal*. That script, in turn, having been redone by Samuel G. Engel and Winston Miller, was filmed by John Ford as *My Darling Clementine* (featuring Henry Fonda, Victor Mature and Linda Darnell), a picture generally recognized as one of the top half dozen westerns of all time. The simple, straightforward and seemingly unpretentious story of the events leading to the famous gunfight at the O.K. Corral was elevated to a highly artistic and entertaining endeavor due to the masterful direction, irresistibly beautiful photography (with dozens of unforgettable frames), suitable musical score (based on folk themes) and a number of first-rate performances. Particularly effective among the actors is Fonda in his understated characterization of Wyatt Earp, the reluctant, modest and upright hero, devoted brother and shy courtier of teacher Clementine (Cathy Downs). The sequences involving the chair bouncing on the boardwalk and his awkward dancing at the church social belong among the most memorable images in the history of the genre. By the most strikingly obvious oversight of the Academy, the movie was not Oscar-nominated even in one category—an oversight which seems to be unfair, especially for Joe MacDonald (there are not many films with equally captivating cinematography) and Ford, who here reached the peak in crystallizing his economical narrative style and promoting the Old West mythology.

Duel in the Sun, produced by David O. Selznick, was envisioned to become another *Gone with the Wind*. There are at least two reasons why those expectations were not fulfilled—the mediocre script, written by the producer himself, inaccurately retelling the story of the superior, lusty 1944 novel by Niven Busch; and the uneven and inconsistent direction (a number of directors had worked on it before it was finished and credited to King Vidor, inevitably leading to a lack of style). Still, it is an interesting and enjoyable picture, worth seeing for a number of reasons—the bold approach to the issue of women's sexuality, Dimitri Tiomkin's superior musical score, decent color photography by four cinematographers, and the long list of distinguished players (Gregory Peck, Jennifer Jones, Joseph Cotten, Lillian Gish, Lionel Barrymore, Walter Huston, and several others), whose different acting styles, however, do not always seem compatible. Two actresses from that movie (Jones and Gish) won—deservedly—an Oscar nomination in the best actress and best supporting actress category, respectively.

Compared to *My Darling Clementine* and *Duel in the Sun*, *Canyon Passage* must appear to be a modest picture, and rightly so, since some of the crew members and actors were at that time involved in medium-budget productions. Yet, the overall result, clearly more rewarding than *Duel in the Sun*, deserves to be praised for a number of merits. It is possibly the most faithful rendition of any work by the legendary Ernest Haycox. Director Jacques Tourneur captured the unique atmosphere of the Oregon pioneering life, with help from cinematographer Edward Cronjager, composers Frank Skinner (score) and Hoagy Carmichael (songs), and the main trio of actors—Dana Andrews, Susan Hayward and Brian Donlevy (who was less effective as Trampas in the same year's *The Virginian*).

It has to be noted that Stuart Gilmore's *The Virginian* of 1946 is the last (to date) big-screen version, rather uninspired and disappointing, of the classic novel by Owen Wister. Joel McCrea gave a decent performance in the titular role; nonetheless, according to some, the part should have been given to Randolph Scott, a true Virginian, who had accent-coached Gary Cooper for the previous 1929 version of the book.

Even though Ford's *Stagecoach* had opened the genre's golden period in 1939, the war years were relatively lean in remarkable westerns, partially due to the engagement in war of some major filmmakers—Ford, Fonda, Tyrone Power, and others. Ford's return to the genre, in particular, shortly after the war revived the artistic western and contributed to its prosperity for years to come.

The most distinguished western-related celebrity among those who passed away in 1946 was indisputably William S. Hart—the first western megastar and the most versatile western filmmaker of the silent period (*Hell's Hinges, The Apostle of Vengeance, Truthful Tulliver, The Toll Gate, Tumbleweeds*).

1947

Outstanding Achievements

PICTURE: *Ramrod*; *Pursued*; *The Sea of Grass*; *Angel and the Badman*; *Trail Street*

NOVEL FILMED: *The Sea of Grass* by Conrad Richter; *Ramrod* by Luke Short; *To the Last Man* by Zane Grey, filmed as *Thunder Mountain*; *Wild Horse Mesa* by Zane Grey; *Twin Sombreros* by Zane Grey, filmed as *Gunfighters*

SCREENPLAY (ORIGINAL): Niven Busch, *Pursued*; James Edward Grant, *Angel and the Badman*

SCREENPLAY (ADAPTATION): Jack Moffitt, Graham Baker, Cecile Kramer, *Ramrod*; Marguerite Roberts, Vincent Lawrence, *The Sea of Grass*

DIRECTION: Raoul Walsh, *Pursued*; André De Toth, *Ramrod*; Elia Kazan, *The Sea of Grass*

CINEMATOGRAPHY (B&W): James Wong Howe, *Pursued*; Russell Harlan, *Ramrod*; Harry Stradling, *The Sea of Grass*

CINEMATOGRAPHY (COLOR): Archie Stout, *Angel and the Badman*; Ray Rennahan, *California*

MUSIC: Adolph Deutsch, *Ramrod*; Victor Young, *California*

MALE LEADING ROLE: Joel McCrea, *Ramrod*; Robert Mitchum, *Pursued*; Spencer Tracy, *The Sea of Grass*

FEMALE LEADING ROLE: Katharine Hepburn, *The Sea of Grass*; Teresa Wright, *Pursued*; Veronica Lake, *Ramrod*

MALE SUPPORTING ROLE: Harry Carey, *Angel and the Badman*; Dean Jagger, *Pursued*

FEMALE SUPPORTING ROLE: Arleen Whelan, *Ramrod*; Judith Anderson, *Pursued*

Births. Composer Ry Cooder.

Deaths. Writer Willa Cather (b. 1873); cinematographer Joseph H. August (b. 1890); actors Harry Carey, Sr. (b. 1878), J. Warren Kerrigan (b. 1889); actresses Olive Borden (b. 1907), Mabel Van Buren (b. 1878).

No western masterpiece was released in 1947; nevertheless, the year's top achievements illustrate an interesting variety of styles and themes.

Ramrod is a conventional story of range war and manipulation, extremely well told by the original author Luke Short (novel of 1943), screenwriters Jack Moffitt, Graham Baker and Cecile Kramer, and director Andre De Toth. Impressively photographed (Russell Harlan) and scored (Adolph Deutsch), it boasts a few memorable characterizations. Joel McCrea appears suitably vulnerable as the straightforward foreman, Dave Nash, tortured by the past; and Veronica Lake (in one of her two westerns) is intriguing in the role of his boss, Connie Dickason, using her glamour and schemes to accomplish her selfish goals. Both the film and the book upon which it was based are truly rewarding works; unfortunately, they are also generally underrated.

Raoul Walsh's *Pursued*, clearly aspiring to be a western film-noir, emerges as a novelty in the genre. Its original story, written by Niven Busch, is *de facto* a drama of crime and mystery, told in flashbacks. James Wong Howe's excellent stark and shadowy compositions suitably enhance the director's concept. Outstanding in the cast is Robert Mitchum, who—even though he proved himself perfect for this kind of role—would have to wait until the mid-1970s to portray the most famous private eye, Philip Marlowe, in a couple of Raymond Chandler adaptations.

Conrad Richter's 1937 novel *The Sea of Grass* is a well recognized, if now rather forgotten, piece of literature. Its highly realistic tone, combined with serious psychological and social issues, puts the book on the margin of western fiction, far from the formula western, and encourages comparisons with Willa Cather or Walter Van Tilburg Clark. Consequently, Metro-Goldwyn-Mayer, which took up the project of its film adaptation, hired for the job people who were not usually associated with the genre. Thus, the movie was directed—competently but without the feel for the West—by Elia Kazan, and the leading parts were given to Spencer Tracy (as Colonel James Brewton), Katharine Hepburn (Lutie Cameron), Melvyn Douglas (Brice Chamberlain) and Robert Walker (Brock Brewton). Although the picture emerged as a highly professional piece of work (despite some major discrepancies between the book and the script), impressing with Harry Stradling's superb outdoor photography, the outcome

Gail Russell and John Wayne in *Angel and the Badman*, a fairly enjoyable western directed by James Edward Grant.

was a less-than-remarkable example of the genre.

Less original and realistic, but more pleasing as a western film, was *Angel and the Badman*, written and directed by James Edward Grant. John Wayne, who starred opposite Gail Russell, gave a nice performance, but his acting was not on a par with that of McCrea, Tracy or Mitchum, and certainly on a different artistic level than his towering characterization of Thomas Dunson in *Red River*, a movie released the following year. Coincidentally, both *Angel and the Badman* and *Red River* (and *The Sea of Grass*, for that matter) featured Harry Carey, a distinguished actor who passed away in 1947, and to whom John Ford would dedicate his 1948 screen version of Peter B. Kyne's novel *The Three Godfathers*.

1948

Outstanding Achievements

PICTURE: *Red River; Fort Apache; Yellow Sky; Four Faces West; Blood on the Moon; 3 Godfathers; Whispering Smith; The Man from Colorado; Station West*

NOVEL FILMED: *The Chisholm Trail* by Borden Chase, filmed as *Red River; Whispering Smith* by Frank H. Spearman; *The Three Godfathers* by Peter B. Kyne, filmed as *3 Godfathers; Gunman's Chance* by Luke Short, filmed as *Blood on the Moon; Coroner Creek* by Luke Short

SHORT STORY/NOVELLA FILMED: "Paso por Aqui" by Eugene Manlove Rhodes, filmed as *Four Faces West;* "Massacre" by James Warner Bellah, filmed as *Fort Apache*

SCREENPLAY (ORIGINAL): Borden Chase, Robert D. Andrews, Ben Maddow, *The Man from Colorado*

SCREENPLAY (ADAPTATION): Borden Chase, Charles Schnee, *Red River;* Frank S. Nugent, *Fort Apache;* W.R. Burnett, Lamar Trotti, *Yellow Sky*

DIRECTION: Howard Hawks, *Red River;* John Ford, *Fort Apache;* William A. Wellman, *Yellow Sky*

CINEMATOGRAPHY (B&W): Archie Stout, *Fort Apache;* Russell Harlan, *Red River;* Joseph MacDonald, *Yellow Sky*

CINEMATOGRAPHY (COLOR): Winton C. Hoch, *3 Godfathers;* Ray Rennahan, *Whispering Smith*

MUSIC: Dimitri Tiomkin, *Red River;* Richard Hageman, *Fort Apache;* Alfred Newman, *Yellow Sky*

SONG: Dimitri Tiomkin, "Settle Down" from *Red River;* Leigh Harline, Mort Greene, "The Sun Shining Warm" from *Station West*

MALE LEADING ROLE: John Wayne, *Red River;* Henry Fonda, *Fort Apache;* Gregory Peck, *Yellow Sky*

FEMALE LEADING ROLE: Anne Baxter, *Yellow Sky;* Joanne Dru, *Red River;* Frances Dee, *Four Faces West*

MALE SUPPORTING ROLE: Walter Brennan, *Red River;* Charles Bickford, *Four Faces West;* Ward Bond, *Fort Apache*

FEMALE SUPPORTING ROLE: Irene Rich, *Fort Apache;* Coleen Gray, *Red River;* Jane Darwell, *3 Godfathers*

Academy Award Nominations

Red River—AAN: motion-picture story (Borden Chase); editing (Christian Nyby).

Deaths. Cinematographer Gregg Toland (b. 1904); actor Samuel S. Hinds (b. 1875); actress Nora Lane (b. 1905).

One of the greatest years in the history of the western film, 1948 brought about an impressive number of aesthetically pleasing productions. The artistic quality was provided especially by the endeavors of such distinguished directors as Howard Hawks, John Ford and William A. Wellman.

Hawks had worked on westerns before but had never been credited for one until he made *Red River*. He would make only four more (mostly remarkable) westerns over the next 22 years. Almost everything in *Red River* is perfect—Borden Chase and Charles Schnee's screenplay from the former's short but captivating novel (1946), Russell Harlan's dynamic black-and-white cinematography, Dimitri Tiomkin's heroic score, and at least half a dozen characterizations. Hawks, who himself made the story even more psychologically plausible with some major alterations in the main characters' relationships, deserves an additional credit for his masterful staging, especially of the outdoor sequences, and highly skillful guidance of the actors. It was Hawks who

made it possible to match the acting styles of John Wayne and Montgomery Clift; it was Hawks who, having extracted a mature, first-class performance from Wayne, helped the actor discover his talent and become a megastar. *Red River* turned out to be a masterpiece, by now generally recognized as one of the very top achievements of the genre, and was selected by the Western Writers of America as one of the best 15 western films of all time in their 1995 poll. Its artistic quality, however, went unnoticed by the Academy; instead of winning several Oscars, the picture received only two nominations.

When John Ford decided to make *Fort Apache*, he introduced to the genre two outstanding writers—James Warner Bellah, the author of the short story "Massacre" (1947), and ex-critic Frank S. Nugent, who received the job of adapting the story for the screen. The film that Ford made from that script, impressively depicting the life at a Cavalry post in Arizona, became a major success and, consequently, was soon followed by two more movies on the same theme—both based on Bellah's prose and one also scripted by Nugent. Thus, *Fort Apache* emerged as the first part of the Cavalry trilogy—three remarkable pictures, beautifully staged, photographed and scored, whose additional common denominator was the participation of three actors from the director's ensemble: John Wayne, Victor McLaglen and Jack Pennick. Several actors appeared in two of the three: John Agar, Harry Carey, Jr. and Ben Johnson. In *Fort Apache*, however, the best performance was delivered by Henry Fonda, who was cast against type as the arrogant and ambitious commandant, Colonel Owen Thursday. As the three movies differ in emphasis and merits, the main intellectual value of *Fort Apache* is the fair treatment of the Indians, along with the charges brought against the white men—the commandant and the sutler, in particular—for the unnecessary conflict and bloodshed. The ambiguity of the ending provides an additional flavor and anticipates the multilevel interpretation of Ford's *The Man Who Shot Liberty Valance* (1962).

In comparison to *Red River* and *Fort Apache*, two pictures overwhelming with their epic grandeur, *Yellow Sky* appears to be a simple and modest drama, focused on the moral dilemma of the protagonist, gang leader Stretch (Gregory Peck). Nevertheless, with the impressively shot (by Joe MacDonald) scenery of the desert and ghost town, fine musical score by Alfred Newman and good acting by most of the players (Anne Baxter, Richard Widmark, John Russell), it is a superior western movie which proved that Wellman was one of the best directors of the genre. The Writers Guild of America honored W.R. Burnett (the author of the original story) and Lamar Trotti (the author of the script) with an award for the "Best Written American Western" of 1949.

The majority of the quality westerns of 1948 were adaptations of well-known literary works. Popular novelist Luke Short, whose excellent book *Ramrod* had been filmed the previous year, contributed superior literary material to as many as four western movies—*Blood on the Moon* (from *Gunman's Chance*, 1941), *Coroner Creek* (1946), *Station West* (1946) and *Albuquerque* (from *Dead Freight for Piute*, 1939). Furthermore, Alfred E. Green's *Four Faces West* was inspired by "Pasi por

Opposite, top: John Wayne and Coleen Gray in the stunningly photographed opening sequence from Howard Hawks' masterful *Red River*. *Bottom:* Montgomery Clift (Matthew Garth) and John Wayne (Thomas Dunson) in the climactic scene from *Red River*.

Aqui," an acclaimed novella by Eugene Manlove Rhodes; Ford's *3 Godfathers* (featuring John Wayne, Harry Carey, Jr. and Pedro Armendariz) was the fifth and last (to date) big screen version of Peter B. Kyne's popular 1912 novel; and Leslie Fenton's *Whispering Smith* (starring Alan Ladd, Brenda Marshall and Robert Preston) was the third rendition of the famous 1906 railroad novel by Frank H. Spearman.

It needs to be noted that one of the best movies of the year was *The Treasure of the Sierra Madre*, a quasi-western based on a superior book by the legendary author B. Traven. The film was honored with one Academy Award (for supporting actor Walter Huston) and three additional nominations—in the category of best picture, screenplay and direction (the last two by John Huston).

The 1948 obituaries did not list many western-related celebrities. However, the list included one true legend of the camera, the distinguished cinematographer Gregg Toland (*The Westerner* and *The Outlaw*), whose deep-focus technique contributed to the artistry of some outstanding pictures directed by William Wyler, Orson Welles and John Ford.

1949

Outstanding Achievements

PICTURE: *She Wore a Yellow Ribbon; Colorado Territory; Streets of Laredo; Lust for Gold*

NOVEL FILMED: *Thunder God's Gold* by Barry Storm, filmed as *Lust for Gold*

NONFICTION BOOK FILMED: *The Texas Rangers: A Century of Frontier Defense* by Walter Prescott Webb, filmed as *Streets of Laredo*

SHORT STORY FILMED: "War Party" by James Warner Bellah, filmed as *She Wore a Yellow Ribbon*

SCREENPLAY (ADAPTATION): Frank S. Nugent and Laurence Stallings, *She Wore a Yellow Ribbon*

DIRECTION: John Ford, *She Wore a Yellow Ribbon*; Raoul Walsh, *Colorado Territory*

CINEMATOGRAPHY (B&W): Sid Hickox, *Colorado Territory*; Archie Stout, *Lust for Gold*

CINEMATOGRAPHY (COLOR): Winton Hoch, *She Wore a Yellow Ribbon*; Ray Rennahan, *Streets of Laredo*

MUSIC: Richard Hageman, *She Wore a Yellow Ribbon*; Victor Young, *Streets of Laredo*; George Duning, *Lust for Gold*

MALE LEADING ROLE: John Wayne, *She Wore a Yellow Ribbon*; Joel McCrea, *Colorado Territory*; Glenn Ford, *Lust for Gold*

FEMALE LEADING ROLE: Virginia Mayo, *Colorado Territory*; Joanne Dru, *She Wore a Yellow Ribbon*; Ida Lupino, *Lust for Gold*

MALE SUPPORTING ROLE: Victor McLaglen, *She Wore a Yellow Ribbon*; Morris Ankrum, *Colorado Territory*; Harry Carey, Jr. *She Wore a Yellow Ribbon*

FEMALE SUPPORTING ROLE: Mildred Natwick, *She Wore a Yellow Ribbon*; Dorothy Malone, *Colorado Territory*

Academy Awards

She Wore a Yellow Ribbon—AA: color cinematography.

Deaths. Writer Rex Beach (b. 1877); directors Victor Fleming (b. 1883), Sam Wood (b. 1883); composer Herbert Stothart (b. 1885); actors Wallace Beery (b. 1885), Harry Davenport (b. 1866), Richard Dix (b. 1894), Bert Sprotte (b. 1870).

After such a prolific year as 1948, 1949 indicated an obvious decline in the production of quality westerns. And, truly, there were not many significant westerns (and certainly no masterpiece) released in that year, but at least two—*She Wore a Yellow* Ribbon (featuring John Wayne, Joanne Dru, John Agar, Victor McLaglen and Harry Carey, Jr.) and *Colorado Territory* (starring Joel McCrea, Virginia Mayo and Dorothy Malone)—deserve a special consideration and a relatively important place in the genre's history.

She Wore a Yellow Ribbon is the second part of John Ford's Cavalry trilogy, the main assets of which are the nostalgic atmosphere (enhanced by Winton C. Hoch's Oscar-winning color cinematography) and the story itself, which here, much more than in the other parts of the trilogy (only remotely inspired by his tales), is owed to James Warner Bellah's writing. In addition to closely following his 1948 short story "War Party," the script also takes some ideas from two of his other short stories, "Command" (1946) and "Big Hunt" (1947). John Wayne gives possibly the greatest performance of his career in the role of Captain Nathan Brittles, an aging officer who goes beyond the call of duty to prevent another Indian war. Unlike in *Red River*, where his character Dunson's dominating traits are obsession and rage, or *Fort Apache*, where most of the time he passively watches his superior's incompetence, here the actor demonstrates sensitivity. He is especially moving in two sequences—when speaking to his wife at her grave and when accepting the watch, a farewell gift from his soldiers. *She Wore a Yellow Ribbon* was chosen one of the best 15 western films of all time by the Western Writers of America in their 1995 poll.

Colorado Territory was Raoul Walsh's remake of his own 1941 gangster movie *High Sierra* (starring Humphrey Bogart and Ida Lupino), which was based on W.R. Burnett's crime novel of the same name. Even though Sid Hickox's stark black-and-white photography tends to enhance the script's hard-boiled literary source, *Colorado Territory* (featuring fine performances from Joel McCrea, Virginia Mayo, Dorothy Malone and Morris Ankrum) is first of all a thoroughly enjoyable psychological and fatalistic melodrama, with the ending borrowed from Carol Reed's *Odd Man Out*.

The year's third best western—Leslie Fenton's *Streets of Laredo* (starring William Holden, Macdonald Carey and Mona Freeman)—is a competent, relatively enjoyable but minor production. It was a remake of King Vidor's 1936 picture *The Texas Rangers*, which claimed to have been inspired by Walter Prescott Webb's first-rate 1935 nonfiction book of the same title. This, however, is difficult to prove, as neither the characters nor the story line of both movies resemble any of the people or episodes described on the pages of the lengthy book.

1950

Outstanding Achievements

PICTURE: *The Gunfighter; Rio Grande; Broken Arrow; Winchester '73; Wagon Master; The Furies; Ambush; Devil's Doorway; Rocky Mountain; Two Flags West*

NOVEL FILMED: *The Furies* by Niven Busch; *Ambush* by Luke Short; *Singing Guns* by Max Brand; *Thunder in the Dust* by Alan LeMay, filmed as *The Sundowners*

NONFICTION BOOK FILMED: *Blood Brother* by Elliott Arnold, filmed as *Broken Arrow*

SHORT STORY FILMED: "Mission with No Record" by James Warner Bellah, filmed as *Rio Grande*

SCREENPLAY (ORIGINAL): William Bowers, André De Toth, William Sellers,

The Gunfighter; Stuart N. Lake, Borden Chase, Robert L. Richards, *Winchester '73*

SCREENPLAY (ADAPTATION): Michael Blankfort, *Broken Arrow;* James Kevin McGuinness, *Rio Grande;* Charles Schnee, *The Furies*

DIRECTION: Henry King, *The Gunfighter;* John Ford, *Rio Grande;* Delmer Daves, *Broken Arrow*

CINEMATOGRAPHY (B&W): Victor Milner, *The Furies;* Arthur C. Miller, *The Gunfighter;* Bert Glennon, *Wagon Master*

CINEMATOGRAPHY (COLOR): Ernest Palmer, *Broken Arrow;* Karl Freund, *Montana;* Ernest Haller, *Dallas*

MUSIC: Richard Hageman, *Wagon Master;* Victor Young, *Rio Grande;* Hugo Friedhofer, *Broken Arrow*

SONG: Fred Glickman, Hy Heath, Johnny Lange, "Mule Train" from *Singing Guns;* Stan Jones, "Wagons West" from *Wagon Master*

MALE LEADING ROLE: Gregory Peck, *The Gunfighter;* James Stewart, *Broken Arrow;* John Wayne, *Rio Grande*

FEMALE LEADING ROLE: Barbara Stanwyck, *The Furies;* Maureen O'Hara, *Rio Grande;* Debra Paget, *Broken Arrow*

MALE SUPPORTING ROLE: Jeff Chandler, *Broken Arrow;* Millard Mitchell, *The Gunfighter;* Ben Johnson, *Rio Grande*

FEMALE SUPPORTING ROLE: Judith Anderson, *The Furies;* Jean Parker, *The Gunfighter*

Academy Award Nominations

Broken Arrow — AAN: supporting actor Jeff Chandler; color cinematography.

The Gunfighter — AAN: motion picture story (William Bowers, Andre De Toth).

The Furies — AAN: B&W cinematography.

Singing Guns — AAN: song "Mule Train."

Deaths. Writer Ernest Haycox (b. 1899); screenwriter Sam Hellman (b. 1885), George Hively (b. 1889); cinematographer Harry Vallejo (b. 1882); actors Walter Huston (b. 1884), Charles Kemper (b. 1900).

Among the considerable number of significant westerns released in 1950 there are two milestones of the genre: *The Gunfighter* and *Broken Arrow*. The former is a gloomy and fatalistic account of the aging gunslinger Jimmy Ringo (Gregory Peck). Superbly staged by Henry King, it has been praised by the critics "because," as Dwight Taylor put it (*On the Movies*, 1969), "it shows movie types behaving realistically instead of in the usual terms of romantic cliché." The latter, on the other hand, being the first western in the sound era to sympathize with the Indians — though impressively directed (by Delmer Daves in his western debut), acted, photographed and scored — owes its place in film history more to its message than artistic quality. The two pictures belong to the most influential works in Hollywood's history; frequently imitated, they have deservedly earned the status of classics.

John Ford came up with two lighter westerns — *Wagon Master*, with a somewhat disappointing story despite its obvious aesthetic assets (the film is the director's own favorite), and *Rio Grande*, the final part of his Cavalry trilogy, which turned out to be a captivating drama, even though he made it as Republic's prerequisite for approving the later production of *The Quiet Man* (with the same stars). Ford extracted fine performances from Ben Johnson, Joanne Dru and Harry Carey, Jr. in *Wagon Master*, while John Wayne and Maureen O'Hara were typically warm and unforgettable as Lt. Col. Kirby Yorke and his wife Kathleen in *Rio Grande*.

Anthony Mann, who in 1950 made a spectacular debut in the genre with three

Claude Jarman, Jr., and John Wayne in *Rio Grande*, the final part of John Ford's famous Cavalry trilogy inspired by James Warner Bellah's short stories.

films (*Winchester '73*, *The Furies* and *Devil's Doorway*), deserves to be additionally praised for the discovery of James Stewart's potential to reveal violence, and for widening the actor's range in the roles of the avenger in *Winchester '73* and four subsequent westerns made in the early 1950s. Indeed, Stewart gave a fine performance as Lin McAdams in *Winchester '73*, but he was even better, despite some critics' complaints about his mannerisms, as Tom Jeffords in *Broken Arrow*. In the latter, he was abetted by Jeff Chandler in the role of Cochise and Debra Paget as Sonseeahray.

The growing interest in the artistic western at the threshold of the new decade can be well illustrated by the number of major directors entering the field. The veterans of the genre, such as Ford, Hathaway, Hawks, Walsh, Wellman and others, were joined in 1950 by Mann and Daves. Those men, soon to be reinforced by Robert Aldrich, John Sturges, Budd Boetticher and Andrew V. McLaglen, would continue making westerns for years to come, and—with the assistance from the old leading men and the new (Burt Lancaster, Kirk Douglas, Richard Widmark)—would provide quality and a special, unforgettable flavor to numerous modest and large-scale productions of the 1950s.

With the gradual increase in the overall number of films shot in color, there were less and less westerns that impressed with their black-and-white cinematography. Thus, 1950 was probably the last year with a significant number of major westerns shot in monochrome. They include—in addition to the ones singled out in the above listing—*Rio Grande* (photographed by Bert Glennon), *Two Flags West* (Leon Shamroy), *Ambush* (Harold Lipstein), *Rocky Mountain* (Ted McCord) and *Devil's Doorway* (John Alton).

The year 1950 marked two events related to literature. While the western fiction fans could cherish the first Pulitzer Prize for a western novel, granted to A.B. Guthrie, Jr. for his second book, *The Way West* (published the previous year but not to be filmed until 1967), they also mourned the passing away of Ernest Haycox, a talented author of numerous novels and short stories that revealed merits far beyond the formula western (*Canyon Passage*, *Man in the Saddle*, *Bugles in the Afternoon*).

The other genre-related people that died in 1950 were Walter Huston, a brilliant actor who started his film career playing Trampas in the first sound version of *The Virginian* and concluded with the role of T.C. Jeffords, Barbara Stanwyck's father, in *The Furies*; and Sam Hellman, whose major accomplishment was the screenplay adapted from Stuart N. Lake's book *Wyatt Earp: Frontier Marshal*, filmed as *Frontier Marshal* in 1939 and used again as the basis for the script of Ford's *My Darling Clementine* (1946).

1951

Outstanding Achievements

PICTURE: *Rawhide*; *Across the Wide Missouri*; *Along the Great Divide*; *Man in the Saddle*; *Vengeance Valley*; *Only the Valiant*; *Branded*

NOVEL FILMED: *Vengeance Valley* by Luke Short; *Man in the Saddle* by Ernest Haycox; *Montana Rides!* by Evan Evans (Max Brand), filmed as *Branded*; *Sugarfoot* by Clarence Budington Kelland; *South of Rio Grande* by Max Brand, filmed as *My Outlaw Brother*; *High Vermilion* by Luke Short, filmed as *Silver City*

NONFICTION BOOK FILMED: *Across the Wide Missouri* by Bernard De Voto

SCREENPLAY (ORIGINAL): Dudley Nichols, *Rawhide*; Kenneth Gamet, *Man in the Saddle*; Walter Doniger, Lewis Meltzer, *Along the Great Divide*

SCREENPLAY (ADAPTATION): Irving Ravetch, *Vengeance Valley*; Edmund H. North, Harry Brown, *Only the Valiant*

DIRECTION: Henry Hathaway, *Rawhide*; William A. Wellman, *Across the Wide Missouri*; Raoul Walsh, *Along the Great Divide*

CINEMATOGRAPHY (B&W): Milton Krasner, *Rawhide*; Sid Hickox, *Along the Great Divide*; Lionel Lindon, *Only the Valiant*

CINEMATOGRAPHY (COLOR): William C. Mellor, *Across the Wide Missouri*; Charles B. Lang, Jr. *Branded*

MUSIC: David Buttolph, *Along the Great Divide*; Sol Kaplan, *Rawhide*; Roy Webb, *Branded*

SONG: Lionel Newman, Bob Russell, "A Rollin' Stone" from *Rawhide*; Harold Lewis, Ralph Murphy, "Man in the Saddle" from *Man in the Saddle*

MALE LEADING MAN: Tyrone Power, *Rawhide*; Clark Gable, *Across the Wide Missouri*; Gregory Peck, *Only the Valiant*

FEMALE LEADING ROLE: Susan Hayward, *Rawhide*; Virginia Mayo, *Along the Great Divide*

MALE SUPPORTING ROLE: Hugh Marlowe, *Rawhide*; Alexander Knox, *Man in the Saddle*; Joseph Calleia, *Branded*

FEMALE SUPPORTING ROLE: Maria Elena Marques, *Across the Wide Missouri*; Selena Royle, *Branded*

Deaths. Writer Kenneth Perkins (b. 1890); director Edwin L. Marin (b. 1899); cinematographer C. Edgar Schoenbaum (b. 1893); actors Warner Baxter (b. 1891), Jack Holt (b. 1888), Vester Pegg (b. 1889).

A lack of westerns among the films winning Academy Award nominations does not necessarily indicate a poor year for the genre. However, 1951 was just such a case. Except for *Rawhide*, which is a thoroughly rewarding picture, the other major westerns of the year were disappointments, in spite of superior production values. The movies suffered from mediocre or poor scripts, even though several superior, albeit conventional, literary works were used as their bases. This tendency was particular conspicuous in the case of two books by Max Brand/Evan Evans—*South of Rio Grande* (1936) and *Montana Rides!* (1933), as well as Clarence Budington Kelland's *Sugarfoot* (1942) and Luke Short's *High Vermilion* (1949), which all were turned into ordinary and routine productions that only occasionally revealed traces of the original author's talent. Furthermore, Luke Short's remarkable novel *Vengeance Valley* (1949) became a little more than a mediocre picture (starring Burt Lancaster, Joanne Dru and Robert Walker) due to Richard Thorpe's uninspired direction; while Andre De Toth's movie *Man in the Saddle* (featuring Randolph Scott, Joan Leslie, Ellen Drew and Alexander Knox), based on Ernest Haycox's engaging 1938 book, retained few of the novel's merits.

Two movies that looked promising and had potential to become major box-office successes were William A. Wellman's *Across the Wide Missouri* (starring Clark Gable and John Hodiak) and Raoul Walsh's *Along the Great Divide* (with Kirk Douglas, Virginia Mayo and Walter Brennan). While Wellman's Indian/ecological western seems confused and uneven primarily due to the distortion of the original ideas by MGM's editing, the major weakness of Walsh's mystery/detective western was the erratic script by Walter Doniger and Lewis Meltzer. Moreover, neither Wellman nor Walsh was at his best at that time. *Across the Wide Missouri* was loosely based on the adventures of David Dawson Mitchell (Flint Mitchell in the film), a real-life trapper mentioned on ten pages of Bernard De Voto's excellent 1947 book of the same name (chosen as the number 2 nonfiction book by the Western Writers of America in their 1995 survey), whose detailed and accurate narrative of nearly 400 pages covers the mountain fur trade from 1832 through 1838.

On the other hand, *Rawhide* is an interesting and highly entertaining hold-up western, skillfully written by Dudley Nichols, who achieves the suspense through the application of the classical unities, and remarkably photographed in black and white by Milton Krasner. Henry Hathaway directs it vigorously and extracts vivid performances from Tyrone Power, Susan Hayward, Hugh Marlowe and newcomer Jack Elam. While *Rawhide* anteceded *High Noon* (released the following year) in the use of the classical unities, André De Toth's *Man in the Saddle* deserves credit for another novelty that is frequently attributed to Zinnemann's classic. The title song of the movie, just like in *High Noon*, is performed (by Ernie Ford) over the credits and throughout the action, contributing to the atmosphere of tension.

1952

Outstanding Achievements

PICTURE: *High Noon; Bend of the River; The Big Sky; Rancho Notorious; Ride the Man Down; Hangman's Knot; Westward* the Women; Bugles in the Afternoon; Springfield Rifle

NOVEL FILMED: *The Big Sky* by A.B. Guthrie, Jr.; *Bugles in the Afternoon* by Ernest Haycox; *Ride the Man Down* by Luke Short; *Bend of the Snake* by Bill Gulick, filmed as *Bend of the River*; *The Renegade* by L.L. Foreman, filmed as *The Savage*; *The Iron Mistress* by Paul I. Wellman

SHORT STORY FILMED: "The Outcasts of Poker Flat" and "The Luck of Roaring Camp" by Bret Harte, filmed as *The Outcasts of Poker Flat*; "The Tin Star" by John M. Cunningham, filmed as *High Noon*; "The Bride Comes to Yellow Sky" by Stephen Crane, filmed as a segment of *Face to Face*

SCREENPLAY (ORIGINAL): Daniel Taradash, *Rancho Notorious*; Roy Huggins, *Hangman's Knot*

SCREENPLAY (ADAPTATION): Carl Foreman, *High Noon*; Borden Chase, *Bend of the River*; Dudley Nichols, *The Big Sky*

DIRECTION: Fred Zinnemann, *High Noon*; Anthony Mann, *Bend of the River*; Howard Hawks, *The Big Sky*

CINEMATOGRAPHY (B&W): Russell Harlan, *The Big Sky*; Floyd Crosby, *High Noon*

CINEMATOGRAPHY (COLOR): Irving Glassberg, *Bend of the River*; Hal Mohr, *Rancho Notorious*; Jack Marta, *Ride the Man Down*

MUSIC: Dimitri Tiomkin, *High Noon*; Hugo Friedhofer, *Rancho Notorious*; Hans Salter, *Bend of the River*

SONG: Dimitri Tiomkin, Ned Washington, "High Noon" from *High Noon*; Ken Darby, "Get Away, Young Man" from *Rancho Notorious*

MALE LEADING ROLE: Gary Cooper, *High Noon*; James Stewart, *Bend of the River*; Kirk Douglas, *The Big Sky*

FEMALE LEADING ROLE: Marlene Dietrich, *Rancho Notorious*; Julia Adams, *Bend of the River*; Grace Kelly, *High Noon*

MALE SUPPORTING ROLE: Arthur Hunnicutt, *The Big Sky*; Lloyd Bridges, *High Noon*; Lee Marvin, *Hangman's Knot*

FEMALE SUPPORTING ROLE: Katy Jurado, *High Noon*; Barbara Britton, *Ride the Man Down*; Eve McVeagh, *High Noon*

Academy Awards/ Nominations

High Noon—AA: music; title song; actor Gary Cooper; editing (Elmo Williams, Harry Gerstad); AAN: picture; screenplay; direction.

The Big Sky—AAN: B&W cinematography; supporting actor Arthur Hunnicutt.

Deaths. Screenwriter Lamar Trotti (b. 1900); director Jack Conway (b. 1887); actor J. Farrell MacDonald (b.1875); actress Molly Malone (b. 1897).

Among the significant westerns released in 1952, *High Noon* holds a special position. Despite the persecutions of some of its makers (Carl Foreman, in particular) at the time of its production and release, and the strong attacks on the film from several distinguished filmmakers immediately afterwards and years later (John Wayne, for example), *High Noon* remains an unquestioned masterpiece, possibly the number 1 western of all time. The highly intellectual and amazingly logical script written by Foreman from John M. Cunningham's 1947 short story can perfectly function on any of the four levels—as a timeless morality tale, a psychological melodrama, a sociological treatise, and a political (McCarthy-era) metaphor. By replacing the outdoor scenery with interior shots and giving up action in favor of extensive dialogue, Fred Zinnemann proved the flexibility of the western canon—however, not without criticism from the western traditionalists/purists. While the movie is excellent in all respects, the

Katy Jurado, Grace Kelly, Gary Cooper and Lloyd Bridges in *High Noon*, one of three movies inspired by John M. Cunningham's short stories.

capacities deserving special praise include Zinnemann's meticulous direction, Dimitri Tiomkin's musical score and title song (with lyrics by Ned Washington, playing an unusual commentarial role), and, above all, Gary Cooper's brilliant performance of unparalleled intuition and sensitivity. As the lonely and tired marshal Will Kane, fighting for his life and threatened integrity, the actor delivers the performance of his career, possibly the best by any actor in a western film, and defeated in the Oscar run such actors as Alec Guinness, Marlon Brando, Kirk Douglas and Jose Ferrer. Altogether, *High Noon* was honored with four Oscars (music, song and editing were the other three categories) and three additional nominations (picture, direction and screenplay). Despite the unprecedented generosity on the part of the Academy (usually more reserved towards westerns), the movie deserved at least two more Oscars—one for Zinnemann (who lost it to Ford for *The Quiet Man*) and one for the picture itself, especially considering the year's winner, Cecil B. DeMille clichéd *The Greatest Show on Earth*. *High Noon* merited one more nomination as well—for Floyd's Crosby's first-rate, suitably unromantic black-and-white photography, which—along with the editing—contributes to the film's unique suspense. *High Noon* is not only a great western, but also a marvelous movie, which—for its perfect

High Noon, Fred Zinnemann's masterpiece starring Gary Cooper and Grace Kelly. For his role as Marshal Will Kane, the actor received one of the four Oscars granted to the movie by the Academy.

fusion of form and content—can compete for honors with the most distinguished works of world cinema. The Western Writers of America, in their 1995 survey, selected *High Noon* as the number 2 best western film of all time, and Cunningham's "The Tin Star" as one of the best 12 western short stories.

The other two films that clearly stand out among the 1952 westerns are Anthony Mann's *Bend of the River* and Howard Hawks' *The Big Sky*. Both excellently photographed and both based on superior literary material, the pictures are perfect examples of using the motif of the road—a wagon train heading for Oregon in 1880 and an exploration up the Missouri in 1830, respectively—to tell a fascinating tale of mystery, betrayal and revenge. Two outstanding writers wrote the scripts; while Dudley Nichols's alterations of A.B. Guthrie, Jr.'s text (his first book of 1947, chosen as the number 1 western novel in the Western Writers of America's 1995 survey) seem rather anonymous, Borden Chase's adaptation of Bill Gulick's 1950 book bears typical traits of Chase's writing and even includes lines that echo Thomas Dunson threatening Matthew Garth in *Red River*.

The most controversial western of the year—highly recognized in Europe but almost unnoticed in America—was probably Fritz Lang's *Rancho Notorious* (starring Marlene Dietrich, Arthur Kennedy and Mel Ferrer), a movie with an interesting script by Daniel Taradash, fine color photography by Hal Mohr, a superior musical score by Hugo Friedhofer and a couple of songs performed by Dietrich. The other major westerns of 1952 include two adaptations of literary material by two masters of quality western yarns. While Luke Short's *Ride the Man Down* (1942) became a minor masterpiece in the capable hands of director Joseph Kane, who extracted solid performances from all of the cast (Rod Cameron, Ella Raines, Forrest Tucker, Brian Donlevy and Barbara Britton), Roy Rowland's rendition (featuring Ray Milland, Helena Carter, Hugh Marlowe and Forrest Tucker) of Ernest Haycox's *Bugles in the Afternoon* (1944) suffered from a lack of vigor and inspiration.

It needs to be noted that all the short stories filmed in 1952—"The Outcasts of Poker Flat," "The Luck of Roaring Camp," "The Tin Star" and Stephen Crane's "The Bride Comes to Yellow Sky" (which was the basis of one episode of Brataigne Windust's movie *Face to Face*, starring Robert Preston and Marjorie Steele)—were included among the best 12 western short stories of all time in the 1995 poll.

Lamar Trotti, the distinguished screenwriter who wrote the scripts for two of William A. Wellman's best westerns—*The Ox-Bow Incident* and *Yellow Sky*—was among the celebrities that passed away in 1952.

NOVEL FILMED: *Shane* by Jack Schaefer; *Wicked Water* by MacKinlay Kantor, filmed as *Hannah Lee; Adobe Walls* by W.R. Burnett, filmed as *Arrowhead; First Blood* by Jack Schaefer, filmed as *The Silver Whip*

SHORT STORY FILMED: "The Gift of Cochise" by Louis L'Amour, filmed as *Hondo;* "Yankee Gold" by John M. Cunningham, filmed as *The Stranger Wore a Gun*

SCREENPLAY (ORIGINAL): Sam Rolfe, Harold Jack Bloom, *The Naked Spur;* Irving Wallace, Roy Huggins, *Gun Fury*

SCREENPLAY (ADAPTATION): A.B. Guthrie, Jr. (and Jack Sher, additional dialogue), *Shane;* James Edward Grant, *Hondo*

DIRECTION: George Stevens, *Shane;* Anthony Mann, *The Naked Spur;* John Farrow, *Hondo*

CINEMATOGRAPHY (B&W): Burnett Guffey, *The Last Posse*

CINEMATOGRAPHY (COLOR): Loyal Griggs, *Shane;* William C. Mellor, *The Naked Spur;* Robert Burks, Archie Stout, *Hondo*

MUSIC: Victor Young, *Shane;* Bronislau Kaper, *The Naked Spur;* Emil Newman, Hugo Friedhofer, *Hondo*

SONG: Emil Newman, Johnny Lehman, "Elaine" from *War Paint*

MALE LEADING ROLE: Alan Ladd, *Shane;* James Stewart, *The Naked Spur;* John Wayne, *Hondo*

FEMALE SUPPORTING ROLE: Jean Arthur, *Shane;* Geraldine Page, *Hondo;* Janet Leigh, *The Naked Spur*

MALE SUPPORTING ROLE: Jack Palance, *Shane;* Brandon De Wilde, *Shane;* Millard Mitchell, *The Naked Spur*

FEMALE SUPPORTING ROLE: Ellen Corby, *Shane*

1953

Outstanding Achievements

PICTURE: *Shane; The Naked Spur; Hondo; Gun Fury; Arrowhead; The Last Posse; The Stranger Wore a Gun*

Academy Awards/ Nominations

Shane—AA: color cinematography; AAN: picture; motion picture story (A.B.

1953

Guthrie, Jr.); direction; supporting actor Jack Palance; supporting actor Brandon De Wilde.

The Naked Spur—AAN: story and screenplay.

Hondo—AAN: supporting actress Geraldine Page.

Births. Actor/director Ron Howard.

Deaths. Screenwriter H. Tipton Steck (b. 1888); cinematographers George Barnes (b. 1893), Clyde De Vinna (b. 1892); actors Cliff Clark (b. 1893), William Farnum (b. 1876), Francis Ford (b. 1882), Porter Hall (b. 1888), Joe Harris (b. 1870), Paul Hurst (b. 1888), Chris-Pin Martin (b. 1893), Millard Mitchell (b. 1900).

After the year of the controversial, albeit excellent, town-bound drama *High Noon* came the year of *Shane*, a film generally regarded as the purest western of all. Written by two giants of western fiction (Jack Schaefer, the author of the 1949 novel, and A.B. Guthrie, Jr., the author of the script), *Shane* was directed by George Stevens, who brought to perfection his individual style—a meticulous approach combined with the his famous "technique of intense simplicity generating a complex drama" (*BFI Film Classics: Shane* by Edward Countryman and Evonne von Heusse-Countryman). As the quintessential western telling the story of the errant knight and the struggle of good and evil, *Shane* has earned an outstanding position in the history of the genre. Often imitated, quoted, referred to or even remade in a somewhat disguised manner (as Clint Eastwood's *Pale Rider*), it is an absolute classic, selected by the Western Writers of America as number 1 western film in their 1995 poll. At the same time, Schaefer's work was listed as number 2 western novel of all time. The film won six Academy Award nominations, but only one of the nominees—cinematographer Loyal Griggs, for his breathtaking color compositions of Jackson Hole, Wyoming, with the peaks of the Grand Tetons in the background—became a winner. The fact that Alan Ladd, whose brilliant characterization of the rider from nowhere was definitely his best (and possibly one of the top half-dozen performances by any actor in a western movie), was not even nominated remains an obvious oversight, often attributed to studio politics.

The other westerns of 1953 that deserve a special recognition are *The Naked Spur*, the third out of the five pictures in the revenge cycle of Anthony Mann and James

Poster for *Shane* (starring Alan Ladd, Jean Arthur and Van Heflin), George Stevens' masterful rendition of the classic novel by Jack Schaefer.

John Wayne, Ward Bond and James Arness in John Farrow's *Hondo*, the first movie derived from Louis L'Amour's prose.

Stewart, and *Hondo*, a likeable movie directed by John Farrow, which suffered from comparisons to *Shane*. While the former was made from an original, Oscar-nominated screenplay by Sam Rolfe and Harold Jack Bloom, the latter was an adaptation of Louis L'Amour's excellent short story "The Gift of Cochise" (1952). The superior script by James Edward Grant was subsequently novelized by L'Amour himself and the book was published at the time of the movie's release. In their 1995 survey, the Western Writers of America chose L'Amour's *Hondo* as one of the 12 best novels, probably forgetting that it was just a novelization, but failed to list "The Gift of Cochise" among the top 12 western short stories.

The players that passed away in 1953 included two remarkable character actors. Francis Ford, who arrived in Hollywood (and became a writer-director-actor) before his younger brother John, appeared in many classic westerns made by his brother (*Stagecoach*, *My Darling Clementine*, *She Wore a Yellow Ribbon*) and other directors (William A. Wellman's *The Ox-Bow Incident*). Millard Mitchell's filmography, on the other hand, is very short—due to his premature death—but includes three major westerns (*The Gunfighter*, *Winchester '73* and *The Naked Spur*).

The year 1953 marked a significant event for the promotion of the literature of the American West. The Western Writers of America, Inc. was founded, and the organization immediately established their Spur Awards, which would be granted annually in recognition of distinguished writing about the West.

1954

Outstanding Achievements

PICTURE: *Vera Cruz; Johnny Guitar; Broken Lance; Apache; Escape from Fort Bravo; River of No Return; Track of the Cat; Drum Beat; Garden of Evil; Silver Lode*

NOVEL FILMED: *The Track of the Cat* by Walter Van Tilburg Clark; *Broncho Apache* by Paul I. Wellman, filmed as *Apache; The Wild Horse* by Les Savage, Jr., filmed as *Black Horse Canyon; Arrow in the Dust* by L.L. Foreman

SCREENPLAY (ORIGINAL): Roland Kibbee, James R. Webb, Borden Chase, *Vera Cruz*; Frank Fenton, *River of No Return*; Philip Rock, Michael Pate, Frank Fenton, *Escape from Fort Bravo*

SCREENPLAY (ADAPTATION): Richard Murphy, *Broken Lance*; A.I. Bezzerides, *Track of the Cat*; Philip Yordan, *Johnny Guitar*

DIRECTION: Robert Aldrich, *Vera Cruz*; Nicholas Ray, *Johnny Guitar*; Edward Dmytryk, *Broken Lance*

CINEMATOGRAPHY (COLOR): Joseph MacDonald, *Broken Lance*; Harry Stradling, *Johnny Guitar*; Ernest Laszlo, *Vera Cruz*

MUSIC: Victor Young, *Johnny Guitar*; Cyril Mockridge, *River of No Return*; Hugo Friedhofer, *Vera Cruz*

SONG: Victor Young, Peggy Lee, "Johnny Guitar" from *Johnny Guitar*; Lionel Newman, Ken Darby, "River of No Return" from *River of No Return*; Stan Jones, "Yellow Stripes" from *Escape from Fort Bravo*

MALE LEADING ROLE: Gary Cooper, *Vera Cruz*; Burt Lancaster, *Apache*; Spencer Tracy, *Broken Lance*

FEMALE LEADING ROLE: Joan Crawford, *Johnny Guitar*; Marilyn Monroe, *River of No Return*; Eleanor Parker, *Escape from Fort Bravo*

MALE SUPPORTING ROLE: John McIntire, *Apache*; Scott Brady, *Johnny Guitar*; Hugh Marlowe, *Garden of Evil*

FEMALE SUPPORTING ROLE: Katy Jurado, *Broken Lance*; Mercedes McCambridge, *Johnny Guitar*; Beulah Bondi, *Track of the Cat*

Academy Awards/ Nominations

Broken Lance—AA: motion picture story (Philip Yordan); AAN: supporting actress Katy Jurado.

Deaths. Writer William MacLeod Raine (b. 1871); director William K. Howard (b. 1899); cinematographer Harry Fowler (b. 1884); actors Lionel Barrymore (b. 1878), Moroni Olsen (b. 1889), Eugene Pallette (b. 1889), Tom Tyler (b. 1903); actresses Florence Bates (b. 1888), Lillian Rich (b. 1900).

Even though the list of major westerns of 1954 is quite long, it hardly includes a true masterpiece. On the contrary, all the nine pictures are only above average westerns, all on more or less the same artistic level. In fact, a reverse order of the items would probably not raise objections from many western fans.

Nevertheless, the best westerns of the year offer an interesting and unique mixture of artistic and entertainment values. While Robert Aldrich's *Vera Cruz* may be the most enjoyable film, rightly regarded as the forerunner of such "mercenary" westerns as *The Magnificent Seven*, *The Professionals* and *The Wild Bunch*, Nicholas

Ray's *Johnny Guitar* is probably the most controversial one. Often described with such adjectives as passionate, lyrical, baroque, oneiric and metaphysical, the picture is definitely one of the most unusual works conceived by Hollywood in the 1950s, even though it also earned the reputation of a 'good bad movie.' Both *Johnny Guitar* and the much more modest *Silver Lode* (starring John Payne, Dan Duryea and Lizabeth Scott), directed by Allan Dwan, are political westerns, both surpassing *High Noon* in their attack on the McCarthy witch hunt.

The other unusual westerns of the year include Aldrich's *Apache*, a superior pro–Indian film based on Paul I. Wellman's 1936 book *Broncho Apache*; Edward Dmytryk's *Broken Lance*, a domestic picture with references to Dostoyefsky's *The Brothers Karamazov*; and William A. Wellman's controversial rendition of Walter Van Tilburg Clark's 1949 novel *The Track of the Cat*, clearly influenced by Herman Melville and Eugene O'Neill.

The year 1954 abounded in memorable performances, especially by leading men. Gary Cooper provided his usual dignity and authority playing a soldier of fortune in both *Vera Cruz* and Henry Hathaway's *Garden of Evil*. Burt Lancaster was charismatic as both Indian Massai in *Apache* and outlaw Joe Erin in *Vera Cruz*. Robert Mitchum turned in a fine performance as ex-convict Matt Calder in Otto Preminger's *River of No Return*, and as the arrogant Curt Bridges in *Track of the Cat*. Also, Richard Widmark appeared successfully in two westerns, playing the role of the evil brother Ben Devereaux in *Broken Lance* and the philosophizing gambler-turned-hero Fiske in *Garden of Evil*. Recommendable were also Spencer Tracy in his towering characterization of the patriarch Matt Devereaux in *Broken Lance*, William Holden in the role of the heroic cavalry officer Captain Roper in John Sturges' *Escape from Fort Bravo*, and Sterling Hayden as the gun-crazy Johnny "Guitar" Logan in *Johnny Guitar*.

1955

Outstanding Achievements

PICTURE: *The Man from Laramie; The Far Country; Man Without a Star; Run for Cover; The Tall Men; The Indian Fighter; A Man Alone; The Violent Men; Wichita; The Kentuckian*

NOVEL FILMED: *Destry Rides Again* by Max Brand, filmed as *Destry*; *Man Without a Star* by Dee Linford; *The Man from Laramie* by T.T. Flynn; *The Vanishing American* by Zane Grey; *Smoky Valley* by Donald Hamilton, filmed as *The Violent Men*; *The Tall Men* by Clay Fisher (Will Henry); *The Gabriel Horn* by Felix Holt, filmed as *The Kentuckian*; *Robbers' Roost* by Zane Grey

SHORT STORY/NOVELLA FILMED: "Tennessee's Partner" by Bret Harte; "The Rider of the Ruby Hills" by Louis L'Amour, filmed as *Treasure of the Ruby Hills*

SCREENPLAY (ORIGINAL): Borden Chase, *The Far Country;* Harriet Frank, Jr. & Irving Ravetch, William C. Thomas, *Run for Cover*

SCREENPLAY (ADAPTATION): Borden Chase, D.D. Beauchamp, *Man Without a Star*; Philip Yordan, Frank Burt, *The Man from Laramie*

DIRECTION: Anthony Mann, *The Far Country*; King Vidor, *Man Without a Star;* Jacques Tourneur, *Wichita*

CINEMATOGRAPHY (B&W): Ellsworth Fredricks, *Seven Angry Men*; Ray Rennahan, *A Lawless Street*

CINEMATOGRAPHY (COLOR): Burnett Guffey, W. Howard Greene, *The Violent Men*; William Daniels, *The Far*

Country; Russell Metty, *Man Without a Star*

MUSIC: Max Steiner, *The Violent Men;* Victor Young, *The Tall Men;* George Duning, *The Man from Laramie*

SONG: Hans J. Salter, Ned Washington, "Wichita" from *Wichita;* Ken Darby, "The Tall Men" from *The Tall Men;* Louis Forbes, Dave Franklin, "Heart of Gold" from *Tennessee's Partner*

MALE LEADING ROLE: James Stewart, *The Man from Laramie;* Kirk Douglas, *Man Without a Star;* Clark Gable, *The Tall Men*

FEMALE LEADING ROLE: Barbara Stanwyck, *The Violent Men;* Ruth Roman, *The Far Country;* Jane Russell, *The Tall Men*

MALE SUPPORTING ROLE: Brian Keith, *The Violent Men;* John McIntire, *The Far Country;* Jean Hersholt, *Run for Cover*

FEMALE SUPPORTING ROLE: Claire Trevor, *Man Without a Star;* Aline MacMahon, *The Man from Laramie;* Jean Parker, *A Lawless Street*

Births. Actors Sam Bottoms, Kevin Costner.

Deaths. Screenwriter Horace McCoy (b. 1897); director Lloyd Bacon (b. 1890); actors James Millican (b. 1910), Tom Powers (b. 1890), Chief Thundercloud (b. 1899); actresses Suzan Ball, Janet Beecher (b. 1884).

The year 1955 marked the conclusion of the unusually fruitful collaboration of Anthony Mann and James Stewart, which commenced in 1950. Having worked together already on three western and three nonwestern pictures, the men reached the peak of their artistic partnership with two westerns released in the same year. Although *The Far Country* and *The Man from Laramie* are both remarkable films offering two more variations on the motif of revenge, it is the latter that is usually regarded as the apotheosis of the director-actor association. The movies differ in many respects, the temperature of the location included. *The Far Country,* made from an original screenplay by Borden Chase, is a vigorous and spectacular adventure telling a relatively conventional story in an unusual Northern setting. On the other hand, *The Man from Laramie,* scripted by Philip Yordan and Frank Burt from a novel by T.T. Flynn, is an emotionally and psychologically complex tale reminiscent of ancient tragedy, more restrained location-wise, and largely depending on the performances of the key players. The acting is commendable in both films; but, whereas the veteran westerners (John McIntire, Walter Brennan, Jay C. Flippen, Harry Morgan, John Doucette) are cast so well that they almost fuse with the scenery of *The Far Country,* some of the distinguished players of *The Man from Laramie* (Arthur Kennedy, Donald Crisp, Alex Nicol) may appear to be out of place. Still, the two westerns make a suitable climax for the prematurely ended collaboration. Mann made another western the same year—the unremarkable *The Last Frontier* (featuring Victor Mature, Guy Madison, Robert Preston and Anne Bancroft); and Stewart went on with the project that caused the split—*Night Passage* (1957), directed by James Neilson, which turned out to be a modest accomplishment.

Another major director of the genre, Raoul Walsh, also made two westerns in 1955 with the same actor (Clark Gable this time) in the leading role, but the outcome was far less appealing. While *The Tall Men,* based on a decent 1954 novel by Clay Fisher (Will Henry), was fairly enjoyable mainly due to the superior characterizations by Gable, Jane Russell, Robert Ryan and Cameron Mitchell, *The King and Four*

Queens (co-starring Eleanor Parker and Jean Willes) seems pretentious and boring. The actor that scored almost as high as Stewart was Kirk Douglas. In addition to being cast as Dempsey in King Vidor's splendid and ambitious, albeit rather inaccurate, adaptation of Dee Linford's remarkable *Man Without a Star* (1952), the actor turned in a likeable performance in André De Toth's conventional yarn *The Indian Fighter* (featuring Elsa Martinelli and Walter Matthau), the first movie produced by Douglas' own company.

Despite the large number of major westerns released in 1955, no standard western was even nominated for an Academy Award. That honor, however, was given to two quasi-westerns: Fred Zinnemann's controversial musical *Oklahoma!* (a winner of two Oscars and two nominations) and John Sturges's excellent contemporary drama *Bad Day at Black Rock*, which was nominated in three categories—script, direction and actor (Spencer Tracy).

Clark Gable in Raoul Walsh's likeable *The Tall Men*, one of seven westerns based on the novels of Clay Fisher/Will Henry.

1956

Outstanding Achievements

PICTURE: *The Searchers; Seven Men from Now; The Last Hunt; The Last Wagon; Jubal; Tribute to a Bad Man; Backlash; The Fastest Gun Alive; The Proud Ones*

NOVEL FILMED: *The Searchers* by Alan LeMay; *The Last Hunt* by Milton Lott; *The Spoilers* by Rex Beach; *To Follow a Flag* by Will Henry, filmed as *Pillars of the Sky*; *Jubal Troop* by Paul I. Wellman, filmed as *Jubal*; *The Burning Hills* by Louis L'Amour; *The Rawhide Years* by Norman A. Fox; *The Maverick Queen* by Zane Grey

SHORT STORY FILMED: "Jeremy Rodock" by Jack Schaefer, filmed as *Tribute to a Bad Man*

SCREENPLAY (ORIGINAL): Burt Kennedy, *Seven Men from Now;* James Edward Grant, Delmer Daves, Gwen Bagni Gielgud, *The Last Wagon*; Russel Rouse, *The Fastest Gun Alive*

SCREENPLAY (ADAPTATION): Frank S. Nugent, *The Searchers*; Michael Blank-

1956

fort, *Tribute to a Bad Man;* Russell S. Hughes, Delmer Daves, *Jubal*

DIRECTION: John Ford, *The Searchers;* Budd Boetticher, *Seven Men from Now;* Richard Brooks, *The Last Hunt*

CINEMATOGRAPHY (B&W): William H. Clothier, *Gun the Man Down;* Walter Strenge, *Stagecoach to Fury;* George Folsey, *The Fastest Gun Alive*

CINEMATOGRAPHY (COLOR): Winton C. Hoch, *The Searchers;* Robert Surtees, *Tribute to a Bad Man;* Russell Harlan, *The Last Hunt*

MUSIC: Miklos Rozsa, *Tribute to a Bad Man;* Max Steiner, *The Searchers;* David Raksin, *Jubal*

SONG: Victor Young, Ned Washington, "The Maverick Queen" from *The Maverick Queen;* Stan Jones, "The Searchers" from *The Searchers;* Josef Myrow, Robert Wells, "The Ballad of Wes Tancred" from *Tension at Table Rock*

MALE LEADING ROLE: John Wayne, *The Searchers;* Robert Taylor, *The Last Hunt;* Robert Ryan, *The Proud Ones*

FEMALE LEADING ROLE: Gail Russell, *Seven Men from Now;* Irene Papas, *Tribute to a Bad Man;* Vera Miles, *The Searchers*

MALE SUPPORTING ROLE: Lee Marvin, *Seven Men from Now;* Ward Bond, *The Searchers;* Eduard Franz, *The Burning Hills*

FEMALE SUPPORTING ROLE: Natalie Wood, *The Searchers;* Olive Carey, *The Searchers;* Valerie French, *Jubal*

Academy Award Nomination

Stagecoach to Fury—AAN: B&W cinematography.

Deaths. Writer Clarence Edward Mulford (b. 1883); screenwriter Edward E. Paramore, Jr. (b. 1895); cinematographer W. Howard Greene (b.?); composer Victor Young (b. 1900); actors George Bancroft (b. 1882), Bob Burns (b. 1893); actress Katherine MacDonald (b. 1881).

In spite of the large number of superior westerns released in that year, 1956 was definitely the year of *The Searchers*. Considered by many to be the greatest American epic, abounding in symbolism and references, the film (featuring John Wayne, Jeffrey Hunter, Vera Miles and Natalie Wood) was based on a first-rate novel (1954) by Alan LeMay, an author who until then was associated primarily with the formula western. Screenwriter Frank S. Nugent changed the ending and softened the character Ethan (Amos, in the book) Edwards, played by Wayne, without losing the spirit of the novel, and John Ford turned the intelligent script into an extremely appealing movie. Though the reviews were not unanimously enthusiastic at the time of its release, the film has grown throughout the years into a legend. However, despite its numerous and obvious merits, including the color cinematography (Winton C. Hoch) and music (Max Steiner), there are certain aspects (Wayne's characterization being one) of the picture that remain controversial. Lindsay Anderson (in *About John Ford*) described the Duke's performance as one "that gives no sense of having been consistently thought through and relapses too often into the rough, easy-going geniality which represents the director's as well as the actor's most comfortable, most natural style." On the other hand, William K. Zinsser wrote (in the *New York Herald Tribune,*) "Wayne is fascinating for his sheer hardness. There's no kindness in his nature—he is crafty and arrogant and his eyes are cold as ice."

The Duke played characters like that (i.e. characters whose actions we do not entirely approve of) in several films. Consequently, traits of those characters have become a part of his screen image, and, as

John Wayne and Jeffrey Hunter on a lobby card for John Ford's masterpiece *The Searchers*, scripted by Frank S. Nugent from Alan LeMay's outstanding novel of the same name.

Garry Wills pointed out in *John Wayne's America*, it is the content of such roles and not the quality of the performances that is often accountable for Wayne's reputation as an actor. Some people did/do not like him because they did/do not like the characters he played, which—paradoxically—proves how good an actor he really was.

Ford and Wayne's artistic relationship was certainly the most fruitful in Hollywood's history and one that can be compared to that of Akira Kurosawa and Toshiro Mifune in Japan, Federico Fellini and Marcello Mastroianni in Italy, and Luis Buñuel and Fernando Rey in Spain. While *The Searchers* represents the apotheosis of their combined creativity, they would work together for seven more years, and the total number of their movies would reach 17, including nine westerns. Thus, it was at the peak of their partnership, and a year after Mann and Stewart terminated their collaboration, when two new director-star associations relevant for the western genre were born. One of them, that of Budd Boetticher and Randolph Scott, owes it to Wayne and his prolonged involvement in *The Searchers* and later in *The Wings of Eagles*. Wayne, who purchased Burt Kennedy's script of *Seven Men from Now* and hoped to star in this first production by his own company, Batjac, was eventually forced to turn the role over to Scott. Thus, the collaboration commenced, and, by 1960, Boetticher and Scott would make altogether seven medium-budget, compact westerns focusing on an aging, revenge-seeking hero. At least four entries in this celebrated cycle (including *Seven Men from Now*, co-starring Gail Russell and Lee Marvin) are regarded as minor classics.

Just like Boetticher and Scott, Delmer Daves and Glenn Ford had had a number of successful westerns to their credit when they discovered each other on the set of *Jubal* (featuring Ernest Borgnine, Rod Steiger, Felicia Farr and Valerie French), a spectacular psychological melodrama inspired by the first chapter of Paul I. Wellman's lengthy novel *Jubal Troop* (1939). The film was not a masterpiece, but the director and the actor developed a mutual respect and understanding while working on it. Consequently, they would make two more significant westerns together during the next two years.

Among the numerous novels that were turned into movies in 1956 was Milton Lott's outstanding 1954 book *The Last Hunt*. Though Richard Brooks, the director and screenwriter of the film adaptation, did his best to save the novel's strong ecological message, and Robert Taylor (as the obsessive and sadistic buffalo hunter Charley Gilson) gave one of his most interesting performances, the complexity of the psychological juxtaposition of the two antithetical personalities (the other one being the sensitive Sandy McKenzie, played by Stewart Granger) is lost, just like the multi-level symbolism of Lott's narrative. To Brooks' credit, however, the shift of the protagonists' clash (which in the book takes place somewhere in the middle) to the end of the movie certainly enhanced the climactic resolution.

The Western Writers of America in their 1995 poll selected *The Searchers* as number 3 western film. Surprisingly, the only standard western that was recognized by the Academy in 1956 was the minor, clichéd picture *Stagecoach to Fury* (featuring Forrest Tucker, Mari Blanchard, Wallace Ford and Paul Fix), directed by William F. Claxton, which was nominated for Walter Strenge's black-and-white cinematography. The movie that received due recognition was George Stevens' contemporary western epic *Giant* (starring Rock Hudson, Elizabeth Taylor and James Dean), which received one Oscar (for best direction) and nine additional nominations, including one for best picture.

A great loss to the western genre came with the death of Victor Young, an Oscar-winning composer who scored numerous classic westerns, including *Wells Fargo*, *Arizona*, *Rio Grande*, *Shane* and *Johnny Guitar*.

1957

Outstanding Achievements

PICTURE: *3:10 to Yuma; The Tin Star; Gunfight at the O.K. Corral; The Tall T; The True Story of Jesse James; Run of the Arrow; Forty Guns; Trooper Hook; Decision at Sundown; Gun for a Coward*

NOVEL FILMED: *Buffalo Grass* by Frank Gruber, filmed as *The Big Land*; *Night Passage* by Norman A. Fox; *The Guns of Fort Petticoat* by C. William Harrison; *Utah Blaine* by Louis L'Amour; *Decision at Sundown* by Michael Carder

SHORT STORY/NOVELLA FILMED: "Three-Ten to Yuma" by Elmore Leonard; "Sergeant Houck" by Jack Schaefer, filmed as *Trooper Hook*; "The Captives" by Elmore Leonard, filmed as *The Tall T*; "Showdown Trail" by Louis L'Amour, filmed as *The Tall Stranger*

SCREENPLAY (ORIGINAL): Barney Slater, Joel Kane, Dudley Nichols, *The Tin Star*; Samuel Fuller, *Forty Guns*

SCREENPLAY (ADAPTATION): Halsted Welles, *3:10 to Yuma*; Burt Kennedy, *The Tall T*

DIRECTION: Delmer Daves, *3:10 to Yuma;* Anthony Mann, *The Tin Star;* John Sturges, *Gunfight at the O.K. Corral*

CINEMATOGRAPHY (B&W): Charles Lawton, Jr., *3:10 to Yuma;* Loyal Griggs, *The Tin Star;* Joseph Biroc, *Forty Guns*

CINEMATOGRAPHY (COLOR): Charles Lang, Jr., *Gunfight at the O.K. Corral;* Charles Lawton, Jr., *The Tall T;* Joseph Biroc, *Run of the Arrow*

MUSIC: George Duning, *3:10 to Yuma;* Dimitri Tiomkin, *Gunfight at the O.K. Corral;* Elmer Bernstein, *The Tin Star*

SONG: George Duning, Ned Washington, "3:10 to Yuma" from *3:10 to Yuma;* Dimitri Tiomkin, Ned Washington, "Gunfight at the O.K. Corral" from *Gunfight at the O.K. Corral;* Victor Young, Harold Adamson, "God Has His Arms Around Me" from *Forty Guns*

MALE LEADING ROLE: Henry Fonda, *The Tin Star;* Glenn Ford, *3:10 to Yuma;* Van Heflin, *3:10 to Yuma*

FEMALE LEADING ROLE: Maureen O'Sullivan, *The Tall T;* Betsy Palmer, *The Tin Star;* Rhonda Fleming, *Gunfight at the O.K. Corral*

MALE SUPPORTING ROLE: Richard Jaeckel, *3:10 to Yuma;* Arthur Hunnicutt, *The Tall T;* Noah Beery, Jr., *Decision at Sundown*

FEMALE SUPPORTING ROLE: Jo Van Fleet, *Gunfight at the O.K. Corral;* Valerie French, *Decision at Sundown;* Leora Dana, *3:10 to Yuma*

Academy Award Nominations

Gunfight at the O.K. Corral—AAN: sound (George Dutton); editing (Warren Low).

The Tin Star—AAN: story and screenplay written directly for the screen.

Deaths. Writers Peter B. Kyne (b. 1880), Kenneth Roberts (b. 1885); directors Fred F. Sears (b. 1913), Tim Whelan (b. 1893); cinematographer Alvin Wyckoff (b. 1877); actors Alfonso Bedoya (b. 1904), Humphrey Bogart (b. 1899), Russell Hicks (b. 1895), Gene Lockhart (b. 1891); actress Elinor Fair (b. 1903).

The numerous westerns that had been so far influenced by *High Noon* included such minor productions as Allan Dwan's *Silver Lode* (1954), Alfred Werker's *At Gunpoint* (1955) and Robert D. Webb's *The Proud Ones* (1956). A 1957 film that owed even more to *High Noon* (but did not need, by any means, to be ashamed of it) was *3:10 to Yuma*, the second and best picture of the Delmer Daves-Glenn Ford

Poster for *Gunfight at the O.K. Corral,* John Sturges' version of the frequently-filmed legendary story, starring Burt Lancaster as Wyatt Earp and Kirk Douglas as Doc Holliday.

1957

Van Heflin, Felicia Farr, Glenn Ford and Ford Rainey on a lobby card for Delmer Daves' *3:10 to Yuma*, an excellent, if generally underrated, western based on a superb short story by Elmore Leonard.

partnership. The movie resembles Zinnemann's classic in at least four respects— the integrity and loneliness of the protagonist, the suspense built up by means of the passing time, the focus on dialogue in indoor settings, and the extensive use of the title song. Regardless of the similarities, however, *3:10 to Yuma* (co-starring Van Heflin, Felicia Farr and Leora Dana) is a truly original western, an unquestioned masterpiece with a number of its own merits. They are contained in Halsted Welles' excellent script (based on Elmore Leonard's remarkable 1953 short story), Charles Lawton, Jr.'s splendid black-and-white photography (avoiding reflected light in the shadows), and George Duning's attractive musical score.

As an interesting novelty, the titular ballad sung by Frankie Laine (who, nota bene, had included the song from *High Noon* in his repertoire) was recorded prior to the shooting and played on the set to create the right atmosphere. Moreover, Daves, whose direction is masterful, extracts first-rate performances from both Heflin in the role of the hero, Dan Evans, and Ford as the likeable villain Ben Wade.

While James Stewart worked in *Night Passage* (co-starring Audie Murphy), a movie significant mainly because of the actor's on-screen musical performance (accordion and vocal), Anthony Mann (who had walked out of that project) was involved in *The Tin Star* (featuring Henry Fonda, Anthony Perkins and Betsy Palmer), an intelligent and socially engaged western reminiscent of both *High Noon* and *Shane*. Since *The Tin Star*, scripted by Dudley Nichols from a screen story by Barney Slater and Joel Kane (earning an Academy Award nomination for the three of them), was a black-and-white picture (superbly photographed by Loyal Griggs), 1957 should be remembered as the last year with two top western achievements shot in monochrome.

Budd Boetticher and Randolph Scott came up with two items in their revenge cycle, of which *The Tall T* (co-starring Maureen O'Sullivan and Richard Boone), clearly the superior of the two, was based on another fine short story by Elmore Leonard ("The Captives," 1956) while *Decision at Sundown* (featuring John Carroll, Karen Steele and Valerie French), based on a decent 1955 novel by Michael Carder, is interesting mostly because of its initial situation (a wedding interrupted by a revenge-seeking man), which is a reversal of that in *Silver Lode* (which in turn is a modification of that in *High Noon*).

Two 1957 westerns that cannot go unnoticed are *Run of the Arrow* (featuring Rod Steiger, Brian Keith, Sarita Montiel and Ralph Meeker) and *Forty Guns* (starring Barbara Stanwyck, Barry Sullivan and Gene Barry). Made by the legendary director Samuel Fuller, the two pictures represent major examples of the primitive cinema. Their extraordinary atmosphere is created as much by Fuller's unconventional direction as by the bizarre camera work by Joseph Biroc—in color and black and white, respectively.

In 1957 the genre lost Peter B. Kyne, an author of many novels and short stories that found their way to the big screen. Highly popular and respected in the first half of the twentieth century, Kyne, whose 1912 novel *The Three Godfathers* is among the works most frequently filmed, is now almost completely forgotten by readers and publishers alike.

1958

Outstanding Achievements

PICTURE: *The Big Country; The Sheepman; From Hell to Texas; Man of the West; The Bravados; Saddle the Wind; Cowboy; The Law and Jake Wade; The Left Handed Gun; Fort Dobbs*

NOVEL FILMED: *The Hell Bent Kid* by Charles O. Locke, filmed as *From Hell to Texas; The Big Country* by Donald Hamilton; *The Border Jumpers* by Will C. Brown, filmed as *Man of the West; The Name's Buchanan* by Jonas Ward, filmed as *Buchanan Rides Alone; Last Stand at Papago Wells* by Louis L'Amour, filmed as *Apache Territory*

NONFICTION BOOK FILMED: *My Reminiscences as a Cowboy* by Frank Harris, filmed as *Cowboy*

SHORT STORY FILMED: "Raiders Die Hard" by John M. Cunningham, filmed as *Day of the Bad Man*

SCREENPLAY (ORIGINAL): James Edward Grant, William Bowers, William Roberts, *The Sheepman*; Rod Serling, Thomas Thompson, *Saddle the Wind*

SCREENPLAY (ADAPTATION): James R. Webb, Sy Bartlett, Robert Wilder, Jessamyn West, *The Big Country*; Philip Yordan, *The Bravados*; Reginald Rose, *Man of the West*

DIRECTION: William Wyler, *The Big Country*; George Marshall, *The Sheepman*; Henry Hathaway, *From Hell to Texas*

CINEMATOGRAPHY (B&W): William H. Clothier, *Fort Dobbs*; J. Peverll Marley, *The Left Handed Gun*; John M. Nicholaus, Jr., *Showdown at Boot Hill*

CINEMATOGRAPHY (COLOR): Franz Planer, *The Big Country*; Ernest Haller, *Man of the West*; Robert Surtees, *The Law and Jake Wade*

MUSIC: Jerome Moross, *The Big*

1958

Country; Jeff Alexander, *Saddle the Wind;* Leigh Harline, *Man of the West*

SONG: Jay Livingston, Ray Evans, "Saddle the Wind" from *Saddle the Wind;* Marilyn and Joe Hoove, "Don't Even Pretend at Love" from *Showdown at Boot Hill*

MALE LEADING ROLE: Gregory Peck, *The Big Country;* Glenn Ford, *The Sheepman;* Gary Cooper, *Man of the West*

FEMALE LEADING ROLE: Jean Simmons, *The Big Country;* Shirley MacLaine, *The Sheepman;* Julie London, *Man of the West*

MALE SUPPORTING ROLE: Burl Ives, *The Big Country;* Charles Bickford, *The Big Country;* Edgar Buchanan, *The Sheepman*

FEMALE SUPPORTING ROLE: Carroll Baker, *The Big Country;* Katy Jurado, *The Badlanders;* Lita Milan, *The Left Handed Gun*

Academy Awards/ Nominations

The Big Country—AA: supporting actor Burl Ives; AAN: scoring of dramatic or comedy picture.

The Sheepman—AAN: story and screenplay.

Cowboy—AAN: editing (William A. Lyon, Al Clark).

Deaths. Writer Les Savage, Jr.; screenwriter Russell Hughes (b. 1910); director Marshall Neilan (b. 1891), Kurt Neumann (b. 1906); cinematographer George Robinson (b. 1890).

The films released in 1958 included a significant number of solid westerns, the majority of which were inspired by superior literary material. Except for *Saddle the Wind* and *The Left Handed Gun* (directed by newcomers Robert Parrish and Arthur Penn, respectively), the major westerns of the year were made by directors already experienced in the genre. In fact, most of them were distinguished contributors to the western film—Henry Hathaway (*From Hell to Texas*), Anthony Mann (*Man of the West*), Delmer Daves (*Cowboy*), William Wyler (*The Big Country*), Henry King (*The Bravados*), John Sturges (*The Law and Jake Wade*) and Gordon Douglas (*Fort Dobbs*).

Excluding his Civil War drama *Friendly Persuasion* (1956), William Wyler had not made a western movie since *The Westerner* (1940). His new, and last, western, *The Big Country* was one of the biggest projects and most ambitious endeavors in the genre's history. The script by James R. Webb, Sy Bartlett, Robert Wilder and Jessamyn West (the author of the novel *The Friendly Persuasion*), based on the good 1957 novel by Donald Hamilton, offered an intellectual challenge and some iconoclastic ideas that only a director of Wyler's caliber could handle. With fine help from the first-rate cast (Gregory Peck, Jean Simmons, Carroll Baker, Charlton Heston, Charles Bickford and the Oscar-winning Burl Ives), Wyler created a captivating drama that was further enhanced by Jerome Moross's splendid, Oscar-nominated score (including the very well known theme) and Franz Planner's breathtaking color and Technirama photography (shot in two Californian locations, Stockton and Red Rock Canyon). "This is preeminently a director's picture and among Westerns a real beauty" opineds Paul V. Beckley in the *New York Herald Tribune*. "Those verbal encounters and violent battles are like something on the windy plains of Troy," stated Bosley Crowther in the *New York Times*.

While *The Big Country* is a western masterpiece in all respects, and a serious morality tale, *The Sheepman* (co-starring Shirley MacLaine and Leslie Nielsen) stands out among the 1958 productions for its top-notch entertainment values. It

Chuck Connors, Gregory Peck and Carroll Baker in *The Big Country*, William Wyler's iconoclastic masterpiece, one of two westerns based on Donald Hamilton's prose.

marked a successful reunion of director Marshall and Glenn Ford, who here, even more than in their *Texas* (1941), created—with significant help from screenwriters James Edward Grant, William Bowers and William Roberts—a perfect combination of action and humor, neither of which quality stood in the other's way.

There are three somewhat controversial westerns of 1958 that illustrate different accomplishments in the area of adapting a book. While *Man of the West* (with Gary Cooper, Julie London and Lee J. Cobb) represents an accurate rendition of Will C. Brown's decent novel *The Border Jumpers* (1955), making good use of the original author's ideas, *From Hell to Texas* (featuring Don Murray, Diane Varsi and Chill Wills), an otherwise rewarding western, shows how an excellent novel (Charles O. Locke's *The Hell Bent Kid*, 1957) can—in the process of adaptation—lose its power by being deprived of its fatalistic tone due to the unsuitable happy ending. *The Bravados* (starring Gregory Peck, Joan Collins and Stephen Boyd) is an example of how an unremarkable formula western book (*The Bravados*, 1957, by Frank O'Rourke) can be turned into a thought-provoking picture by a good screenwriter (Philip Yordan) and director.

In 1958, Delmer Daves and Glenn Ford concluded their collaboration with a so-so rendition of the popular biographical book *My Reminiscences as a Cowboy* (1930) by Frank Harris (portrayed by Jack Lemmon), which received the title *Cowboy*. Budd Boetticher and Randolph Scott

1959

Gary Cooper in Anthony Mann's controversial western *Man of the West* (co-starring Julie London and Lee J. Cobb).

continued their partnership with *Buchanan Rides Alone* (co-starring Jennifer Holden), a lesser picture in their cycle, derived from an entertaining novel, *The Name's Buchanan* (1956), by Jonas Ward.

The Freudian elements which had been traced in a few westerns before—most obviously in *Pursued* (1947) and *The Furies* (1950), both written by Niven Busch—can be also found (to a greater or lesser degree) in three westerns of 1958: *Saddle the Wind* (starring Robert Taylor, John Cassavetes and Julie London), *The Left Handed Gun* (featuring Paul Newman, John Dehner and Lita Milan) and Gene Fowler, Jr.'s *Showdown at Boot Hill* (with Charles Bronson and Carole Mathews).

Outstanding Achievements

PICTURE: *Rio Bravo; Warlock; Last Train from Gun Hill; The Hanging Tree; The Wonderful Country; The Horse Soldiers; Ride Lonesome; They Came to Cordura; These Thousand Hills; Face of a Fugitive*

NOVEL FILMED: *The Wonderful Country* by Tom Lea; *The Horse Soldiers* by Harold Sinclair; *These Thousand Hills* by A.B. Guthrie, Jr.; *Warlock* by Oakley Hall; *They Came to Cordura* by Glendon Swarthout; *Yellowstone Kelly* by Clay Fisher (Will Henry)

NOVELLA FILMED: "The Hanging Tree" by Dorothy M. Johnson

SCREENPLAY (ORIGINAL): B.H. McCampbell, Jules Furthman, Leigh Brackett, *Rio Bravo;* Burt Kennedy, *Ride Lonesome*

SCREENPLAY (ADAPTATION): Robert Alan Aurthur, *Warlock;* Wendell Mayes, Halsted Welles, *The Hanging Tree;* Robert Ardrey, *The Wonderful Country*

DIRECTION: Howard Hawks, *Rio Bravo;* Edward Dmytryk, *Warlock;* Delmer Daves, *The Hanging Tree*

CINEMATOGRAPHY (B&W): Russell Harlan, *Day of the Outlaw;* Loyal Griggs, *The Hangman;* William H. Clothier, *Escort West*

CINEMATOGRAPHY (COLOR): Russell Harlan, *Rio Bravo;* William H. Clothier, *The Horse Soldiers;* Ted McCord, *The Hanging Tree*

MUSIC: Dimitri Tiomkin, *Rio Bravo;* Max Steiner, *The Hanging Tree;* Alex North, *The Wonderful Country*

SONG: Dimitri Tiomkin, Paul Francis Webster, "My Rifle, My Pony and Me" from *Rio Bravo;* Dimitri Tiomkin, Ned Washington, "Strange Are the Ways of Love" from *The Young Land;* Jerry Livingston, Mack David, "The Hanging Tree" from *The Hanging Tree*

MALE LEADING ROLE: Henry Fonda, *Warlock;* John Wayne, *Rio Bravo;* Gary Cooper, *The Hanging Tree*
FEMALE LEADING ROLE: Angie Dickinson, *Rio Bravo;* Dorothy Malone, *Warlock;* Maria Schell, *The Hanging Tree*
MALE SUPPORTING ROLE: Walter Brennan, *Rio Bravo;* Karl Malden, *The Hanging Tree;* Pedro Gonzalez-Gonzalez, *Rio Bravo*
FEMALE SUPPORTING ROLE: Carolyn Jones, *Last Train from Gun Hill;* Dolores Michaels, *Warlock;* Estelita Rodriguez, *Rio Bravo*

Academy Award Nomination

The Young Land—AAN: song "Strange Are the Ways of Love."

Deaths. Directors George Archainbaud (b. 1890), Irving Cummings (b. 1888), Cecil B. De Mille (b. 1881); composer George Antheil (b. 1900); actors William Bishop, Errol Flynn (b. 1909), James Gleason (b. 1886), Charles Halton (b. 1876), Victor McLaglen (b. 1886), Russell Simpson (b. 1878), Grant Withers (b. 1904).

Just like the whole second half of the decade, 1959 saw the release of a significant number of remarkable westerns, the titles of which still evoke a thrill of nostalgic excitement. Although the majority of them were renditions of excellent literary material, the most outstanding western of the year, Howard Hawks' *Rio Bravo* (featuring John Wayne, Dean Martin, Angie Dickinson and Ricky Nelson), was made from an original screenplay. Scripted by Jules Furthman and Leigh Bracket from a screen story by B.H. McCampbell (the director's daughter), *Rio Bravo* was Hawks and Wayne's reaction to *High Noon*, a movie they did not like and considered anti–American. Regardless of the intentions, however, the picture turned out to be, above all, a large-scale, highly relaxed, and extremely enjoyable and amiable western, which constitutes the summing up of everything that had been best in the work of Hawks and his prime screenwriter, Furthman. Even though Hawks and Wayne had worked together only once before (*Red River*, 1948), they seemed to form a team blessed with perfect mutual understanding, which would eventually

Ricky Nelson (Colorado) and John Wayne (Sheriff John T. Chance) in a scene from Howard Hawks' *Rio Bravo,* **one of the most beloved westerns of all time.**

1959

One of the most distinguished character actors, Walter Brennan, provided a dose of humor and warmth with his outstanding performance as jailer Stumpy in *Rio Bravo*.

result in five movies altogether, including *El Dorado* (1967) and *Rio Lobo* (1970), two variations on the plot of *Rio Bravo* (creating a loose trilogy). As Sheriff John T. Chance, John Wayne turned in a towering performance, both literally and figuratively speaking, demonstrating everything he had learned so far and making the role seem extremely easy. In 1959 he was still in his prime, but from then on his advancement in years, affecting his appearance and physical fitness, would—despite his growing experience—gradually reduce the plausibility of his on-screen heroics (unless the script turned such shortcomings into assets, as, for example, in *True Grit* and *The Shootist*).

The second best western of 1959, Edward Dmytryk's *Warlock* (starring Henry Fonda, Richard Widmark and Anthony Quinn), is also a captivating town-bound drama resolved through an attractive mixture of action and dialogue. Unlike *Rio Bravo*, however, whose success benefited considerably from its abundant humor, *Warlock* is an extremely earnest picture, rightly compared to an ancient tragedy. Since the main character, the hired law enforcer Clay Blaisdell, is modeled after Wyatt Earp, Fonda's role can be seen as a continuation of his previous characterizations in *My Darling Clementine* and, possibly, *The Tin Star*. Although the actor has appeared in many remarkable westerns and delivered unforgettable performances in most of them, those three roles of his, in which he wears (at least at a certain time) a lawman's star, constitute a gem in the genre's history.

Anthony Quinn, an actor often underrated and somehow neglected by western historians, plays an important, tragic role in both *Warlock* and *Last Train from Gun Hill*. The latter (co-starring Kirk Douglas and Carolyn Jones) is a very economically structured film (rightly compared to a symphony), which, however, owes a lot to both *3:10 to Yuma* and, indirectly, *High Noon*. The musical score of *Last Train from Gun Hill* was written by Dimitri Tiomkin, a distinguished and hardworking composer whose credits in 1959 include two more westerns, *Rio Bravo* and *The Young Land*, which he furnished with memorable songs.

Four successful, if not masterful, screen adaptations were made by four major directors. Delmer Daves crafted *The Hanging Tree* (starring Gary Cooper, in his best western role since *High Noon*, and Maria Schell) from Dorothy M. Johnson's excellent 1957 novella (selected as one of the 12 best short stories in the Western Writers of America's 1995 survey); Robert Parrish filmed Tom Lea's splendid 1952 novel *The Wonderful Country*, with fine characterizations by Robert Mitchum,

Julie London and Charles McGraw; John Ford turned Harold Sinclair's superior Civil War book *The Horse Soldiers* (1956) into an enjoyable movie with John Wayne, William Holden and Constance Towers; and Robert Rossen made *They Came to Cordura* (starring Gary Cooper, Rita Hayworth and Van Heflin) from a good psychological 1958 novel by Glendon Swarthout. On the other hand, A.B. Guthrie, Jr.'s major novel *These Thousand Hills* (1956, a sequel to *The Way West*, 1949) became a disappointing movie (with Don Murray, Lee Remick and Richard Egan), mainly because of the uninspired direction by Richard Fleischer.

Ride Lonesome (featuring Randolph Scott, Karen Steele and Pernell Roberts) was the fifth (and one of the best) picture in the interesting cycle resulting from the partnership of Scott and director Budd Boetticher. Just like *Seven Men from Now*, *The Tall T* and *Comanche Station* (to be released in 1960), it was superbly scripted by Burt Kennedy.

A pioneer filmmaker, Cecil B. De Mille, the director of the first screen adaptation of *The Virginian*, the three versions of *The Squaw Man*, as well as of *The Plainsman* and *Union Pacific*, was among the celebrities that passed away in 1959.

1960

Outstanding Achievements

PICTURE: *The Magnificent Seven; Sergeant Rutledge; Comanche Station; The Unforgiven; North to Alaska; The Alamo; Heller in Pink Tights; Flaming Star; Cimarron*

NOVEL FILMED: *Cimarron* by Edna Ferber; *The Unforgiven* by Alan LeMay; *Flaming Lance* by Clair Huffaker, filmed as *Flaming Star; Heller with a Gun* by Louis L'Amour, filmed as *Heller in Pink Tights; Captain Buffalo* by James Warner Bellah, filmed as *Sergeant Rutledge; Seven Ways from Sundown* by Clair Huffaker; *Guns of the Timberlands* by Louis L'Amour, filmed as *Guns of the Timberland*

SCREENPLAY (ORIGINAL): Burt Kennedy, *Comanche Station*

SCREENPLAY (ADAPTATION): William Roberts, *The Magnificent Seven*; Dudley Nichols, Walter Bernstein, *Heller in Pink Tights*; Nunnally Johnson, Clair Huffaker, *Flaming Star*

DIRECTION: John Sturges, *The Magnificent Seven*; Henry Hathaway, *North to Alaska*; John Ford, *Sergeant Rutledge*

CINEMATOGRAPHY (B&W): Walter Strenge, *Oklahoma Territory*

CINEMATOGRAPHY (COLOR): William H. Clothier, *The Alamo*; Charles Lang, Jr., *The Magnificent Seven*; Franz Planer, *The Unforgiven*

MUSIC: Elmer Bernstein, *The Magnificent Seven*; Dimitri Tiomkin, *The Alamo*; Dimitri Tiomkin, *The Unforgiven*

SONG: Dimitri Tiomkin, Paul Francis Webster, "The Green Leaves of Summer" from *The Alamo*; Jerry Livingston, Mack David, "Captain Buffalo" from *Sergeant Rutledge*; Sid Wayne, Sherman Edwards, "Flaming Star" from *Flaming Star*

MALE LEADING ROLE: Yul Brunner, *The Magnificent Seven*; Burt Lancaster, *The Unforgiven*; Randolph Scott, *Comanche Station*

FEMALE LEADING ROLE: Audrey Hepburn, *The Unforgiven*; Sophia Loren, *Heller in Pink Tights*; Maria Schell, *Cimarron*

MALE SUPPORTING ROLE: Chill Wills, *The Alamo*; Eli Wallach, *The Magnificent Seven*; John McIntire, *Flaming Star*

FEMALE SUPPORTING ROLE: Lillian Gish, *The Unforgiven*; Dolores Del Rio,

1960

Flaming Star; Rosenda Monteros, *The Magnificent Seven*

Academy Awards/ Nominations

The Alamo—AA: sound (Gordon E. Sawyer, Fred Hynes); AAN: picture; color cinematography; scoring of a dramatic or comedy picture; song "The Green Leaves of Summer"; supporting actor Chill Wills; editing (Stuart Gilmore).

Cimarron—AAN: color art direction-set decoration (George W. Davis, Addison Hehr; Henry Grace, Hugh Hunt, Otto Siegel); sound (Franklin E. Milton)

The Magnificent Seven—AAN: scoring of a dramatic or comedy picture.

Deaths. Writer Norman A. Fox (b. 1911); screenwriters Jules Furthman (b. 1888), Dudley Nichols (b. 1895); directors Alfred E. Green (1889), Frank Lloyd (b. 1888), Ben Stoloff (b. 1895); cinematographers Edward Cronjager (b. 1904), Sol Polito (b. 1892); actors Ward Bond (b. 1903), Clark Gable (b. 1901), Louis Jean Heydt (b. 1905), Douglas Spencer (b. 1910); actress Hope Emerson (b. 1897).

Since his film debut in 1946, John Sturges had made several remarkable movies, including a few westerns, but somehow had not gained the recognition he deserved. In 1960, however, he made *The Magnificent Seven,* a picture that assured him a reputation as a first-rate filmmaker and master of the western genre. The brilliant script, based on Akira Kurosawa's *Seven Samurai* (1954), was originally written by Walter Newman and subsequently revised and credited to William Roberts. Sturges, who turned it into one of the most enjoyable and celebrated westerns of all time, deserves to be praised for the masterful staging, especially of the action sequences, but, even more, for the excellent casting of the seven protagonists, who all create strong and original characterizations. Yul Brynner is particularly effective as the leader of the hired gun-

James Coburn, Brad Dexter, Robert Vaughn, Charles Bronson, Horst Buchholz, Steve McQueen and Yul Brynner as *The Magnificent Seven,* **an outstanding western directed by John Sturges.**

slingers, but the others are not far behind. A part of the enormous success of the movie is rightly attributed to the grand color and Cinemascope photography by Charles Lang, Jr. (who had worked with Sturges on two other westerns, *Gunfight at the O.K. Corral* and *Last Train from Gun Hill*), and the excellent, Oscar-nominated symphonic score by Elmer Bernstein (including a popular theme). An extremely influential western, *The Magnificent Seven* launched the careers of a few actors, especially Steve McQueen, Charles Bronson and James Coburn, who all—probably not by accident—would appear in Sturges' last hit, the World War II POW adventure *The Great Escape* (1963).

An undertaking comparable in terms of scale to *The Magnificent Seven* was *The Alamo* (featuring John Wayne, Richard Widmark and Laurence Harvey), the Duke's directorial debut. The movie has a few outstanding components, such as the score and songs by Dimitri Tiomkin, and the color cinematography by William H. Clothier but due to the erratic script by James Edward Grant, episodic and full of historical inaccuracies, and the overwhelming problems Wayne had to face as a producer (leading to his bankruptcy), *The Alamo* did not fulfill the actor-director-producer's expectations and also failed at the box office. Despite winning one Oscar and several nominations, it was not an artistic success, either.

There were three major 1960 westerns that surprised the audiences with their bold approach to the problem of racial prejudice. John Ford's *Sergeant Rutledge* (featuring Jeffrey Hunter, Woody Strode and Constance Towers) is a courtroom drama about a black soldier accused of murdering a white girl. John Huston's *The Unforgiven* (starring Burt Lancaster,

Richard Widmark (Jim Bowie) and John Wayne (Davy Crockett) in Wayne's controversial directorial debut, *The Alamo*.

Audrey Hepburn and Audie Murphy, in possibly his best performance), based on Alan LeMay's novel (1957), offers an interesting reversal of the situation in *The Searchers*, another movie from LeMay's prose, made four years earlier. While in the latter a white girl captured by the Comanches is sought by two of her relatives, in the former an Indian girl raised by a white family is claimed by her Kiowa brother. What is interesting in the comparison of the two pictures (and novels, for that matter) is the way the conflict is resolved—with the white people being the winners and keeping the girl in both. Finally, Don Siegel's *Flaming Star* (with Elvis Presley in his by far greatest performance) constitutes a pessimistic study of what happens to the family of a white man living among the whites with his Indian wife and two sons, one of which is a half-breed.

In 1960, Budd Boetticher and Randolph Scott made the last two of their seven oaters. While *Westbound* (co-starring Virginia Mayo and Karen Steele) is a clichéd and unremarkable film, *Comanche Station* (featuring Nancy Gates and Claude Akins) stands out as possibly the best item in the cycle. Considered to be one of the top ten westerns of all time by critic Andrew Farris, *Comanche Station* resembles—in more ways than one—Sam Peckinpah's *Ride the High Country*, a movie released two years later.

Among the remaining major westerns of the year were two adaptations of popular and acclaimed books. If Anthony Mann's rendition (starring Glenn Ford, Maria Schell and Anne Baxter) of Edna Ferber's *Cimarron* (1930) disappointed both the critics and the public (being clearly inferior to the first, 1931 screen version), George Cukor's only western, *Heller in Pink Tights* (featuring Anthony Quinn, Sophia Loren and Steve Forrest), based on Louis L'Amour's *Heller with a Gun* (1955), is a quite original, intelligent and rewarding film. The major alterations in the latter's story line (by screenwriters Dudley Nichols and Walter Bernstein) did not stop L'Amour from regarding the film as the second best adaptation of his prose.

Several distinguished celebrities passed away in 1960. In addition to two major screenwriters—Dudley Nichols (*Stagecoach*, *The Big Sky*, *The Tin Star*) and Jules Furthman *(The Outlaw, Rio Bravo)*, the western film lost one popular character actor, Ward Bond. An important member of John Ford's stock company, Bond appeared in numerous pictures opposite his close friend John Wayne, either under the guidance of Ford (*Fort Apache*) or other directors (*Tall in the Saddle, Hondo, Rio Bravo*).

1961

Outstanding Achievements

PICTURE: *One-Eyed Jacks; The Comancheros; The Last Sunset; Two Rode Together; The Deadly Companions*

NOVEL FILMED: *The Authentic Death of Hendry Jones* by Charles Neider, filmed as *One-Eyed Jacks; The Comancheros* by Paul I. Wellman; *Posse from Hell* by Clair Huffaker; *Sundown at Crazy Horse* by Vechel Howard (Howard Rigsby), filmed as *The Last Sunset; Yellowleg* by A.S. Fleischman, filmed as *The Deadly Companions*

SCREENPLAY (ADAPTATION): James Edward Grant, Clair Huffaker, *The Comancheros;* Dalton Trumbo, *The Last Sunset;* Calder Willingham, Guy Trosper, *One-Eyed Jacks*

DIRECTION: Robert Aldrich, *The Last Sunset;* John Ford, *Two Rode Together;* Michael Curtiz, *The Comancheros*

CINEMATOGRAPHY (COLOR): Charles Lang, Jr., *One-Eyed Jacks;* Charles

Lawton, Jr., *Two Rode Together;* William H. Clothier, *The Deadly Companions*

MUSIC: Ernest Gold, *The Last Sunset;* Elmer Bernstein, *The Comancheros;* Hugo Friedhofer, *One-Eyed Jacks*

SONG: Charles B. FitzSimons, Marlin Skiles, "A Dream of Love" from *The Deadly Companions;* Ken Darby, "This Is Canada" from *The Canadians*

MALE LEADING ROLE: Kirk Douglas, *The Last Sunset;* James Stewart, *Two Rode Together;* Marlon Brando, *One-Eyed Jacks*

FEMALE LEADING ROLE: Dorothy Malone, *The Last Sunset;* Maureen O'Hara, *The Deadly Companions;* Pina Pellicer, *One-Eyed Jacks*

MALE SUPPORTING ROLE: Ben Johnson, *One-Eyed Jacks;* Lee Marvin, *The Comancheros;* Chill Wills, *The Deadly Companions*

FEMALE SUPPORTING ROLE: Katy Jurado, *One-Eyed Jacks;* Carol Lynley, *The Last Sunset;* Linda Cristal, *Two Rode Together*

Academy Award Nomination

One-Eyed Jacks—AAN: color cinematography.

Deaths. Screenwriter John Stone (b. 1888); directors Edward F. Cline (b. 1892), George Melford (b. 1889); actors Jeff Chandler, Gary Cooper (b. 1901), Henry O'Neill (b. 1891); actress Gail Russell.

The western films released in 1961 do not include a masterpiece, but the five pictures that stand out—all major productions with prestigious names, and all adaptations of more or less successful novels—represent a mixture of interesting failures that are significant in the genre's history for one reason or another. Marlon Brando's directorial debut, *One-Eyed Jacks* (featuring Brando, Karl Malden, Pina Pellicer and Katy Jurado) is an extravaganza memorable for the excellent color cinematography by Charles Lang, Jr., including rare (in a western) and marvellous footage of the California coast, and a handful of fine performances, especially from Pellicer, Jurado and Ben Johnson (as one of the villains). The screenplay by Calder Willingham and Guy Trosper fails to reveal the quality of the compelling 1956 novel by Charles Neider, on which it was allegedly based; nor does it make any innuendo (unlike the book) that it is a disguised story of Billy the Kid and his relationship with Pat Garrett. Oddly, however, since Sam Peckinpah was an uncredited collaborator on the script, some of Neider's ideas and situations would survive in *Pat Garrett and Billy the Kid* (1973), albeit without being credited to the author.

As a director, Peckinpah made an interesting, though rather unnoticed, big-screen debut with *The Deadly Companions* (starring Maureen O'Hara and Brian Keith), an unremarkable western that nevertheless shows some traces of the director's talent and style.

Three other major westerns were released in 1961. *The Comancheros* (with John Wayne, Stuart Whitman and Ina Balin) was an enjoyable traditional western notable for being the last film directed by Michael Curtiz (who would die in 1962) and the last western derived from the prose by Paul I. Wellman (a novel of 1952). *The Last Sunset* (featuring Rock Hudson, Kirk Douglas, Dorothy Malone and Carol Lynley), Robert Aldrich's third western, was significant for the motif of incestuous love (absent in Vechel Howard's 1957 novel, *Sundown at Crazy Horse*, on which it was based), which made critics compare it to an ancient tragedy. *Two Rode Together* (starring James Stewart and Richard Widmark) was John Ford's return to the theme of *The Searchers* (the search for Indian captives) and the first collaboration of Ford and Stewart (further widening the actor's range and enriching his screen image with some negative traits).

The obituaries of 1961 reported the death of two major western leading men—Jeff Chandler, who appeared in a dozen westerns, including *Broken Arrow*, *The Spoilers* and *Pillars of the Sky*; and the legendary Gary Cooper, the only actor qualified to compete with John Wayne for the title of number 1 western star, whose credits include such gems as *The Virginian*, *The Plainsman*, *The Westerner*, *High Noon*, *Vera Cruz*, *Man of the West* and *The Hanging Tree*.

1962

Outstanding Achievements

PICTURE: *Ride the High Country*; *The Man Who Shot Liberty Valance*
SHORT STORY FILMED: "The Man Who Shot Liberty Valance" by Dorothy M. Johnson
SCREENPLAY (ORIGINAL): N.B. Stone, Jr., *Ride the High Country*
SCREENPLAY (ADAPTATION): James Warner Bellah, Willis Goldbeck, *The Man Who Shot Liberty Valance*
DIRECTION: Sam Peckinpah, *Ride the High Country*; John Ford, *The Man Who Shot Liberty Valance*
CINEMATOGRAPHY (B&W): William H. Clothier, *The Man Who Shot Liberty Valance*
CINEMATOGRAPHY (COLOR): Lucien Ballard, *Ride the High Country*; Winton C. Hoch, *Sergeants 3*; Maury Gertsman, *Six Black Horses*
MUSIC: Cyril Mockridge, *The Man Who Shot Liberty Valance*; George Bassman, *Ride the High Country*
MALE LEADING ROLE: Joel McCrea, *Ride the High Country*; Randolph Scott, *Ride the High Country*; John Wayne, *The Man Who Shot Liberty Valance*
FEMALE LEADING ROLE: Vera Miles, *The Man Who Shot Liberty Valance*; Mariette Hartley, *Ride the High Country*
MALE SUPPORTING ROLE: Edmond O'Brien, *The Man Who Shot Liberty Valance*; R.G. Armstrong, *Ride the High Country*; Edgar Buchanan, *Ride the High Country*
FEMALE SUPPORTING ROLE: Jeanette Nolan, *The Man Who Shot Liberty Valance*; Jennie Jackson, *Ride the High Country*

Academy Award Nomination

The Man Who Shot Liberty Valance—AAN: B&W costume design (Edith Head).

Births. Actor Lou Diamond Phillips.

Deaths. Directors Michael Curtiz (b. 1888), Louis King (b. 1898); actors James Barton (b. 1890), Hoot Gibson (b. 1892), Thomas Mitchell (b. 1892), Vladimir Sokoloff (b. 1889), Guinn ("Big Boy") Williams (b. 1899), Will Wright (b. 1891); actress Marilyn Monroe.

The radical decrease in the number of superior western films in 1962 indicated a conspicuous decline of interest in the genre by the major directors in Hollywood. Still, it was a special year as both *Ride the High Country* and *The Man Who Shot Liberty Valance* are unique westerns, more significant and influential than any other western of the early 1960s (with the possible exception of *The Magnificent*

Opposite: **Poster for** *The Man Who Shot Liberty Valance,* **one of several movies inspired by Dorothy M. Johnson's excellent short stories.**

Seven). Directed by Sam Peckinpah and John Ford, respectively, the two films have a lot in common. In addition to being aesthetically and intellectually compelling, and revealing their directors' pronounced styles, they resemble each other in three respects: they are both focused on two protagonists, one noble and one pragmatic; they both accentuate moral values; and they both have strong elegiac qualities. Within these similarities, however, they are considerably different. If *Ride the High Country* is a straightforward story, probably the ultimate morality tale ("All I want to do is enter my house justified"), *The Man Who Shot Liberty Valance* vacillates towards a political treatise with an ambiguous message ("When the legend becomes fact, print the legend"). While Peckinpah laments the predicament of two aging and impoverished ex-lawmen, challenges their friendship and resolves the conflict with the death of the idealist (thus saving the other hero's threatened integrity), Ford begins his film with a funeral of the practical hero and, in flashbacks, tells the story of how his selfless deed paved the way for the idealist's political career.

Regardless of this juxtaposition, which may point out *Liberty Valance* (based on Dorothy M. Johnson's excellent 1949 tale, included among the top 12 western short stories in the Western Writers of America's 1995 poll) as a more complex movie, *Ride the High Country* (selected as one of the best 15 western films in the same survey) is the better picture, more effective

Both Randolph Scott (pictured) and Joel McCrea interrupted their retirement to star in *Ride the High Country*.

and consistent as a drama. It is also superior in the casting of the two leading men. While the participation of Joel McCrea (as Steve Judd) and Randolph Scott (Gil Westrum) contributes a great deal to the excellent story of *Ride the High Country*, John Wayne and James Stewart (in the roles of Tom Doniphon and Ranse Stoddard) seem clearly too old for their parts, their excellent performances notwithstanding.

Ford and Peckinpah each made one western in 1961 and in 1962, and there would be no more year like that (i.e. a year offering the opportunity to compare the work of the two foremost western filmmakers). *Ride the High Country* was Peckinpah's second film and western, and *Liberty Valance* was one of Ford's last few pictures and his penultimate western (if we do not count his modest contribution to *How the West Was Won*). Thus, 1962 can be regarded as the year dividing two periods in the genre's history, the end of Ford's era and the commencement of the period of Sam Peckinpah. The color cinematography (by Lucien Ballard) and the new faces (R.G. Armstrong, Warren Oates, L.Q. Jones and John Davis Chandler—all to become a part of Peckinpah's ensemble) of *Ride the High Country*, as opposed to the black-and-white photography (by William H. Clothier) and the old faces (Wayne, Vera Miles, Andy Devine, John Qualen, Jeanette Nolan and several others from Ford's stock) of *Liberty Valance* further indicated the differences between the directors' styles and announced that changes would take place in the genre in the forthcoming years.

The alcoholic intellectual in *The Man Who Shot Liberty Valance* was brilliantly portrayed by Edmond O'Brien. Years ago a similar role in a movie directed by Ford brought an Academy Award to Thomas Mitchell (*Stagecoach*, 1939), who, however, did not appear in the director's last outstanding western. The distinguished actor (also memorable for his solid characterizations in such westerns as *The Outlaw*, *Buffalo Bill*, *High Noon* and *Destry*) was one of the celebrities that died in 1962.

1963

Outstanding Achievements

PICTURE: *How the West Was Won; McLintock!*

NOVEL FILMED: *Savage Sam* by Fred Gipson

SCREENPLAY (ORIGINAL): James R. Webb, *How the West Was Won;* James Edward Grant, *McLintock!*

DIRECTION: Henry Hathaway, John Ford, George Marshall, *How the West Was Won;* Andrew V. McLaglen, *McLintock!*

CINEMATOGRAPHY (COLOR): William H. Daniels, Milton Krasner, Charles Lang, Jr., Joseph LaShelle, *How the West Was Won;* William H. Clothier, *McLintock!*

MUSIC: Alfred Newman, *How the West Was Won;* Frank De Vol, *McLintock!*

SONG: Alfred Newman, Ken Darby, "How the West Was Won" from *How the West Was Won;* Frank De Vol, "By" Dunham, "Love in the Country" from *McLintock!;* Robert P. Marcucci, Russ Faith, "A Searcher for Love" from *The Gun Hawk*

MALE LEADING ROLE: James Stewart, *How the West Was Won;* John Wayne, *McLintock!*

FEMALE LEADING ROLE: Maureen O'Hara, *McLintock!;* Carroll Baker, *How the West Was Won*

MALE SUPPORTING ROLE: Robert Preston, *How the West Was Won;* Walter Brennan, *How the West Was Won;* Chill Wills, *McLintock!*

FEMALE SUPPORTING ROLE: Yvonne De Carlo, *McLintock!;* Thelma Ritter, *How the West Was Won*

1963

Academy Awards/ Nominations

How the West Was Won—AA: story and screenplay written directly for the screen; sound (Franklin E. Milton); editing (Harold F. Kress); AAN: picture; color cinematography; music score substantially original (Alfred Newman, Ken Darby); color art direction-set decoration (George W. Davis, William Ferrari, Addison Hehr; Henry Grace, Don Greenwood, Jr., Jack Mills); color costume design (Walter Plunkett).

Deaths. Writer Walter Prescott Webb (b. 1888); screenwriters Charles Schnee, Louis Stevens (b. 1899), Guy Trosper (b. 1911); directors Edward L. Cahn (b. 1899), John Farrow (b. 1904), Lewis Seiler (b. 1891); cinematographers William C. Mellor (b. 1904), Paul Perry (b. 1891); songwriter Stan Jones; actors Pedro Armendariz (b. 1912), Clem Bevans (b. 1880), Monte Blue (b. 1890), James Kirkwood (b. 1883), Tom London (b. 1893).

Just like in the previous year, there were only two notable standard westerns released in 1963, but their quality was far less impressive. The Cinerama epic *How the West Was Won* was composed of five segments: "The Rivers," "The Plains" and "The Outlaws" directed by Henry Hath-

Edgar Buchanan, Maureen O'Hara and John Wayne in a muddy scene from Andrew V. McLaglen's humorous *McLintock!*

and consistent as a drama. It is also superior in the casting of the two leading men. While the participation of Joel McCrea (as Steve Judd) and Randolph Scott (Gil Westrum) contributes a great deal to the excellent story of *Ride the High Country*, John Wayne and James Stewart (in the roles of Tom Doniphon and Ranse Stoddard) seem clearly too old for their parts, their excellent performances notwithstanding.

Ford and Peckinpah each made one western in 1961 and in 1962, and there would be no more year like that (i.e. a year offering the opportunity to compare the work of the two foremost western filmmakers). *Ride the High Country* was Peckinpah's second film and western, and *Liberty Valance* was one of Ford's last few pictures and his penultimate western (if we do not count his modest contribution to *How the West Was Won*). Thus, 1962 can be regarded as the year dividing two periods in the genre's history, the end of Ford's era and the commencement of the period of Sam Peckinpah. The color cinematography (by Lucien Ballard) and the new faces (R.G. Armstrong, Warren Oates, L.Q. Jones and John Davis Chandler—all to become a part of Peckinpah's ensemble) of *Ride the High Country*, as opposed to the black-and-white photography (by William H. Clothier) and the old faces (Wayne, Vera Miles, Andy Devine, John Qualen, Jeanette Nolan and several others from Ford's stock) of *Liberty Valance* further indicated the differences between the directors' styles and announced that changes would take place in the genre in the forthcoming years.

The alcoholic intellectual in *The Man Who Shot Liberty Valance* was brilliantly portrayed by Edmond O'Brien. Years ago a similar role in a movie directed by Ford brought an Academy Award to Thomas Mitchell (*Stagecoach*, 1939), who, however, did not appear in the director's last outstanding western. The distinguished actor (also memorable for his solid characterizations in such westerns as *The Outlaw*, *Buffalo Bill*, *High Noon* and *Destry*) was one of the celebrities that died in 1962.

1963

Outstanding Achievements

PICTURE: *How the West Was Won*; *McLintock!*

NOVEL FILMED: *Savage Sam* by Fred Gipson

SCREENPLAY (ORIGINAL): James R. Webb, *How the West Was Won*; James Edward Grant, *McLintock!*

DIRECTION: Henry Hathaway, John Ford, George Marshall, *How the West Was Won*; Andrew V. McLaglen, *McLintock!*

CINEMATOGRAPHY (COLOR): William H. Daniels, Milton Krasner, Charles Lang, Jr., Joseph LaShelle, *How the West Was Won*; William H. Clothier, *McLintock!*

MUSIC: Alfred Newman, *How the West Was Won*; Frank De Vol, *McLintock!*

SONG: Alfred Newman, Ken Darby, "How the West Was Won" from *How the West Was Won*; Frank De Vol, "By" Dunham, "Love in the Country" from *McLintock!*; Robert P. Marcucci, Russ Faith, "A Searcher for Love" from *The Gun Hawk*

MALE LEADING ROLE: James Stewart, *How the West Was Won*; John Wayne, *McLintock!*

FEMALE LEADING ROLE: Maureen O'Hara, *McLintock!*; Carroll Baker, *How the West Was Won*

MALE SUPPORTING ROLE: Robert Preston, *How the West Was Won*; Walter Brennan, *How the West Was Won*; Chill Wills, *McLintock!*

FEMALE SUPPORTING ROLE: Yvonne De Carlo, *McLintock!*; Thelma Ritter, *How the West Was Won*

1963

Academy Awards/ Nominations

How the West Was Won—AA: story and screenplay written directly for the screen; sound (Franklin E. Milton); editing (Harold F. Kress); AAN: picture; color cinematography; music score substantially original (Alfred Newman, Ken Darby); color art direction-set decoration (George W. Davis, William Ferrari, Addison Hehr; Henry Grace, Don Greenwood, Jr., Jack Mills); color costume design (Walter Plunkett).

Deaths. Writer Walter Prescott Webb (b. 1888); screenwriters Charles Schnee, Louis Stevens (b. 1899), Guy Trosper (b. 1911); directors Edward L. Cahn (b. 1899), John Farrow (b. 1904), Lewis Seiler (b. 1891); cinematographers William C. Mellor (b. 1904), Paul Perry (b. 1891); songwriter Stan Jones; actors Pedro Armendariz (b. 1912), Clem Bevans (b. 1880), Monte Blue (b. 1890), James Kirkwood (b. 1883), Tom London (b. 1893).

Just like in the previous year, there were only two notable standard westerns released in 1963, but their quality was far less impressive. The Cinerama epic *How the West Was Won* was composed of five segments: "The Rivers," "The Plains" and "The Outlaws" directed by Henry Hath-

Edgar Buchanan, Maureen O'Hara and John Wayne in a muddy scene from Andrew V. McLaglen's humorous *McLintock!*

away; "The Civil War" directed by John Ford; and "The Railroad" directed by George Marshall. In many respects—budget, running time, time period covered by the stories, number of characters, number of themes and number of stars involved (James Stewart, Gregory Peck, Henry Fonda, Carroll Baker, Debbie Reynolds, George Peppard, John Wayne, Richard Widmark and many others)—the movie is without a doubt the biggest western of all time. And, even though it is also quite entertaining and historically accurate, artistically it is unoriginal and inferior to many westerns made on a much smaller budget.

McLintock!, on the other hand, is an enjoyable western vacillating towards comedy, in the good tradition of such unforgettable pictures as *Destry Rides Again*, *The Sheepman* and *North to Alaska*. It does not break any aesthetic or intellectual grounds, but it is interesting as yet another version of the unusual and likeable on-screen relationship between John Wayne and Maureen O'Hara, with the intended similarity to both *Rio Grande* and *The Quiet Man* (both loosely derived from Shakespeare's *The Taming of the Shrew*) emphasized by the heroine's first name, Katherine. *McLintock!* had a special personal significance for Wayne, as it was scripted by James Edward Grant around the Duke's screen image, and two of his children, Patrick and Aissa, appeared in supporting roles.

The early 1960s brought about three remarkable contemporary westerns of a rare elegiac power—John Huston's *The Misfits* (1961, with Clark Gable, Marilyn Monroe and Montgomery Clift), scripted by Arthur Miller from his own 1957 short story; David Miller's *Lonely Are the Brave* (1962, starring Kirk Douglas, Gena Rowlands and Walter Matthau), based on the novel *The Brave Cowboy* (1956) by Edward Abbey; and Martin Ritt's *Hud* (1963, featuring Paul Newman, Patricia Neal, Melvyn Douglas and Brandon De Wilde), derived from Larry McMurtry's first novel, *Horseman, Pass By* (1961). The latter picture was honored by the Academy with three Oscars (actress Neal, supporting actor Douglas and black-and-white cinematography by James Wong Howe) and four additional nominations (screenplay by Irving Ravetch and Harriet Frank, Jr., direction, actor Newman and art direction-set decoration).

1964

Outstanding Achievements

PICTURE: *Cheyenne Autumn; A Fistful of Dollars; A Distant Trumpet; The Outrage; Rio Conchos*

NOVEL FILMED: *A Distant Trumpet* by Paul Horgan; *Company of Cowards* by Jack Schaefer, filmed as *Advance to the Rear*; *Guns of Rio Conchos* by Clair Huffaker, filmed as *Rio Conchos*; *Taggart* by Louis L'Amour

NONFICTION BOOK FILMED: *Cheyenne Autumn* by Mari Sandoz

SCREENPLAY (ADAPTATION): Sergio Leone, Duccio Tessari, *A Fistful of Dollars*; Clair Huffaker, Joseph Landon, *Rio Conchos*

DIRECTION: Sergio Leone, *A Fistful of Dollars*; John Ford, *Cheyenne Autumn*; Raoul Walsh, *A Distant Trumpet*

CINEMATOGRAPHY (B&W): James Wong Howe, *The Outrage*

CINEMATOGRAPHY (COLOR): William H. Clothier, *Cheyenne Autumn*; Joseph MacDonald, *Rio Conchos*; William H. Clothier, *A Distant Trumpet*

MUSIC: Ennio Morricone, *A Fistful of Dollars*; Max Steiner, *A Distant Trumpet*; Alex North, *Cheyenne Autumn*

MALE LEADING ROLE: Clint Eastwood, *A Fistful of Dollars;* Richard Widmark, *Cheyenne Autumn*; Richard Boone, *Rio Conchos*

FEMALE LEADING ROLE: Carroll Baker, *Cheyenne Autumn;* Claire Bloom, *The Outrage*

MALE SUPPORTING ROLE: Edward G. Robinson, *Cheyenne Autumn*; Gilbert Roland, *Cheyenne Autumn;* Pat Hingle, *Invitation to a Gunfighter*

FEMALE SUPPORTING ROLE: Dolores Del Rio, *Cheyenne Autumn*

Academy Award Nominations

Cheyenne Autumn—AAN: color cinematography.

Deaths. Writers Roy Chanslor (b. 1899), Will Cook, Clarence Budington Kelland (b. 1881), Stuart N. Lake (b. 1889), Alan LeMay (b. 1899); director Rudolph Maté (b. 1898); cinematographers J. Peverell Marley (b. 1901), George Schneiderman (b. 1894), Leo Tover (b. 1902); actors Morris Ankrum (b. 1896), Ed Brendel (b. 1890), Alan Ladd (b. 1913), Jack Pennick (b. 1895), Harry Shannon (b. 1890), Charles Stevens (b. 1893).

Two veteran directors made their last westerns in 1964, and though the films were inspired by highly acclaimed literary works, and both were photographed by one of Hollywood's most distinguished cinematographers, the results were unfortunately not satisfactory and far from the filmmakers' best achievements. John Ford concluded his western career with an unfaithful rendition of Mari Sandoz's 1953 book *Cheyenne Autumn*, included among the 13 best nonfiction books in the Western Writers of America's 1995 survey. Since James R. Webb's script shifted the emphasis from the Indians' unfair treatment and hardships (almost leading to their extermination) to the dilemmas faced by the sympathetic white people, a Cavalry officer (Richard Widmark) and reservation schoolmarm (Carroll Baker), Ford's intention to repay the Native Americans for Hollywood's misrepresentation of their character (a penance the director himself hardly needed to do anyway) turned out only partially successful. Nonetheless, the movie has some undeniable merits, such as William H. Clothier's Panavision and color cinematography, Alex North's score, and a number of decent performances, especially that given by Edward G. Robinson in the part of the secretary of the interior, Carl Schurz.

A life at a remote military post, Fort Delivery, Arizona, is the theme of Paul Horgan's lengthy and old-fashioned novel *A Distant Trumpet* (1951). Though it seemed like perfect material for a Ford project, the screen version of the book was made by Raoul Walsh, whose *They Died with Their Boots On*, dealing with a similar subject matter, had been an artistic and box-office success over 20 years before. However, unexpectedly, Walsh missed the opportunity to create an epic and failed to accomplish any of the atmosphere prevalent in Ford's famous Cavalry trilogy. Instead, he made a mediocre soap opera with characters lacking magnetism, played without conviction by Troy Donahue (as Lt. Matthew Hazard), Suzanne Pleshette (Kitty Mainwaring), Diane McBain (Laura) and James Gregory (General Alexander Upton Quait). Thus, the vivid musical score by Max Steiner and Clothier's superior Panavision and color photography are the picture's main assets, along with the original ideas, somewhat hidden or distorted here (the literary Matt gives up his extremely promising military career in response to the Department of War's injustice done to the Indian chiefs, his devoted scout in particular), from the superior novel.

1965

the international stardom of Clint Eastwood and began a new trend in the world cinema soon to be known as "spaghetti western."

It needs to be recognized that the ultimate commercial success of the spaghetti western was made possible, to a large degree, by the previous popularity of the multiple adaptations of the juvenile novels by the influential German writer Karl May (1842–1912). Made in the early and mid-1960s, usually as a German-French-Italian-Yugoslav co-production, the films were based on such novels as *Winnetou* (1893), *Der Schatz im Silbersee* (*The Treasure in Silver Lake*, 1894) and *Old Surehand* (1894–1896). The May heroes were portrayed by Pierre Brice (Winnetou), Lex Barker (Old Shatterhand) and Stewart Granger (Old Surehand).

Clint Eastwood as the Man with No Name in Sergio Leone's *A Fistful of Dollars*, a movie that began a subgenre known as "spaghetti western."

The discovery of the Japanese cinema continued to enrich the western genre in the mid-1960s. Following the example of John Sturges' *The Magnificent Seven*, which was based on Akira Kurosawa's *Seven Samurai*, Martin Ritt and Sergio Leone transposed two other classics of the distinguished Japanese director. If Ritt's *The Outrage* (featuring Paul Newman, Claire Bloom, Laurence Harvey and Edward G. Robinson), inspired by *Rashomon* (1950), turned out to be an awkward misunderstanding, with James Wong Howe's Panavision and black-and-white photography being the only asset, Leone's *A Fistful of Dollars*, based on *Yojimbo* (The Bodyguard, 1961), became a major hit. Furthermore, the latter picture launched

The 1964 obituaries list five western writers—including the original authors of such classic movies as *Arizona* (Clarence Budington Kelland), *My Darling Clementine* (Stuart N. Lake) and *The Searchers* (Alan LeMay)—and one western star, Alan Ladd, who will always be remembered as the rider from nowhere, *Shane*.

1965

Outstanding Achievements

PICTURE: *Major Dundee; Shenandoah; For a Few Dollars More; Cat Ballou; The Sons of Katie Elder*

NOVEL FILMED: *The Ballad of Cat*

1965

Ballou by Roy Chanslor, filmed as *Cat Ballou*; *Hallelujah Train* by Bill Gulick, filmed as *The Hallelujah Trail*

SCREENPLAY (ORIGINAL): Harry Julian Fink, Oscar Saul, Sam Peckinpah, *Major Dundee*; James Lee Barrett, *Shenandoah*

SCREENPLAY (ADAPTATION): Walter Newman, Frank R. Pierson, *Cat Ballou*

DIRECTION: Sam Peckinpah, *Major Dundee*; Andrew V. McLaglen, *Shenandoah*; Sergio Leone, *For a Few Dollars More*

CINEMATOGRAPHY: Sam Leavitt, *Major Dundee*; William H. Clothier, *Shenandoah*; Lucien Ballard, *The Sons of Katie Elder*

MUSIC: Ennio Morricone, *For a Few Dollars More*; Frank De Vol, *Cat Ballou*; Daniele Amfitheatrof, *Major Dundee*

SONG: Jerry Livingston, Mack David, "The Ballad of Cat Ballou" from *Cat Ballou*; Daniele Amfitheatrof, Ned Washington, "Major Dundee March" from *Major Dundee*

MALE LEADING ROLE: Lee Marvin, *Cat Ballou*; James Stewart, *Shenandoah*; Charlton Heston, *Major Dundee*

FEMALE LEADING ROLE: Jane Fonda, *Cat Ballou*; Senta Berger, *Major Dundee*

MALE SUPPORTING ROLE: Gian Maria Volonte, *For a Few Dollars More*; R.G. Armstrong, *Major Dundee*; George Kennedy, *Shenandoah*

Academy Awards/ Nominations

Cat Ballou—AA: actor Lee Marvin; AAN: screenplay based on material from another medium; scoring of music, adaptation or treatment; song "The Ballad of Cat Ballou"; editing (Charles Nelson).

Shenandoah—AAN: sound (Waldon O. Watson).

Deaths. Screenwriters Frank S. Nugent (b. 1908), C. Gardner Sullivan (b. 1879); directors Ray Enright (b. 1896), John Waters (b. 1893); cinematographers Faxon M. Dean (b. 1890), Charles Lawton, Jr. (b. 1904), Archie Stout (b. 1886); actors Steve Cochran, Ray Collins (b. 1888), William ("Wild Bill") Elliott (b. 1903), Jack Hoxie (b. 1885); actress Linda Darnell.

The major westerns of 1965 interestingly reflected the then-current tendencies in the genre. At the same time as Sam Peckinpah came up with his third movie (a somewhat disappointing but, at the same time, generally underrated western dealing, like many of his works, with challenged friendship), Sergio Leone made his second spaghetti western, understandably on a considerably bigger budget, in which he provided the Man with No Name (Clint Eastwood) with a partner, another gunman and professional bounty hunter (Lee Van Cleef). Though Peckinpah's *Major Dundee* (starring Charlton Heston, Richard Harris and Senta Berger) is by far the superior picture, more complex and sophisticated, it was inevitably compared to Leone's *For a Few Dollars More*, as both films display an abundance of violent sequences that were not artistically justified, at least in the eyes of the critics of that period. While the major asset of *For a Few Dollars More* is the captivating score by Ennio Morricone, *Major Dundee* has a number of merits, such as the original script by Harry Julian Fink, Oscar Saul and Peckinpah, Sam Leavitt's photography and some fine performances, notably by the two leading men and by James Coburn, who in this film joined several old members of the director's stock company (R.G. Armstrong, L.Q. Jones, Warren Oates and John Davis Chandler).

The other major western films of the year include *Shenandoah* (featuring James

Stewart, Rosemary Forsyth and Katharine Ross), possibly Andrew V. McLaglen's best film, whose pacifistic undertones reflected America's contemporary feelings about the Vietnam war; *Cat Ballou* (starring Jane Fonda and Lee Marvin), Elliot Silverstein's enjoyable, if rather unreasonable, attempt to turn Roy Chanslor's earnest 1956 novel into a spoof, with Marvin's dual performance (defeating in the Oscar competition such distinguished actors as Laurence Olivier, Richard Burton, Rod Steiger and Oskar Werner) and the songs (including the Oscar-nominated "The Ballad of Cat Ballou") performed by Nat King Cole and Stubby Kaye being its major assets; and *The Sons of Katie Elder* (with John Wayne, Dean Martin and Martha Hyer), Henry Hathaway's predictable mystery western, which nonetheless is a solid example of traditional entertainment.

Among the western-related celebrities that passed away in 1965, there was one distinguished screenwriter, Frank S. Nugent (*Fort Apache*, *She Wore a Yellow Ribbon*, *The Searchers*), two major cinematographers, Charles Lawton, Jr. (*3:10 to Yuma*, *The Tall T*, *Comanche Station*) and Archie Stout (*Angel and the Badman*, *Fort Apache*, *Hondo*), and one glamorous actress, Linda Darnell, best remembered as Chihuahua in *My Darling Clementine*.

Among the winners honored by the Western Writers of America was the distinguished, but relatively unknown, author Vardis Fisher, who received the Spur Award for his excellent novel *Mountain Man*, to be filmed by Sydney Pollack in 1972.

1966

Outstanding Achievements

PICTURE: *The Professionals*; *The Good, the Bad and the Ugly*; *A Bullet for the General*; *Duel at Diablo*; *Stagecoach*; *Nevada Smith*; *Ride in the Whirlwind*

NOVEL FILMED: *Apache Rising* by Marvin H. Albert, filmed as *Duel at Diablo*; *A Mule for the Marquesa* by Frank O'Rourke, filmed as *The Professionals*; *The Appaloosa* by Robert MacLeod; *Guns of North Texas* by Will Cook, filmed as *The Tramplers*; *Kid Rodelo* by Louis L'Amour

SHORT STORY FILMED: "Stage to Lordsburg" by Ernest Haycox, filmed as *Stagecoach*

SCREENPLAY (ORIGINAL): Luciano Vincenzoni, Sergio Leone, *The Good, the Bad and the Ugly*; Salvatore Laurani, Franco Solinas, *A Bullet for the General*

SCREENPLAY (ADAPTATION): Richard Brooks, *The Professionals*; Marvin H. Albert, Michael M. Grilikhes, *Duel at Diablo*; John Michael Hayes, *Nevada Smith*

DIRECTION: Richard Brooks, *The Professionals*; Sergio Leone, *The Good, the Bad and the Ugly*; Damiano Damiani, *A Bullet for the General*

CINEMATOGRAPHY: Conrad Hall, *The Professionals*; William H. Clothier, *Stagecoach*; Lucien Ballard, *Nevada Smith*

MUSIC: Ennio Morricone, *The Good, the Bad and the Ugly*; Maurice Jarre, *The Professionals*; Elmer Bernstein, *Return of the Seven*

SONG: John Green, Johnny Mercer, "Alvarez Kelly" from *Alvarez Kelly*

MALE LEADING ROLE: Burt Lancaster, *The Professionals*; Lee Marvin, *The Professionals*; Lee Van Cleef, *The Good, the Bad and the Ugly*

FEMALE LEADING ROLE: Claudia Cardinale, *The Professionals*; Maureen O'Hara, *The Rare Breed*; Ann-Margret, *Stagecoach*

MALE SUPPORTING ROLE: Jack Palance, *The Professionals*; Brian Keith, *Nevada Smith*; Van Heflin, *Stagecoach*

FEMALE SUPPORTING ROLE: Stefanie Powers, *Stagecoach*; Josephine Hutchinson, *Nevada Smith*

1966

Academy Award Nominations

The Professionals—AAN: screenplay based on material from another medium; direction; color cinematography.

Return of the Seven—AAN: scoring of music, adaptation or treatment.

Births. Actor Kiefer Sutherland.

Deaths. Writers Mari Sandoz (b. 1896), Paul I. Wellman (b. 1898); screenwriter James Edward Grant (b. 1902); composers Richard Hageman (b. 1882), Howard Jackson (b. 1900); actors Wallace Ford (b. 1898), Robert Keith (b. 1896), Nestor Paiva (b. 1905), Chief Yowlachie (b. 1891); actresses Emma Dunn (b. 1875), Seena Owen (b. 1894), Estelita Rodriguez.

Widescreen color photography, ponderous musical scores, increased running time, extensive and frequent action sequences, and multiple-star casts were some of the dominating traits of the westerns of the late 1960s. *The Professionals* (featuring Lee Marvin, Burt Lancaster, Robert Ryan, Woody Strode, Claudia Cardinale and Jack Palance) is not only the best example of the above, but it stands out as one of the best westerns of the decade, ranking among the top 25 of all time. Its top-notch production values were reinforced by Richard Brooks' first-rate, Oscar-nominated direction and script (from Frank O'Rourke's formula 1964 novel *A Mule for the Marquesa*), and by the remarkable performances from all members of the excellent cast. Though artistically superior to all the other westerns of the year, this highly enjoyable mercenary/caper movie was surpassed by two spaghetti westerns—Sergio Leone's *The Good, the Bad and the Ugly* and Damiano Damiani's *A Bullet for the General*—in terms of the presented bloodshed. While the former product from Italy (starring Clint Eastwood, Lee Van Cleef and Eli Wallach) was the longest, loudest, most bloody and possibly most controversial of Leone and Eastwood's loose trilogy featuring the Man with No Name, the latter (with Gian Maria Volonte and Lou Castel), by far less famous, is one of the most eloquent and thoughtful examples of the spaghetti western.

Three of the remaining major westerns of the year are not as rewarding as the first three, but are significant at least for their respective literary sources. Ralph Nelson's *Duel at Diablo* (featuring James Garner, Sidney Poitier and Bibi Andersson) is a fairly accurate rendition of Marvin H. Albert's possibly best novel, *Apache Rising* (1957), interestingly retelling the book's theme of a woman freed from Indian captivity with her half-breed child (cf. *Trooper Hook*, 1957, and *The Stalking Moon*, 1969). Gordon Douglas' *Stagecoach* (starring Alex Cord, Ann-Margret, Bing Crosby and Van Heflin) is a color and widescreen remake of Ford's classic, and thus based on Dudley Nichols' script, which in turn was inspired by Ernest Haycox's short story. And Henry Hathaway's *Nevada Smith* (with Steve McQueen, Karl Malden, Arthur Kennedy and Brian Keith) is an unremarkable revenge drama derived from a retrospective chapter of Harold Robbins' best-selling nonwestern novel *The Carpetbaggers* (1961).

A curiosity in the genre, marginal in their reception and impact (and therefore released a few years after their production), are two 1966 pictures filmed back to back in Utah by Monte Hellman, both starring Jack Nicholson (prior to his recognition and stardom) and Millie Perkins. If *The Shooting* may appear to be awkward, pretentious and bizarre, *Ride in the Whirlwind* is a captivating and logically constructed drama scripted, nota bene, by Nicholson himself.

Two of the celebrities that passed

away in 1966 made an especially significant contribution to the western film: screenwriter James Edward Grant (*Angel and the Badman*, *The Last Wagon*, *The Alamo*, *McLintock!*) and composer Richard Hageman (*Stagecoach*, *Angel and the Badman*, *Fort Apache*, *She Wore a Yellow Ribbon*, *Wagon Master*), both involved in many westerns starring John Wayne.

1967

Outstanding Achievements

PICTURE: *Hombre; El Dorado; Hour of the Gun; The War Wagon; Welcome to Hard Times; The Way West*

NOVEL FILMED: *The Way West* by A.B. Guthrie, Jr.; *Hombre* by Elmore Leonard; *Welcome to Hard Times* by E.L. Doctorow; *The Stars in Their Courses* by Harry Brown, filmed as *El Dorado*; *Badman* by Clair Huffaker, filmed as *The War Wagon*

SCREENPLAY (ORIGINAL): Edward Anhalt, *Hour of the Gun*

SCREENPLAY (ADAPTATION): Irving Ravetch, Harriet Frank, Jr., *Hombre*; Burt Kennedy, *The War Wagon*; Leigh Brackett, *El Dorado*

DIRECTION: Howard Hawks, *El Dorado*; Martin Ritt, *Hombre*; John Sturges, *Hour of the Gun*

CINEMATOGRAPHY: Lucien Ballard, *Hour of the Gun*; Harold Rosson, *El Dorado*; James Wong Howe, *Hombre*

MUSIC: Nelson Riddle, *El Dorado*; Jerry Goldsmith, *Hour of the Gun*; Bronislaw Kaper, *The Way West*

SONG: Nelson Riddle, John Gabriel, "El Dorado" from *El Dorado*; Bronislaw Kaper, Mack David, "The Way West" from *The Way West*; Dimitri Tiomkin, Ned Washington, "Ballad of the War Wagon" from *The War Wagon*

MALE LEADING ROLE: Paul Newman, *Hombre*; James Garner, *Hour of the Gun*; Robert Mitchum, *El Dorado*

FEMALE LEADING ROLE: Jean Simmons, *Rough Night in Jericho*; Lola Albright, *The Way West*

MALE SUPPORTING ROLE: Robert Ryan, *Hour of the Gun*; Arthur Hunnicutt, *El Dorado*; Martin Balsam, *Hombre*

FEMALE SUPPORTING ROLE: Barbara Rush, *Hombre*; Diane Cilento, *Hombre*; Sally Field, *The Way West*

Deaths. Screenwriter Frank Butler (b. 1890); director Anthony Mann (b. 1906); cinematographers Carl E. Guthrie (b. 1905), Ben F. Reynolds (b. c. 1891); actors Mischa Auer (b. 1905), Charles Bickford (b. 1889), Chief Big Tree (b. 1865), Smiley Burnette (b. 1911), Antonio Moreno (b. 1886), House Peters (b. 1880), Spencer Tracy (b. 1900); actresses Jane Darwell (b. 1879), Winifred Kingston (b. 1895), Barbara Payton, Ann Sheridan.

The top three western achievements of 1967 were each some kind of continuation of the filmmaker's previous work. *Hombre* (featuring Paul Newman, Fredric March and Diane Cilento) was just one link, if a very important one, in the series of films made by director Martin Ritt and actor Newman, a series including *Hud* and *The Outrage* in the previous few years. Though some of the ideas of *Hombre* seem to have been borrowed from such pictures as *Stagecoach* and *The Tall T*, it is nevertheless a quite original movie, both in the thoughtful story line and the characterizations of the main participants of the intense drama.

Howard Hawks' *El Dorado* (starring John Wayne, Robert Mitchum and James Caan) revisits the protagonists of the director's earlier *Rio Bravo*, with changes of names and certain shifts of their characteristics, and retells the story of a group of devoted friends fighting for law and order in a small Texas town. Thus, Mitchum takes over Dean Martin's part as the alcoholic lawman, Wayne is again his friend (but a deputy rather than the sheriff), Caan as Mississippi replaces Ricky Nelson as Colorado, and Arthur Hunnicutt takes over Walter Brennan's part as the old-timer and comic relief. With several situations paraphrased from the original, *El Dorado* was sometimes criticized for lack of originality. However, it has its own charm, and those who loved *Rio Bravo* would definitely accept this one as well, since both evoke the same kind of sense of immunity and elation that is generated by the unusual camaraderie of the Hawksian heroes.

In *Hour of the Gun*, John Sturges goes back to Tombstone and picks up the story in the place where his *Gunfight at the O.K. Corral* ended. As, according to history, the conflict was not concluded yet, his heroes—Wyatt Earp (James Garner, replacing Burt Lancaster) and Doc Holliday (Jason Robards, Jr., taking over Kirk Douglas' part)—continue fighting the gang led by Ike Clanton (Robert Ryan).

John Wayne as Cole Thornton, a gunslinger on the right side of the law, in *El Dorado*.

Except for *Hour of the Gun*, all the major westerns of the year were based on novels, mostly by famous authors. A.B. Guthrie, Jr.'s Pulitzer Prize–winning *The Way West* (1949) was turned into a disappointing adaptation by Andrew V. McLaglen, despite the participation of the genre's three major leading men—Kirk Douglas (as Senator Captain William J. Tadlock), Robert Mitchum (Dick Summers) and Richard Widmark (Lije Evans). E.L Doctorow's *Welcome to Hard Times* (1960) became a nihilistic, thus controversial, picture and a rather unusual item in the filmographies of director Burt Kennedy and actor Henry Fonda. *Hombre* is a faithful rendition of Elmore Leonard's acclaimed 1961 book, selected as the number 24 western novel in the 1977 poll of the Western Writers of America, while the story line of *El Dorado* hardly resembles the plot of Harry Brown's *The Stars in Their Courses* (1960), a westernized version of the *Iliad* and the nominal source of the script. Finally, Burt Kennedy's enjoyable and action-packed movie *The War Wagon* (starring John Wayne, Kirk Douglas and Howard Keel) is a fairly accurate rendition of Clair Huffaker's formula western novel *Badman* (1958), even though one of the film's two leading characters, gunslinger

Lomax (Douglas), was created by Huffaker in the script rather than in the book.

Among the western-related celebrities who died in 1967 were one major director, Anthony Mann (a maker of 11 westerns, including *Bend of the River, The Man from Laramie, The Tin Star, Man of the West*), one distinguished character actor, Charles Bickford (*Hell's Heroes, The Plainsman, Four Faces West, The Big Country*), and one memorable supporting actress, Jane Darwell (*Fighting Caravans, Jesse James, The Ox-Bow Incident, My Darling Clementine*).

While the Academy honored Gregory Peck with the Jean Hersholt Humanitarian Award, the literary highlight of the year was the Spur Award received by Lee Hoffman for her novel *The Valdez Horses*, which would be turned into a movie by John Sturges in 1973.

1968

Outstanding Achievements

PICTURE: *The Scalphunters; Will Penny; Journey to Shiloh; Firecreek; Hang 'Em High; Custer of the West*

NOVEL FILMED: *Journey to Shiloh* by Will Henry; *Shalako* by Louis L'Amour

SCREENPLAY (ORIGINAL): William Norton, *The Scalphunters;* Tom Gries, *Will Penny*

SCREENPLAY (ADAPTATION): Gene Coon, *Journey to Shiloh*

DIRECTION: Sydney Pollack, *The Scalphunters;* Tom Gries, *Will Penny*

CINEMATOGRAPHY: Duke Callaghan, Richard Moore, *The Scalphunters;* Lucien Ballard, *Will Penny;* William H. Clothier, *Firecreek*

MUSIC: Elmer Bernstein, *The Scalphunters;* Dominic Frontiere, *Hang 'Em High;* David Raksin, *Will Penny*

SONG: David Raksin, Robert Wells, "The Lonely Rider" from *Will Penny;* Don Costa, Floyd Huddleston, "The Ballad of Josie" from *The Ballad of Josie*

MALE LEADING ROLE: Burt Lancaster, *The Scalphunters;* Charlton Heston, *Will Penny;* James Stewart, *Firecreek*

FEMALE LEADING ROLE: Joan Hackett, *Will Penny;* Inger Stevens, *Hang 'Em High*

MALE SUPPORTING ROLE: Telly Savalas, *The Scalphunters;* Robert Ryan, *Custer of the West;* Pat Hingle, *Hang 'Em High*

FEMALE SUPPORTING ROLE: Shelley Winters, *The Scalphunters;* Brenda Scott, *Journey to Shiloh*

Deaths. Writers Edna Ferber (b. 1887), Vardis Fisher (b. 1895) William Colt MacDonald (b. 1891), Conrad Richter (b. 1890); screenwriter Laurence Stallings (b. 1894); cinematographers Charles P. Boyle (b. 1892), Joseph MacDonald (b. 1906); composer Frank Skinner (b. 1898); songwriter Henry Russell (b. 1913); actors Wendell Corey, Albert Dekker (b. 1904), Dan Duryea (b. 1907), Francis J. McDonald (b. 1891), Howard Petrie (b. 1906), Harry Woods (b. 1889); actress Mae Marsh (b. 1895), Eva Puig (b. 1894).

Only two westerns released in 1968 are truly rewarding pictures: *The Scalphunters* and *Will Penny*. Although *The Scalphunters* was Sydney Pollack's first western, made early in the director's career, it is an intelligent and enjoyable movie with the characters played by Burt Lancaster and Ossie Davis developing a sort of Crusoe–Man Friday relationship. Furthermore, with Davis' role being at least as big as that of Woody Strode in *Sergeant Rutledge*, the film was also a big step towards the appropriate representation of the African-Americans in the western genre. *Will Penny* (with superior performances from Charlton Heston and Joan Hackett), on the other hand, is one of director Tom Gries' last westerns and his foremost accomplishment, rightly regarded as an outstanding account of the American cowboy's life. Despite some minor reservations regarding both pictures—the execution of certain sequences in the former and the indulgence in violence in the latter—*The Scalphunters* and *Will Penny* are remarkable examples of the genre, which, by now, have deservedly earned the status of classics.

The other four notable westerns of the year, by far less appealing, are each significant for at least one reason—William Hale's *Journey to Shiloh* (featuring James Caan, Michael Sarrazin and Brenda Scott) for the literary source, Will Henry's excellent historical novel (1960); Vincent McEveety's *Firecreek* for the rare co-appearance of two outstanding western leading men and very good friends, James Stewart and Henry Fonda, the latter as the villain; Ted Post's *Hang 'Em High* for being Clint Eastwood's first American western after his return from Europe; and Robert Siodmak's *Custer of the West* (starring Robert Shaw, Mary Ure and Jeffrey Hunter) for offering yet one more, albeit unconvincing, version of the Custer phenomenon, with a stealing performance by Robert Ryan.

The year 1968 marked the death of two well known writers—Edna Ferber, who had the luck to have seen the two versions (1931, 1960) of her classic western novel *Cimarron*, and Vardis Fisher, who passed away before his great novel *Mountain Man* was adapted for the screen (as *Jeremiah Johnson*, 1972). The obituaries also listed Joseph MacDonald, a distinguished cinematographer (*My Darling Clementine, Yellow Sky, Broken Lance, Warlock*), and Dan Duryea, a talented character actor with a distinctive persona of villainy (*Along Came Jones, Winchester '73, Silver Lode, Six Black Horse*).

1969

Outstanding Achievements

PICTURE: *The Wild Bunch; Butch Cassidy and the Sundance Kid; True Grit; Once Upon a Time in the West; Support Your Local Sheriff; Tell Them Willie Boy Is Here; Mackenna's Gold; The Stalking Moon; Death of a Gunfighter*

NOVEL FILMED: *True Grit* by Charles Portis; *Man Without a Star* by Dee Linford, filmed as *A Man Called Gannon; Mackenna's Gold* by Will Henry; *Death of a Gunfighter* by Lewis B. Patten; *The Stalking Moon* by Theodore V. Olsen; *Who Rides with Wyatt* by Will Henry, filmed as *Young Billy Young*

NONFICTION BOOK FILMED: *Willie Boy* by Harry Lawton, filmed as *Tell Them Willie Boy Is Here*

SCREENPLAY (ORIGINAL): William Goldman, *Butch Cassidy and the Sundance Kid;* Walon Green, Roy N. Sickner, Sam Peckinpah, *The Wild Bunch;* William Bowers, *Support Your Local Sheriff*

SCREENPLAY (ADAPTATION): Marguerite Roberts, *True Grit*

DIRECTION: Sam Peckinpah, *The Wild Bunch;* George Roy Hill, *Butch Cassidy and the Sundance Kid;* Henry Hathaway, *True Grit*

CINEMATOGRAPHY: Conrad Hall, *Butch Cassidy and the Sundance Kid;* Lucien Ballard, *True Grit;* Joseph MacDonald, *Mackenna's Gold*

MUSIC: Burt Bacharach, *Butch Cassidy and the Sundance Kid;* Jerry Fielding, *The Wild Bunch;* Ennio Morricone, *Once Upon a Time in the West*

SONG: Burt Bacharach, Hal David, "Raindrops Keep Fallin' on My Head" from *Butch Cassidy and the Sundance Kid;* Elmer Bernstein, Don Black, "True Grit" from *True Grit;* Quincy Jones, Freddie Douglass, "Old Turkey Buzzard" from *Mackenna's Gold*

MALE LEADING ROLE: John Wayne, *True Grit;* Paul Newman, *Butch Cassidy and the Sundance Kid;* William Holden, *The Wild Bunch*

FEMALE LEADING ROLE: Katharine Ross, *Butch Cassidy and the Sundance Kid;* Eva Marie Saint, *The Stalking Moon;* Kim Darby, *True Grit*

MALE SUPPORTING ROLE: Robert Ryan, *The Wild Bunch;* Strother Martin, *True Grit;* Walter Brennan, *Support Your Local Sheriff*

FEMALE SUPPORTING ROLE: Susan Clark, *Tell Them Willie Boy Is Here;* Lena Horne, *Death of a Gunfighter*

Academy Awards/ Nominations

Butch Cassidy and the Sundance Kid — AA: story and screenplay (based on material not previously published or produced); cinematography; original score; song "Raindrops Keep Fallin' on my Head"; AAN: picture; direction; sound (William Edmundson, Daniel Dockendorf).

True Grit — AA: actor John Wayne; AAN: song "True Grit."

The Wild Bunch — AAN: story and screenplay (based on material not previously published or produced); original score.

Deaths. Writer Frank Gruber (b. 1904); director Lambert Hillyer (b. 1889); composer Leigh Harline (b. 1907); actors James Anderson, Roy Barcroft (b. 1902), Paul Birch (b. 1912), John Boles (b. 1895), George "Gabby" Hayes (b. 1885), Jeffrey Hunter, Barton MacLane (b. 1902), Alan Mowbray (b. 1893), Robert Taylor (b. 1911), Rhys Williams (b. 1897), Charles Winninger (b. 1884); actress Thelma Ritter (b. 1905).

A number of major western books were made into movies in 1969. Will Henry provided literary material for two—J. Lee Thompson's *Mackenna's Gold* (starring Gregory Peck and Omar Sharif), which was a fairly accurate but rather disappointing rendition of his superior 1963 novel of the same name; and Burt Kennedy's *Young Billy Young* (featuring Robert Mitchum, Robert Walker, Jr. and Angie Dickinson), which was an extremely inaccurate and clichéd adaptation of the author's 1954 novel *Who Rides with Wyatt*, focusing (unlike the film) on the relationship between Wyatt Earp and Johnny Ringo. Partially successful were the screen versions of T.V. Olsen's *The Stalking Moon* (1965), filmed by Richard Mulligan with Peck and Eva Marie Saint; Lewis B. Patten's *Death of a Gunfighter* (1968), made into a movie (starring Richard Widmark and John Saxon) by Robert Totten and Don Siegel (under the pseudonym Allen Smithee); and Harry Lawton's documentary account *Willie Boy* (1960), which emerged as Abraham Polonsky's picture *Tell Them Willie Boy Is Here* (featuring Robert Redford, Robert Blake, Katharine Ross and Susan Clark). The adaptations which were even less rewarding include James Goldstone's *A Man Called Gannon* (with Anthony Franciosa and Michael Sarrazin), a remake of King Vidor's *Man Without a Star* (1955); Tom Gries' *100 Rifles* (starring Jim Brown, Raquel Welch and Burt Reynolds), from Robert MacLeod's 1966 novel *The Californio*; and Hy Averback's *The Great Bank Robbery* (featuring Zero Mostel, Kim Novak and Clint Walker), based on Frank O'Rourke's 1961 novel of the same title. Indisputably the best novel filmed in 1969 was Charles Portis' *True Grit* (1968), which Henry Hathaway turned into a movie with John Wayne, Kim Darby and Glen Campbell.

The screen version of *True Grit* emerged as one of the best western pictures, possibly number 3, of the year, inferior only to such acclaimed masterpieces

1969

Robert Redford and Paul Newman as the titular heroes of George Roy Hill's *Butch Cassidy and the Sundance Kid*.

as *The Wild Bunch* and *Butch Cassidy and the Sundance Kid*—both made from an original screenplay and both glorifying outlaws, even though in diametrically different tones. While Peckinpah's picture was almost ignored by the Academy (winning only two nominations and no Oscar, probably due to the indigestive amount of violence), the film directed by George Roy Hill was one of the major contenders of the year and won four well-deserved Oscars: for best original story and screenplay, cinematography, original score, and song (performed by B.J. Thomas). The movie also won three additional Oscar nominations; however, in two of the three categories, best picture and best director; it can be strongly challenged by another western. Possibly even more deserving of those nominations are *The Wild Bunch* (a film more mature and complex) and its director (one of a few giants of the genre), for whom this picture is the most successful and complete artistic achievement. In their 1995 poll, the Western Writers of America included both *Butch Cassidy and the Sundance Kid* and *The Wild Bunch* among the 15 best western films of all time.

John Wayne, having been Oscar nominated only once before (for the war movie *Sands of Iwo Jima*, 1949), finally received the best actor Academy Award for his brilliant performance as Marshal Rooster Cogburn in *True Grit*. The award was well deserved, even though the actor can boast a few superior acting achievements in the past (*Red River*, *She Wore a Yellow Ribbon* and *The Searchers*, to name but three). Having delivered a western performance superior to those by such remarkable actors as Peck, Mitchum, Redford (each in two western films), Newman, Holden, Widmark and James Garner, in the Oscar chase the Duke outran two accomplished British actors (Richard Burton for *Anne of the Thousand Days* and Peter O'Toole for *Goodbye Mr. Chips*), as well as two rising American stars (Dustin Hoffman and Jon Voight, both nominated for *Midnight Cowboy*). Oddly and ironically, Wayne's name is mentioned on the radio on the bus that takes Joe Buck (Voight) from Albuquerque to New York City in an early sequence of *Midnight Cowboy*.

The year 1969 was abundant in superior performances by supporting actors. In *The Wild Bunch* alone, there are at least half a dozen players who deserve a special mention. The top achievement in this capacity is the performance delivered by Robert Ryan, who should be praised for his difficult part as Deke Thornton, the ex-member of the gang and reluctant informer, a key role which best explains Peckinpah's message in the film and in his artistic heritage in general. Strother Martin, on the other hand, managed to give a remarkable performance in the top three westerns of the year, and is especially memorable for his characterization of horse-trader Colonel G. Stonehill in *True Grit*.

Katharine Ross played two "small" leading parts. Quite effective as the Indian girl in *Tell Them Willie Boy Is Here*, she was even better as schoolteacher Etta Place in *Butch Cassidy and the Sundance Kid*. Eva Marie Saint gave a memorable performance as the Indian captive and mother of the chief's two sons in *The Stalking Moon*, and so did Susan Clark as the idealistic missionary Dr. Elizabeth Arnold (Clara True in Lawton's book) in *Tell Them Willie Boy Is Here*.

One of the very best years in the history of the genre, 1969 had its western representative among the strongest contenders and winners of the Academy Awards, an accomplishment that had taken place before in 1930–1931, 1939, 1940, 1952, 1953 and 1963, and would happen again in 1990 and 1992. Furthermore, it brought

Top: John Wayne in his Oscar-winning role as Rooster Cogburn in Henry Hathaway's accurate adaptation of Charles Portis' *True Grit*. *Bottom:* James Garner played the charming hero in both *Support Your Local Sheriff* and its less successful sequel, *Support Your Local Gunfighter* (1971), both directed by Burt Kennedy.

about two enjoyable and intellectual masterpieces of the genre which both deserve to be ranked among the top dozen western films of all time. And, moreover, the impressive number of remarkable westerns that were released in that year offers an interesting diversity of themes and styles, a diversity that would help keep the genre alive for the next six years.

1970

Outstanding Achievements

PICTURE: *The Ballad of Cable Hogue; Little Big Man; Monte Walsh; A Man Called Horse; Soldier Blue; Rio Lobo; Chisum; Two Mules for Sister Sara*

NOVEL FILMED: *Monte Walsh* by Jack Schaefer; *Little Big Man* by Thomas Berger; *Arrow in the Sun* by Theodore V. Olsen, filmed as *Soldier Blue*

SHORT STORY FILMED: "A Man Called Horse" by Dorothy M. Johnson

SCREENPLAY (ORIGINAL): John Crawford, Edmund Penny, *The Ballad of Cable Hogue*

SCREENPLAY (ADAPTATION): Lukas Heller, David Zelag Goodman, *Monte Walsh*; Calder Willingham, *Little Big Man*

DIRECTION: Sam Peckinpah, *The Ballad of Cable Hogue*; William A. Fraker, *Monte Walsh*; Arthur Penn, *Little Big Man*

CINEMATOGRAPHY: David M. Walsh, *Monte Walsh*; Lucien Ballard, *The Ballad of Cable Hogue*; Robert Hauser, *Soldier Blue*

MUSIC: Jerry Goldsmith, *The Ballad of Cable Hogue*; John Barry, *Monte Walsh*; Ennio Morricone, *Two Mules for Sister Sara*

SONG: Jerry Goldsmith, Richard Gillis, "Tomorrow Is the Song I Sing" from *The Ballad of Cable Hogue*; Buffy Sainte-Marie, "Soldier Blue" from *Soldier Blue*; John Barry, Hal David, "The Good Times Are Comin'" from *Monte Walsh*

MALE LEADING ROLE: Lee Marvin, *Monte Walsh*; Jason Robards, *The Ballad of Cable Hogue*; Dustin Hoffman, *Little Big Man*

FEMALE LEADING ROLE: Jeanne Moreau, *Monte Walsh*; Candice Bergen, *Soldier Blue*; Stella Stevens, *The Ballad of Cable Hogue*

MALE SUPPORTING ROLE: Chief Dan George, *Little Big Man*; Jack Palance, *Monte Walsh*; David Warner, *The Ballad of Cable Hogue*

FEMALE SUPPORTING ROLE: Judith Anderson, *A Man Called Horse*; Faye Dunaway, *Little Big Man*; Allyn Ann McLerie, *Monte Walsh*

Academy Award Nominations

Little Big Man—AAN: supporting actor Chief Dan George.

Deaths. Screenwriter Jack Natteford (b. 1894); cinematographers William H. Daniels (b. 1895), Arthur Edeson (b. 1891), Ernest Haller (b. 1896), Arthur C. Miller (b. 1895); composers Alfred Newman (b. 1901), Paul Sawtell (b. 1906), Leith Stevens (b. 1909); songwriter Dave Franklin (b. 1895); actors Robert H. Barrat (b. 1891), Ed Begley (b. 1901), Preston Foster (b. 1900), Arthur Shields (b. 1896), Frank Silvera; actresses Mari Blanchard, Inger Stevens, Vola Vale (b. 1897).

The death of the Old West was one of the two themes most successfully represented in the western films of 1970. Sam Peckinpah in *The Ballad of Cable Hogue* and William A. Fraker in *Monte Walsh* reached a striking similarity in their depiction of the vanishing West and in their sentimental and humorous, yet quite realistic, characterizations of the protagonists—adventurer/entrepreneur Cable Hogue (Jason Robards) and cowboy/

bronco rider Monte Walsh (Lee Marvin). Their heroes, engaged in the doomed struggle to survive in the new and unwelcome reality, are tough Westerners but also kind, gentle and vulnerable human beings, both involved in an unusual relationship with a warm-hearted prostitute—Hildy (Stella Stevens) and Martine Bernard (Jeanne Moreau), respectively. The elegiac tone of the screenplays (regardless of the alterations in *Monte Walsh*, where, unlike in Jack Schaefer's outstanding novel of 1963, Chet Rollins, played by Jack Palance, dies instead of Walsh) is further enhanced by the superb direction, the remarkable cinematography and the suitable musical scores, including some catchy song(s), in both pictures.

The Indian issues were taken up in three major westerns of 1970. Two of them—Arthur Penn's *Little Big Man* (starring Dustin Hoffman as Jack Crabb and Faye Dunaway as Mrs. Pendrake) and Ralph Nelson's *Soldier Blue* (with Candice Bergen in the role of Cresta Marybelle Lee and Peter Strauss as Private Honus Gant) are impressive but rather inaccurate (especially the latter) renditions of well-known novels—Thomas Berger's *Little Big Man* (1964, to be continued in 1999 as *The Return of Little Big Man*) and Theodore V. Olsen's *Arrow in the Sun* (1969). Due to their focus on the Cavalry's atrocities on the Indian race, the two movies can be viewed as either Hollywood's top examples of revisionism or its misplaced response

Dustin Hoffman as Jack Crabb, the unorthodox protagonist of Arthur Penn's *Little Big Man*.

1971

Clint Eastwood in Don Siegel's *Two Mules for Sister Sara*, one of the actor's lesser westerns made between his European experience and the time he decided to direct himself.

years after his retirement, the 1970 obituaries included many outstanding names. Especially distinguished was the western work of cinematographer Arthur C. Miller and composer Alfred Newman, who both had worked on Henry King's classic western *The Gunfighter*.

In their 1995 survey, the Western Writers of America would include both Schaefer's *Monte Walsh* and Berger's *Little Big Man* among the 12 best western novels of all time, while Penn's *Little Big Man* would be chosen as one of the best 15 western films.

to the current events in Indochina. The third one, Elliot Silverstein's *A Man Called Horse* (featuring Richard Harris and Judith Anderson), puts the emphasis on the impact of Indian customs on a white man's life, without—however—being historically accurate or doing justice to Dorothy M. Johnson's excellent 1949 tale (selected as the number 1 short story in the Western Writers of America's 1995 survey) by which it was inspired.

Outside of the two strands is *Rio Lobo* (featuring John Wayne, Jorge Rivero and Christopher Mitchum), a conservative, yet quite enjoyable, picture that turned out to be the conclusion of the unique career of veteran director Howard Hawks.

While Hawks would live seven more

1971

Outstanding Achievements

PICTURE: *Valdez Is Coming; McCabe & Mrs. Miller; Man in the Wilderness; The Hired Hand; Shoot Out; Big Jake; A Gunfight*

NOVEL FILMED: *McCabe* by Edmund Naughton, filmed as *McCabe & Mrs. Miller*; *Valdez Is Coming* by Elmore Leonard; *Catlow* by Louis L'Amour

NONFICTION BOOK FILMED: *Lone Cowboy: My Life Story* by Will James, filmed as *Shoot Out*

SCREENPLAY (ORIGINAL): Alan Sharp, *The Hired Hand*; Pete Hamill, *Doc*; Jack De Witt, *Man in the Wilderness*

SCREENPLAY (ADAPTATION): Roland Kibbee, David Rayfiel, *Valdez Is Coming*; Robert Altman, Brian McKay, *McCabe & Mrs. Miller*

DIRECTION: Edwin Sherin, *Valdez Is Coming*; Robert Altman, *McCabe & Mrs. Miller*; Richard C. Sarafian, *Man in the Wilderness*

CINEMATOGRAPHY: William H. Clothier, *Big Jake*; Earl Rath, *Shoot Out*; Gerry Fisher, *Man in the Wilderness*

MUSIC: Elmer Bernstein, *Big Jake*;

1971

Laurence Rosenthal, *A Gunfight*; Dave Grusin, *Shoot Out*

SONG: Leonard Cohen, "Sisters of Mercy" from *McCabe & Mrs. Miller*; Johnny Cash, "A Gunfight" from *A Gunfight*; Leonard Cohen, "The Stranger Song" from *McCabe & Mrs. Miller*

MALE LEADING ROLE: Burt Lancaster, *Valdez Is Coming*; Warren Beatty, *McCabe & Mrs. Miller*; Richard Harris, *Man in the Wilderness*

FEMALE LEADING ROLE: Julie Christie, *McCabe & Mrs. Miller*; Susan Clark, *Valdez Is Coming*; Maureen O'Hara, *Big Jake*

MALE SUPPORTING ROLE: Frank Silvera, *Valdez Is Coming*; Jeff Corey, *Shoot Out*; Robert Wilke, *A Gunfight*

FEMALE SUPPORTING ROLE: Jane Alexander, *A Gunfight*; Shelley Duvall, *McCabe & Mrs. Miller*; Dawn Lyn, *Shoot Out*

Academy Award Nominations

McCabe & Mrs. Miller—AAN: actress Julie Christie.

Deaths. Writers Borden Chase (b. 1900), Walter Van Tilburg Clark (b. 1909); screenwriter Kenneth Gamet (b.1903); cinematographers Robert De Grasse (b. 1900), Lionel Lindon (b. 1905); composer Max Steiner (b. 1888); songwriter Jack Brooks (b. 1912); actors Gilbert M. 'Broncho Billy' Anderson (b. 1880), Jay C. Flippen (b.

Burt Lancaster gave a towering performance in Edwin Sherin's screen rendition of Elmore Leonard's superior novel *Valdez Is Coming*.

1898), Billy Gilbert (b. 1893), Raymond Hatton (b. 1887), Van Heflin (b. 1910), Percy Helton (b. 1894), Kermit (Tex) Maynard (b. 1902), Audie Murphy, Walter Sande (b. 1906), James Westerfield (b. 1912), Carleton Young (b. 1907); actress Bebe Daniels (b. 1901).

Among the top seven western achievements of the year, there were two movies inspired by highly acclaimed novels. Edwin Sherin's *Valdez Is Coming* is an enjoyable film and a faithful rendition of Elmore Leonard's relatively traditional novel (1970), with a towering performance from Burt Lancaster as the persevering lawman who, while seeking justice for a poor Mexican widow, wins an uneven war against an arrogant cattle baron along with the opponent's woman (Susan Clark). Robert Altman's *McCabe & Mrs. Miller* is, on the other hand, a controversial adaptation of an offbeat 1959 book by Edmund Naughton, featuring Warren Beatty and Julie Christie in the titular roles of an unusual pair of Old West entrepreneurs. The most apparent difference between the book and the film is the protagonists' character and attitude in the critical part of the story. While Naughton's John McCabe dies like a hero fighting for his dignity with the loyal and caring Constance Miller scolding him for the unnecessary sacrifice, in the movie they are both pathetic individuals—he desperately fighting for his life after losing his dignity (in the unsuccessful attempt to sell out cheaply), and she, under the influence of opium, oblivious of the shoot-out and her man lying dead in the snow. Hence, comparisons of the climax to *High Noon* have more grounds in the case of the novel than in the case of the picture. A controversial, albeit interesting, decision was the use of three songs from Leonard Cohen's first LP—"The Stranger Song," "Sisters of Mercy" and "Winter Lady"—in order to enhance the unusual atmosphere of Altman's picture.

Even though the two movies have their devoted advocates, they are only partially rewarding endeavors, just like the other five films on the list—interesting for some reasons, but uneven and disappointing in more ways than one. Three of them—*Man in the Wilderness* (with Richard Harris and John Huston), *The Hired Hand* (starring Peter Fonda and Warren Oates) and *A Gunfight* (featuring Kirk Douglas and Johnny Cash)—were made by representatives of the new generation of filmmakers: Richard C. Sarafian (who began his career directing such television series as *Gunsmoke* and *Maverick*), Peter Fonda (ex-"Wild Angel") and Lamont John-

John Wayne and Maureen O'Hara concluded their unusual on-screen relationship in George Sherman's *Big Jake*.

son (another television-trained director). Their films clearly reveal the new strands in the genre, allusions to the current affairs and self-consciousness above all. *Shoot Out* and *Big Jake*, on the other hand, are typical examples of the old school, and are "swan songs" in the western careers of Henry Hathaway and George Sherman. The former (starring Gregory Peck) is a rather disappointing movie that had nothing (except the protagonist's prison time) to do with Will James' genuine 1930 book *Lone Cowboy: My Life Story*, upon which it claims to be based. The latter was the culmination of the on-screen relationship between John Wayne (for whom it was also one more family enterprise) and Maureen O'Hara.

Among the people that passed away in 1971 were two outstanding writers—Walter Van Tilburg Clark and Borden Chase, the original authors of *The Ox-Bow Incident* and *Red River*, respectively; one great composer, Max Steiner (*The Searchers*); and one underrated actor, Van Heflin, who had contributed to the grandeur of such western masterpieces as *Shane* and *3:10 to Yuma*.

It should be noted that the Western Writers of America granted one of their 1971 awards to a filmmaker: the Spur Award in the Movie Script category went to Pete Hamill for the screenplay of *Doc*, Frank Perry's controversial picture featuring Stacy Keach (as Doc Holliday), Faye Dunaway (Kate Fisher) and Harris Yulin (Wyatt Earp).

Though Julie Christie was the only 1971 Academy Award nominee for a standard western, it needs to be recognized that there was one quasi-western, Peter Bogdanovich's *The Last Picture Show*, based on an excellent novel by Larry McMurtry, which won eight Oscar nominations. Supporting actor Ben Johnson, who gave a brilliant performance as Thalia's old-timer, turned out to be the movie's only winner of the statuette.

1972

Outstanding Achievements

PICTURE: *Jeremiah Johnson*; *Ulzana's Raid*; *The Cowboys*; *Bad Company*; *The Life and Times of Judge Roy Bean*

NOVEL FILMED: *Mountain Man* by Vardis Fisher, filmed as *Jeremiah Johnson*; *The Cowboys* by William Dale Jennings

NONFICTION BOOK FILMED: *Crow Killer* by Raymond W. Thorp and Robert Bunker, filmed as *Jeremiah Johnson*

SCREENPLAY (ORIGINAL): David Newman, Robert Benton, *Bad Company*; Alan Sharp, *Ulzana's Raid*

SCREENPLAY (ADAPTATION): Irving Ravetch, Harriet, Frank, Jr., *The Cowboys*; John Milius, Edward Anhalt, *Jeremiah Johnson*

DIRECTION: Robert Aldrich, *Ulzana's Raid*; Sydney Pollack, *Jeremiah Johnson*; Robert Benton, *Bad Company*

CINEMATOGRAPHY: Duke Callaghan, *Jeremiah Johnson*; Joseph Biroc, *Ulzana's Raid*; Robert Surtees, *The Cowboys*

MUSIC: John Williams, *The Cowboys*; Maurice Jarre, *The Life and Times of Judge Roy Bean*; John Rubinstein, Tim McIntire, *Jeremiah Johnson*

SONG: Maurice Jarre, Marilyn & Alan Bergman, "Marmalade, Molasses and Honey" from *The Life and Times of Judge Roy Bean*

MALE LEADING ROLE: Burt Lancaster, *Ulzana's Raid*; John Wayne, *The Cowboys*; Robert Redford, *Jeremiah Johnson*

FEMALE LEADING ROLE: Vera Miles, *Molly and Lawless John*; Susan Clark, *Showdown*

MALE SUPPORTING ROLE: Roscoe Lee Browne, *The Cowboys*; Will Geer, *Jeremiah Johnson*; Jim Davis, *Bad Company*

FEMALE SUPPORTING ROLE: Delle

1972

Bolton, *Jeremiah Johnson*; Ava Gardner, *The Life and Times of Judge Roy Bean*; Allyn Ann McLerie, *Jeremiah Johnson*

Academy Award Nominations

The Life and Times of Judge Roy Bean—AAN: song "Marmalade, Molasses and Honey."

Deaths. Director Harmon Jones (b. 1911), Edward Sloman (b. 1886); cinematographer Victor Milner (b. 1893); actors William Boyd (b. 1895), Bruce Cabot (b. 1904), Lane Chandler (b. 1899), Brandon De Wilde, Brian Donlevy (b. 1899), John Litel (b. 1894), Akim Tamiroff (b. 1899).

The year 1972 brought about a variety of good-looking westerns with superior production values, solid direction and some unforgettable performances. The themes dealt with by the most notable westerns of that year include a trapper's rigorous life in the mid–1800s (*Jeremiah Johnson*), an Indian hunt (*Ulzana's Raid*), a cattle drive (*The Cowboys*), juvenile outlawry (*Bad Company*) and a biography of a historical figure (*The Life and Times of Judge Roy Bean*).

John Milius and Edward Anhalt's otherwise competent script of *Jeremiah Johnson* must appear to be disappointing, especially to those who have read either Raymond W. Thorp and Robert Bunker's book *Crow Killer* (1958), an engaging account of the adventurous life of John Johnston, also known as Liver-Eating Johnson or *Dapiek Absaroka* (the Killer of Crows), or Vardis Fisher's outstanding ecological novel *Mountain Man* (1965), depicting selected episodes from Johnston's (Samson John Minard) life. This is not just because of the minor alterations in the story line, which can be considered irrelevant (except for the omission of both books' most dramatic part—the capture and escape episode), but mostly because the movie fails to exploit the major merits of Fisher's novel, such as the extensive references to the arts, music in particular, frequently combined with the description of nature and primitive life. If, despite this and the episodic structure, the movie is still worth seeing, it's mainly for Duke Callaghan's breathtaking Panavision and color cinematography. Robert Redford in the titular role seems out of place in this rugged land-

Robert Redford played the titular hero in Sydney Pollack's *Jeremiah Johnson*, an only partially successful adaptation of two outstanding books.

scape, his attractive appearance and personality notwithstanding.

A more linear story was offered by *Ulzana's Raid*, a picture in which director Robert Aldrich and actor Burt Lancaster returned to the theme of their 1954 movie, *Apache*. While in the old movie Lancaster played a Chiricahua warrior hunted by a group of white men, here he is the scout helping a Cavalry squad chase a band of Apache renegades. The major asset of the picture is the sense of omnipresent threat and the fatalistic atmosphere, enhanced by Lancaster's mature and elegiac performance and Joseph Biroc's gorgeous color cinematography.

In Mark Rydell's *The Cowboys*, John Wayne once again becomes a herd owner and cattle drive boss. Hence the movie offers an interesting comparison with *Red River*. However, since Wil Andersen (Wayne) bosses and fathers a bunch of teenage cowboys and dies in their defense, the actor's characterization here considerably differs from that of the obsessive Thomas Dunson. The film is beautifully scored by John Williams, nicely photographed by Robert Surtees, and boasts a superior script, quite faithfully retelling the story line of the superior 1971 novel by William Dale Jennings, with some reservations to the plausibility of both. Particular praise, among the actors, should go to Roscoe Lee Browne for his charismatic performance as cook Jedediah (Charlie, in the book) Nightinger.

Regardless of the above-mentioned reservations, *Jeremiah Johnson*, *Ulzana's Raid* and *The Cowboys* are thoroughly enjoyable pictures, a compliment that, unfortunately, cannot be paid to the remaining two films on the list. *Bad Company* (starring Jeff Bridges, Barry Brown and John Savage) has a number of flaws—such as the unoriginal score, and characters lacking charm and depth—despite the evident traces of screenwriters David Newman and Robert Benton's former glory (*Bonnie and Clyde*). *The Life and Times of Judge Roy Bean* (featuring Paul Newman, Anthony Perkins and Jacqueline Bisset) has a poor, pretentious script that fails to hold the story together. Fortunately, the picture is impressively scored by Maurice Jarre, and the touch of John Huston's genius is unquestionable, though the actors are guided in a rather unorganized manner.

While no Academy Award was granted to any 1972 western film, an Honorary Oscar was given to Edward G. Robinson ("who achieved greatness as a player, a patron of the arts, a dedicated citizen … in sum, a Renaissance man"), an outstanding actor who hated westerns but appeared in a few—*Silver Dollar*, *The Violent Men*, *The Outrage*, *Cheyenne Autumn* and *Mackenna's Gold*.

1973

Outstanding Achievements

PICTURE: *Pat Garrett and Billy the Kid*; *High Plains Drifter*; *Kid Blue*

NOVEL FILMED: *The Valdez Horses* by Lee Hoffman, filmed as *Valdez, the Halfbreed*; *The Man Called Noon* by Louis L'Amour; *The Man Who Loved Cat Dancing* by Marilyn Durham

SCREENPLAY (ORIGINAL): Ernest Tidyman, *High Plains Drifter*; Rudolph Wurlitzer, *Pat Garrett and Billy the Kid*

DIRECTION: Sam Peckinpah, *Pat Garrett and Billy the Kid*; Clint Eastwood, *High Plains Drifter*

CINEMATOGRAPHY: John Coquillon, *Pat Garrett and Billy the Kid*; Bruce Surtees, *High Plains Drifter*

MUSIC: Bob Dylan, *Pat Garrett and Billy the Kid*; Ennio Morricone, *My Name Is Nobody*

1973

SONG: Bob Dylan, Main Title Theme ("Billy"/"Far Away from Home") from *Pat Garrett and Billy the Kid*; Bob Dylan, "Knockin' on Heaven's Door" from *Pat Garrett and Billy the Kid*; John Rubinstein, Tim McIntire, "Kid Blue" from *Kid Blue*

MALE LEADING ROLE: Clint Eastwood, *High Plains Drifter;* James Coburn, *Pat Garrett and Billy the Kid*

FEMALE LEADING ROLE: Verna Bloom, *High Plains Drifter*

MALE SUPPORTING ROLE: Slim Pickens, *Pat Garrett and Billy the Kid*; Warren Oates, *Kid Blue*; R.G. Armstrong, *Pat Garrett and Billy the Kid*

FEMALE SUPPORTING ROLE: Katy Jurado, *Pat Garrett and Billy the Kid*; Lee Purcell, *Kid Blue*

Deaths. Writer Fred Gipson (b. 1908); screenwriter Warren Duff (b. 1904); directors Harry Joe Brown (b. 1890), John Ford (b. 1895); actors Lex Barker, James Bell (b. 1891), David Brian, Lon Chaney, Jr. (b. 1906), Ted De Corsia (b. 1904), Tim Holt, Douglas Kennedy, Allan ("Rocky") Lane (b. 1904), George Macready (b. 1899), Ken Maynard (b. 1895), J. Carrol Naish (b. 1897), Carl Benton Reid (b. 1893), Edward G. Robinson (b. 1893), Buddy Roosevelt (b. 1898), Robert Ryan (b. 1909), Glenn Strange (b. 1899); actress Peggie Castle.

Though the number of major westerns dropped drastically in 1973, the top two achievements of the year—clearly standing out—are still vivid examples of the genre's best qualities, the indulgence in violence in both notwithstanding. Though inferior to the director's best achievements (*The Wild Bunch*, *Ride the High Country*), Sam Peckinpah's *Pat Garrett and Billy the Kid* (starring James Coburn and Kris Kristofferson) is a rewarding picture and one more version of the director's recurrent theme of threatened friendship, again in the context of the passing of the Old West. Clint Eastwood challenges Peckinpah's romantic and sentimental vision with his cold, almost nihilistic, approach in *High Plains Drifter* (with Eastwood, Verna Bloom and Marianna Hill), a gloomy and mystical picture taking for its target, just like *High Noon*, the cowardice and hypocrisy of a small western town citizenry.

James Frawley's *Kid Blue* (featuring Dennis Hopper, Warren Oates and Peter Boyle)—a much more modest endeavor—is a tender and warm farewell to the Old West, even though the story of

Clint Eastwood (the Stranger) and Billy Curtis (Mordecai) in *High Plains Drifter*, the first western (but not film) directed by Eastwood himself.

an outlaw's unsuccessful attempts to go straight in the new, civilized society is told in ironic and satirical tones.

As *Pat Garrett* was Peckinpah's final western, and *High Plains Drifter* was the first western directed by Eastwood, 1973 can be seen as the year of the succession of the title of the genre's chief filmmaker. Ironically, John Ford, who had ruled in the genre before Peckinpah and made a dozen western classics, including *The Iron Horse, Stagecoach, My Darling Clementine* and *The Searchers*, passed away in 1973, thus making the coronation of Eastwood complete and definite.

The year's obituaries also listed Robert Ryan, possibly the most underrated actor in Hollywood's history, whose numerous western credits include *Best of the Badmen, The Naked Spur, The Tall Men, The Proud Ones, The Professionals, Hour of the Gun* and *The Wild Bunch*.

American poster for *High Plains Drifter* (Univ., 1973), an interesting, if controversial, western with clearly mystical/surrealistic undertones.

1974

Outstanding Achievements

PICTURE: *The Spikes Gang*; *Zandy's Bride*

NOVEL FILMED: *The Stranger* by Lillian Bos Ross, filmed as *Zandy's Bride*; *The Bank Robbers* by Giles Tippette, filmed as *The Spikes Gang*

SCREENPLAY (ADAPTATION): Irving Ravetch, Harriet Frank, Jr., *The Spikes Gang*; Marc Norman, *Zandy's Bride*

DIRECTION: Richard Fleischer, *The Spikes Gang*; Jan Troell, *Zandy's Bride*

CINEMATOGRAPHY: Jordan Croneweth, *Zandy's Bride*; Brian West, *The Spikes Gang*

MUSIC: Fred Karlin, *The Spikes Gang*; Michael Franks, *Zandy's Bride*

MALE LEADING ROLE: Lee Marvin, *The Spikes Gang*; Gene Hackman, *Zandy's Bride*

FEMALE LEADING ROLE: Liv Ullmann, *Zandy's Bride*; Ann-Margret, *The Train Robbers*

MALE SUPPORTING ROLE: Arthur Hunnicutt, *The Spikes Gang*

FEMALE SUPPORTING ROLE: Eileen Heckart, *Zandy's Bride*

Deaths. Screenwriter James R. Webb (b. 1909); director Lewis R. Foster (b. 1900); cinematographers Russell Harlan (b. 1903), Harold Lipstein (b. 1898), Hal Mohr (b. 1894), Leon Shamroy (b. 1901); actors Rodolfo Acosta, Walter Brennan (b. 1894), Johnny Mack Brown (b. 1904), Donald Crisp (b. 1880), Chubby Johnson (b. 1903), Otto Kruger (1885), Tex Ritter (b. 1905); actresses Betty Compson (b. 1897), Agnes Moorehead (b. 1906).

The least impressive year of the early 1970s, 1974 did not offer even one thoroughly rewarding western film. One of its obvious failures was John Wayne's *The Train Robbers* (co-starring Ann-Margret), directed by Burt Kennedy, which is possibly the most embarrassing picture in the last 15 years of the Duke's career. Richard Fleischer's *The Spikes Gang* (featuring Lee Marvin, Gary Grimes and Ron Howard) and Jan Troell's *Zandy's Bride* (starring Gene Hackman, Liv Ullmann and Sam Bottoms) are both promising but ultimately disappointing movies, by far inferior to the two major westerns of 1973. *Zandy's Bride* is significant for being the final part of Troell's loose Scandinavian trilogy, including *The Emigrants* (nominated for an Oscar in four categories, 1972) and *The New Land*.

James R. Webb, who wrote or co-wrote the screenplays of such memorable westerns as *Apache*, *Vera Cruz*, *The Big Country*, *How the West Was Won* and *Cheyenne Autumn*, died in 1974. Other western-related celebrities that passed away in that year include Russell Harlan and Walter Brennan, an outstanding cinematographer and a brilliant character actor, who happened to work together on two masterpieces of the genre—*Red River* and *Rio Bravo*. The two pictures also shared in the credits the names of actor John Wayne, composer Dimitri Tiomkin and director Howard Hawks. The latter—incidentally—received one of the 1974 Honorary Oscars as "a master American filmmaker whose creative efforts hold a distinguished place in world cinema."

1975

Outstanding Achievements

PICTURE: *Bite the Bullet*; *Posse*; *Rooster Cogburn*

SCREENPLAY (ORIGINAL): Richard Brooks, *Bite the Bullet*; William Roberts, Christopher Knopf, *Posse*

DIRECTION: Richard Brooks, *Bite the Bullet*; Kirk Douglas, *Posse*; Stuart Millar, *Rooster Cogburn*

CINEMATOGRAPHY: Harry Stradling, Jr., *Bite the Bullet*; Harry Stradling, Jr., *Rooster Cogburn*; Fred Koenekamp, *Posse*

MUSIC: Alex North, *Bite the Bullet*; Maurice Jarre, *Posse*; Laurence Rosenthal, *Rooster Cogburn*

MALE LEADING ROLE: Gene Hackman, *Bite the Bullet*; John Wayne, *Rooster Cogburn*; Kirk Douglas, *Posse*

FEMALE LEADING ROLE: Katharine Hepburn, *Rooster Cogburn*; Candice Bergen, *Bite the Bullet*

MALE SUPPORTING ROLE: Ben Johnson, *Bite the Bullet*; Bo Hopkins, *Posse*; Anthony Zerbe, *Rooster Cogburn*

Academy Award Nominations

Bite the Bullet—AAN: original score; sound (Arthur Piantodosi, Les Fresholtz, Richard Tyler, Al Overton, Jr.).

Deaths. Writer Luke Short (b. 1908); directors Joseph Kane (b. 1897), George Marshall (b. 1891), George Stevens (b. 1904), William A. Wellman (1896), Alfred Werker (b. 1896); cinematographers Wilfrid M. Cline (b. 1903), Paul C. Vogel (b. 1899); actors Joseph Calleia (1897), Richard Conte, John Dierkes (b. 1905), Roy Roberts (b. 1900); actresses Susan Hayward, Marjorie Main (b. 1890).

No literary work was turned into a western movie in 1975. Thus, all three major examples of the genre were made from original screenplays, even though Stuart Millar's *Rooster Cogburn* was based on the character created by Charles Portis. The sequel to Henry Hathaway's *True Grit* is clearly inferior to the original, but the teaming of John Wayne with Katharine Hepburn, while borrowing some ideas from *The African Queen*, was not the worst that could happen to the Duke's penultimate picture.

Bite the Bullet (featuring Gene Hackman, James Coburn and Candice Bergen) does not stand out among Richard Brooks' achievements and is probably not as good as either of the director's previous westerns—*The Last Hunt* and *The Professionals*, both based on popular books. However, it tells a relatively original story in a quite entertaining manner. On the other hand, Kirk Douglas' directorial debut, *Posse* (starring Douglas and Bruce Dern), is perhaps the most pretentious of the three westerns, but not necessarily the best. It is definitely one of the most politically oriented westerns, with an ambiguous message that may appear to be out of place.

The 1975 obituaries listed five directors significant to the genre—two associated mainly with low and medium-budget westerns, Joe Kane (*Dakota, Wyoming, Ride the Man Down*) and Alfred Werker (*The Last Posse, Three Hours to Kill, At Gunpoint*) and three famous for large-scale productions, William A. Wellman (*The Conquerors, The Ox-Bow Incident, Yellow Sky, Across the Wide Missouri*), George Marshall (*Destry Rides Again, Texas, The Sheepman*) and George Stevens (*Annie Oakley, Shane, Giant*). The other celebrities that died in that year include Luke Short, an underrated author of quality western fiction (*Ramrod, Vengeance Valley, Ride the Man Down*), and Susan Hayward, a charismatic and glamorous leading lady (*Canyon Passage, Rawhide, Garden of Evil, The Revengers*).

The absolute highlight of the year was the Spur Award granted to Glendon Swarthout for his remarkable novel *The Shootist*, a book that would soon be turned into John Wayne's screen testament.

1976

Outstanding Achievements

PICTURE: *The Shootist; The Outlaw Josey Wales; The Return of a Man Called Horse; The Missouri Breaks; The Last Hard Men*

NOVEL FILMED: *The Shootist* by Glendon Swarthout; *Gone to Texas* by Forrest Carter, filmed as *The Outlaw Josey Wales*; *Gun Down* by Brian Garfield, filmed as *The Last Hard Men*

SCREENPLAY (ORIGINAL): Thomas McGuane, *The Missouri Breaks*

SCREENPLAY (ADAPTATION): Miles Hood Swarthout, Scott Hale, *The Shootist*; Philip Kaufman, Sonya Chernus, *The Outlaw Josey Wales*

DIRECTION: Don Siegel, *The Shootist*; Clint Eastwood, *The Outlaw Josey Wales*

CINEMATOGRAPHY: Bruce Surtees, *The Outlaw Josey Wales*; Bruce Surtees, *The Shootist*; Owen Roizman, *The Return of a Man Called Horse*

1976

MUSIC: Elmer Bernstein, *The Shootist;* Jerry Fielding, *The Outlaw Josey Wales;* John Williams, *The Missouri Breaks*

MALE LEADING ROLE: John Wayne, *The Shootist;* Clint Eastwood, *The Outlaw Josey Wales;* Richard Harris, *The Return of a Man Called Horse*

FEMALE LEADING ROLE: Lauren Bacall, *The Shootist;* Barbara Hershey, *The Last Hard Men;* Sondra Locke, *The Outlaw Josey Wales*

MALE SUPPORTING ROLE: James Stewart, *The Shootist;* Chief Dan George, *The Outlaw Josey Wales;* Hugh O'Brian, *The Shootist*

FEMALE SUPPORTING ROLE: Sheree North, *The Shootist;* Gale Sondergaard, *The Return of a Man Called Horse*

Academy Award Nominations

The Shootist—AAN: art direction-set decoration (Robert F. Boyle; Arthur Jeph Parker).

The Outlaw Josey Wales—AAN: original score.

Deaths. Writer James Warner Bellah (b. 1899); screenwriters Martin Rackin, John Twist (b. 1898); directors Norman Foster (b. 1900), Joseph Henabery (b. 1888), Fritz Lang (b. 1890), Irvin Willat (b. 1892); cinematographers James Wong Howe (b. 1899), William V. Skall (b. 1898); songwriter Ned Washington (b. 1901); actors Richard Arlen (b. 1899), Lee J. Cobb (b. 1911), Fuzzy Knight (b. 1901), Sal Mineo, Ray Teal (b. 1902), Victor Varconi (b. 1896); actress Cathy Downs.

The top two western achievements of 1976, *The Shootist* (starring John Wayne, Lauren Bacall and Ron Howard) and *The Outlaw Josey Wales* (featuring Clint Eastwood, Sondra Locke and Chief Dan George), were directed by Don Siegel and Clint Eastwood, respectively, two men who had made several movies together operating on the opposite sides of the camera. Moreover, both films were photographed by a talented second-generation cinematographer, Bruce Surtees, who had collaborated with both directors more than once before. And, to add one more thing in common, both were based on a respectable literary work—the former upon Glendon Swarthout's Spur Award–winning, psychological novel (1975) of the same name, and the latter upon a Civil War/post–Civil War revenge/adventure book, *Gone to Texas* (1973) by Forrest Carter. While Swarthout's book would be selected as one of the top 12 western novels in

A farewell of two giants: John Wayne in his last screen appearance as John Bernard Books, and James Stewart in his last western role as Dr. Hostetler in Don Siegel's elegiac *The Shootist* (co-starring Lauren Bacall and Ron Howard), based on the excellent novel by Glendon Swarthout.

the 1995 poll by the Western Writers of America, both movies would be included among the best 15 western films in the same survey.

With the elimination of the pessimistic message of Swarthout's book (regardless of the fact that the original author's son, Miles Hood Swarthout, collaborated on the script), the emphasis in Siegel's movie was changed enough to make it a suitable testament and elegy for John Wayne, for whom (just like for the aging gunslinger John Bernard Books), due to a terminal illness, it would be the final show. Samples of the gunman's proficiency in different stages of his life are demonstrated in the prologue by means of the footage from the actor's previous movies—*Red River*, *Hondo*, *Rio Bravo* and *El Dorado*—a device that enhanced the valedictory aspect of the picture. (The same idea would be used again over 20 years later by director John Asher, who would insert clips from 1949's *Champion* in his comedy *Diamonds*, also featuring Lauren Bacall, to illustrate the boxing past of the character played by Kirk Douglas.) And thus, 1976 became a truly meaningful year for the genre, concluding—in a quite becoming way—the era of the Duke, the screen cowboy with the longest and most impressive career. Challenged only by Gary Cooper, an actor more sensitive and versatile, Wayne wins the competition for the number 1 western leading man due to the unique persona which he had managed to develop throughout the years and the unsurpassed number of classic westerns in which he had starred.

With the other major western stars either dead, retired or semi-retired (*The Shootist* was also Jimmy Stewart's last western), Wayne's disappearance from the scene sealed Eastwood's succession as the genre's master filmmaker—now in both capacities, as actor and director. In *The Outlaw Josey Wales*, Eastwood, now 46 years old, tells a fascinating and quite original story in his own individual style, which—understandably influenced by Sergio Leone and Don Siegel—had been developing since his directorial debut in 1971. As the Man with No Name had been symbolically buried in *High Plains Drifter*, Eastwood's new hero, Josey Wales, reveals more humanity and, following the up-lifting ending of Carter's novel, manages—eventually—to put his guns away and peacefully settle down.

Each of the other notable western films of the year, controversial to say the least, is worth mentioning for one reason or another. As a sequel to Elliot Silverstein's *A Man Called Horse*, Irvin Kershner's *The Return of a Man Called Horse* (with Richard Harris resuming the titular role) is indirectly tied to the excellent short story by Dorothy M. Johnson. Yet the sequel is even more disappointing than the original, and clearly more inaccurate, at least in the representation of the author's ideas. Arthur Penn's *The Missouri Breaks* managed to attract the audiences with the appearance of two legends of the screen—Marlon Brando and Jack Nicholson. However, the eccentricity of their performances, amazing rather than amusing, contributed to the artistic failure of the otherwise interesting and intelligent project. And *The Last Hard Men* (featuring Charlton Heston, James Coburn and Barbara Hershey) is a relatively faithful rendition of Brian Garfield's decent detective/chase novel *Gun Down* (1971), but Andrew V. McLaglen's uninspired direction was able to elevate it only a bit above mediocrity.

Despite their obvious flaws, these three movies, coupled with the two frontrunners, add up to an impressive year of western entertainment, thus making 1976 the final chapter in the period of the genre's prosperity. From then on, western films would be scarce and usually unremarkable. Sporadically, there would be a single and rather unexpected triumph (*Dances with Wolves, Unforgiven*), but most of the westerns released after 1976 would suffer from unauthenticity, banality and triteness—three major "sins" resulting from either the exhaustion of ideas in the subject matter or, more likely, from the lack of continuity in the tradition and practice of western filmmaking.

The obituaries of 1976 reported the death of James Warner Bellah, the original author of the short stories that inspired John Ford's Cavalry trilogy; James Wong Howe, an Oscar-winning cinematographer with a number of superior western credits (*Pursued, The Outrage, Hombre*); and Ray Teal, an extremely popular character actor who appeared in dozens of westerns (*Canyon Passage, Hangman's Knot, Saddle the Wind, One-Eyed Jacks*).

1977

Outstanding Achievements

PICTURE: *Another Man, Another Chance*
NOVEL FILMED: *The White Buffalo* by Richard Sale
DIRECTION: Claude Lelouch, *Another Man, Another Chance*
MUSIC: Francis Lai, *Another Man, Another Chance*; John Barry, *The White Buffalo*
MALE LEADING ROLE: James Caan, *Another Man, Another Chance*

Deaths. Writers MacKinlay Kantor (b. 1904), Charles O. Locke (b.?); screenwriter Nunnally Johnson (b. 1897); directors William Castle, Delmer Daves (b. 1904), Tom Gries, Howard Hawks (b. 1896), William McGann (b. 1895), Jacques Tourneur (b. 1904); actors Willis Bouchey (b. 1907), Stephen Boyd, Andy Devine (b. 1905), Richard Egan, Henry Hull (b. 1890), Robert Middleton (b. 1911), Elvis Presley, Eddy Waller (b. 1889); actress Joan Crawford (b. 1904).

In the first year of the latest lean period for the genre, which would last until now (with occasional glimpses of greatness), no remarkable western was released. One that is worth mentioning is Claude Lelouch's French-American co-production *Another Man, Another Chance* (with likeable performances from James Caan and Geneviève Bujold), a warm and charming, though rather disappointing, attempt at a European approach to the Old West legend. Interestingly, Francis Lai, the author of the sound track, used Beethoven's V Symphony to emphasize the European viewpoint.

It needs to be noted that Charlton Heston, a distinguished, Oscar-winning actor who had appeared in numerous westerns, including *Arrowhead, The Big Country, Major Dundee* and *Will Penny*, was the 1977 winner of the Jean Hersholt Humanitarian Award; while William Kelley's "Cully Madigan" (a segment of the mini-series *How the West Was Won*) received the Spur Award for best television script.

Among the filmmakers that passed away in 1977 were two major directors of the genre: Howard Hawks (*Red River, The Big Sky, Rio Bravo, El Dorado* and *Rio Lobo*) and Delmer Daves (*Broken Arrow, Jubal, 3:10 to Yuma, Cowboy, The Hanging Tree*).

1978

Outstanding Achievements

PICTURE: *Goin' South*
DIRECTION: Jack Nicholson, *Goin' South*

CINEMATOGRAPHY: Nestor Almendros, *Goin' South*

FEMALE LEADING ROLE: Mary Steenburgen, *Goin' South*

Deaths. Screenwriters Leigh Brackett, Howard Estabrook (b. 1884), Lillie Hayward (b. 1892), Barney Slater; director Leslie Fenton (b. 1902); cinematographers Lee Garmes (b. 1898), Lloyd Griggs (b. 1907), Russell Metty (b. 1906); actors Trevor Bardette (b. 1902), Frank Ferguson (b. 1899), Will Geer (b. 1902), Ian MacDonald, Tim McCoy (b. 1891), Jack Oakie (b. 1903), Karl Swenson (b. 1908), Chill Wills (b. 1903); actress Claire Adams (b. 1898).

Another poor year brought about one noteworthy western, Jack Nicholson's *Goin' South* (featuring Nicholson, Mary Steenburgen, Christopher Lloyd and John Belushi). While the movie's main assets include Steenburgen's warm performance, Almendros' marvelous photography and Nicholson's competent direction, the whole, albeit quite humorous, is only partially rewarding.

One of the 1978 recipients of the Academy's Honorary Award was King Vidor—"for incomparable achievements as a cinematic creator and innovator." At the same time, Richard Farnsworth was nominated as best supporting actor for his performance in the modern western *Comes a Horseman* (starring James Caan, Jane Fonda and Jason Robards), directed by Alan J. Pakula. Moreover, Dennis Lynton Clark received the Spur Award for the movie script of *Comes a Horseman*, while Calvin Clemets, John Mantley and Earl W. Wallace shared the Spur Award for the TV script of *How the West Was Won*.

Chill Wills was one of several character actors who died in 1978. His western credits include such remarkable pictures as *The Westerner*, *Rio Grande*, *From Hell to Texas*, *The Alamo*, *McLintock!* and *Pat Garrett and Billy the Kid*.

1979

Outstanding Achievements

PICTURE: *Butch and Sundance: The Early Days*

DIRECTION: Richard Lester, *Butch and Sundance: The Early Days*

CINEMATOGRAPHY: Laszlo Kovacs, *Butch and Sundance: The Early Days*

MALE LEADING ROLE: Tom Berenger, *Butch and Sundance: The Early Days*; William Katt, *Butch and Sundance: The Early Days*

MALE SUPPORTING ROLE: Jeff Corey, *Butch and Sundance: The Early Days*

Academy Award Nomination

Butch and Sundance: The Early Days— AAN: costume design (William Theiss).

Deaths. Writer Thomas T. Flynn (b. 1902); screenwriters Robert Carson (b. 1909), Willis Goldbeck (b. 1900); directors David Butler (b. 1894), Stuart Heisler (b. 1894), Nicholas Ray (b. 1911), Lesley Selander (b. 1900); cinematographers Lucien Andriot (b. 1897), Winton C. Hoch (b. 1905), John F. Seitz (b. 1893); composers Cyril J. Mockridge (b. 1896), Dimitri Tiomkin (b. 1894); actors George Brent (1904), Edgar Buchanan (b. 1902), Dick Foran (b. 1910), Arthur Hunnicutt (b. 1911), Victor Kilian (b. 1891), Wally Wales (aka Hal Taliaferro, b. 1887), John Wayne (b. 1907); actresses Joan Blondell (b. 1909), Virginia Brissac (b. 1895), Marjorie Daw (b. 1902), Ann Dvorak (b. 1912).

A 'prequel' to *Butch Cassidy and The Sundance Kid*, Richard Lester's *Butch and*

1980

Sundance: The Early Days (featuring Tom Berenger, William Katt and Jeff Corey) cannot compare with the original; however, it has a beauty and charm of its own, and the young actors did a commendable job. The movie is definitely better and less pretentious than Sydney Pollack's contemporary essay *The Electric Horseman* (starring Robert Redford, Jane Fonda and Valerie Perrine), a disappointing picture that the Academy recognized with one nomination (in the category of best sound).

The 1979 obituaries were full of western-related names. The biggest blow for the western fans was the death of John Wayne, the greatest of the screen cowboys, whose classic westerns include films directed by John Ford (*Stagecoach*, Cavalry trilogy, *The Searchers*, *The Man Who Shot Liberty Valance* and others), Howard Hawks (*Red River*, *Rio Bravo*, *El Dorado* and *Rio Lobo*), Henry Hathaway (*The Shepherd of the Hills*, *North to Alaska*, *The Sons of Katie Elder* and *True Grit*) and Raoul Walsh (*The Big Trail* and *Dark Command*). Incidentally, among the celebrities that passed away in that year were also two filmmakers that contributed a great deal to the artistry of Wayne's westerns: Dimitri Tiomkin, a brilliant composer (*Red River*, *Rio Bravo*, *The Alamo* and *The War Wagon* with the Duke, and *High Noon* among his other outstanding achievements), and Winton C. Hoch, a distinguished cinematographer (*3 Godfathers*, *She Wore a Yellow Ribbon*).

The Western Writers of America granted the movie script Spur Award to John Hunter for *The Grey Fox*, a picture that would not be released until 1982.

Outstanding Achievements

PICTURE: *Heaven's Gate*; *The Long Riders*

DIRECTION: Walter Hill, *The Long Riders*; Michael Cimino, *Heaven's Gate*

CINEMATOGRAPHY: Ric Waite, *The Long Riders*; John Alonzo, *Tom Horn*; Vilmos Zsigmond, *Heaven's Gate*

MUSIC: Michel Legrand, *The Mountain Men*

MALE LEADING ROLE: David Carradine, *The Long Riders*; Steve McQueen, *Tom Horn*; Kris Kristofferson, *Heaven's Gate*

FEMALE LEADING ROLE: Linda Evans, *Tom Horn*; Isabelle Huppert, *Heaven's Gate*

MALE SUPPORTING ROLE: James Whitmore, *The Long Riders*; Jeff Bridges, *Heaven's Gate*; Richard Farnsworth, *Tom Horn*

FEMALE SUPPORTING ROLE: Pamela Reed, *The Long Riders*

Deaths. Writer Elliott Arnold (b. 1912); directors Henry Levin (b. 1909), Raoul Walsh (b. 1887); cinematographer Ray Rennahan (b. 1896); composers Adolph Deutsch (b. 1897), Jerry Fielding; actors Don "Red" Barry (b. 1912), Strother Martin, Charles McGraw, Steve McQueen, Jay Silverheels, Milburn Stone (b. 1904); actresses Barbara Britton, Edith Evanson (b. 1896), Florence Lake (b. 1904), Gail Patrick (b. 1911).

The major 1980 westerns—Michael Cimino's *Heaven's Gate* (featuring Kris Kristofferson, Christopher Walken, Isabelle Huppert, John Hurt, Jeff Bridges, Sam Waterston and Joseph Cotten) and Walter Hill's *The Long Riders* (starring David, Keith and Robert Carradine as the

Younger brothers; James and Stacy Keach as Jesse and Frank James; and Dennis and Randy Quaid as the Millers)—constitute a good illustration of some of the tendencies in the contemporary cinema. Large-scale, pretentious, spectacular and historical, the two movies are disappointing and controversial, despite some undeniable assets, such as superb photography and some good acting, both by the leading men and by many supporting actors. William Wiard's *Tom Horn* (starring Steve McQueen and Linda Evans), referring to the same historical event as *Heaven's Gate*—the Johnson County War—can be summed up in the same way as the above, except that it is by far a less impressive picture as a whole.

The Academy granted the 1980 Honorary Award to Henry Fonda, "the consummate actor, in recognition of his brilliant accomplishments and enduring contributions to the art of motion pictures." At the same time, Michael Landon received a Spur Award for his television script "May We Make Them Proud," a segment of the series *Little House on the Prairie*.

1981

Outstanding Achievements

PICTURE: *Cattle Annie and Little Britches*
NOVEL: *Cattle Annie and Little Britches* by Robert Ward
CINEMATOGRAPHY: Larry Pizer, *Cattle Annie and Little Britches*
MUSIC: Sanh Berti, Tom Slocum, *Cattle Annie and Little Britches*
MALE LEADING ROLE: Burt Lancaster, *Cattle Annie and Little Britches*
MALE SUPPORTING ROLE: Rod Steiger, *Cattle Annie and Little Britches*
FEMALE SUPPORTING ROLE: Diane Lane, *Cattle Annie and Little Britches*

Deaths. Directors Allan Dwan (b. 1885), William Wyler (b. 1902); composers Hugo Friedhofer (b. 1902), Marlin Skiles (b. 1906); actors Richard Boone, Jim Davis, Frank De Kova (b. 1910), Melvyn Douglas (b. 1901), Chief Dan George (b. 1899), Russell Hayden (b. 1912), William Holden, Arthur O'Connell (b. 1908); actresses Beulah Bondi (b. 1892), Dorothy Dwan (b. 1906), Gloria Grahame, Wanda Hendrix.

Robert Ward's 1977 novel *Cattle Annie and Little Britches*, about two teenage girls joining the Doolin-Dalton gang, is a superior piece of western prose. However, its screen version, directed by Lamont Johnson, is only partially successful, despite a number of first-rate performances (Burt Lancaster, Rod Steiger, Diane Lane), good music and fine cinematography.

An obvious highlight of the year is the Honorary Award granted by the Academy to Barbara Stanwyck "for superlative creativity and unique contribution to the art of screen acting." At the same time, Paul Cooper received the Spur Award for the television script of "Establish Thou the Work of Our Hands," a segment of the series *Father Murphy*.

The 1981 obituaries listed a number of western-related celebrities. The outstanding ones include directors Allan Dwan (*Frontier Marshal, Silver Lode*) and William Wyler (*The Westerner, The Big Country*), composer Hugo Friedhofer (*Broken Arrow, Vera Cruz*), and actors William Holden (*Arizona, The Horse Soldiers, The Wild Bunch*), Jim Davis (*The Big Sky, Monte Walsh, Bad Company*) and Richard Boone (*Man Without a Star, The Tall T, Hombre*).

An event indirectly related to the western film was the inauguration of the 40th president of the United States. Ronald Reagan (born in 1911) had been a

1982

Ronald Reagan, the only screen cowboy to find a way to the White House.

movie star for nearly 30 years and appeared in a half dozen westerns (including *Santa Fe Trail*, *Law and Order*, *Cattle Queen of Montana* and *Tennessee's Partner*) before his political career that culminated in two terms as president.

1982

Outstanding Achievements

PICTURE: *The Grey Fox*; *Barbarosa*
SCREENPLAY (ORIGINAL): John Hunter, *The Grey Fox*
DIRECTION: Phillip Borsos, *The Grey Fox*; Fred Schepisi, *Barbarosa*
CINEMATOGRAPHY: Frank Tidy, *The Grey Fox*
MUSIC: Michael Conway, *The Grey Fox*
MALE LEADING ROLE: Richard Farnsworth, *The Grey Fox*; Willie Nelson, *Barbarosa*
FEMALE LEADING ROLE: Jackie Burroughs, *The Grey Fox*

Deaths. Screenwriter Michael Blankfort (b. 1910); directors Henry King (b. 1888), King Vidor (b. 1894); cinematographer Sidney Hickox (b. 1895); composer Roy Webb (b. 1888); actors Henry Fonda (b. 1905), Victor Jory (b. 1902), Hugh Marlowe (b. 1911), Warren Oates, Joe Sawyer (b. 1906), Tom Tully (b. 1908); actress Ruth Donnelly (b. 1896).

A big surprise for the western fans was Phillip Borsos' Canadian production *The Grey Fox*, a beautiful, elegiac picture in which a so-far unrecognized character actor, Richard Farnsworth, gave an extremely effective and likeable performance as stagecoach robber Bill Miner. Fred Schepisi's *Barbarosa* (featuring Willie Nelson, Gary Busey and Gilbert Roland), though hardly a masterpiece, offered an interesting and rewarding combination of the old values and the new trends in the cinema. While *The Grey Fox*, 'a breath of fresh air,' is possibly the most appealing western since *The Shootist*, *Barbarosa* stands out among the minor westerns of the early 1980s.

Mickey Rooney, an actor who appeared in a few westerns (*My Outlaw Brother*, *The Twinkle in God's Eye*), was the 1982 recipient of the Academy's Honorary Award—"for 50 years of versatility in a variety of memorable film performances."

The most distinguished celebrity among those that died in 1982 was undoubtedly Henry Fonda, a brilliant actor who starred in at least a dozen western classics, including *Jesse James, The Ox-Bow Incident, My Darling Clementine, Fort Apache, The Tin Star, Warlock* and *Once Upon a Time in the West*. The obituaries also listed two major directors, Henry King (*Jesse James, The Gunfighter, The Bravados*) and King Vidor (*Billy the Kid, Duel in the Sun, Man Without a Star*), and at least one outstanding character actor, Warren Oates, most famous for his roles in Sam Peckinpah's films (*Ride the High Country, Major Dundee, The Wild Bunch*).

The Western Writers of America gave the best television script Spur Award to Don Balluck for "Knights of the White Camelia," a segment of the *Father Murphy* series.

1983

Outstanding Achievements

SONG: George Garvarentz, Buddy Kaye, "He's Coming Back" from *Triumphs of a Man Called Horse*

Deaths. Screenwriter Harold Shumate (b. 1893); director Robert Aldrich; cinematographers Charles G. Clarke (b. 1899), Burnett Guffey (b. 1905); composers Daniele Amfitheatrof (b. 1901), David Buttolph (b. 1902), Bronislau Kaper (b. 1902), Jerome Moross (b. 1913); actors Rod Cameron (b. 1910), Larry "Buster" Crabbe (b. 1907), William Demarest (b. 1892), Paul Fix (b. 1901), Christopher George, Raymond Massey (b. 1896), Slim Pickens; actresses Dolores Del Rio (b. 1905), Jacqueline Logan (b. 1901), Lois Wilson (b. 1896).

Top: Henry Fonda, one of the top half dozen western leading men, died in 1982. The photograph comes from the television series *The Deputy* (1959–61). *Bottom:* Rod Cameron, who starred in numerous medium- and low-budget westerns (*Frontier Gal, Short Grass, Ride the Man Down*), died in 1983.

Ironically, the only significant achievement of 1983 was the song "He's Coming Back," beautifully performed by Rita Coolidge for John Hough's disappointing picture *Triumphs of a Man Called Horse* (starring Michael Beck and Ana De Sade), which concluded the *A Man Called Horse* trilogy started by the superior 1970 movie derived from Dorothy M. Johnson's masterful short story.

The long list of celebrities that died in 1983 included such important for the genre names as Robert Aldrich, the director of *Apache*, *Vera Cruz* and *Ulzana's Raid*; Bronislau Kaper, the author of the musical score for *Ride, Vaquero!*, *The Naked Spur* and *The Way West*; and Slim Pickens, a character actor memorable for roles in such westerns as *One-Eyed Jacks*, *Major Dundee*, *Pat Garrett and Billy the Kid* and many, many others.

Oddly, a year after the death of director Robert Aldrich, the motion picture industry also lost Ernest Laszlo, the distinguished cinematographer who photographed some of Aldrich's best westerns (*Apache*, *Vera Cruz*, *The Last Sunset*) and nonwesterns (*The Big Knife*). The other major western-related people that passed away in 1984 include Dorothy M. Johnson, the author of the short stories that inspired *The Hanging Tree*, *The Man Who Shot Liberty Valance* and *A Man Called Horse*; Carl Foreman, the screenwriter of *High Noon*; and Paul Francis Webster, a songwriter who wrote the lyrics for such memorable westerns as *Rio Bravo*, *The Alamo* and *Cimarron*.

1984

Outstanding Achievements

None!

Deaths. Writer Dorothy M. Johnson (b. 1905); screenwriters Carl Foreman, Frances Goodrich (b. 1891), Roland Kibbee; directors Byron Haskin (b. 1899), H. Bruce Humberstone (b. 1903); cinematographers Ernest Laszlo (b. 1905), William E. Snyder (b. 1901); songwriter Paul Francis Webster (b. 1907); actors Richard Basehart, William Powell (b. 1892); actress Ann Little (b. 1891).

The only highlight associated with 1984 was the Honorary Award granted by the Academy to James Stewart "for 50 years of meaningful performances, for his high ideals, both on and off the screen, with the respect and admiration of his colleagues."

1985

Outstanding Achievements

PICTURE: *Pale Rider*; *Silverado*
SCREENPLAY (ORIGINAL): Michael Butler, Dennis Shryack, *Pale Rider*; Lawrence Kasdan, Mark Kasdan, *Silverado*
DIRECTION: Clint Eastwood, *Pale Rider*; Lawrence Kasdan, *Silverado*
CINEMATOGRAPHY: Bruce Surtees, *Pale Rider*; John Bailey, *Silverado*
MUSIC: Bruce Broughton, *Silverado*; Lennie Niehaus, *Pale Rider*
MALE LEADING ROLE: Clint Eastwood, *Pale Rider*; Kevin Kline, *Silverado*; Scott Glenn, *Silverado*
FEMALE LEADING ROLE: Carrie Snodgress, *Pale Rider*
MALE SUPPORTING ROLE: Michael Moriarty, *Pale Rider*; Richard Dennehy, *Silverado*
FEMALE SUPPORTING ROLE: Linda Hunt, *Silverado*; Rosanna Arquette, *Silverado*

Academy Awards Nominations

Silverado—AAN: original score; sound (Donald O. Mitchell, Rick Kline, Kevin O'Connell, David Ronne).

Deaths. Directors Henry Hathaway (b. 1898), Jesse Hibbs (b. 1906), Phil Karlson (b. 1908), Sam Peckinpah; cinematographers Floyd Crosby (b. 1899), Harry Perry (b. 1888), Robert L. Surtees (b. 1906); composers Nelson Riddle, Heinz Roemheld (b. 1901), Paul J. Smith (1906), Herman Stein; actors Scott Brady, Yul Brynner, George Chandler (b. 1902), James Craig (b. 1912), Frank Faylen (b. 1905), Rock Hudson, Lloyd Nolan (b. 1902), Edmond O'Brien, George O'Brien (b. 1900), Kent Smith (b. 1907); actresses Anne Baxter, Connie Gilchrist (b. 1901).

As an obvious, albeit unexpected, rise in the production of the genre, two major westerns were released in 1985—Clint Eastwood's *Pale Rider* (starring Eastwood, Carrie Snodgress and Michael Moriarty) and Lawrence Kasdan's *Silverado* (featuring Kevin Kline, Scott Glenn, Kevin Costner, Danny Glover, Brian Dennehy, Linda Hunt, Rosanna Arquette, John Cleese and Jeff Goldblum). Though the two films are definite examples of large-scale and ambitious endeavors, with a number of assets providing a great deal of fun and satisfaction for the audience, they do not offer anything strikingly new in the development of the genre, nor do they reach the aesthetic heights of the cinema. While Eastwood was criticized mostly for lack of new ideas and too obvious references to (or borrowings from) both *Shane* and *High Plains Drifter*, *Silverado* was perceived as a return to the clichés of the B western, strongly relying on the story of the Three Mesquiteers.

A winner of the 1985 Spur Award for screenplay, *Pale Rider* received the following review from Andrew Sarris in *The Village Voice*: "On the whole, Eastwood's instincts as an artist are well-nigh inspiring in the context of the temptations he must face all the time to play it completely safe. Consequently, even his mistakes contribute to his mystique ... Eastwood has managed to keep the genre alive ... through the ghostly intervention of his heroic persona."

Another Spur Award, for best western novel, was granted to *Lonesome Dove*, Larry McMurtry's masterpiece epic which

Polish poster (by Jakub Erol, 1986) for Clint Eastwood's *Pale Rider*, a picture filled with conspicuous allusions to *Shane*.

would become a hit television mini-series and would be followed by three more major novels dealing with the same characters— *Streets of Laredo* (1993), *Dead Man's Walk* (1995) and *Comanche Moon* (1997).

Two out of the three recipients of the Academy's 1985 Honorary Award were Paul Newman, who starred in a half dozen westerns, including *The Left Handed Gun*, *Hombre* and *Butch Cassidy and the Sundance Kid*; and Alex North, who scored a few major westerns, including *Man with the Gun, The Wonderful Country, Cheyenne Autumn* and *Bite the Bullet*. The western credits that the two filmmakers have in common are *The Outrage* and *Pocket Money*.

A big loss for the western fans was the death of two outstanding directors— Henry Hathaway, a pioneer filmmaker whose western credits include *Rawhide, From Hell to Texas, North to Alaska* and *True Grit,* and Sam Peckinpah, one of the true masters of the genre, who demonstrated his unusual talent and individual style in such movie gems as *Ride the High Country, The Wild Bunch, The Ballad of Cable Hogue* and *Pat Garrett and Billy the Kid*.

1986

Outstanding Achievements

None!

Yakima Canutt, a man who made an enormous contribution to the western genre in multiple capacities—stunts, assistant directing, second unit directing and acting—died in 1986.

Deaths. Writer Harry Brown; director Ray Nazarro (b. 1902); cinematographer Daniel L. Fapp (b. 1904); actors James Cagney (b. 1899), Broderick Crawford (b. 1911), Leif Erickson (b. 1911), Emilio Fernandez (b. 1904), Sterling Hayden, Ray Milland (b. 1907), Charles Starrett (b. 1903), Forrest Tucker, Keenan Wynn; actresses Susan Cabot, Virginia Gregg, Bessie Love (b. 1898); stuntman/actor/second unit director Yakima Canutt (b. 1895).

The only highlight of the year was the Pulitzer Prize granted to Larry McMurtry's novel *Lonesome Dove*, as the second western book (after A.B. Guthrie, Jr.'s *The Way West*) to win this prestigious distinction.

1987

Outstanding Achievements

None!

Deaths. Screenwriter William Bowers; directors Hugo Fregonese (b. 1908), John Huston (b. 1906), Harry Keller (b. 1913), Albert S. Rogell (b. 1901); songwriter Jerry Livingston (b. 1909); actors Lorne Greene, Lee Marvin, Emile Meyer (b. 1908), Robert Preston, John Qualen (b. 1899), Randolph Scott (b. 1898); actress Geraldine Page.

The Western Writers of America granted the 1987 screenplay Spur Award to Gordon Dawson for *Independence*.

In addition to one major screenwriter, William Bowers (*The Gunfighter, The Sheepman, Support Your Local Sheriff*), and one star director, John Huston (*The Unforgiven, The Life and Times of Judge Roy Bean*), the motion picture industry lost two outstanding actors important to the western genre. While Randolph Scott was a leading man almost from the beginning of his acting career in the early 1930s, and appeared in dozens of westerns, including *Jesse James, Western Union, The Desperadoes, Seven Men from Now, The Tall T, Comanche Station* and *Ride the High Country*, Lee Marvin had a long climb to stardom, and his leading parts in standard westerns, albeit remarkable, are scarce: *Cat Ballou, The Professionals, Monte Walsh*.

Randolph Scott, who struggled for law and order in an impressive number of superior westerns, died in 1987.

1988

Outstanding Achievements

PICTURE: *Young Guns*
DIRECTION: Christopher Cain, *Young Guns*
CINEMATOGRAPHY: John Fusco, *Young Guns*
MALE LEADING ROLE: Kiefer Sutherland, *Young Guns*
MALE SUPPORTING ROLE: Jack Palance, *Young Guns*

Deaths. Writer Louis L'Amour (b. 1908); screenwriters Gerald Drayson Adams (b. 1900), Jesse Lasky, Jr. (b. 1908), Jack Sher (b.1913); cinematographers Lucien Ballard (b. 1908), George J. Folsey (b. 1898), Milton Krasner (b. 1901), Harold Rosson (b. 1895); composer Joseph Gershenson (b. 1904); actors John Carradine (b. 1906), Stuart Randall (b. 1909), Bob

Charlie Sheen, Dermot Mulroney, Kiefer Sutherland, Emilio Estevez, Casey Siemaszko and Lou Diamond Phillips in Christopher Cain's *Young Guns*.

Steele (b. 1906); actresses Olive Carey (b. 1895), Colleen Moore (b. 1900), Eva Novak (b. 1899), Ella Raines, Irene Rich (b. 1891).

Significantly more than just a "Brat Pack" western, Christopher Cain's *Young Guns* (featuring Emilio Estevez as Billy the Kid, Kiefer Sutherland, Lou Diamond Phillips, Charlie Sheen, Casey Siemaszko, Jack Palance, Terence Stamp, and Patrick Wayne as Pat Garrett) is a quite interesting and relatively authentic-looking movie, despite its forced modern approach, focus on action and abundance of juvenile stuff. With Cain's inspired direction and a number of solid performances, in particular by Sutherland and Palance, *Young Guns* stands out as possibly the most important western of the late 1980s.

The television mini-series *Lonesome Dove* (featuring Tommy Lee Jones, Robert Duvall, Diane Lane, Danny Glover, Robert Urich and Anjelica Huston), directed by Simon Wincer, emerged as a major surprise, a picture that can easily compete with many theatrical westerns. While the film would be selected as the number 1 mini-series by the Western Writers of America in their 1995 poll, Larry McMurtry's book on which the series was based would be chosen as the number 3 (a tie with Elmer Kelton's *The Time It Never Rained*) western novel in the same survey.

Among the western-related people who passed away in 1988, two made especially remarkable contributions to the genre—Louis L'Amour, an extremely popular and prolific writer whose prose inspired over a dozen films, including *Hondo, The Burning Hills, The Tall Stranger, Heller*

Robert Duvall and Tommy Lee Jones in the excellent television mini-series *Lonesome Dove*, based on the Pulitzer Prize–winning novel by Larry McMurtry.

in Pink Tights and *Shalako*; and Lucien Ballard, a distinguished cinematographer whose credits include such classics as *Ride the High Country, Hour of the Gun, Will Penny, The Wild Bunch* and *True Grit*.

1989

Outstanding Achievements

None!

Deaths. Screenwriters James Lee Barrett, Robert H. Buckner (b. 1906), Marguerite Roberts (b. 1905); directors

1990

As no standard western was released in 1989, the genre's fans' attention was drawn by two remarkable quasi-westerns—Edward Zwick's Civil War reconstruction *Glory* (featuring Matthew Broderick, Denzel Washington, Cary Elwes and Morgan Freeman) and Luis Puenzo's biographical *Old Gringo* (starring Jane Fonda, Gregory Peck and Jimmy Smits). The former picture won three Academy Awards (supporting actor Washington, cinematography by Freddie Francis and sound) and two nominations (art direction and editing).

The 1989 obituaries listed many western-related filmmakers, including Sergio Leone, the creator and top representative of the spaghetti western (*A Fistful of Dollars*, *For a Few Dollars More*, *The Good, the Bad and the Ugly*, *Once Upon a Time in the West*); Lionel Newman, a prolific composer (*The Last Wagon*, *Love Me Tender*, *The Bravados* and *North to Alaska*); and, oddly, two character actors who appeared together in *High Noon* as members of Frank Miller's gang—Lee Van Cleef ("Colby," also memorable from *Gunfight at the O.K. Corral*, *The Man Who Shot Liberty Valance*, *How the West Was Won* and numerous spaghetti westerns, notably *The Good, the Bad and the Ugly*) and Robert J. Wilke ("Pierce," whose other major credits include *The Far Country*, *Man of the West*, *The Magnificent Seven* and *A Gunfight*). Sergio Leone, R.G. Springsteen (b. 1904); cinematographer Joseph LaShelle (b. 1900); composers Jeff Alexander (b. 1910), Lionel Newman; actors Jack Buetel, Joe De Santis (b. 1909), Jock Mahoney, John Payne (b. 1912), Lee Van Cleef, Cornel Wilde, Robert J. Wilke (b. 1911); actresses Amanda Blake, Jean Willes.

1990

Outstanding Achievements

PICTURE: *Dances with Wolves*
NOVEL FILMED: *Dances with Wolves* by Michael Blake
SCREENPLAY (ADAPTATION): Michael Blake, *Dances with Wolves*
DIRECTION: Kevin Costner, *Dances with Wolves*
CINEMATOGRAPHY: Dean Semler, *Dances with Wolves;* Dean Semler, *Young Guns II*
MUSIC: John Barry, *Dances with Wolves;* Alan Silvestri, *Young Guns II*
SONG: Jon Bon Jovi, "Blaze of Glory" from *Young Guns II*
MALE LEADING ROLE: Kevin Costner, *Dances with Wolves*
MALE SUPPORTING ROLE: Graham Greene, *Dances with Wolves*
FEMALE SUPPORTING ROLE: Mary McDonnell, *Dances with Wolves*

Academy Awards/ Nominations

Dances with Wolves—AA: picture; adapted screenplay; direction; cinematography; original score; editing (Neil Travis); sound (Russell Williams II, Jeffrey Perkins, Bill W. Benton, Greg Watkins); AAN: actor Kevin Costner; supporting actor Graham Greene; supporting actress Mary McDonnell; art direction (Jeffrey Beecroft, Lisa Dean); costume design (Elsa Zamparelli).

Young Guns II—AAN: song "Blaze of Glory."

Deaths. Writer Clair Huffaker; screenwriters Sydney Boehm (b. 1908), Edmund H. North (b. 1911), Irving Wallace; directors Martin Ritt, Charles Marquis Warren (b. 1912), Robert D. Webb (b.

1903); cinematographer Karl Brown (b. 1896); composer Sol Kaplan; actors Henry Brandon (b. 1912), Sunset Carson, Robert Cummings (b. 1908), Howard Duff (b. 1913), Alan Hale, Jr., Arthur Kennedy, Mike Mazurki (b. 1909), Joel McCrea (b. 1905), Gary Merrill; actresses Valerie French, Jill Ireland, Jane Novak (b. 1896), Barbara Stanwyck (b. 1907).

A major event in the genre and a breath of fresh air in the treatment of the Indian theme was the 1988 publication of Michael Blake's almost sensational novel *Dances with Wolves*, which was followed by Kevin Costner's meticulous screen adaptation, featuring Costner as Lieutenant John Dunbar, Mary McDonnell as Christine, Graham Greene as Kicking Bird and Rodney A. Grant as Wind in His Hair. While both the book and the movie received positive receptions from the critics and the audience alike, the film upping the authenticity quotient by making the Indians speak their own language, was recognized by the Academy. The movie set a record among westerns, receiving altogether seven Oscars, including one for best picture (over *Awakenings*, *Ghost*, *The Godfather Part III* and *GoodFellas*), and five additional nominations. Kevin Costner, nominated for best actor, won an Oscar for direction (even though the nominees included such distinguished directors as Francis Ford Coppola and Martin Scorsese)—an unprecedented distinction in the

Morris Ankrum and Barbara Stanwyck in Allan Dwan's *Cattle Queen of Montana* (1954). The talented actress died in 1990.

genre, even though there had been a few filmmakers nominated for directing a western before: Irving Cummings, Wesley Ruggles, John Ford, Fred Zinnemann and George Stevens.

A winner of the 1990 Spur Award for a motion picture, and one of the best 15 western films in the Western Writers of America's 1995 poll, Costner's epic western received the following review from David Ansen in *Newsweek*: "*Dances with Wolves* is vulnerable both to charges of sentimentality and anachronism—the hero exhibits a sensibility at times dubiously contemporary. But if one's mind sometimes balks, one's heart embraces the movie's fine, wide-open spirit, its genuine respect for a culture we destroyed without a second thought.... It's an engrossing tale, and Costner directs with the confidence of a Hollywood veteran well aware that entertainment comes before earnestness."

Another Spur Award, for a television screenplay, was granted to "Dust in the Wind," a segment of the series *Guns of Paradise*.

The sequel to *Young Guns*, Geoff Murphy's *Young Guns II* (featuring Emilio Estevez, Kiefer Sutherland, Lou Diamond Phillips, Christian Slater and William Petersen), did not meet the fans' expectations, in spite of some good moments, fine cinematography by Dean Semler (who also photographed *Dances with Wolves*) and a superior musical score by Alan Silvestri (decorated with two songs written and performed by Jon Bon Jovi—"Blaze of Glory," a winner of an Academy Award nomination and a Golden Globe Award, and "Billy Get Your Guns"). The major flaw of the movie was John Fusco's script (based on the characters he created for the original), which overemphasized action and violence and gave no chance to the protagonists to develop.

The two celebrities that clearly stand out among those that died in 1990 are Joel McCrea and Barbara Stanwyck—a leading man and a leading lady who appeared in numerous major westerns and co-starred in three: *Union Pacific*, *The Great Man's Lady* and *Trooper Hook*.

1991

Outstanding Achievements

None!

Deaths. Writers Niven Busch (b. 1903), A.B. Guthrie, Jr. (b. 1901), Jack Schaefer (b. 1907); directors George Sherman (b. 1908), Donald Siegel (b. 1912), Richard Thorpe (b. 1896); composer Alex North (b. 1910); actors Iron Eyes Cody (b. 1907), Ken Curtis, Dean Jagger (b. 1903), Fred MacMurray (b. 1908), John McIntire (b. 1907), John Russell, Regis Toomey (b. 1902); actresses Jean Arthur (b. 1905), Nancy Kulp, Aline MacMahon (b. 1899), Gene Tierney.

In a year of no standard western movies, a welcome item was Stuart Rosenberg's modern rodeo/family drama *My Heroes Have Always Been Cowboys* (starring Scott Glenn, Kate Capshaw, Ben Johnson and Tess Harper). Nicely photographed by Bernd Heinl, and pleasantly scored by James Horner (with the title song performed by Willie Nelson), it is a fine quasi-western, albeit not on a par with Sam Peckinpah's masterful *Junior Bonner* (1972; also featuring Ben Johnson, this time opposite Steve McQueen, Ida Lupino and Robert Preston).

Another quasi-western, Ron Underwood's comedy *City Slickers* (starring Billy Crystal and Daniel Stern), was a good opportunity to recognize the talent of Jack Palance, who won his only Oscar for the part of Curly, the old cattle drive boss. The movie would be soon followed by a sequel, Paul Weiland's *City Slickers 2: The Legend of Curly's Gold*, to be released in 1994.

The 1991 obituaries announced the death of many people distinguished in the western genre. The especially notable ones include three writers—A.B. Guthrie, Jr. (*The Way West, The Big Sky, These Thousand Hills*), Jack Schaefer (*Shane, Monte Walsh*) and Niven Busch (*Duel in the Sun, The Furies*); one director—Donald Siegel (*Flaming Star, Two Mules for Sister Sara, The Shootist*); one leading lady—Jean Arthur (*The Plainsman, Arizona, Shane*); and one character actor—John McIntire (*Apache, The Far Country, The Tin Star, Flaming Star*).

1992

Outstanding Achievements

PICTURE: *Unforgiven*
SCREENPLAY (ORIGINAL): David Webb Peoples, *Unforgiven*
DIRECTION: Clint Eastwood, *Unforgiven*
CINEMATOGRAPHY: Jack N. Green, *Unforgiven*
MUSIC: Lennie Niehaus, *Unforgiven*
MALE LEADING ROLE: Clint Eastwood, *Unforgiven*
MALE SUPPORTING ROLE: Gene Hackman, *Unforgiven;* Morgan Freeman, *Unforgiven;* Richard Harris, *Unforgiven*
FEMALE SUPPORTING ROLE: Frances Fisher, *Unforgiven*

Academy Awards/ Nominations

Unforgiven—AA: picture; direction; supporting actor Gene Hackman; editing (Joel Cox); AAN: original screenplay; cinematography; actor Clint Eastwood; art direction (Henry Bumstead, Janice Blackie-Goodine); sound (Les Fresholtz, Vern Poore, Dick Alexander, Rob Young).

Deaths. Writer Glendon Swarthout; screenwriter Ben Maddow (b. c. 1909); directors Jack Arnold, Richard Brooks (b. 1912), John Sturges (b. 1910); cinematographer Lester Shorr (b. c. 1907); songwriter Ken Darby (b. 1909); actors John Anderson, Dana Andrews (b. 1912), Malcolm Atterbury (b. 1907), Neville Brand, Steve Brodie, Chuck Connors, Ray Danton, John Dehner, John Ireland, John Lund (b. 1913), Anthony Perkins, Bill Williams (b. c. 1916), Ian Wolfe (b. 1896), Hank Worden (b. 1901); actresses Judith Anderson (b. 1898), Mae Clarke (b.1907), Marlene Dietrich (b. 1901).

Clint Eastwood, who started directing his own films in the early 1970s, surprised audiences once again with a picture that can easily be considered the last western movie masterpiece to date. *Unforgiven* (starring Eastwood, Gene Hackman, Morgan Freeman and Richard Harris) is an extremely mature and multidimensional work in which Eastwood accomplished a number of things—he enriched it with numerous allusions to both classic westerns (e.g. Peckinpah) and classical literature (Homer), concluded the gradual humanization of his western hero (originating with Leone's Man with No Name), brought his individual style to perfection, and sealed his remarkable contribution to the genre with a film that is often perceived as his western testament (not making another western movie till now). At the same time, Eastwood, who had never even been nominated for an Oscar in any category before, finally won the respect and recognition of the Academy. While the movie received the best picture Oscar

1992

Clint Eastwood won the best director Oscar and was nominated as best actor for his magisterial western *Unforgiven*, which also won the best picture Academy Award.

(over *The Crying Game*, *A Few Good Men*, *Howard's End* and *Scent of a Woman*), Eastwood himself not only became the second filmmaker to win an Oscar for directing a western (after Kevin Costner, also primarily an actor!)—in a competition against Robert Altman, Martin Brest, James Ivory and Neil Jordan—but he also joined those few stars that had been nominated for best actor in a western film (the only Oscar winners among which are Warner Baxter, Gary Cooper, Lee Marvin and John Wayne). (The 1992 best actor statuette went to Al Pacino for *Scent of a Woman*.) Todd McCarthy noted in *Variety*: "A classic western for the ages. Clint Eastwood has crafted a tense, hard-edged, superbly dramatic yarn that is also an exceedingly intelligent meditation on the West, its myths and its heroes." "Dedicated to Sergio [Leone] and Don [Siegel]," two directors that played the greatest role in creating Eastwood's persona and making his ultimate success possible, *Unforgiven* would be included among the best 15 western films in the Western Writers of America's 1995 survey.

Since *Unforgiven* is the last western movie to win multiple Academy Awards and nominations (all well deserved), it is possible to do the Oscar/western statistics right here. The top scorers on the list are #1. *Dances with Wolves* (7 Oscars plus 5 nominations); #2. *Unforgiven* (4 Oscars plus 5 nominations); #3/4. *High Noon* and *Butch Cassidy and the Sundance Kid* (both winning 4 Oscars plus 3 nominations); #5. *Cimarron* (1931, 3 Oscars plus 4 nominations); #6/7. *Stagecoach* (1939) and *How the West Was Won* (both winning 2 Oscars plus 5 nominations); #8. *The Alamo* (1 Oscar plus 6 nominations); #9. *Shane* (1 Oscar plus 5 nominations); #10/11/12. *In Old Arizona*, *North West Mounted Police* and *Cat Ballou* (each a winner of 1 Oscar plus 4 nominations); #13/14. *The Westerner* and *Legends of the Fall* (each winning 1 Oscar plus two nominations); #15/16/17. *Broken Lance*, *The Big Country* and *True Grit* (each a winner of 1 Oscar plus 1 nomination). However, the statistics should not be treated too seriously, as there are many outstanding western pictures that have not received even one Academy Award nomination—*My Darling Clementine*, *Rio Bravo*, *The Searchers*, *3:10 to Yuma* and *Ride the High Country*, to mention only the most obvious examples.

The 1992 Spur Award for a movie script went to David Webb Peoples for *Unforgiven*, and the best television script award went to John Miglis for *Keep the Change*.

The western-related celebrities that passed away in 1992 include the distinguished writer Glendon Swarthout (*They Came to Cordura*, *The Shootist*); two major directors, John Sturges (*Gunfight at the*

O.K. Corral, Last Train from Gun Hill, The Magnificent Seven) and Richard Brooks (The Last Hunt, The Professionals, Bite the Bullet); and one important leading man, Dana Andrews (The Ox-Bow Incident, Canyon Passage, Three Hours to Kill).

1993

Outstanding Achievements

PICTURE: *Tombstone*
SCREENPLAY: Kevin Jarre, *Tombstone;* John Milius, Larry Gross, *Geronimo: An American Legend*
DIRECTION: George P. Cosmatos, *Tombstone*
CINEMATOGRAPHY: William A. Fraker, *Tombstone;* Lloyd Ahern, *Geronimo: An American Legend*
MUSIC: Bruce Broughton, *Tombstone;* Jerry Goldsmith, *Bad Girls*
MALE LEADING ROLE: Val Kilmer, *Tombstone;* Kurt Russell, *Tombstone*
MALE SUPPORTING ROLE: Robert Duvall, *Geronimo, An American Legend;* Michael Biehn, *Tombstone;* Sam Elliott, *Tombstone*
FEMALE SUPPORTING ROLE: Joanna Pacula, *Tombstone;* Drew Barrymore, *Bad Girls*

Academy Award Nomination

Geronimo: An American Legend— AAN: Sound (Bill W. Benton, Chris Carpenter, Doug Hemphill, Lee Orloff).

Deaths. Writer Theodore V. Olsen; screenwriter Wells Root (b. 1900); director Gordon Douglas (b. 1909); cinematographer Ellsworth Fredricks (b. 1904); songwriter Mack David (b. 1912); actors Leon Ames (b. 1903), Raymond Burr, Glenn Corbett, Stewart Granger (b. 1913), Vincent Price (b. 1911), Dan Seymour, Robert Shayne (b. c. 1902), Richard Webb; actresses Claire DuBrey (b. 1893), Lillian Gish (b. 1896), Alexis Smith, Arleen Whelan.

Two major westerns—George P. Cosmatos's *Tombstone* (starring Kurt Russell, Val Kilmer, Michael Biehn, Powers Boothe, Sam Elliott and Bill Paxton) and Walter Hill's *Geronimo: An American Legend* (featuring Jason Patric, Gene Hackman, Robert Duvall and Wes Studi)— were released in 1993, but only the former is a wholly rewarding picture. Unfortunately, John Milius and Larry Gross' literate *Geronimo* script, which focused on the last raid and surrender of Geronimo (Studi), was rather wasted due to Hill's uninspired direction. As for *Tombstone*— except for the final 40 minutes (filled with the Earp faction's one-sided chases and killings), which make the whole movie rather anticlimactic—it is a fairly successful update of the very well known and frequently filmed story. The major assets of the film include Val Kilmer's magnetic characterization of Doc Holliday, and William A. Fraker's stunning photography. As *My Darling Clementine* remains the best, albeit least accurate, account of the Earps vs. Clantons conflict, it is interesting to notice how the two pictures managed to illustrate Doc Holliday's refined taste and education. While Victor Mature's Doc in Ford's classic helps an itinerant actor (Alan Mowbray) recite Hamlet's soliloquy, Kilmer's Doc shows off by playing one of Chopin's nocturns in a saloon. The Western Writers of America would select *Tombstone* as one of the best 15 western films in their 1995 poll.

Another 1993 western, Mario Van Peebles' *Posse* (featuring Van Peebles, Stephen Baldwin, Billy Zane, "Tiny" Lister and Charles Lane), turned out to be an unsuccessful attempt at a 'black' western.

Kurt Russell (Wyatt Earp) and Val Kilmer (Doc Holliday) in George P. Cosmatos' *Tombstone*.

Brimming with nonsensical action and excessive violence, the movie appears to be a job of amateurs, almost a total artistic disaster. The only reason why it is worth mentioning is the appearance of Woody Strode (as the Old Man), a remarkable character player whose western credits include *Sergeant Rutledge*, *The Man Who Shot Liberty Valance*, *The Professionals* and *Once Upon a Time in the West*. The great actor would die on December 31, 1994, shortly after completing his work on *The Quick and the Dead*.

Jonathan Kaplan's *Bad Girls* (starring Madeleine Stowe, Andie MacDowell, Mary Stuart Masterson and Drew Barrymore) is equally unremarkable among the 1993 productions, although it is decorated with several beautiful faces and a superior musical score by Jerry Goldsmith.

The Western Writers of America's Spur Award for a motion picture script went to Nicholas Meyer and Sarah Kernochan for *Sommersby* (starring Richard Gere, Jodie Foster and Bill Pullman), Jon Amiel's Civil War morality tale, which was based on the French movie *The Return of Martin Guerre*. At the same time, John Wilder received the Spur Award for his television script of the mini-series *Return to Lonesome Dove*, which was inspired by Larry McMurtry's characters but none of his books. And Paul Newman, the unforgettable Butch Cassidy, was honored by the Academy with the Jean Hersholt Humanitarian Award.

1994

Outstanding Achievements

NOVELLA FILMED: "Legends of the Fall" by Jim Harrison
CINEMATOGRAPHY: John Toll, *Legends of the Fall*; Owen Roizman, *Wyatt Earp*
MUSIC: James Horner, *Legends of the Fall*; James Newton Howard, *Wyatt Earp*
SONG: Randy Newman, "Ride Gambler Ride" from *Maverick*; James Horner, Brock Walsh, "Twilight and Mist" from *Legends of the Fall*
MALE SUPPORTING ROLE: James Garner, *Maverick*; James Coburn, *Maverick*
FEMALE SUPPORTING ROLE: Mare Winningham, *Wyatt Earp*; Linda Hunt, *Maverick*

Academy Awards/Nominations

Legends of the Fall—AA: cinematography; AAN: art direction (Lilly Kilvert, Dorree Cooper); sound (Paul Massey, David Campbell, Christopher David, Douglas Ganton).
Wyatt Earp—AAN: cinematography.
Maverick—AAN: costume design (April Ferry).

Deaths. Composer Hans J. Salter (b. 1896); actors Claude Akins, Noah Beery, Jr. (b. 1913), Macdonald Carey (b. 1913), William Conrad, Joseph Cotten (b. 1905), Nick Cravat (b. 1911), John Doucette, Charles Drake, Robert Emhardt, Burt Lancaster (b. 1913), John Larch, Stephen McNally (b. 1913), Cameron Mitchell, Dennis Morgan (b. 1910), George Peppard, Fernando Rey, Gilbert Roland (b. 1905), Cesar Romero (b. 1907), Telly Savalas, Woody Strode, Barry Sullivan (b. 1912), Dub Taylor (b. 1908), Gian Maria Volonte; actresses Helen Brown, Esther Ralston (b. 1902).

Two good-looking but disappointing westerns were released in 1994. While Edward Zwick's *Legends of the Fall* (starring Brad Pitt, Anthony Hopkins, Aidan Quinn and Julia Ormond) works, at least to some extent, as a romance and family drama, Lawrence Kasdan's *Wyatt Earp* (featuring Kevin Costner, Dennis Quaid, Gene Hackman, Michael Madsen and Catherine O'Hara) emerges as an overblown biography rather than a suspenseful western, despite its care for historical accuracy. Costner, who had worked with Kasdan before on *Silverado*, and who by himself managed to score high with *Dances with Wolves*, participated in this over-ambitious endeavor and contributed to its failure in two ways—by interfering

Kevin Costner as the titular hero in Lawrence Kasdan's controversial western *Wyatt Earp.*

with the production and by creating one of the weakest Earps in western history. Dennis Quaid gives a far better performance as Doc Holliday, even though his characterization does not compare well with Val Kilmer's from the previous year. The movie, nevertheless, won the Spur Award in the drama script category, and the recipients were Dan Gordon and Lawrence Kasdan.

A great loss for the western genre, and for the movie industry in general, came with was the death of Burt Lancaster, an outstanding actor and one of the top ten screen cowboys, whose western credits include such classics as *Apache, Vera Cruz, Gunfight at the O.K. Corral, The Unforgiven, The Professionals, The Scalphunters* and *Ulzana's Raid*. Incidently, the 1994 obituaries also listed Nick Cravat, Lancaster's good friend, who played major roles in Lancaster's two swashbuckling hits (*The Flame and the Arrow* and *The Crimson Pirate*) and bit parts in many movies, including *The Scalphunters*.

1995

Outstanding Achievements

PICTURE: *Wild Bill*

PLAY FILMED: *Fathers and Sons* by Thomas Babe, filmed—together with Pete Dexter's book *Deadwood*—as *Wild Bill*

SCREENPLAY (ADAPTATION): Walter Hill, *Wild Bill*

DIRECTION: Walter Hill, *Wild Bill*

CINEMATOGRAPHY: Lloyd Ahern, *Wild Bill*; Dante Spinotti, *The Quick and the Dead*

MUSIC: Alan Silvestri, *The Quick and the Dead*; Van Dyke Parks, *Wild Bill*

MALE LEADING ROLE: Jeff Bridges, *Wild Bill*; Gene Hackman, *The Quick and the Dead*

FEMALE LEADING ROLE: Ellen Barkin, *Wild Bill*

MALE SUPPORTING ROLE: James Gammon, *Wild Bill*; Leonardo DiCaprio, *The Quick and the Dead*; Lance Henriksen, *The Quick and the Dead*

FEMALE SUPPORTING ROLE: Diane Lane, *Wild Bill*

Deaths. Writer Will C. Brown (b. 1905); screenwriters Albert Hackett (b. 1900), Lewis Meltzer (b. 1911); directors Robert Parrish, Roy Rowland (b. 1910); cinematographer Philip H. Lathrop; composer Miklos Rozsa (b. 1907); actors Elisha Cook, Jr. (b. 1906), John Howard (b. 1913), Burl Ives (b. 1909), Alexander Knox (b. 1907), Dean Martin, Doug McClure, Timothy Scott , Jeff York (b. 1912); actresses Katherine De Mille (b. 1911), Mary Beth Hughes, Ida Lupino.

In the year of the last rise of the genre, two standard western films were released. While Walter Hill's *Wild Bill* (starring Jeff Bridges, Ellen Barkin, John Hurt and Diane Lane) was a complete triumph for both Hill the screenwriter and Hill the director, who managed to accomplish an original variation of an adult and deeply psychological western, Sam Raimi's *The Quick and the Dead* (featuring Sharon Stone, Gene Hackman, Russell Crowe and Leonardo DiCaprio) is a picture which, on the one hand, fascinates in more than one way and, on the other hand, amazes with its difficult to define approach. Partly trashy, partly bizarre, it evokes *Johnny Guitar* in both its aesthetic appeal and its heroine's characterization.

The celebrities that passed away in 1995 include two remarkable actor/singers—Dean Martin, who starred in about a dozen westerns, including *Rio Bravo, The Sons of Katie Elder* and *Bandolero!*; and Burl Ives, who gave a few memorable western performances, notably in such films as *Station West*, *The Big Country* and *Day of the Outlaw*.

The 1995 recipient of the Honorary Oscar was Kirk Douglas, a distinguished actor who rode in many westerns, including *The Big Sky*, *Man Without a Star*, *Gunfight at the O.K. Corral*, *Last Train from Gun Hill* and *The Last Sunset*, and gave an unforgettable performance in the modern elegy *Lonely Are the Brave*.

1996

Outstanding Achievements

None!

Deaths. Writer Marvin H. Albert; screenwriter George Zuckerman; cinematographers John Alton (b. 1901), Joseph F. Biroc (b. 1903), William H. Clothier (b. 1903); actors Martin Balsam, Whit Bissell (b. 1909), Ben Johnson, Lash La Rue, Guy Madison, Willard Parker (b. 1912); actresses Luana Anders, Virginia Christine, Joanne Dru.

The only highlight of the year was the Academy Award nomination granted to the modern western mystery *Lone Star* (starring Chris Cooper, Kris Kristofferson and Ron Canada) for the original screenplay by John Sayles, who also directed the picture.

The 1996 obituaries reported the death of many western-related people, including William H. Clothier, a distinguished cinematographer who photographed westerns for William A. Wellman (*Track of the Cat*), John Ford (*The Horse Soldiers, The Man Who Shot Liberty Valance, Cheyenne Autumn*), Sam Peckinpah (*The Deadly Companions*), Howard Hawks (*Rio Lobo*) and several other major directors of the genre; and Ben Johnson, who portrayed cowboys in many unforgettable westerns under the guidance of Ford (*She Wore a Yellow Ribbon, Wagon Master, Rio Grande*), Peckinpah (*Major Dundee, The Wild Bunch*), George Stevens (*Shane*), Richard Brooks (*Bite the Bullet*) and many others.

1997

Outstanding Achievements

None!

Deaths. Screenwriters Harry Essex (b. 1910), William Roberts (b. 1913); directors Samuel Fuller (b. 1911), Fred Zinnemann (b. 1907); actors Richard Jaeckel, Brian Keith, Burgess Meredith (b. 1908), Robert Mitchum, Denver Pyle, James Stewart (b. 1908); actresses Sally Blane (b. 1910), Billie Dove (b. 1900), Eve McVeagh.

While there were no standard western films released in 1997, the genre's fans mourned the death of two outstanding screen cowboys—James Stewart and Robert Mitchum. Stewart, who managed to develop a successful and original western persona, appeared in nearly 20 western movies, including such classics as *Destry Rides Again, Broken Arrow, Bend of the River, The Man from Laramie, The Man Who Shot Liberty Valance, Shenandoah* and *The Shootist*. And Mitchum starred in about the same number of westerns, the most important ones of which include *Blood on the Moon, River of No Return, Track of the Cat, The Wonderful Country, The Way West* and *El Dorado*.

1998

Outstanding Achievements

None!

Deaths. Cinematographer Charles B. Lang, Jr. (b. 1902); actors Lloyd Bridges (b. 1913), Richard Denning, John Derek, Gene Evans, Roddy McDowall, Roy Rogers (b. 1911), Frank Sinatra, Robert Young (b. 1907); actresses Josephine Hutchinson (b. 1903), Jeanette Nolan (b. 1911), Maureen O'Sullivan (b. 1911), Helen Westcott.

In the absence of a standard western in 1998, there were a couple of quasi-westerns that were enjoyed by the public and somewhat recognized by the Academy. Robert Redford's modern melodrama *The Horse Whisperer* (starring Redford, Kristin Scott Thomas and Sam Neill) was nominated for the song "A Soft Place to Fall," written by Allison Moorer and Gwil Owen. Martin Campbell's Old-California swashbuckling adventure *The Mask of Zorro* (featuring Antonio Banderas, Anthony Hopkins, Catherine Zeta-Jones and Stuart Wilson)—nota bene, inspired more by Alexandre Dumas' *The Count of Monte Cristo* than the characters created by Johnson McCulley—won two nominations: for sound and sound effects editing.

Among the celebrities that passed away in 1998, two seem most important to the genre—Roy Rogers, the king of the B western, and Charles B. Lang, Jr., an outstanding cinematographer whose western credits include such gems as *The Man from Laramie*, *Gunfight at the O.K. Corral*, *Last Train from Gun Hill*, *The Magnificent Seven* and *How the West Was Won*.

Three stars of the "B" western: Roy Rogers (1911–1998), Dale Evans (1912–2001) and George "Gabby" Hayes (1885–1969).

1999

Outstanding Achievements

None!

Deaths. Screenwriter Harold Jack Bloom; cinematographer Maury Gertsman (b. 1907); composer Frank De Vol (b. 1911); songwriter Terry Gilkyson; actors Rory Calhoun, Henry Jones (b. 1912), DeForest Kelley, Victor Mature; actresses Ellen Corby (b. 1911), Ruth Roman.

With the audiences apparently less and less interested in the standard western, the only 1999 picture related to the genre was Barry Sonnenfeld's spoof *Wild Wild West* (starring Will Smith, Kevin Kline and Kenneth Branagh). Focused on gadgets and special effects, the movie was far less successful than Mel Brooks' *Blazing Saddles* (featuring Cleavon Little, Gene Wilder and Slim Pickens) from 1974. Although *Wild Wild West* was scored by Elmer Bernstein himself, the sound track features an anachronistic song, "Wild Wild West," written by Stevie Wonder, Will Smith and Mohanndas DeWese.

2000

Outstanding Achievements

None!

Rory Calhoun, a star of many western pictures (*The Silver Whip*, *River of No Return*, *The Spoilers*, 1956), passed away in 1999.

Deaths. Directors James B. Clark (b. 1908), Joseph H. Lewis (b. 1907); composer George Duning (b. 1908); actors Richard Farnsworth, Leo Gordon, Walter Matthau, George Montgomery, Jason Robards, Jr.; actresses Ann Doran (b. 1911), Julie London, Jean Peters, Gloria Talbott, Claire Trevor (b. 1909), Marie Windsor, Loretta Young (b. 1913).

Again, no standard western. Instead, the western fans were offered four pictures indirectly related to the genre. They included one post–World War II drama set mostly in Mexico—*All the Pretty Horses* (starring Matt Damon, Henry Thomas, Lucas Black and Penelope Cruz), an adaptation of Cormac McCarthy's 1992 excellent novel, which director Billy Bob Thornton failed to turn into a masterful movie; and one Revolutionary War drama—*The Patriot* (featuring Mel Gibson, Heath Ledger and Joey Richardson), which became a moderate success in the hands of director Roland Emmerick. Furthermore, the year saw two interesting hybrids: one oriental/occidental comedy, *Shanghai Noon* (with Jackie Chan, Owen Wilson and Lucy Liu), which director Tom Dey turned into a lot of fun and filled with numerous allusions to such western pictures as *Red Sun*, *Butch Cassidy and the Sundance Kid* and *The Quick and the Dead*; and one science-fiction adventure, *Space Cowboys* (starring Clint Eastwood, Tommy Lee Jones, Donald Sutherland and James Garner), in which producer/director Eastwood, with help from his regulars (cinematographer Jack N. Green and composer Lennie Niehaus), captured a rare kind of nostalgic flavor, greatly

2001

George Montgomery, who appeared in numerous medium- and low-budget westerns (*The Texas Rangers*, 1951, *Gun Belt*, *Robbers' Roost*), died in 2000.

Outstanding Achievements

CINEMATOGRAPHY: Russell Boyd, *American Outlaws;* Daryn Okada, *Texas Rangers*

MALE SUPPORTING ROLE: Timothy Dalton, *American Outlaws*; Tom Skerritt, *Texas Rangers*

FEMALE SUPPORTING ROLE: Kathy Bates, *American Outlaws*

Deaths. Writers Dan Cushman (b. 1909), Tom Lea (b. 1907), Charles Neider; director Budd Boetticher; songwriter Jay Livingston; actors John Mitchum, Anthony Quinn; actresses Dale Evans (b. 1912), Kathleen Freeman.

Even though, at last, two standard westerns were released— Les Mayfield's *American Outlaws* (starring Colin Farrell, Scott Caan, Ali Larter and Gabriel Macht) and Steve Miner's *Texas Rangers* (featuring James Van Der Beek, Dylan McDermott, Usher Raymond and Ashton Kutcher)—neither of them deserves to be recognized as a successful picture. In both cases, the juvenile and clichéd script could not be saved by either mediocre and miscast actors or uninspired direction. Only the remarkable photography and some good performances by the supporting players make the movies worth seeing. Let us hope that the announcements of the genre's demise have not come true yet.

In addition to Anthony Quinn, an Oscar-winning actor who appeared in numerous westerns, including *The Plainsman, Union Pacific, The Ox-Bow Incident, Last Train from Gun Hill, Warlock* and *Heller in Pink Tights*, western fans lost one remarkable director, Budd Boetticher

benefiting from the charismatic stars' performances as well as the references to well-known western situations.

The people with the greatest contribution to the genre among those that died in 2000 include Claire Trevor, the talented actress who starred in such westerns as *Stagecoach, Texas, The Desperadoes* and *Man Without a Star*; Jason Robards, a brilliant character actor who appeared in several outstanding westerns, including *Hour of the Gun, The Ballad of Cable Hogue* and *Pat Garrett and Billy the Kid*; and George Duning, a distinguished composer who scored such classics as *The Man from Colorado, The Man from Laramie* and *3:10 to Yuma*.

(*Seven Men from Now*, *The Tall T*, *Ride Lonesome*, *Comanche Station*), and three major writers who each contributed to the genre with at least one superior novel: Tom Lea (*The Wonderful Country*), Charles Neider (*The Authentic Death of Hendry Jones*, filmed as *One-Eyed Jacks*) and Dan Cushman (*Timberjack*; *Stay Away, Joe*).

Although some of the greatest western writers are gone, western literature is far from dead: there are more and more new people trying their hand at the western novel, short story or poetry. Those who have discovered the beauty, the moral power and the universality of western fiction, along with its unquestioned historical and mythological assets, will never doubt the importance of such books as *The Virginian*, *The Ox-Bow Incident*, *Monte Walsh* and *Lonesome Dove*. They will read the works of authors such as Owen Wister, Walter Van Tilburg Clark, Jack Schaefer and Larry McMurtry, and impatiently look out for their successors. As Jon Tuska put it in his introduction to *Western Stories: A Chronological Anthology*, "Only when courage and hope are gone will the Western story cease to be relevant to all of us." Let us hope that the people in charge of movie production will also and always be aware of that axiom.

Appendix A

Top 100 Films

Below is the list of the pictures without which I could not imagine the history of the western film, but it should be recognized that there are at least fifty more movies that deserve to be included here. I regret that I was not able to include several more silent pictures (in particular, John Ford's *The Outcasts of Poker Flat* and *Three Bad Men*, Cecil B. De Mille's *The Squaw Man* and *The Virginian* [both 1914], Henry King's *The Winning of Barbara Worth*, and a few films with William S. Hart and Tom Mix) and some early talkies (William Wyler's *Hell's Heroes*, Raoul Walsh's *The Big Trail* and Edward L. Cahn's *Law and Order)*. However, the most obvious runners-up are some westerns made in the golden years of the genre—Henry Hathaway's *Rawhide* and *North to Alaska*; Delmer Daves' *The Last Wagon*, *Jubal* and *Cowboy*; William A. Wellman's *The Great Man's Lady* and *Buffalo Bill*; George Marshall's *Texas* and *When the Daltons Rode*; Fritz Lang's *The Return of Frank James*; Sergio Leone's *A Fistful of Dollars* and *For a Few Dollars More*; Budd Boetticher's *Ride Lonesome*; Robert Aldrich's *Apache* and *The Last Sunset*; Joseph Kane's *Ride the Man Down*; Anthony Mann's *The Furies*; Robert Parrish's *The Wonderful Country*; Edwin Sherin's *Valdez Is Coming*; Phillip Borsos's *The Grey Fox*; and Ford's *3 Godfathers* and *The Horse Soldiers*.

1. *High Noon* (UA, 1952). Sc. Carl Foreman, from the short story "The Tin Star" by John M. Cunningham. Dir. Fred Zinnemann. Phot. Floyd Crosby. Music by Dimitri Tiomkin. Song "Do Not Forsake Me, Oh My Darlin'" by Dimitri Tiomkin and Ned Washington. The cast: Gary Cooper (Will Kane), Grace Kelly (Amy Kane), Thomas Mitchell (Jonas Henderson), Katy Jurado (Helen Ramirez), Lloyd Bridges (Harvey Pell), Henry Morgan (William Fuller), Otto Kruger (Judge Percy Mettrick), Lon Chaney, Jr. (Martin Howe), Eve McVeagh (Mildred Fuller), James Millican (Herb Baker), Morgan Farley (minister), Ian Mac Donald (Frank Miller), Sheb Wooley (Ben Miller), Lee Van Cleef (Jack Colby), Robert Wilke (James Pierce).

Four Academy Awards and three nominations (including one for best picture).

2. *Stagecoach* (UA, 1939). Sc. Dudley Nichols, from the short story "Stage to Lordsburg" by Ernest Haycox. Dir. John Ford. Phot. Bert Glennon. Music by Richard Hageman, W. Franke Harling, John Leipold and Leo Shuken. The cast: Claire Trevor (Dallas), John Wayne

(Ringo Kid), Thomas Mitchell (Dr. Josiah Boone), George Bancroft (Sheriff Curley Wilcox), Andy Devine (Buck Rickabaugh), John Carradine (Hatfield), Louise Platt (Lucy Mallory), Donald Meek (Samuel Peacock), Berton Churchill (Henry Gatewood), Tim Holt (Lt. Blanchard), Chris-Pin Martin (Chris), Francis Ford (Billy Pickett), Tom Tyler (Luke Plummer), Yakima Canutt (Cavalry scout).

Two Academy Awards and five nominations (including one for best picture).

3. *Red River* (UA, 1948). Sc. Borden Chase and Charles Schnee, from the novel *The Chisholm Trail* by Borden Chase. Dir. Howard Hawks. Phot. Russell Harlan. Music by Dimitri Tiomkin. Song "Settle Down" by Dimitri Tiomkin. The cast: John Wayne (Thomas Dunson), Montgomery Clift (Matthew Garth), Joanne Dru (Tess Millay), Walter Brennan (Groot Nadine), John Ireland (Cherry Valance), Coleen Gray (Fen), Noah Beery, Jr. (Buster McGee), Harry Carey, Sr. (Mr. Melville), Harry Carey, Jr. (Dan Latimer), Paul Fix (Teeler Yacey), Mickey Kuhn (Matt as a boy), Chief Yowlachie (Quo), Hank Worden (Sims), Hal Taliaferro (Old Leather), Tom Tyler (a quitter), Glenn Strange (Naylor), Shelley Winters (dancehall girl).

Two Academy Award nominations.

4. *My Darling Clementine* (20th C-F, 1946). Sc. Samuel G. Engel and Winston Miller, from the screenplay by Sam Hellman, based on the book *Wyatt Earp: Frontier Marshal* by Stuart N. Lake. Dir. John Ford. Phot. Joseph MacDonald. Music by Cyril Mockridge. The cast: Henry Fonda (Wyatt Earp), Victor Mature (Doc Holliday), Linda Darnell (Chihuahua), Walter Brennan (Old Man Clanton), Ward Bond (Morgan Earp), Tim Holt (Virgil Earp), Cathy Downs (Clementine), John Ireland (Billy Clanton), Alan Mowbray (Thorndyke), Roy Roberts (mayor), Jane Darwell (Kate) Grant Withers (Ike Clanton), J. Farrell MacDonald (bartender), Russell Simpson (John Simpson), Don Garner (James Earp), Francis Ford (town drunk), Harry Woods (marshal), Charles Stevens (Indian Charlie).

5. *Rio Bravo* (WB, 1959). Sc. Jules Furthman and Leigh Brackett, from a story by B.H. McCampbell. Dir. Howard Hawks. Phot. Russell Harlan. Music by Dimitri Tiomkin. Songs "Rio Bravo" and "My Rifle, My Pony and Me" by Dimitri Tiomkin and Paul Francis Webster. The cast: John Wayne (John T. Chance), Dean Martin (Dude), Ricky Nelson (Colorado Ryan), Angie Dickinson (Feathers), Walter Brennan (Stumpy), Ward Bond (Pat Wheeler), John Russell (Nathan Burdette), Claude Akins (Joe Burdette), Pedro Gonzalez-Gonzalez (Carlos), Estelita Rodriguez (Consuela), Malcolm Atterbury (Jake), Bob Steele (Matt Harris), Myron Healey (barfly), Fred Graham (gunman).

6. *Shane* (Par., 1953). Sc. A.B. Guthrie, Jr. (Additional Dialogue by Jack Sher), from the novel *Shane* by Jack Schaefer. Dir. George Stevens. Phot. Loyal Griggs. Music by Victor Young. The cast: Alan Ladd (Shane), Jean Arthur (Marian Starrett), Van Heflin (Joe Starrett), Brandon De Wilde (Joey Starrett), Jack Palance (Jack Wilson), Ben Johnson (Chris Callaway), Edgar Buchanan (Fred Lewis), Emile Meyer (Rufus Ryker), Elisha Cook, Jr. (Stonewall Torrey), Douglas Spencer (Shipstead), John Dierkes (Morgan Ryker), Ellen Corby (Mrs. Torrey), Paul McVey (Sam Grafton), Edith Evanson (Mrs. Shipstead).

One Academy Award and five nominations (including one for best picture).

7. *The Searchers* (WB, 1956). Sc. Frank S. Nugent, from the novel *The*

Searchers by Alan LeMay. Dir. John Ford. Phot. Winton C. Hoch. Music by Max Steiner. Title song by Stan Jones. The cast: John Wayne (Ethan Edwards), Jeffrey Hunter (Martin Pauley), Vera Miles (Laurie Jorgensen), Ward Bond (Capt. Rev. Clayton), Natalie Wood (Debbie Reynolds), John Qualen (Lars Jorgensen), Olive Carey (Mrs. Jorgensen), Ken Curtis (Charlie MacCorry), Henry Brandon (Chief Scar), Harry Carey, Jr. (Brad Jorgensen), Antonio Moreno (Emilio Figueroa), Hank Worden (Mose Harper), Patrick Wayne (Lt. Greenhill), Walter Coy (Aaron Edwards), Dorothy Jordan (Martha Edwards), Pippa Scott (Lucy Edwards).

8. *3:10 to Yuma* (Col., 1957). Sc. Halsted Welles, from the story "3:10 to Yuma" by Elmore Leonard. Dir. Delmer Daves. Phot. Charles Lawton, Jr. Music by George Duning. Title song by George Duning and Ned Washington. The cast: Glenn Ford (Ben Wade), Van Heflin (Dan Evans), Felicia Farr (Emmy), Leora Dana (Alice Evans), Henry Jones (Alex Potter), Richard Jaeckel (Charlie Prince), Robert Emhardt (Mr. Butterfield), George Mitchell (bartender), Robert Ellenstein (Ernie Collins), Ford Rainey (marshal), Barry Curtis (Matthew).

9. *The Wild Bunch* (WB-7 Arts, 1969). Sc. Walon Green, Roy N. Sickner and Sam Peckinpah. Dir. Sam Peckinpah. Phot. Lucien Ballard. Music by Jerry Fielding. The cast: William Holden (Pike Bishop), Ernest Borgnine (Dutch Engstrom), Robert Ryan (Deke Thornton), Edmond O'Brien (Sykes), Warren Oates (Lyle Gorch), Jaime Sanchez (Angel), Ben Johnson (Tector Gorch), Emilio Fernandez (Mapache), Strother Martin (Coffer), L.Q. Jones (T.C.), Albert Dekker (Pat Harrigan), Bo Hopkins (Crazy Lee), Dub Taylor (Mayor Wainscoat), Barry Sullivan (Chisum, in the director's cut only).

Two Academy Award nominations.

10. *Butch Cassidy and the Sundance Kid* (20th C-F, 1969). Sc. William Goldman. Dir. George Roy Hill. Phot. Conrad Hall. Music by Burt Bacharach. Song "Raindrops Keep Fallin' on My Head" by Burt Bacharach and Hal David. The cast: Paul Newman (Butch Cassidy), Robert Redford (Sundance Kid), Katharine Ross (Etta Place), Strother Martin (Percy Garris), Henry Jones (bicycle vender), Jeff Corey (Sheriff Bledsoe), Cloris Leachman (Agnes), Ted Cassidy (Harvey Logan), Kenneth Mars (marshal), Donnelly Rhodes (Macon), Sam Elliott (card player), Percy Helton (little man).

Four Academy Awards and three nominations (including one for best picture).

11. *Ride the High Country* (MGM, 1962). Sc. N.B. Stone, Jr. Dir. Sam Peckinpah. Phot. Lucien Ballard. Music by George Bassman. The cast: Randolph Scott (Gil Westrum), Joel McCrea (Steve Judd), Ronald Starr (Heck Longtree), Mariette Hartley (Elsa Knudsen), R.G. Armstrong (Joshua Knudsen), James Drury (Billy Hammond), Edgar Buchanan (Judge Tolliver), Jennie Jackson (Kate), John Anderson (Elder Hammond), L.Q. Jones (Sylvus Hammond), Warren Oates (Henry Hammond), John Davis Chandler (Jimmy Hammond), Percy Helton (banker).

12. *The Westerner* (UA, 1940). Sc. Stuart N. Lake, Jo Swerling and Niven Busch. Dir. William Wyler. Phot. Gregg Toland. Music by Dimitri Tiomkin. The cast: Gary Cooper (Cole Hardin), Walter Brennan (Judge Roy Bean), Doris Davenport (Jane-Ellen Mathews), Fred Stone (Caliphet Mathews), Paul Hurst (Chickenfoot), Chill Wills (Southeast), Charles Halton (Mort Borrow), Forrest Tucker (Wade Harper), Tom Tyler (King Evans), Arthur Aylesworth (Mr. Dixon), Lupita Tovar (Teresita), Lillian Bond (Lily Langtry), Dana Andrews (Bart Cobble), Jack Pennick (Bantry), Trevor Bardette (Shad Wilkins), Jim Corey (Lee Webb).

One Academy Award and two nominations.

13. *The Ox-Bow Incident* (20th C-F, 1943). Sc. Lamar Trotti, from the novel by Walter Van Tilburg Clark. Dir. William A. Wellman. Phot. Arthur C. Miller. Music by Cyril J. Mockridge. The cast: Henry Fonda (Gil Carter), Dana Andrews (Donald Martin), Mary Beth Hughes (Rose Mapen), Anthony Quinn (Mexican), William Eythe (Gerald Tetley), Henry Morgan (Art Croft), Jane Darwell (Ma Grier), Francis Ford (old man), Matt Briggs (Judge Tyler), Harry Davenport (Arthur Davies), Frank Conroy (Major Tetley), Marc Lawrence (Jeff Farnley), Victor Kilian (Darby), Paul Hurst (Monty Smith), Chris-Pin Martin (Pancho), Willard Robertson (sheriff), George Meeker (Mr. Swanson).

One Academy Award nomination (for best picture).

14. *The Magnificent Seven* (UA, 1960). Sc. William Roberts, from the original screenplay for *The Seven Samurai*. Dir. John Sturges. Phot. Charles Lang, Jr. Music by Elmer Bernstein. The cast: Yul Brynner (Chris), Steve McQueen (Vin), Horst Buchholz (Chico), Eli Wallach (Calvera), James Coburn (Britt), Charles Bronson (Bernardo O'Reilly), Robert Vaughn (Lee), Brad Dexter (Harry Luck), Vladimir Sokoloff (old man), Rosenda Monteros (Mexican girl), Robert Wilke (man that challenged Britt), Whit Bissell (undertaker), Val Avery and Bing Russell (men in town).

One Academy Award nomination.

15 *The Big Country* (UA, 1958). Sc. James R. Webb, Sy Bartlett, Robert Wilder, Jessamyn West and Robert Wyler, from the novel by Donald Hamilton. Dir. William Wyler. Phot. Franz Planer. Music by Jerome Moross. The cast: Gregory Peck (James McKay), Jean Simmons (Julie Maragon), Carroll Baker (Patricia Terrill), Charlton Heston (Steve Leech), Burl Ives (Rufus Hannassey), Charles Bickford (Maj. Henry Terrill), Alfonso Bedoya (Ramon), Chuck Connors (Buck Hannassey), Chuck Hayward (Rafe Hannassey).

One Academy Award and one nomination.

16. *Unforgiven* (WB, 1992). Sc. David Webb Peoples. Dir. Clint Eastwood. Phot. Jack N. Green. Music by Lennie Niehaus. The cast: Clint Eastwood (William Munny), Gene Hackman (Little Bill Daggett), Morgan Freeman (Ned Logan), Richard Harris (English Bob), Jaimz Woolvett (The "Schofield Kid"), Saul Rubinek (W.W. Beauchamp), Frances Fisher (Strawberry Alice), Anna Thomson (Delilah Fitzgerald), David Mucci (Quick Mike), Bob Campbell (Davey Bunting), Anthony James (Skinny Dubois), Tara Dawn Frederick (Little Sue).

Four Academy Awards (including one for best picture) and five nominations.

17. *Destry Rides Again* (Univ., 1939). Sc. Felix Jackson, Gertrude Purcell and Henry Myers, from the novel by Max Brand. Dir. George Marshall. Phot. Hal Mohr. Music by Frank Skinner. Songs "Little Joe the Wrangler," "You've Got That Look" and "The Boys in the Back Room" by Frederick Hollander and Frank Loesser. The cast: James Stewart (Tom Destry), Marlene Dietrich (Frenchy), Mischa Auer (Boris Callahan), Charles Winninger (Wash Dimsdale), Brian Donlevy (Kent), Allen Jenkins (Gyp Watson), Warren Hymer (Bugs Watson), Irene Hervey (Janice Tyndall), Una Merkel (Lily Belle Callahan), Tom Fadden (Lem Claggett), Samuel S. Hinds (Judge Hiram

Slade), Billy Gilbert (bartender), Virginia Brissac (Sophie Claggett), Jack Carson (Jack Tyndall).

18. *The Man Who Shot Liberty Valance* (Par., 1962). Sc. James Warner Bellah and Willis Goldbeck, from the short story by Dorothy M. Johnson. Dir. John Ford. Phot. William H. Clothier. Music by Cyril Mockridge. The cast: John Wayne (Tom Doniphon), James Stewart (Ranse Stoddard), Vera Miles (Hallie), Lee Marvin (Liberty Valance), Edmond O'Brien (Dutton Peabody), Andy Devine (Link Appleyard), Ken Murray (Dr. Willoughby), Jeanette Nolan (Nora), John Qualen (Peter), Woody Strode (Pompey), Willis Bouchey (Jason Tully), Carleton Young (Maxwell Scott), Denver Pyle (Amos Carruthers), Strother Martin (Floyd), Lee Van Cleef (Reese), Robert F. Simon (Handy Strong), Paul Birch (Mayor Winders), O.Z. Whitehead (Ben Carruthers).

One Academy Award nomination.

19. *Fort Apache* (RKO, 1948). Sc. Frank S. Nugent, from the short story "Massacre" by James Warner Bellah. Dir. John Ford. Phot. Archie Stout. Music by Richard Hageman. The cast: John Wayne (Capt. Kirby York), Henry Fonda (Lt. Col. Owen Thursday), Shirley Temple (Philadelphia Thursday), John Agar (Lt. Michael O'Rourke), Ward Bond (Sgt. Maj. Michael O'Rourke), George O'Brien (Capt. Sam Collingwood), Victor McLaglen (Sgt. Mulcahy), Pedro Armendariz (Sgt. Beaufort), Anna Lee (Mrs. Collingwood), Irene Rich (Mrs. O'Rourke), Miguel Inclan (Chief Cochise), Dick Foran (Sgt. Quincannon), Jack Pennick (Sgt. Shattuck), Guy Kibbee (Dr. Wilkens), Grant Withers (Silas Meacham), Mae Marsh (Martha Gates), Hank Worden (Southern recruit), Francis Ford (Fen, the stage guard), Cliff Clark (stage driver), Frank Ferguson (newspaperman).

20. *She Wore a Yellow Ribbon* (RKO, 1949). Sc. Frank S. Nugent and Laurence Stallings, from the short stories "War Party," "Command" and "Big Hunt" by James Warner Bellah. Dir. John Ford. Phot. Winton C. Hoch. Music by Richard Hageman. The cast: John Wayne (Capt. Nathan Brittles), Joanne Dru (Olivia Dandridge), John Agar (Lt. Flint Cohill), Ben Johnson (Sgt. Tyree), Harry Carey, Jr. (Lt. Ross Pennell), Victor McLaglen (Sgt. Quincannon), Mildred Natwick (Mrs. Allshard), George O'Brien (Maj. Allshard), Arthur Shields (Dr. O'Laughlin), Francis Ford (bartender), Harry Woods (Karl Rynders), Noble Johnson (Red Shirt), Cliff Lyons (Cliff), Tom Tyler (Capt. Mike Quayne), Michael Dugan (Sgt. Hochbauer), Mickey Simpson (Wagner).

One Academy Award.

21. *The Ballad of Cable Hogue* (WB, 1970). Sc. John Crawford and Edmund Penney. Dir. Sam Peckinpah. Phot. Lucien Ballard. Music by Jerry Goldsmith. Songs "Tomorrow Is the Song I Sing" by Jerry Goldsmith and Richard Gillis; "Wait for Me, Sunrise" and "Butterfly Mornings" by Richard Gillis. The cast: Jason Robards (Cable Hogue), Stella Stevens (Hildy), David Warner (Joshua Duncan Sloane), Strother Martin (Samuel Bowen), J.Q. Jones (Taggart), Slim Pickens (Ben), Felix Nelson (stage guard), R.G. Armstrong (Quittner), Kathleen Freeman (stage passenger), Gene Evans (Clete).

22. *The Professionals* (Col., 1966). Sc. and Dir. Richard Brooks (from the novel *A Mule for the Marquesa* by Frank O'Rourke). Phot. Conrad Hall. Music by Maurice Jarre. The cast: Burt Lancaster (Bill Dolworth), Lee Marvin (Henry Rico Fardan), Robert Ryan (Hans Ehrengard), Woody Strode (Jake Sharp), Jack Palance (Jesus Raza), Claudia Cardinale (Maria Grant), Ralph Bellamy (Joe Grant).

Three Academy Award nominations.

23. *Bend of the River* (Univ., 1952). Sc. Borden Chase, from the novel *Bend of the Snake* by Bill Gulick. Dir. Anthony Mann. Phot. Irving Glassberg. Music by Hans J. Salter. The cast: James Stewart (Glyn McLyntock), Arthur Kennedy (Cole Garrett), Julia Adams (Laura Baile), Rock Hudson (Trey Wilson), Lori Nelson (Marjie Baile), Jay C. Flippen (Jeremy Baile), Harry Morgan (Shorty), Chubby Johnson (Cap'n Mello), Howard Petrie (Tom Hendrickson), Royal Dano (Long Tom), Stepin Fetchit (Adam), Jack Lambert (Red), Frank Ferguson (Don Grundy), Frances Bavier (Mrs. Prentiss).

24. *The Gunfighter* (20th C-F, 1950). Sc. William Bowers, Andre De Toth, and William Sellers. Dir. Henry King. Phot. Arthur C. Miller. Music by Alfred Newman. The cast: Gregory Peck (Jimmy Ringo), Helen Westcott (Peggy Walsh), Millard Mitchell (Marshal Mark Strett), Jean Parker (Molly), Karl Malden (Mac), Skip Homeier (Hunt Bromley), Anthony Ross (Charlie), Ellen Corby (Mrs. Devlin), Richard Jaeckel (Eddie), Alan Hale, Jr. (first brother), David Clarke (second brother), John Pickard (third brother), Cliff Clark (Jerry Marlowe), Verna Felton (Mrs. Pennyfeather), D.G. Norman (Jimmie).

One Academy Award nomination.

25. *Warlock* (20th C-F, 1959). Sc. Robert Alan Aurthur, from the novel by Oakley Hall. Dir. Edward Dmytryk. Phot. Joseph MacDonald. Music by Leigh Harline. The cast: Richard Widmark (Johnny Gannon), Henry Fonda (Clay Blaisdell), Anthony Quinn (Tom Morgan), Dorothy Malone (Lily Dollar), Dolores Michaels (Jessie Marlow), Wallace Ford (Judge Holloway), Tom Drake (Abe McQuown), Richard Arlen (Bacon), DeForest Kelley (Curley Burne), Regis Toomey (Skinner), Vaughn Taylor (Richardson), Don Beddoe (Dr. Wagner), Whit Bissell (Mr. Petrix), Ian MacDonald (MacDonald), L.Q. Jones (Jiggs).

26. *The Tin Star* (Par., 1957). Sc. Barney Slater, Joel Kane, Dudley Nichols. Dir. Anthony Mann. Phot. Loyal Griggs. Music by Elmer Bernstein. The cast: Henry Fonda (Morg Hickman), Anthony Perkins (Ben Owens), Betsy Palmer (Nona Mayfield), Michel Ray (Kip Mayfield), Neville Brand (Bart Bogardus), John McIntire (Doc Joseph McCord), Mary Webster (Millie Parker), Peter Baldwin (Zeke McGaffey), Lee Van Cleef (Ed McGaffey), Richard Shannon (Buck Henderson), James Bell (Judge Thatcher), Howard Petrie (Harvey King), Russell Simpson (Clem Hall).

One Academy Award nomination.

27. *Gunfight at the O.K. Corral* (Par., 1957). Sc. Leon Uris, from an article by George Scullin. Dir. John Sturges. Phot. Charles Lang, Jr. Music by Dimitri Tiomkin. Title song by Dimitri Tiomkin and Ned Washington. The cast: Burt Lancaster (Wyatt Earp), Kirk Douglas (Doc Holliday), Rhonda Fleming (Laura Denbow), Jo Van Fleet (Kate Fisher), John Ireland (Ringo), Lyle Bettger (Ike Clanton), Frank Faylen (Cotton Wilson), Earl Holliman (Charles Bassett), Ted De Corsia (Shanghai Pierce), Dennis Hopper (Billy Clanton), Whit Bissell (John P. Clum), George Mathews (John Shanssey), John Hudson (Virgil Earp), DeForest Kelley (Morgan Earp), Kenneth Tobey (Bat Masterson), Lee Van Cleef (Ed Bailey), Olive Carey (Mrs. Clanton), Joan Camden (Betty Earp), Brian Hutton (Rick).

Two Academy Award nominations.

28. *Hombre* (20th C-F, 1967). Sc. Irving Ravetch and Harriet Frank, Jr., from the novel by Elmore Leonard. Dir. Martin Ritt. Phot. James Wong Howe. Music by David Rose. The cast: Paul

Newman (John Russell, "Hombre"), Fredric March (Alexander Favor), Richard Boone (Cicero Grimes), Diane Cilento (Jessie Brown), Cameron Mitchell (Sheriff Frank Braden), Barbara Rush (Audra Favor), Martin Balsam (Henry Mendez), Peter Lazer (Billy Lee Blake), Margaret Blye (Doris Lee Blake), Frank Silvera (Mexican bandit), David Canary (Lamar), Larry Ward (a soldier), Val Avery (Delgado).

29. *The Shootist* (WB, 1976). Sc. Miles Hood Swarthout and Scott Hale, from the novel by Glendon Swarthout. Dir. Don Siegel. Phot. Bruce Surtees. Music by Elmer Bernstein. The cast: John Wayne (John Bernard Books), Lauren Bacall (Bond Rogers), Ron Howard (Gillom Rogers), James Stewart (Dr. Hostetler), Richard Boone (Sweeney), Hugh O'Brian (Pulford), Bill McKinney (Cobb), Harry Morgan (Marshal Thibido), John Carradine (Beckum), Sheree North (Serepta), Richard Lenz (Dobkins), Scatman Crothers (Moses), Alfred Dennis (barber).

One Academy Award nomination.

30. *Dances with Wolves* (TIG, 1990). Sc. Michael Blake from his own novel. Dir. Kevin Costner. Phot. Dean Semler. Music by John Barry. The cast: Kevin Costner (Lt. John Dunbar), Mary McDonnell (Christine), Graham Greene (Kicking Bird), Rodney A. Grant (Wind in His Hair).

Seven Academy Awards (including one for best picture) and five nominations.

31. *The Man from Laramie* (Col., 1955). Sc. Philip Yordan and Frank Burt, from the novel by T.T. Flynn. Dir. Anthony Mann. Phot. Charles Lang, Jr. Music by George Duning. The cast: James Stewart (Will Lockhart), Arthur Kennedy (Vic Hansbro), Donald Crisp (Alec Waggoman), Cathy O'Donnell (Barbara Waggoman), Alex Nicol (Dave Waggoman), Aline MacMahon (Kate Canaday), Wallace Ford (Charley O'Leary), Jack Elam (Chris Boldt), John War Eagle (Frank Darrah), James Millican (Sheriff Tom Quigby), Gregg Barton (Fritz), Boyd Stockman (Spud Oxton), Frank De Kova (Padre).

32. *True Grit* (Par., 1969). Sc. Marguerite Roberts, from the novel by Charles Portis. Dir. Henry Hathaway. Phot. Lucien Ballard. Music by Elmer Bernstein. Title song by Elmer Bernstein and Don Black. The cast: John Wayne (Rooster Cogburn), Glen Campbell (La Boef), Kim Darby (Mattie Ross), Robert Duvall (Ned Pepper), Jeff Corey (Tom Chaney), Dennis Hopper (Moon), Jeremy Slate (Emmett Quincy), Strother Martin (Col. G. Stonehill), John Fiedler (Lawyer Daggett), Alfred Ryder (Goudy), James Westerfield (Judge Parker), John Doucette (sheriff), Donald Woods (Barlow), John Pickard (Frank Ross), Elizabeth Harrower (Mrs. Ross), Carlos Rivas (Dirty Bob), Isabel Boniface (Mrs. Bagby).

One Academy Award and one nomination.

33. *Hell's Hinges* (TRI, 1916). Sc. C. Gardner Sullivan. Dir. William S. Hart and Charles Swickard. Phot. Joseph August. The cast: William S. Hart (Blaze Tracy), Clara Williams (Faith Henley), Jack Standing (Rev. Robert Henley), Alfred Hollingsworth (Silk Miller), Robert McKim (clergyman), J. Frank Burke (Zeb Taylor), Louise Glaum (Dolly).

34. *Rio Grande* (Rep., 1950). Sc. James Kevin McGuinness, from the short story "Mission with No Record" by James Warner Bellah. Dir. John Ford. Phot. Bert Glennon. Music by Victor Young. Songs by Stan Jones. The cast: John Wayne (Lt. Col. Kirby Yorke), Maureen O'Hara (Kathleen Yorke), Ben Johnson (Trooper Travis Tyree), Claude Jarman, Jr. (Jeff

York), Harry Carey, Jr. (Trooper Daniel 'Sandy' Boone), J. Carrol Naish (General Sheridan), Victor McLaglen (Sgt Maj. Quincannon), Chill Wills (Dr. Wilkins), Grant Withers (US Deputy Marshal), Stan Jones (sergeant), Jack Pennick (sergeant).

35 *The Virginian* (Par., 1929). Sc. Howard Estabrook, Grover Jones, Keene Thompson and Edward E. Paramore, Jr., from the novel by Owen Wister and the play by Owen Wister and Kirk La Shelle. Dir. Victor Fleming. Phot. J. Roy Hunt and Edward Cronjager. The cast: Gary Cooper (The Virginian), Walter Huston (Trampas), Mary Brian (Molly Stark Wood), Richard Arlen (Steve), Helen Ware (Mrs. Taylor), Chester Conklin (Uncle Hughey), Eugene Pallette ("Honey" Wiggin), Victor Potel (Nebrasky), E.H. Calvert (Judge Henry), Tex Young (Shorty), Charles Stevens (Pedro), Jack Pennick (Slim), George Chandler (ranch hand), Willie Fung (Hong, the cook).

36. *Once Upon a Time in the West* (Rafran–San Marco/Par., Italy/US, 1969). Sc. Sergio Leone, Sergio Donati, Dario Argento and Bernardo Bertolucci. Dir. Sergio Leone. Phot. Tonino Delli Colli. Music by Ennio Morricone. The cast: Henry Fonda (Frank), Claudia Cardinale (Jill McBain), Charles Bronson (the Man "Harmonica"), Jason Robards (Cheyenne), Frank Wolff (Brett McBain), Gabriele Ferzetti (Morton), Keenan Wynn (Sheriff), Paolo Stoppa (Sam), Lionel Stander (bartender), Jack Elam (Knuckles), Woody Strode (Stony).

37. *Little Big Man* (Cinema Center, 1970). Sc. Calder Willingham, from the novel by Thomas Berger. Dir. Arthur Penn. Phot. Harry Stradling, Jr. Music by John Hammond. The cast: Dustin Hoffman (Jack Crabb), Chief Dan George (Old Lodge Skins), Richard Mulligan (George Armstrong Custer), Faye Dunaway (Louise Pendrake), Martin Balsam (Allardyce M. Meriweather), Jeff Corey (Wild Bill Hickok), Carol Androsky (Caroline Crabb), Kelly Jean Peters (Olga), Amy Eccles (Sunshine), Cal Bellini (Younger Bear), Robert Little Star (Little Horse), James Anderson (sergeant), Thayer David (Rev. Silas Pendrake), William Hickey (historian).

One Academy Award nomination.

38. *The Outlaw Josey Wales* (WB, 1976). Sc. Philip Kaufman, from the novel *Gone to Texas* by Forrest Carter. Dir. Clint Eastwood. Phot. Bruce Surtees. Music by Jerry Fielding. The cast: Clint Eastwood (Josey Wales), Chief Dan George (Lone Wolf), Sondra Locke (Laura Lee), Bill McKinney (Terrill), John Vernon (Fletcher), Paula Trueman (Grandma Sarah), Sam Bottoms (Jamie), Geraldine Keams (Little Moonlight), Sheb Wooley (Cobb), Matt Clark (Kelly), Will Sampson (Ten Bears), John Quade (Comanchero leader).

One Academy Award nomination.

39. *The Far Country* (Univ., 1955). Sc. Borden Chase. Dir. Anthony Mann. Phot. William Daniels. Music by Hans J. Salter. The cast: James Stewart (Jeff Webster), Ruth Roman (Ronda Castle), Corinne Calvet (Renee Vallon), Walter Brennan (Ben Tatum), John McIntire (Gannon), Jay C. Flippen (Rube), Henry Morgan (Ketchum), Seve Brodie (Ives), Connie Gilchrist (Hominy), Robert Wilke (Madden), Chubby Johnson (Dusty), Royal Dano (Luke), Jack Elam (Newberry), Kathleen Freeman (Grits).

40. *Pat Garrett and Billy the Kid* (MGM, 1973). Sc. Rudolph Wurlitzer. Dir. Sam Peckinpah. Phot. John Coquillon. Music by Bob Dylan. Songs "Far Away from Home"/"Billy" and "Knockin' on Heaven's Door" by Bob Dylan. The cast: James Coburn (Pat Garrett), Kris

Kristofferson ((Billy the Kid), Bob Dylan (Alias), John Beck (John W. Poe), Richard Bright (Holly), Luke Askew (Eno), Harry Dean Stanton (Luke Hight), Matt Clark (J.W. Bell), R.G. Armstrong (Bob Ollinger), Jason Robards (Governor Lew Wallace), Slim Pickens (Sheriff Baker), Katy Jurado (Mrs. Baker), Richard Jaeckel (Sheriff Kip McKinney), Jack Elam (Alamosa Bill Kermit), Chill Wills (Lemuel Jones), L.Q. Jones (Black Harris), John Chandler (Norris), Charles Martin Smith (Charlie Bowdre), Barry Sullivan (Chisum), Emilio Fernandez (Paco), Gene Evans (Horrell), Dub Taylor (Josh), Paul Fix (Pete Maxwell).

41. *The Naked Spur* (MGM, 1953). Sc. Sam Rolfe and Harold Jack Bloom. Dir. Anthony Mann. Phot. William C. Mellor. Music by Bronislau Kaper. The cast: James Stewart (Howard Kemp), Janet Leigh (Lina Patch), Robert Ryan (Ben Vandergroat), Ralph Meeker (Roy Anderson), Millard Mitchell (Jesse Tate).
One Academy Award nomination.

42. *The Iron Horse* (Fox, 1924). Sc. John Russell Kenyon, Charles Kenyon. Dir. John Ford. Phot. George Schneiderman and Burnett Guffey. Music by Erno Rapee. The cast: George O'Brien (Davy Brandon), Madge Bellamy (Miriam Marsh), Cyril Chadwick (Peter Jesson), Fred Kohler (Bauman), Gladys Hulette (Ruby), James Marcus (Judge Haller), Francis Powers (Sgt. Slattery), J. Farrell MacDonald (Cpl. Casey), James Welch (Pvt. Schultz), Walter Rogers (Gen. Dodge), Delbert Mann (Charles Crocker), Chief Big Tree (Cheyenne chief).

43. *Yellow Sky* (20th C-F, 1948). Sc. W.R. Burnett, Lamar Trotti. Dir. William A. Wellman. Phot. Joseph MacDonald. Music by Alfred Newman. The cast: Gregory Peck (Stretch), Anne Baxter (Mike), Richard Widmark (Dude), Robert Arthur (Bull Run), John Russell (Lengthy), Henry Morgan ((Half Pint), James Barton (Grandpa), Charles Kemper (Walrus), Robert Adler (Jed), Victor Kilian (bartender), Paul Hurst (drunk), Chief Yowlachie (Colorado), Hank Worden (rancher), Jay Silverheels (Indian).

44. *Last Train from Gun Hill* (Par., 1959). Sc. Les Crutchfield, James Poe. Dir. John Sturges. Phot. Charles B. Lang, Jr. Music by Dimitri Tiomkin. The cast: Kirk Douglas (Matt Morgan), Anthony Quinn (Craig Beldon), Carolyn Jones (Linda), Earl Holliman (Rick Beldon), Ziva Rodann (Catherine Morgan), Brad Dexter (Beero), Brian Hutton (Lee), Bing Russell (Skag), Val Avery (bartender), Walter Sande (Sheriff Bartlett), Lars Henderson (Petey Morgan), Henry Wills (Jake), Charles Stevens (Keno), Glenn Strange (saloon bouncer).

45. *Vera Cruz* (UA, 1954). Sc. Roland Kibbee and James R. Webb. Dir. Robert Aldrich. Phot. Ernest Laszlo. Music by Hugo Friedhofer. The cast: Gary Cooper (Benjamin Trane), Burt Lancaster (Joe Erin), Denise Darcel (Countess Marie Duvarre), Cesar Romero (Marquis de Labordere), Sarita Montiel (Nina), George Macready (Emperor Maximilian), Ernest Borgnine (Donnegan), Henry Brandon (Danette), Charles Bronson (Pittsburgh), Morris Ankrum (Gen. Aguilar), Jack Lambert (Charlie), Jack Elam (Tex), Juan Garcia (Pedro).

46. *Broken Arrow* (20 C-F, 1950). Sc. Michael Blankfort, from the book *Blood Brother* by Elliott Arnold. Dir. Delmer Daves. Phot. Ernest Palmer. Music by Hugo Friedhofer. The cast: James Stewart (Tom Jeffords), Jeff Chandler (Cochise), Debra Paget (Sonseeahray), Basil Ruysdael (Gen. Howard), Will Geer (Ben Slade), Joyce MacKenzie (Terry), Arthur Hunnicutt (Duffield), Raymond

Bramley (Col. Bernall), Jay Silverheels (Goklia), Argentina Brunetti (Nalikadeya), Jack Lee (Bocher), Robert Adler (Lonergan), Robert Griffin (Lowrie), Mickey Kuhn (Chip Slade).

Two Academy Award nominations.

47. *Colorado Territory* (WB, 1949). Sc. John Twist and Edmund H. North, from the crime novel *High Sierra* by W.R. Burnett. Dir. Raoul Walsh. Phot. Sid Hickox. Music by David Buttolph. The cast: Joel McCrea (Wes McQueen), Virginia Mayo (Colorado Carson), Dorothy Malone (Julie Ann), Henry Hull (Winslow), John Archer (Reno Blake), James Mitchell (Duke Harris), Morris Ankrum (marshal), Basil Ruysdael (Dave Rickard), Frank Puglia (Brother Yomas), Ian Wolfe (Wallace), Victor Kilian (sheriff).

48. *The Covered Wagon* (FP/Par., 1923). Sc. Jack Cunningham, from the novel by Emerson Hough. Dir. James Cruze. Phot. Karl Brown. The cast: Lois Wilson (Molly Wingate), J. Warren Kerrigan (Will Banion), Ernest Torrence (Jackson), Charles Ogle (Mr. Wingate), Ethel Wales (Mrs. Wingate), Alan Hale (Sam Woodhull), Tully Marshall (Bridger), Guy Oliver (Kit Carson), John Fox (Jed Wingate).

49. *Tombstone* (Hollywood Pictures, 1993). Sc. Kevin Jarre. Dir. George P. Cosmatos. Phot. William A. Fraker. Music by Bruce Broughton. The cast: Kurt Russell (Wyatt Earp), Val Kilmer (John 'Doc' Holliday), Michael Biehn (Johnny Ringo), Powers Boothe (Curly Bill), Sam Elliott (Virgil Earp), Joanna Pacula (Kate), Bill Paxton (Morgan Earp), Jason Priestley (Billy Breckinridge), Terry O'Quinn (Ike Clanton), Charlton Heston (Henry Hooker), Harry Carey, Jr. (marshal), Pedro Armendariz, Jr. (priest).

50. *The Scalphunters* (UA, 1968). Sc. William Norton. Dir. Sydney Pollack. Phot. Duke Callaghan and Richard Moore. Music by Elmer Bernstein. The cast: Burt Lancaster (Joe Bass), Ossie Davis (Joseph Winfield Lee), Telly Savalas (Jim Howie), Shelley Winters (Kate), Armando Silvestre (Two Crows), Dan Vadis (Yuma), Nick Cravat (Yancy), Paul Picerni (Frank), Dabney Coleman (Jed).

51. *El Dorado* (Par., 1967). Sc. Leigh Brackett, from the novel *The Stars in Their Courses* by Harry Brown. Dir. Howard Hawks. Phot. Harold Rosson. Music by Nelson Riddle. Song "El Dorado" by Nelson Riddle and John Gabriel. The cast: John Wayne (Cole Thornton), Robert Mitchum (Sheriff J.P. Harrah), James Caan (Alan Bourdillon Traherne, called "Mississippi"), Charlene Holt (Maudie), Michele Carey (Joey MacDonald), Arthur Hunnicutt (Bull Harris), R.G. Armstrong (Kevin MacDonald), Edward Asner (Bart Jason), Paul Fix (Doc Miller), Christopher George (Nelse McLeod), Robert Donner (Milt), Jim Davis (Jason's foreman), Johnny Crawford (Luke MacDonald).

52. *Monte Walsh* (National General, 1970). Sc. Lukas Heller and David Zelag Goodman, from the novel by Jack Schaefer. Dir. William A. Fraker. Phot. David M. Walsh. Music by John Barry. Song "The Good Times Are Comin'" by John Barry and Hal David. The cast: Lee Marvin (Monte Walsh), Jeanne Moreau (Martine Bernard), Jack Palance (Chet Rollins), Mitchell Ryan (Shorty Austin), Jim Davis (Cal Brennan), G.D. Spradlin (Hat Henderson), John Hudkins (Sonny Jacobs), Ray Guth (Sunfish Perkins), John R. McKee (Petey Williams), Michael Conrad (Dally Johnson), Bo Hopkins (Jumpin' Joe Joslin), Allyn Ann McLerie (Mary Eagle), Matt Clark (Rufus Brady), Billy Green Bush (Powder Kent).

53. *Jesse James* (20th C-F, 1939). Sc. Nunnally Johnson, from the historical data assembled by Rosalind Schaeffer and Jo Frances James. Dir. Henry King. Phot. George Barnes and W. Howard Greene. Musical Director Louis Silvers. The cast: Tyrone Power (Jesse James), Henry Fonda (Frank James), Nancy Kelly (Zerelda), Randolph Scott (Will Wright), Henry Hull (Maj. Rufus Cobb), Slim Summerville (jailer), J. Edward Bromberg (Mr. Runyan), John Carradine (Bob Ford), Donald Meek (McCoy), John Russell (Jesse James, Jr.), Jane Darwell (Mrs. Samuels), Charles Tannen (Charles Ford), Claire DuBrey (Mrs. Bob Ford), Willard Robertson (Clarke), Harold Goodwin (Bill), Ernest Whiteman (Pinkie), Eddy Waller (Deputy), Paul Burns (Hank), Spencer Charters (minister), Arthur Aylesworth (Tom Colson).

54. *Major Dundee* (Col., 1965). Sc. Harry Julian Fink, Oscar Saul and Sam Peckinpah. Dir. Sam Peckinpah. Phot. Sam Leavitt. Music by Daniele Amfitheatrof. Song "Major Dundee March" by Daniele Amfitheatrof and Ned Washington. Song "Laura Lee" by Liam Sullivan and Forrest Wood. The cast: Charlton Heston (Maj. Amos Charles Dundee), Richard Harris (Capt. Benjamin Tyreen), Jim Hutton (Lt. Graham), James Coburn (Samuel Potts), Michael Anderson (Tim Ryan), Senta Berger (Teresa Maria Santiago), Mario Adorf (Sgt. Gomez), Brock Peters (Aesop), Warren Oates (O.W. Hadley), Ben Johnson (Sgt. Chillum), R.G. Armstrong (Reverend Dahlstrom), L.Q. Jones (Arthur Hadley), Slim Pickens (Wiley), Karl Swenson (Capt. Waller), Dub Taylor (Priam), John Davis Chandler (Benteen).

55. *Will Penny* (Par., 1968). Sc. & Dir. Tom Gries. Phot. Lucien Ballard. Music by David Raksin. Song "The Lonely Rider" by David Raksin and Robert Wells. The cast: Charlton Heston (Will Penny), Joan Hackett (Catherine Allen), Lee Majors (Blue), Anthony Zerbe (Dutchy), Donald Pleasence (Quint), Jon Francis (Horace Allen), Ben Johnson (Alex), G.D. Spradlin (Anse Howard), Slim Pickens (Ike), Bruce Dern (Rafe Quint), Gene Rutherford (Rufus Quint), Roy Jenson (Sullivan), Quentin Dean (Jennie), William Schallert (Dr. Fraker), Lydia Clarke (Mrs. Fraker), Robert Luster (Shem Bodine), Matt Clark (Romulus), Luke Askew (Foxy).

56. *The Plainsman* (Par., 1936). Sc. Waldemar Young, Harold Lamb, Lynn Riggs and Jeanie MacPherson, from the story "Wild Bill Hickok" by Frank J. Wilstach and the story "The Prince of Pistoleers" by Courtney Ryley Cooper and Grover Jones. Dir. Cecil B. De Mille. Phot. Victor Milner and George Robinson. Music by George Antheil. The cast: Gary Cooper (Wild Bill Hickok), Jean Arthur (Calamity Jane), James Ellison (Buffalo Bill Cody), Charles Bickford (John Latimer), Porter Hall (Jack McCall), Helen Burgess (Louisa Cody), John Miljan (Gen. George Armstrong Custer), Victor Varconi (Painted Horse), Paul Harvey (Chief Yellow Hand), Anthony Quinn (a Cheyenne warrior), George "Gabby" Hayes (Breezy), Fuzzy Knight (Dave), Fred Kohler (Jack).

57. *Shenandoah* (Univ., 1965). Sc. James Lee Barrett. Dir. Andrew V. McLaglen. Phot. William H. Clothier. Music by Frank Skinner. The cast: James Stewart (Charlie), Doug McClure (Sam), Glenn Corbett (Jacob), Patrick Wayne (James), Rosemary Forsyth (Jennie), Philip Alford (Boy), Katharine Ross (Ann), Charles Robinson (Nathan), Paul Fix (Dr. Witherspoon), Denver Pyle (Bjoerling), George Kennedy (Col. Fairchild), Tim McIntire (Henry), James Best (Carter), Warren Oates (Billy Packer), Strother Martin (engineer), Harry Carey, Jr. (Jenkins).

One Academy Award nomination.

58. *Hondo* (WB, 1953). Sc. James Edward Grant, from the short story "The Gift of Cochise" by Louis L'Amour. Dir. John Farrow. Phot. Robert Burks and Archie Stout. Music by Emil Newman and Hugo Friedhofer. The cast: John Wayne (Hondo Lane), Geraldine Page (Angie Lowe), Ward Bond (Buffalo Baker), Michael Pate (Vittorio), James Arness (Lennie), Rodolfo Acosta (Silva), Leo Gordon (Ed Lowe), Lee Aaker (Johnny Lowe).

One Academy Award nomination.

59. *Ulzana's Raid* (Univ., 1972). Sc. Alan Sharp. Dir. Robert Aldrich. Phot. Joseph Biroc. Music by Frank De Vol. The cast: Burt Lancaster (McIntosh), Bruce Davison (Lt. Garnett DeBuin), Jorge Luke (Ke-Ni-Tay), Richard Jaeckel (sergeant), Joaquin Martinez (Ulzana), Lloyd Bochner (Capt. Gates), Karl Swenson (Rukeyser), Douglass Watson (Maj. Cartwright), Dran Hamilton (Mrs. Riordan), John Pearce (corporal), Gladys Holland (Mrs. Rukeyser), Margaret Fairchild (Mrs. Ginsford), Aimee Eccles (McIntosh's Indian woman), Richard Bull (Ginsford), Nick Cravat (trooper).

60. *Man Without a Star* (Univ., 1955). Sc. Borden Chase and D.D. Beauchamp, from the novel by Dee Linford. Dir. King Vidor. Phot. Russell Metty. Music by Joseph Gershenson. Songs "Man Without a Star" by Arnold Hughes and Frederick Herbert; "And the Moon Grew Brighter and Brighter" by Jimmy Kennedy and Lou Singer. The cast: Kirk Douglas (Dempsey Rae), Jeanne Crain (Reed Bowman), Claire Trevor (Idonee), William Campbell (Jeff Jimson), Richard Boone (Steve Miles), Jay C. Flippen (Strap Davis), Myrna Hansen (Tess Cassidy), Mara Corday (Moccasin Mary), Eddy C. Waller (Tom Cassidy), Sheb Wooley (Latigo), George Wallace (Tom Carter), Paul Birch (Mark Tolliver), Roy Barcroft (Sheriff Olson), Jack Elam (tramp).

61. *Jeremiah Johnson* (WB, 1972). Sc. John Milius and Edward Anhalt, from the novel *Mountain Man* by Vardis Fisher and the book *Crow Killer* by Raymond W. Thorp and Robert Bunker. Dir. Sydney Pollack. Phot. Duke Callaghan. Music by John Rubinstein and Tim McIntire. Title song by John Rubinstein and Tim McIntire. The cast: Robert Redford (Jeremiah Johnson), Will Geer (Bear Claw), Stefan Gierasch (Del Gue), Allyn Ann McLerie (crazy woman), Delle Bolton (Swan), Josh Albee (Caleb), Charles Tyner (Robidoux), Joaquin Martinez (Paints His Shirt Red), Paul Benedict (Reverend), Matt Clark (Qualen), Jack Colvin (Lt. Mulvey).

62. *Cimarron* (RKO, 1931). Sc. Howard Estabrook, from the novel by Edna Ferber. Dir. Wesley Ruggles. Phot. Edward Cronjager. Music by Max Steiner. The cast: Richard Dix (Yancey Cravat), Irene Dunne (Sabra Cravat), Dixie Lee (Estelle Taylor), Nance O'Neil (Felice Venable), William Collier, Jr. (the Kid), Roscoe Ates (Jesse Rickey), George E. Stone (Sol Levy), Stanley Fields (Lon Yountis), Robert McWade (Louis Hefner), Edna May Oliver (Mrs. Tracy Wyatt), Nancy Dover (Donna Cravat), Eugene Jackson (Isaiah).

Three Academy Awards (including one for best picture) and four nominations.

63. *Johnny Guitar* (Rep., 1954). Sc. Philip Yordan, from the novel by Roy Chanslor. Dir. Nicholas Ray. Phot. Harry Stradling. Music by Victor Young. Title song by Victor Young and Peggy Lee. The cast: Joan Crawford (Vienna), Sterling Hayden (Johnny "Guitar" Logan), Mercedes McCambridge (Emma Small), Scott Brady (Dancin' Kid), Ward Bond (John McIvers), Ben Cooper (Turkey Ralston), Ernest Borgnine (Bart Lonergan), John

Carradine (Old Tom), Royal Dano (Corey), Frank Ferguson (Marshal Williams), Paul Fix (Eddie), Rhys Williams (Mr. Andrews), Ian MacDonald (Pete), Sheb Wooley (posse member), Denver Pyle (posse member), Will Wright (Ned).

64. *Union Pacific* (Par., 1939). Sc. Walter DeLeon, C. Gardner Sullivan, Jesse Lasky, Jr. and Jack Cunningham, from the novel *Trouble Shooter* by Ernest Haycox. Dir. Cecil B. De Mille. Phot. Victor Milner and Dewey Wrigley. Music by Sigmund Krumgold and John Leipold. The cast: Joel McCrea (Jeff Butler), Barbara Stanwyck (Mollie Monahan), Akim Tamiroff (Fiesta), Robert Preston (Dick Allen), Lynne Overman (Leach Overmile), Brian Donlevy (Sid Campeau), Anthony Quinn (Jack Cordray), Evelyn Keyes (Mrs. Calvin), Robert Barrat (Duke Ring), Stanley Ridges (Gen. Casement), Henry Kolker (Asa M. Barrows), Francis J. McDonald (Gen. Grenville M. Dodge), Regis Toomey (Paddy O'Rourke), Fuzzy Knight (Cookie). One Academy Award nomination.

65. *Dodge City* (WB, 1939). Sc. Robert Buckner. Dir. Michael Curtiz. Phot. Sol Polito. Music by Max Steiner. The cast: Errol Flynn (Wade Hatton), Olivia de Havilland (Abbie Irving), Ann Sheridan (Ruby Gilman), Bruce Cabot (Jeff Surrett), Frank McHugh (Joe Clemens), Alan Hale (Rusty Hart), John Litel (Matt Cole), Henry Travers (Dr. Irving), Henry O'Neill (Col. Dodge), Victor Jory (Yancey), William Lundigan (Lee Irving), Guinn "Big Boy" Williams (Tex Baird), Gloria Holden (Mrs. Cole), Ward Bond (Bud Taylor), Cora Witherspoon (Mrs. McCoy), Russell Simpson (Orth), Clem Bevans (barber).

66. *Tumbleweeds* (WSHP/UA, 1925). Sc. C. Gardner Sullivan, from the novel by Hal G. Evarts. Dir. King Baggot. Phot. Joseph August. The cast: William S. Hart (Don Carver), Barbara Bedford (Molly Lassiter), Lucien Littlefield ("Kentucky Rose"), J. Gordon Russell (Noll Lassiter), Richard R. Neill (Bill Freel), Jack Murphy (Bart Lassiter), Lillian Leighton (Mrs. Riley), Gertrude Claire (old woman), George F. Marion (old man).

67. *Four Faces West* (UA, 1948). Graham Baker, Teddi Sherman and William & Milarde Brent, from the novella "Paso por Aqui" by Eugene Manlove Rhodes. Dir. Alfred E. Green. Phot. Russell Harlan. Music by Paul Sawtell. The cast: Joel McCrea (Ross McEwen), Frances Dee (Fay Hollister), Charles Bickford (Pat Garrett), Joseph Calleia (Monte Marquez), William Conrad (Sheriff Egan), Martin Garralaga (Florencio), Raymond Largay (Dr. Eldridge), Dan White (Clint Waters), Eva Novak (Mrs. Winston), Glenn Strange (lawman on train).

68. *The Hanging Tree* (WB, 1959). Sc. Wendell Mayes and Halsted Welles, from the novella by Dorothy M. Johnson. Dir. Delmer Daves. Phot. Ted McCord. Music by Max Steiner. Song "The Hanging Tree" by Mack David and Jerry Livingston. The cast: Gary Cooper (Doc Joseph Frail), Maria Schell (Elizabeth Mahler), Karl Malden (Frenchy Plante), Ben Piazza (Rune), George C. Scott (Dr. George Grubb), Karl Swenson (Tom Flaunce), Virginia Gregg (Edna Flaunce), John Dierkes (Society Red), King Donovan (Wonder), Guy Wilkerson (home owner), Slim Talbot (stage driver), Bud Osborne (horseman).

69. *The Good, the Bad and the Ugly* (Produzioni Europee, Italy/Spain, 1966). Sc. Age Scarpelli, Luciano Vincenzoni and Sergio Leone. Dir. Sergio Leone. Phot. Tonino Delli Colli. Music by Ennio Morricone. The cast: Clint Eastwood (The Stranger), Lee Van Cleef (Sentenza), Eli Wallach (Tuco).

Appendix A

70. *Sergeant Rutledge* (WB, 1960). Sc. James Warner Bellah and Willis Goldbweck, from the novel *Captain Buffalo* by James Warner Bellah. Dir. John Ford. Phot. Bert Glennon. Music by Howard Jackson. Song "Captain Buffalo" by Mack David and Jerry Livingston. The cast: Jeffrey Hunter (Lt. Thomas Cantrell), Constance Towers (Mary Beecher), Woody Strode (1st Sgt. Braxton Rutledge), Billie Burke (Mrs. Cordelia Fosgate), Juano Hernandez (Sgt. Matthew Luke Skidmore), Willis Bouchey (Fosgate), Carleton Young (Capt. Shattuck), Judson Pratt (Lt. Mulqueen), Jack Pennick (sergeant), Walter Reed (Capt. MacAfee), Mae Marsh (Nellie), Hank Worden (Laredo), Eva Novak (spectator).

71. *The Big Sky* (RKO, 1952). Sc. Dudley Nichols, from the novel by A.B. Guthrie, Jr. Dir. Howard Hawks. Phot. Russell Harlan. Music by Dimitri Tiomkin. Songs by Gordon Clark. The cast: Kirk Douglas (Jim Deakins), Dewey Martin (Boone Caudill), Elizabeth Coyotte Threatt (Teal Eye), Arthur Hunnicutt (Zeb Calloway), Buddy Baer (Romaine), Steven Geray (Jourdonnais), Hank Worden (Poordevil), Jim Davis (Streak), Henri Letondal (Labadie), Robert Hunter (Chouquette), Booth Colman (Pascal), Frank De Kova (Moleface), Guy Wilkerson (Longface), Don Beddoe (townsman), Barbara Hawks (Indian girl). Two Academy Award nominations.

72. *Comanche Station* (Col., 1960). Sc. Burt Kennedy. Dir. Budd Boetticher. Phot. Charles Lawton, Jr. Music Conducted by Mischa Bakaleinikoff. The cast: Randolph Scott (Jefferson Cody), Nancy Gates (Mrs. Lowe), Claude Akins (Ben Lane), Skip Homeier (Frank), Richard Rust (Dobie), Rand Brooks (station man), Dyke Johnson (Mr. Lowe), Foster Hood (Comanche lance bearer), Joe Molina (Comanche chief).

73. *They Died with Their Boots On* (WB, 1942). Sc. Wally Kline and Aeneas MacKenzie. Dir. Raoul Walsh. Phot. Bert Glennon. Music by Max Steiner. The cast: Errol Flynn (George Armstrong Custer), Olivia de Havilland (Elizabeth Bacon Custer), Arthur Kennedy (Ned Sharp), Charley Grapewin (California Joe), Gene Lockhart (Samuel Bacon), Anthony Quinn (Crazy Horse), Stanley Ridges (Maj. Romulus Taipe), John Litel (Gen. Philip Sheridan), Walter Hampden (William Sharp), Sydney Greenstreet (Gen. Winfield Scott), Regis Toomey (Fitzhugh Lee), Hattie McDaniel (Callie), Frank Wilcox (Capt. Webb), Joseph Sawyer (Sgt. Doolittle), Minor Watson (Sgt. Smith).

74. *North of 36* (FP-LAS/Par., 1924). Sc. James Shelley Hamilton, from the novel by Emerson Hough. Dir. Irvin Willat. Phot. Alfred Gilks. The cast: Jack Holt (Don McMasters), Lois Wilson (Taisie Lockheart), Ernest Torrence (Jim Nabours), Noah Beery (Slim Rudabaugh), David Dunbar (Dell Williams), Stephen Carr (Cinquo Centavos), Guy Oliver (Maj. McCoyne), William Carroll (Sanchez), Clarence Geldert (Col. Griswold), George Irving (Pattison), Ella Miller (Milly).

75. *The Texas Rangers* (Par., 1936). Sc. Louis Stevens, King Vidor and Elizabeth Hill Vidor, from the data in the book by Walter Prescott Webb. Dir. King Vidor. Phot. Edward Cronjager. Musical Direction by Boris Morros. The cast: Fred MacMurray (Jim Hawkins), Jack Oakie (Wahoo Jones), Jean Parker (Amanda Bailey), Lloyd Nolan (Sam McGee), Edward Ellis (Maj. Bailey), Bennie Bartlett (David), Frank Shannon (Capt. Stafford), Frank Cordell (Ranger Ditson), Richard Carle (Casper Johnson), Jed Prouty (prosecuting attorney), Fred Kohler, Sr. (Higgins), George "Gabby" Hayes (Judge),

Elena Martinez (Maria), Kathryn Bates (schoolteacher).

One Academy Award nomination.

76. *Cheyenne Autumn* (WB, 1964). Sc. James R. Webb, from the book by Mari Sandoz. Dir. John Ford. Phot. William H. Clothier. Music by Alex North. The cast: Richard Widmark (Capt. Thomas Archer), Carroll Baker (Deborah Wright), Karl Malden (Capt. Oscar Wessels), Sal Mineo (Red Shirt), Dolores Del Rio (Spanish woman), Ricardo Montalban (Little Wolf), Gilbert Roland (Dull Knife), Edward G. Robinson (Carl Schurz), James Stewart (Wyatt Earp), Arthur Kennedy (Doc Holliday), Patrick Wayne (Lt. Scott), Mike Mazurki (Sgt. Wichowsky), Victor Jory (Tall Tree), Elizabeth Allen (Guinevere Plantagenet), John Carradine (Major Jeff Blair), Ken Curtis (Homer).

One Academy Award nomination.

77. *Winchester '73* (Univ., 1950). Sc. Stuart N. Lake, Robert Richards and Borden Chase. Dir. Anthony Mann. Phot. William Daniels. Music Director, Joseph Gershenson. The cast: James Stewart (Lin McAdam), Shelley Winters (Lola Manners), Dan Duryea (Waco Johnny Dean), Stephen McNally (Dutch Henry Brown), Millard Mitchell (High Spade), Charles Drake (Steve Miller), John McIntire (Joe Lamont), Will Geer (Wyatt Earp), Jay C. Flippen (Sgt. Wilkes), Rock Hudson (Young Bull), John Alexander (Jack Riker), Steve Brodie (Wesley), James Millican (Wheeler), Tony Curtis (Doan).

78. *Western Union* (20th C-F, 1941). Sc. Robert Carson, from the novel by Zane Grey. Dir. Fritz Lang. Phot. Edward Cronjager and Allen M. Davey. Music by David Buttolph. The cast: Randolph Scott (Vance Shaw), Robert Young (Richard Blake), Dean Jagger (Edward Creighton), Virginia Gilmore (Sue Creighton), John Carradine (Doc Murdoch), Slim Summerville (Herman), Chill Wills (Homer), Barton MacLane (Jack Slade), Russell Hicks (Governor), Victor Kilian (Charlie), Minor Watson (Pat Grogan), George Chandler (Herb), Chief Big Tree (Chief Spotted Horse), Chief Thundercloud (Indian leader).

79. *Arizona* (Col., 1940). Sc. Claude Binyon, from the novel by Clarence Budington Kelland. Dir. Wesley Ruggles. Phot. Joseph Walker, Harry Hollenberger and Fayte Brown. Music by Victor Young. The cast: Jean Arthur (Phoebe Titus), William Holden (Peter Muncie), Warren William (Jefferson Carteret), Porter Hall (Lazarus Ward), Paul Harvey (Solomon Warner), George Chandler (Haley), Byron Foulger (Pete Kitchen), Regis Toomey (Grant Oury), Paul Lopez (Estevan Ochoa) Edgar Buchanan (Judge Bogardus), Earl Crawford (Joe Briggs).

Two Academy Award nominations.

80. *Ramrod* (MGM, 1947). Sc. Jack Moffit, Graham Baker and Cecile Kramer, from the novel by Luke Short. Dir. Andre De Toth. Phot. Russell Harlan. Music by Adolph Deutsch. The cast: Joel McCrea (Dave Nash), Veronica Lake (Connie Dickason), Don DeFore (Bill Schell), Donald Crisp (Sheriff Jim Crew), Preston Foster (Frank Ivey), Arleen Whelan (Rose Leland), Charlie Ruggles (Ben Dickason), Lloyd Bridges (Red Cates), Nestor Paiva (Curley), Ray Teal (Ed Burma), Housely Stevenson (George Smedley), Robert Wood (Link Thoms), Ian MacDonald (Walt Shipley).

81. *Pursued* (WB, 1947). Sc. Niven Busch. Dir. Raoul Walsh. Phot. James Wong Howe. Music by Max Steiner. The cast: Teresa Wright (Thor Callum), Robert Mitchum (Jeb Rand), Judith Anderson (Medora Callum), Dean Jagger (Grant Callum), Alan Hale (Jake Dingle),

Harry Carey, Jr. (Prentice McComber), John Rodney (Adam Callum), Clifton Young (sergeant), Ernest Severn (Jeb at the age of 11), Peggy Miller (Thor at the age of 10), Charles Bates (Adam at the age of 11), Ray Teal (army captain), Ian Wolfe (coroner).

82. *The Tall T* (Col., 1957). Sc. Burt Kennedy, from the short story "The Captives" by Elmore Leonard. Dir. Budd Boetticher. Phot. Charles Lawton, Jr. Music by Heinz Roemheld. The cast: Randolph Scott (Pat Brennan), Richard Boone (Frank Usher), Maureen O'Sullivan (Doretta Mims), Arthur Hunnicutt (Ed Rintoon), Skip Homeier (Billy Jack), Henry Silva (Chink), John Hubbard (Willard Mims), Robert Burton (Tenvoorde), Robert Anderson (Jace), Fred E. Sherman (Hank Parker), Chris Olsen (Jeff).

83. *The Apostle of Vengeance* (TRI, 1916). Sc. Monte M. Katterjohn. Dir. William S. Hart and Clifford Smith. Phot. Joseph August. The cast: William S. Hart (David Hudson), Nona Thomas (Mary McCoy), Joseph J. Dowling (Tom McCoy), Fanny Midgley ("Marm" Hudson), Jack Gilbert (Willie Hudson), Marvel Stafford (Elsie Hudson).

84. *Broken Lance* (20th C-F, 1954). Sc. Richard Murphy, from a story by Philip Yordan. Dir. Edward Dmytryk. Phot. Joseph MacDonald. Music by Leigh Harline. The cast: Spencer Tracy (Matt Devereaux), Robert Wagner (Joe Devereaux), Jean Peters (Barbara), Richard Widmark (Ben Devereaux), Katy Jurado (Senora Devereaux), Hugh O'Brian (Mike Devereaux), Eduard Franz (Two Moons), Earl Holliman (Danny Devereaux), E.G. Marshall (The Governor), Carl Benton Reid (Clem Lawton), Philip Ober (Van Cleve), Robert Burton (Mac Andrews), Robert Adler (O'Reilly).

One Academy Award and one nomination.

85. *The Unforgiven* (UA, 1960). Sc. Ben Maddow, from the novel by Alan LeMay. Dir. John Huston. Phot. Franz Planer. Music by Dimitri Tiomkin. The cast: Burt Lancaster (Ben Zachary), Audrey Hepburn (Rachel Zachary), Audie Murphy (Cash Zachary), John Saxon (Johnny Portugal), Charles Bickford (Zeb Rawlins), Lillian Gish (Mattilda Zachary), Albert Salmi (Charlie Rawlins), Joseph Wiseman (Abe Kelsey), June Walker (Hagar Rawlins), Kipp Hamilton (Georgia Rawlins), Arnold Merritt (Jude Rawlins), Doug McClure (Andy Zachary), Carlos Rivas (Lost Bird).

86. *Hour of the Gun* (UA, 1967). Sc. Edward Anhalt. Dir. John Sturges. Phot. Lucien Ballard. Music by Jerry Goldsmith. The cast: James Garner (Wyatt Earp), Jason Robards (Doc Holliday), Robert Ryan (Ike Clanton), Albert Salmi (Octavius Roy), Charles Aidman (Horace Sullivan), Steve Ihnat (Warshaw), Michael Tolan (Pete Spence), William Windom (Texas Jack Vermillion), Lonny Chapman (Turkey Creek Johnson), Larry Gates (John P. Clum), William Schallert (Herman Spicer), Karl Swenson (Dr. Charles Goodfellow), Jon Voight (Curly Bill Brocius).

87. *Seven Men from Now* (WB, 1956). Sc. Burt Kennedy. Dir. Budd Boetticher. Phot. William H. Clothier. Music by Henry Vars. Song by Henry Vars and "By" Dunham. The cast: Randolph Scott (Ben Stride), Gail Russell (Annie Greer), Lee Marvin (Big Masters), Walter Reed (John Greer), John Larch (Pate Bodeen), Donald Barry (Clete), Fred Graham (henchman), John Barradino (Clint), John Phillips (Jed), Chuck Roberson (Mason), Steve Mitchell (Fowler), Pamela Duncan (Senorita), Stuart Whitman (Cavalry Lieutenant).

88. *Canyon Passage* (Univ., 1946). Sc. Ernest Pascal, from the novel by Ernest Haycox. Dir. Jacques Tourneur. Phot. Edward Cronjager. Musical Director Frank Skinner. Songs "Rogue River Valley," "I'm Getting Married in the Morning" and "Silver Saddle" by Hoagy Carmichael; "Ole Buttermilk Sky" by Hoagy Carmichael and Jack Brooks. The cast: Dana Andrews (Logan Stuart), Susan Hayward (Lucy Overmire), Brian Donlevy (George Camrose), Patricia Roc (Caroline Dance), Ward Bond (Honey Bragg), Hoagy Carmichael (Hi Linnet), Lloyd Bridges (Johnny Steele), Andy Devine (Ben Dance), Stanley Ridges (Jonas Overmire), Fay Holden (Mrs. Overmire), Onslow Stevens (Lestrade), Ray Teal (Neil Howison), Rose Hobart (Marta Lestrade).

One Academy Award nomination.

89. *Duel in the Sun* (Selznick, 1946). Sc. David O. Selznick and Oliver H.P. Garrett, from the novel by Niven Busch. Dir. King Vidor. Phot. Lee Garmes, Hal Rosson, Ray Rennahan. Music by Dimitri Tiomkin. Song "Gotta Get Me Somebody to Love" by Allie Wrubel. The cast: Jennifer Jones (Pearl Chavez), Gregory Peck (Lewt McCanles), Joseph Cotton (Jesse McCanles), Lionel Barrymore (Senator McCanles), Lillian Gish (Laura Belle McCanles), Walter Huston (the Sin Killer), Herbert Marshall (Scott Chavez), Charles Bickford (Sam Pierce), Harry Carey (Lem Smoot), Joan Tetzel (Helen Langford), Otto Kruger (Mr. Langford), Sidney Blackmer (the lover), Tilly Losch (Mrs. Chavez).

Two Academy Award nominations.

90. *Wagon Master* (RKO, 1950). Sc. Frank Nugent and Patrick Ford. Dir. John Ford. Phot. Bert Glennon. Music by Richard Hageman. Songs "Shadows in the Dust," "Song of the Wagon Master," "Wagons West" and "Chuckawalla Swing" by Stan Jones. The cast: Ben Johnson (Travis Blue), Joanne Dru (Denver), Harry Carey, Jr. (Sandy Owens), Ward Bond (Elder Wiggs), Charles Kemper (Uncle Shiloh Clegg), Alan Mowbray (Dr. A. Locksley Hall), Jane Darwell (Sister Ledeyard), Ruth Clifford (Florie), Russell Simpson (Adam Perkins), Kathleen O'Malley (Prudence Perkins), James Arness (Floyd Clegg), Hank Worden (Luke Clegg), Francis Ford (Mr. Peachtree).

91. *Blood on the Moon* (RKO, 1948). Sc. Lillie Hayward and Harold Shumate from, the novel *Gunman's Chance* by Luke Short. Dir. Robert Wise. Phot. Nicholas Musuraca. Music by Roy Webb. The cast: Robert Mitchum (Jim Garry), Barbara Bel Geddes (Amy Lufton), Robert Preston (Tate Riling), Walter Brennan (Kris Barden), Phyllis Thaxter (Carol Lufton), Frank Faylen (Jack Pindalest), Tom Tully (John Lufton), Charles McGraw (Milo Sweet), Clifton Young (Joe Shotton), Tom Tyler (Frank Reardon), George Cooper (Fritz Barden), Richard Powers (Ted Elser).

92. *The Sheepman* (MGM, 1958). Sc. William Bowers, James Edward Grant and William Roberts. Dir. George Marshall. Phot. Robert Bronner. Music by Jeff Alexander. The cast: Glenn Ford (Jason Sweet), Shirley MacLaine (Dell Payton), Leslie Nielsen (Johnny Bledsoe, Col. Stephen Bedford), Mickey Shanughnessy (Jumbo McCall), Edgar Buchanan (Milt Masters), Willis Bouchey (Mr. Payton), Pernell Roberts (Choctaw), Slim Pickens (marshal), Buzz Henry (Red), Pedro Gonzalez-Gonzalez (Angelo).

One Academy Award nomination.

93. *In Old Arizona* (Fox, 1929). Sc. Tom Barry, from stories by O. Henry. Dir. Raoul Walsh and Irving Cummings. Phot. Arthur Edeson. Song "My Tonia" by Lew Brown, B.G. DeSylva and Ray Henderson. The cast: Warner Baxter (The Cisco Kid), Dorothy Burgess (Tonia Maria), Edmund Lowe (Sergeant Mickey Dunn), J. Farrell MacDonald (Tad), Fred Warren (piano player), Henry Armetta (barber), Frank Campeau (cowpuncher), Tom Santschi (cowpuncher), Pat Harrigan (cowpuncher).

One Academy Award and four nominations (including one for best picture).

94. *From Hell to Texas* (20th C-F, 1958). Sc. Robert Buckner and Wendell Mayes, from the novel *The Hell Bent Kid* by Charles O. Locke. Dir. Henry Hathaway. Phot. Wilfrid M. Cline. Music by Daniele Amfitheatrof. The cast: Don Murray (Tod Lohman), Diane Varsi (Juanita Bradley), Chill Wills (Amos Bradley), Dennis Hopper (Tom Boyd), R.G. Armstrong (Hunter Boyd), Jay C. Flippen (Jake Lefferfinger), Margo (Mrs. Bradley), John Larch (Hal Carmody), Ken Scott (Otis Boyd), Rodolfo Acosta (Bayliss), Harry Carey, Jr. (Trueblood), Malcolm Atterbury (hotel clerk).

95. *Man of the West* (UA, 1958). Sc. Reginald Rose, from the novel *The Border Jumpers* by Will C. Brown. Dir. Anthony Mann. Phot. Ernest Haller. Music by Leigh Harline. The cast: Gary Cooper (Link Jones), Julie London (Billie Ellis), Lee J. Cobb (Dock Tobin), Arthur O'Connell (Sam Beasley), Jack Lord (Coaley), John Dehner (Claude), Royal Dano (Trout), Robert Wilke (Ponch), Jack Williams (Alcutt), Guy Wilkerson (conductor), Chuck Roberson (rifleman), Frank Ferguson (marshal), Emory Parnell (Gribble), Tina Menard (Mexican woman).

96. *Cat Ballou* (Col., 1965). Sc. Walter Newman and Frank R. Pierson, from the novel *The Ballad of Cat Ballou* by Roy Chanslor. Dir. Elliot Silverstein. Phot. Jack Marta. Music by Frank De Vol. Songs by Mack David and Jay Livingston. The cast: Jane Fonda (Cat Ballou), Lee Marvin (Kid Shelleen-Strawn), Michael Callan (Clay Boone), Dwayne Hickman (Jed), Nat King Cole (shouter), Stubby Kaye (shouter), Tom Nardini (Jackson Two-Bears), John Marley (Frankie Ballou), Reginald Denny (Sir Harry Percival), Jay C. Flippen (Sheriff Cardigan), Arthur Hunnicutt (Butch Cassidy), Bruce Cabot (Sheriff Maledon), Burt Mustin (accuser), Paul Gilbert (train messenger).

One Academy Award and four nominations.

97. *Rancho Notorious* (RKO, 1952). Sc. Silvia Richards, Daniel Taradash. Dir. Fritz Lang. Phot. Hal Mohr. Music by Emil Newman. Songs "Legend of Chuck-a-Luck," "Gypsy Davey" and "Get Away Young Man" by Ken Darby. The cast: Marlene Dietrich (Altar Keane), Arthur Kennedy (Vern Haskell), Mel Ferrer (Frenchy Fermont), Gloria Henry (Beth), William Frawley (Baldy Gunder), Lisa Ferraday (Maxine), John Raven (Chuck-a-Luck dealer), Jack Elam (Geary), George Reeves (Wilson), Frank Ferguson (Preacher), Francis McDonald (Harbin), Dan Seymour (Comanche Paul).

98. *Pale Rider* (Malpaso-WB, 1985). Sc. Michael Butler and Dennis Shryack. Dir. Clint Eastwood. Phot. Bruce Surtees. Music by Lennie Niehaus. The cast: Clint Eastwood (Preacher), Michael Moriarty (Hull Barrett), Carrie Snodgress (Sarah Wheeler), Christopher Penn (Josh LaHood), Richard Dysart (Coy LaHood), Sydney Penny (Megan Wheeler), Richard Kiel (Club), Doug McGrath (Spider Conway), John Russell (Stockburn).

99. *How the West Was Won* (MGM, 1963). Sc. James R. Webb, from a series of articles *How the West Was Won* in *Life* magazine. Dir. Henry Hathaway (The Rivers, The Plains, The Outlaws), John

Ford (The Civil War) and George Marshall (The Railroad). Phot. William H. Daniels, Milton Krasner, Charles Lang, Jr. and Joseph LaShelle. Music by Alfred Newman. Songs by Alfred Newman (music), Ken Darby (lyrics of "How the West Was Won"), Sammy Kahn (lyrics of "Home in the Meadow") and Johnny Mercer (lyrics adaptation of "Raise a Ruckus," "Wait for the Hoedown" and "What Was Your Name in the States"). The cast: Carroll Baker (Eve Prescott), Debbie Reynolds (Lilith Prescott), James Stewart (Linus Rawlings), Gregory Peck (Cleve Van Valen), Henry Fonda (Jethro Stuart), George Peppard (Zeb Rawlings), Lee J. Cobb (Marshal Lou Ramsey), Carolyn Jones (Julie Rawlings), Karl Malden (Zebulon Prescott), Robert Preston (Roger Morgan), Eli Wallach (Charlie Gant), John Wayne (Gen. Sherman), Richard Widmark (Mike King), Brigid Bazlen (Dora), Walter Brennan (Col. Hawkins), David Brian (attorney), Andy Devine (Peterson), Raymond Massey (Abraham Lincoln), Harry Morgan (Gen. Grant), Agnes Moorehead (Rebecca Prescott), Thelma Ritter (Agatha Clegg), Russ Tamblyn (Reb soldier), Mickey Shaughnessy (Deputy), Lee Van Cleef (Marty), Jay C. Flippen (Huggins), Joe Sawyer (ship's officer), Rodolfo Acosta (henchman).

One Academy Award and five nominations (including one for best picture).

100. *The Last Hunt* (MGM, 1956). Sc. Richard Brooks, from the novel by Milton Lott. Dir. Richard Brooks. Phot. Russell Harlan. Music by Daniele Amfitheatroff. The cast: Robert Taylor (Charles Gilson), Stewart Granger (Sandy McKenzie), Lloyd Nolan (Woodfoot), Debra Paget (Indian girl), Russ Tamblyn (Jimmy), Constance Ford (Peg), Joe De Santis (Ed Black), Ralph Moody (Indian agent), Fred Graham (bartender), Ed Lonehill (Spotted Hand).

Appendix B

Top 100 Novels Filmed

1. **The Virginian: A Horseman of the Plains** (1902) by Owen Wister, filmed as *The Virginian* (1914, 1923, 1929 and 1946).
2. **The Big Sky** (1947) by A.B. Guthrie, Jr., filmed as *The Big Sky* (1952).
3. **Shane** (1949) by Jack Schaefer, filmed as *Shane* (1953).
4. **The Ox-Bow Incident** (1940) by Walter Van Tilburg Clark, filmed as *The Ox-Bow Incident* (1943).
5. **Riders of the Purple Sage** (1912) by Zane Grey, filmed as *Riders of the Purple Sage* (1918, 1925, 1931, 1941).
6. **Monte Walsh** (1963) by Jack Schaefer, filmed as *Monte Walsh* (1970).
7. **The Searchers** (1954) by Alan LeMay, filmed as *The Searchers* (1956).
8. **True Grit** (1968) by Charles Portis, filmed as *True Grit* (1969).
9. **The Shootist** (1975), by Glendon Swarthout, filmed as *The Shootist* (1976).
10. **The Way West** (1949) by A.B. Guthrie, Jr., filmed as *The Way West* (1967).
11. **Canyon Passage** (1945) by Ernest Haycox, filmed as *Canyon Passage* (1946).
12. **The Sea of Grass** (1937) by Conrad Richter, filmed as *The Sea of Grass* (1947).
13. **Ramrod** (1943) by Luke Short, filmed as *Ramrod* (1947).
14. **The Hell Bent Kid** (1957) by Charles O. Locke, filmed as *From Hell to Texas* (1958).
15. **Little Big Man** (1964) by Thomas Berger, filmed as *Little Big Man* (1970).
16. **Hombre** (1961) by Elmore Leonard, filmed as *Hombre* (1967).
17. **Bugles in the Afternoon** (1944) by Ernest Haycox, filmed as *Bugles in the Afternoon* (1952).
18. **Cimarron** (1930) by Edna Ferber, filmed as *Cimarron* (1931 and 1960).
19. **The Track of the Cat** (1949) by Walter Van Tilburg Clark, filmed as *Track of the Cat* (1954).
20. **The Wonderful Country** (1952) by Tom Lea, filmed as *The Wonderful Country* (1959).
21. **Arizona Nights** (1907) by Stewart Edward White, filmed as *Arizona Nights* (1927).
22. **Mountain Man** (1965) by Vardis Fisher, filmed as *Jeremiah Johnson* (1972).
23. **The Authentic Death of Hendry Jones** (1956) by Charles Neider, filmed as *One-Eyed Jacks* (1961).

24. **The Covered Wagon** (1922) by Emerson Hough, filmed as *The Covered Wagon* (1923).

25. **Ride the Man Down** (1942) by Luke Short, filmed as *Ride the Man Down* (1952).

26. **The Unforgiven** (1957) by Alan LeMay, filmed as *The Unforgiven* (1960).

27. **Ramona** (1884) by Helen Hunt Jackson, filmed as *Ramona* (1916, 1928 and 1936).

28. **The Shepherd of the Hills** (1907) by Harold Bell Wright, filmed as *The Shepherd of the Hills* (1920, 1928, 1941 and 1964).

29. **The Last Hunt** (1954) by Milton Lott, filmed as *The Last Hunt* (1956).

30. **The Chisholm Trail** aka **Blazing Guns on the Chisholm Trail** (1947) by Borden Chase, filmed as *Red River* (1948).

31. **Whispering Smith** (1906) by Frank H. Spearman, filmed as *Whispering Smith* (1916, 1926 and 1948).

32. **The Spoilers** (1906) by Rex Beach, filmed as *The Spoilers* (1914, 1923, 1930, 1942 and 1956).

33. **Vengeance Valley** (1949) by Luke Short, filmed as *Vengeance Valley* (1951).

34. **McCabe** (1959) by Edmund Naughton, filmed as *McCabe & Mrs. Miller* (1971).

35. **The Westerners** (1901) by Stewart Edward White, filmed as *The Westerners* (1919).

36. **The Desert Crucible** aka **The Rainbow Trail** (1915) by Zane Grey, filmed as *The Rainbow Trail* (1918, 1925 and 1932).

37. **Destry Rides Again** (1930) by Max Brand, filmed as *Destry Rides Again* (1932 and 1939) and as *Destry* (1955).

38. **North of 36** (1924) by Emerson Hough, filmed as *North of 36* (1924) and as *The Texans* (1938).

39. **Dances with Wolves** (1988) by Michael Blake, filmed as *Dances with Wolves* (1990).

40. **The Heritage of the Desert** (1910) by Zane Grey, filmed as *Heritage of the Desert* (1924, 1932 and 1939).

41. **Ambush at Blanco Canyon** aka **The Big Country** (1957) by Donald Hamilton, filmed as *The Big Country* (1958).

42. **The Night Horseman** (1920) by Max Brand, filmed as *The Night Horseman* (1921).

43. **Arizona** (1939) by Clarence Budington Kelland, filmed as *Arizona* (1940).

44. **Valdez Is Coming** (1970) by Elmore Leonard, filmed as *Valdez Is Coming* (1971).

45. **Man Without a Star** (1952) by Dee Linford, filmed as *Man Without a Star* (1955) and as *A Man Called Gannon* (1969).

46. **Wicked Water** (1948) by MacKinlay Kantor, filmed as *Hannah Lee* (1953).

47. **The Winning of Barbara Worth** (1911) by Harold Bell Wright, filmed as *The Winning of Barbara Worth* (1926).

48. **Lin McLean** (1898) by Owen Wister, filmed as *A Woman's Fool* (1918).

49. **Arouse and Beware** (1936) by MacKinlay Kantor, filmed as *The Man from Dakota* (1940).

50. **Chip of the Flying U** (1904) by B.M. Bower, filmed as *Chip of the Flying U* (1914, 1926 and 1939) and as *The Galloping Devil* (1920).

51. **The Dark Command** (1938) by W.R. Burnett, filmed as *Dark Command* (1940).

52. **The River's End** (1919) by James Oliver Curwood, filmed as *River's End* (1920, 1931 and 1940).

53. **Broncho Apache** (1936) by Paul I. Wellman, filmed as *Apache* (1954).

54. **The Long Chance** (1914) by Peter B. Kyne, filmed as *The Long Chance* (1922).

55. **Welcome to Hard Times** (1960)

Appendix B

by E.L. Doctorow, filmed as *Welcome to Hard Times* (1967).

56. **To the Last Man** (1922) by Zane Grey, filmed as *To the Last Man* (1923 and 1933) and as *Thunder Mountain* (1947).

57. **The Man from Laramie** (1954) by T.T. Flynn, filmed as *The Man from Laramie* (1955).

58. **Gone to Texas** (1973) by Forrest Carter, filmed as *The Outlaw Josey Wales* (1976).

59. **Duel in the Sun** (1944) by Niven Busch, filmed as *Duel in the Sun* (1946).

60. **The Valdez Horses** (1967) by Lee Hoffman, filmed as *Valdez, the Halfbreed* (1973).

61. **The Wild Horse** (1950) by Les Savage, Jr., filmed as *Black Horse Canyon* (1954).

62. **The Vanishing American** (1922) by Zane Grey, filmed as *The Vanishing American* (1925 and 1955).

63. **The Sky Pilot: A Tale of the Foothills** (1899) by Ralph Connor, filmed as *The Sky Pilot* (1921).

64. **To Follow a Flag** (1952) by Will Henry, filmed as *Pillars of the Sky* (1956).

65. **Trail Town** (1941) by Ernest Haycox, filmed as *Abilene Town* (1946).

66. **A Distant Trumpet** (1951) by Paul Horgan, filmed as *A Distant Trumpet* (1964).

67. **The Gray Dawn** (1915) by Stewart Edward White, filmed as *The Gray Dawn* (1922).

68. **The Horse Soldiers** (1956) by Harold Sinclair, filmed as *The Horse Soldiers* (1959).

69. **The Furies** (1948) by Niven Busch, filmed as *The Furies* (1950).

70. **These Thousand Hills** (1956) by A.B. Guthrie, Jr., filmed as *These Thousand Hills* (1959).

71. **Saint Johnson** (1930) by W.R. Burnett, filmed as *Law and Order* (1932, 1937 and 1953).

72. **Man in the Saddle** (1938) by Ernest Haycox, filmed as *Man in the Saddle* (1951).

73. **Ambush** (1948) by Luke Short, filmed as *Ambush* (1950).

74. **Warlock** (1958) by Oakley Hall, filmed as *Warlock* (1959).

75. **They Came to Cordura** (1958) by Glendon Swarthout, filmed as *They Came to Cordura* (1959).

76. **Company of Cowards** (1957) by Jack Schaefer, filmed as *Advance to the Rear* (1964).

77. **Flaming Lance** (1958) by Clair Huffaker, filmed as *Flaming Star* (1960).

78. **Heller with a Gun** (1955) by Louis L'Amour, filmed as *Heller in Pink Tights* (1960).

79. **Bend of the Snake** (1950) by Bill Gulick, filmed as *Bend of the River* (1952).

80. **The Three Godfathers** (1912) by Peter B. Kyne, filmed as *Three Godfathers* (1916, 1936 and 1948), as *Marked Men* (1919) and as *Hell's Heroes* (1930).

81. **Jubal Troop** (1939) by Paul I. Wellman, filmed as *Jubal* (1956).

82. **The Stars in Their Courses** (1960) by Harry Brown, filmed as *El Dorado* (1967).

83. **Nan of Music Mountain** (1916) by Frank H. Spearman, filmed as *Nan of Music Mountain* (1917).

84. **The Cowboys** (1971) by William Dale Jennings, filmed as *The Cowboys* (1972).

85. **Mackenna's Gold** (1963) by Will Henry, filmed as *Mackenna's Gold* (1969).

86. **"Nevada"** (1926) by Zane Grey, filmed as *Nevada* (1927, 1936 and 1944).

87. **Flying U Ranch** (1912) by B.M. Bower, filmed as *Flying U Ranch* (1927).

88. **The Valley of the Giants** (1916) by Peter B. Kyne, filmed as *Valley of the Giants* (1919, 1927 and 1938).

89. **Gunman's Chance** (1941) by Luke Short, filmed as *Blood on the Moon* (1948).

90. Sundown Jim (1938) by Ernest Haycox, filmed as *Sundown Jim* (1942).

91. Smoky Valley (1954) by Donald Hamilton, filmed as *The Violent Men* (1955).

92. The Renegade (1942) by L.L. Foreman, filmed as *The Savage* (1952).

93. Yellowstone Kelly (1957) by Clay Fisher (Will Henry), filmed as *Yellowstone Kelly* (1959).

94. Apache Rising (1957) by Marvin H. Albert, filmed as *Duel at Diablo* (1966).

95. The Ballad of Cat Ballou (1956) by Roy Chanslor, filmed as *Cat Ballou* (1965).

96. Arrow in the Sun (1969) by Theodore V. Olsen, filmed as *Soldier Blue* (1970).

97. Death of a Gunfighter (1968) by Lewis B. Patten, filmed as *Death of a Gunfighter* (1969).

98. Adobe Walls (1953) by W.R. Burnett, filmed as *Arrowhead* (1953).

99. The Burning Hills (1956) by Louis L'Amour, filmed as *The Burning Hills* (1956).

100. The Stalking Moon (1965) by Theodore V. Olsen, filmed as *The Stalking Moon* (1969).

Appendix C

Top 10 Nonfiction Books Filmed

1. **Across the Wide Missouri** (1947) by Bernard De Voto, filmed as *Across the Wide Missouri* (1951).
2. **The Texas Rangers: A Century of Frontier Defense** (1935) by Walter Prescott Webb, filmed as *The Texas Rangers,* (1936) and as *Streets of Laredo* (1949).
3. **Cheyenne Autumn** (1953) by Mari Sandoz, filmed as *Cheyenne Autumn* (1964).
4. **My Reminiscences as a Cowboy** (1930) by Frank Harris, filmed as *Cowboy* (1958).
5. **Willie Boy** (1960) by Harry Lawton, filmed as *Tell Them Willie Boy Is Here* (1969).
6. **Blood Brother** (1947) by Elliott Arnold, filmed as *Broken Arrow* (1950).
7. **Crow Killer** (1958) by Raymond W. Thorp and Robert Bunker, filmed as *Jeremiah Johnson* (1972).
8. **Wyatt Earp: Frontier Marshal** (1931) by Stuart N. Lake, filmed as *Frontier Marshal* (1934 and 1939) and as *My Darling Clementine* (1946).
9. **The Saga of Billy the Kid** (1926) by Walter Noble Burns, filmed as *Billy the Kid* (1930 and 1941).
10. **Tombstone: An Iliad of the Southwest** (1927) by Walter Noble Burns, filmed as *Tombstone* (1942).

Appendix D

Top 25 Short Stories/Novellas Filmed

1. **The Outcasts of Poker Flat** (1869) by Bret Harte, filmed, together with "The Luck of Roaring Camp," as *The Outcasts of Poker Flat* (1919, 1937 and 1952).

2. **The Luck of Roaring Camp** (1868) by Bret Harte, filmed, together with "The Outcasts of Poker Flat," as *The Outcasts of Poker Flat* (1919, 1937 and 1952); and as *The Luck of Roaring Camp* (1937).

3. **A Man Called Horse** (1949) by Dorothy M. Johnson, filmed as *A Man Called Horse* (1970); the character used also in *The Return of a Man Called Horse* (1976) and *Triumphs of a Man Called Horse* (1983).

4. **Paso por Aqui** (1926) by Eugene Manlove Rhodes, filmed as *Four Faces West* (1948).

5. **Three-Ten to Yuma** (1953) by Elmore Leonard, filmed as *3:10 to Yuma* (1957).

6. **Jeremy Rodock** by Jack Schaefer, filmed as *Tribute to a Bad Man* (1956).

7. **Stage to Lordsburg** (1937) by Ernest Haycox, filmed as *Stagecoach* (1939 and 1966).

8. **The Tin Star** (1947) by John M. Cunningham, filmed as *High Noon* (1952).

9. **The Hanging Tree** (1957) by Dorothy M. Johnson, filmed as *The Hanging Tree* (1959).

10. **The Gift of Cochise** (1952) by Louis L'Amour, filmed as *Hondo* (1953).

11. **A Double-Dyed Deceiver** (1905) by O. Henry, filmed as *The Texan* (1930).

12. **War Party** (1948) by James Warner Bellah, filmed as *She Wore a Yellow Ribbon* (1949).

13. **The Bride Comes to Yellows Sky** (1897) by Stephen Crane, filmed as *Face to Face* (1952).

14. **The Man Who Shot Liberty Valance** (1949) by Dorothy M. Johnson, filmed as *The Man Who Shot Liberty Valance* (1962).

15. **The Gay Caballero** by O. Henry, filmed as *In Old Arizona* (1929).

16. **Tennessee's Partner** (1869) by Bret Harte, filmed as *Tennessee's Partner* (1916 and 1955).

17. **Sergeant Houck** (1951) by Jack Schaefer, filmed as *Trooper Hook* (1957).

18. **The Captives** (1956) by Elmore Leonard, filmed as *The Tall T* (1957).

19. **Salomy Jane's Kiss** (1897) by Bret Harte, filmed as *Salomy Jane* (1914 and 1923).

Appendix D

20. Raiders Die Hard (1952) by John M. Cunningham, filmed as *Day of the Bad Man* (1958).

21. The Parson of Panamint by Peter B. Kyne, filmed as *The Parson of Panamint* (1919 and 1941) and as *While Satan Sleeps* (1922).

22. Massacre (1947) by James Warner Bellah, filmed as *Fort Apache* (1948).

23. M'liss by Bret Harte, filmed as *M'liss* (1915, 1918 and 1936) and as *The Girl Who Ran Wild* (1922).

24. Yankee Gold (1946) by John M. Cunningham, filmed as *The Stranger Wore a Gun* (1953).

25. Mission with No Record (1947) by James Warner Bellah, filmed as *Rio Grande* (1950).

Appendix E

Top 50 Songs Used

1. **High Noon (Do Not Forsake Me, Oh My Darlin')** by Dimitri Tiomkin and Ned Washington (AA), from *High Noon* (1952).

2. **Settle Down/My Rifle, My Pony and Me** by Dimitri Tiomkin and Paul Francis Webster, from *Red River* (1948) and *Rio Bravo* (1959), respectively.

3. **The Green Leaves of Summer** by Dimitri Tiomkin and Paul Francis Webster (AAN), from *The Alamo* (1960).

4. **Johnny Guitar** by Victor Young and Peggy Lee, from *Johnny Guitar* (1954).

5. **River of No Return** by Lionel Newman and Ken Darby, from *River of No Return* (1954).

6. **Raindrops Keep Fallin' on My Head** by Burt Bacharach and Hal David (AA), from *Butch Cassidy and the Sundance Kid* (1969)

7. **3:10 to Yuma** by George Duning and Ned Washington, from *3:10 to Yuma* (1957).

8. **Tomorrow Is the Song I Sing** by Jerry Goldsmith and Richard Gillis, from *The Ballad of Cable Hogue* (1970).

9. **Far Away from Home/Billy** by Bob Dylan, from *Pat Garrett and Billy the Kid* (1973).

10. **The Ballad of Cat Ballou** by Jerry Livingston and Mack David (AAN), from *Cat Ballou* (1965).

11. **True Grit** by Elmer Bernstein and Don Black (AAN), from *True Grit* (1969).

12. **Old Turkey Buzzard** by Quincy Jones and Freddie Douglass, from *Mackenna's Gold* (1969).

13. **Knockin' on Heaven's Door** by Bob Dylan, from *Pat Garrett and Billy the Kid* (1973).

14. **Strange Are the Ways of Love** by Dimitri Tiomkin and Ned Washington (AAN), from *The Young Land* (1959).

15. **The Hanging Tree** by Jerry Livingston and Mack David, from *The Hanging Tree* (1959).

16. **How the West Was Won** by Alfred Newman and Ken Darby, from *How the West Was Won* (1963).

17. **Soldier Blue** by Buffy Sainte-Marie, from *Soldier Blue* (1970).

18. **Saddle the Wind** by Jay Livingston and Ray Evans, from *Saddle the Wind* (1958).

19. **Sisters of Mercy** by Leonard Cohen, from *McCabe & Mrs. Miller* (1971).

20. **A Gunfight** by Johnny Cash, from *A Gunfight* (1971).

21. **Mule Train** by Fred Glickman, Hy Heath and Johnny Lange (AAN), from *Singing Guns* (1950).

22. **Wagons West** by Stan Jones, from *Wagon Master* (1950).

23. **Gunfight at the O.K. Corral** by Dimitri Tiomkin and Ned Washington, from *Gunfight at the O.K. Corral* (1957).
24. **Marmalade, Molasses and Honey** by Maurice Jarre and Marilyn & Alan Bergman (AAN), from *The Life and Times of Judge Roy Bean* (1972).
25. **Yellow Stripes** by Stan Jones, from *Escape from Bravo* (1954).
26. **The Good Times Are Comin'** by John Barry and Hal David, from *Monte Walsh* (1970).
27. **Ramona** by Mabel Wayne and L. Wolf Gilbert, from *Ramona* (1928).
28. **The Boys in the Back Room** by Frederick Hollander and Frank Loesser, from *Destry Rides Again* (1939).
29. **Ole Buttermilk Sky** by Hoagy Carmichael and Jack Brooks (AAN), from *Canyon Passage* (1946).
30. **Butterfly Mornings** by Richard Gillis, from *The Ballad of Cable Hogue* (1970).
31. **One Silver Dollar** by Lionel Newman and Ken Darby, from *River of No Return* (1954).
32. **Wichita** by Hans J. Salter and Ned Washington, from *Wichita* (1955).
33. **The Maverick Queen** by Victor Young and Ned Washington, from *The Maverick Queen* (1956).
34. **Get Away, Young Man** by Ken Darby, from *Rancho Notorious* (1952).
35. **El Dorado** by Nelson Riddle and John Gabriel, from *El Dorado* (1967).
36. **The Tall Men** by Ken Darby, from *The Tall Men* (1955).
37. **The Searchers** by Stan Jones, from *The Searchers* (1956).
38. **Some Sunday Morning** by Ray Heindorf, M.K. Jerome and Ted Koehler (AAN), from *San Antonio* (1945).
39. **A Dream of Love** by Charles B. FitzSimons and Marlin Skiles, from *The Deadly Companions* (1961).
40. **Heart of Gold** by Louis Forbes and Dave Franklin, from *Tennessee's Partner* (1955).
41. **Captain Buffalo** by Jerry Livingston and Mack David, from *Sergeant Rutledge* (1960).
42. **The Way West** by Bronislaw Kaper and Mack David, from *The Way West* (1967).
43. **A Rollin' Stone** by Lionel Newman and Bob Russell, from *Rawhide* (1951).
44. **Man Without a Star** by Arnold Hughes and Frederick Herbert, from *Man Without a Star* (1955).
45. **Flaming Star** by Sid Wayne and Sherman Edwards, from *Flaming Star* (1960).
46. **The Sun Shining Warm** by Leigh Harline and Mort Greene, from *Station West* (1948).
47. **Wait for Me, Sunrise** by Richard Gillis, from *The Ballad of Cable Hogue* (1970).
48. **Major Dundee March** by Daniele Amfitheatrof and Ned Washington, from *Major Dundee* (1965).
49. **Man in the Saddle** by Ralph Murphy and Harold Lewis, from *Man in the Saddle* (1951).
50. **Ballad of the War Wagon** by Dimitri Tiomkin and Ned Washington, from *The War Wagon* (1967).

Appendix F

Top 20 Authors

1. Zane Grey
2. Ernest Haycox
3. Luke Short
4. Jack Schaefer
5. Bret Harte
6. Max Brand/Evan Evans
7. Peter B. Kyne
8. Will Henry/Clay Fisher
9. Owen Wister
10. A.B. Guthrie, Jr.
11. Elmore Leonard
12. Louis L'Amour
13. Alan LeMay
14. Walter Van Tilburg Clark
15. Stewart Edward White
16. Harold Bell Wright
17. Dorothy M. Johnson
18. James Warner Bellah
19. W.R. Burnett
20. Glendon Swarthout

Appendix G

Top 20 Screenwriters

1. Dudley Nichols (AAN for *The Tin Star*, 1957)
2. Frank S. Nugent
3. James R. Webb (AA for *How the West Was Won*, 1963)
4. Borden Chase (AAN for *Red River*, 1948)
5. James Edward Grant (AAN for *The Sheepman*, 1958)
6. William Bowers (AAN for *The Gunfighter*, 1950; AAN for *The Sheepman*, 1958)
7. Philip Yordan (AA for *Broken Lance*, 1954)
8. Lamar Trotti
9. Howard Estabrook (AA for *Cimarron*, 1931)
10. Irving Ravetch & Harriet Frank, Jr.
11. Robert Buckner
12. Winston Miller
13. C. Gardner Sullivan
14. Leigh Brackett
15. James Lee Barrett
16. Sydney Boehm
17. Jack Cunningham
18. Jules Furthman
19. Carl Foreman (AAN for *High Noon*, 1952)
20. William Goldman (AA for *Butch Cassidy and the Sundance Kid*, 1969)

The only other Academy Award winner in the category of writing for a standard western film is Michael Blake (*Dances with Wolves*, 1990), while the other nominees include Tom Barry (*In Old Arizona*, 1929), Stuart N. Lake (*The Westerner*, 1940), A.B. Guthrie, Jr. (*Shane*, 1953), Sam Rolfe & Harold Jack Bloom (*The Naked Spur*, 1953), Barney Slater & Joel Kane (*The Tin Star*, 1957), Charles Lang, Jr. (*One-Eyed Jacks*, 1961), Walter Newman & Frank R. Pierson (*Cat Ballou*, 1965), Richard Brooks (*The Professionals*, 1966), Walon Green, Roy N. Sickner and Sam Peckinpah (*The Wild Bunch*, 1969), and David Webb Peoples (*Unforgiven*, 1992).

Appendix H

Top 20 Directors

1. John Ford (AAN for *Stagecoach*, 1939)
2. Howard Hawks
3. Sam Peckinpah
4. Anthony Mann
5. Delmer Daves
6. John Sturges
7. William A. Wellman
8. Raoul Walsh
9. Henry Hathaway
10. George Marshall
11. William Wyler
12. Henry King
13. William S. Hart
14. Clint Eastwood (AA for *Unforgiven*, 1992)
15. King Vidor
16. Robert Aldrich
17. Budd Boetticher
18. Sergio Leone
19. Burt Kennedy
20. Michael Curtiz

The only other director who won an Academy Award for a standard western film is Kevin Costner (*Dances with Wolves*, 1990). The other directors that were Oscar-nominated for a western picture are Irving Cummings (*In Old Arizona*, 1928–29, co-directed with Raoul Walsh, who—oddly—has never been mentioned as the co-nominee), Wesley Ruggles (*Cimarron*, 1930–31), Fred Zinnemann (*High Noon*, 1952) and George Stevens (*Shane*, 1953).

Appendix I

Top 20 Cinematographers

1. William H. Clothier (AAN for *The Alamo*, 1960; AAN for *Cheyenne Autumn*, 1964)
2. Lucien Ballard
3. Russell Harlan (AAN for *The Big Sky*, 1952)
4. Charles B. Lang, Jr. (AAN for *How the West Was Won*, 1963)
5. Joseph H. August
6. Joseph MacDonald
7. Victor Milner (AAN for *North West Mounted Police*, 1940; AAN for *The Furies*, 1950)
8. Bert Glennon (AAN for *Stagecoach*, 1939)
9. James Wong Howe
10. Loyal Griggs (AA for *Shane*, 1953)
11. W. Howard Greene (AAN for *North West Mounted Police*, 1940)
12. Edward Cronjager (AAN for *Cimarron*, 1930–31)
13. Winton C. Hoch (AA for *She Wore a Yellow Ribbon*, 1949)
14. Harry Stradling
15. Robert Surtees
16. Bruce Surtees
17. Charles Lawton, Jr.
18. Conrad Hall (AAN for *The Professionals*, 1966; AA for *Butch Cassidy and the Sundance Kid*, 1969)
19. Milton Krasner (AAN for *How the West Was Won*, 1963)
20. William H. Daniels (AAN for *How the West Was Won*, 1963)

The only other Academy Award winners in the category of best cinematography for a western picture are Dean Semler (*Dances with Wolves*, 1990) and John Toll (*Legends of the Fall*, 1994). The other nominees include Arthur Edeson (*In Old Arizona*, 1928–29), William V. Skall & Leonard Smith (*Billy the Kid*, 1941), Ernest Palmer (*Broken Arrow*, 1950), Walter Strenge (*Stagecoach to Fury*, 1956), Joseph LaShelle (*How the West Was Won*, 1963), Jack N. Green (*Unforgiven*, 1992), and Owen Roizman (*Wyatt Earp*, 1994).

Appendix J

Top 20 Composers

1. Dimitri Tiomkin (AA for *High Noon*, 1952, score and song; AAN for *The Young Land*, 1959, song; AAN for *The Alamo*, 1960, score and song)
2. Victor Young (AAN for *Man of Conquest*, 1939; AAN for *Arizona*, 1940; AAN for *Dark Command*, 1940; AAN for *North West Mounted Police*, 1940)
3. Max Steiner
4. Alfred Newman (AAN for *How the West Was Won*, 1963)
5. Elmer Bernstein (AAN for *The Magnificent Seven*, 1960; AAN for *Return of the Magnificent Seven*, 1966; AAN for *True Grit*, 1969, song)
6. Ennio Morricone
7. Cyril J. Mockridge
8. George Duning
9. Jerry Goldsmith
10. Daniele Amfitheatrof
11. Richard Hageman (AA for *Stagecoach*, 1939)
12. David Buttolph
13. Jeff Alexander
14. Jerry Fielding (AAN for *The Outlaw Josey Wales*, 1976)
15. Frank Skinner
16. Hugo Friedhofer
17. Leigh Harline
18. Maurice Jarre
19. Alex North
20. Bronislau Kaper

In addition to the above, Burt Bacharach won a double Academy Award, score and song, for *Butch Cassidy and the Sundance Kid* (1969), John Barry won the best score Oscar for *Dances with Wolves* (1990), and the other statuette receivers for best music in *Stagecoach*, besides Richard Hageman, were W. Franke Harling, John Leipold and Leo Shuken. The other Academy Award nominees in the category of musical score for a standard western picture include Walter Scharf (*In Old Oklahoma*, 1943), Gerard Carbonara (*The Kansan*, 1943), Miklos Rozsa (*The Woman of the Town*, 1944), Jerome Moross (*The Big Country*, 1958), Frank De Vol (*Cat Ballou*, 1965), Alex North (*Bite the Bullet*, 1975) and Bruce Broughton (*Silverado*, 1985).

Appendix K

Top 20 Leading Men

1. John Wayne (AA for *True Grit*, 1969)
2. Gary Cooper (AA for *High Noon*, 1952)
3. Henry Fonda
4. James Stewart
5. Burt Lancaster
6. Clint Eastwood (AAN for *Unforgiven*, 1992)
7. Kirk Douglas
8. Randolph Scott
9. Joel McCrea
10. William S. Hart
11. Robert Mitchum
12. Glenn Ford
13. Richard Widmark
14. William Holden
15. Lee Marvin (AA for *Cat Ballou*, 1965)
16. Gregory Peck
17. Harry Carey
18. Alan Ladd
19. Charlton Heston
20. Warner Baxter (AA for *In Old Arizona*, 1928–29)

The other Academy Award nominees in the Best Actor category for a western movie are Richard Dix (*Cimarron*, 1930–31) and Kevin Costner (*Dances with Wolves*, 1990).

Appendix L

Top 20 Leading Ladies

1. Barbara Stanwyck
2. Jean Arthur
3. Claire Trevor
4. Maureen O'Hara
5. Dorothy Malone
6. Winifred Kingston
7. Yvonne De Carlo
8. Anne Baxter
9. Susan Hayward
10. Angie Dickinson
11. Virginia Mayo
12. Vera Miles
13. Olivia de Havilland
14. Joanne Dru
15. Julie Adams
16. Linda Darnell
17. Jane Russell
18. Donna Reed
19. Rhonda Fleming
20. Debra Paget

There were three Academy Award nominees in the category of best actress in a western picture: Irene Dunne (*Cimarron*, 1930–31), Jennifer Jones (*Duel in the Sun*, 1946) and Julie Christie (*McCabe & Mrs. Miller*, 1971).

Appendix M

Top 20 Supporting Actors

1. Walter Brennan (AA for *The Westerner*, 1940)
2. Ben Johnson
3. John McIntire
4. Ward Bond
5. Edgar Buchanan
6. Chill Wills
7. Arthur Hunnicutt (AAN for *The Big Sky*, 1952)
8. Harry Carey, Jr.
9. John Carradine
10. Charles Bickford
11. Dan Duryea
12. Jeff Corey
13. Paul Fix
14. Jim Davis
15. Slim Pickens
16. J. Farrell MacDonald
17. Strother Martin
18. Jack Elam
19. Russell Simpson
20. Lee Van Cleef

The other players winning an Academy Award as best supporting actor in a western film are Thomas Mitchell (*Stagecoach*, 1939), Burl Ives (*The Big Country*, 1958) and Gene Hackman (*Unforgiven*, 1992). The other nominees include Jeff Chandler (*Broken Arrow*, 1950), Jack Palance and Brandon De Wilde (both nominated for *Shane*, 1953), Chief Dan George (*Little Big Man*, 1970) and Graham Greene (*Dances with Wolves*, 1990).

Appendix N

Top 20 Supporting Actresses

1. Jane Darwell
2. Katy Jurado (AAN for *Broken Lance*, 1954)
3. Jeanette Nolan
4. Olive Carey
5. Beulah Bondi
6. Ruth Donnelly
7. Gloria Grahame
8. Agnes Moorehead
9. Aline MacMahon
10. Marjorie Main
11. Kathleen Freeman
12. Ellen Corby
13. Mercedes McCambridge
14. Irene Rich
15. Joan Blondell
16. Josephine Hutchinson
17. Edna May Oliver
18. Hope Emerson
19. Connie Gilchrist
20. Anna Lee

The other actresses who won an Academy Award nomination for a supporting role in a western film are Lillian Gish (*Duel in the Sun*, 1946), Geraldine Page (*Hondo*, 1953) and Mary McDonnell (*Dances with Wolves*, 1990).

Select Bibliography

Anderson, Lindsay. *About John Ford...* (New York: McGraw-Hill, 1981).

Biskind, Peter. *Seeing Is Believing: How Hollywood Taught Us to Stop Worrying and Love the Fifties* (New York: Pantheon Books, 1983).

Buscombe, Edward. *BFI Classics: The Searchers* (London: BFI, 2000).

———. *BFI Film Classics: Stagecoach* (London: BFI, 1992).

———, ed. *The BFI Companion to the Western* (New York: Atheneum, 1988).

Charnez, Casey St. *The Films of Steve McQueen* (New York: Citadel, 1984).

Connelly, Robert. *The Motion Picture Guide: Silent Film* (Chicago: Cinebooks, 1986).

Countryman, Edward, and Evonne von Heussen-Countryman. *BFI Film Classics: Shane* (London: BFI, 1999).

Deschner, Donald. *The Films of Spencer Tracy* (New York: Cadillac, 1968).

Dickens, Homer. *The Complete Films of James Cagney* (New York: Citadel, 1972).

———. *The Films of Gary Cooper* (New York: Citadel, 1970).

Drummond, Phillip. *BFI Film Classics: High Noon* (London: BFI, 1997).

Easton, Robert. *Max Brand: The Big "Westerner"* (Norman: University of Oklahoma Press, 1970).

Essoe, Gabe. *The Films of Clark Gable* (New York: Citadel, 1970).

Estleman, Loren D. *The Wister Trace: Classic Novels of the American Frontier* (Ottawa, IL.: Jameson Books, 1987).

Everson, William K. *A Pictorial History of the Western Film* (New York: Citadel, 1969).

Eyles, Allen. *The Western* (New York: A.S. Barnes, 1975).

Fenin, George N., and William K. Everson. *The Western: From Silents to Cinerama* (New York: Grossman, 1973).

Ford, Thomas W. *A.B. Guthrie, Jr.* (Boston: Twayne, 1981).

Franklin, Joe. *Classics of the Silent Screen: A Pictorial Treasury* (New York: 1959).

Garfield, Brian. *Western Films: A Complete Guide* (New York: Da Capo Press, 1982).

Griggs, John. *The Films of Gregory Peck* (New York: Citadel, 1984).

Guerif, Francois. *Robert Redford* (Paris: PAC, 1976).

Guttmacher, Peter. *Legendary Westerns* (New York: MetroBooks, 1995).

Halliwell, Leslie. *Halliwell's Film Guide* (New York: HarperPerennial, 1991).

Hardy, Phil, ed. *The Overlook Film Encyclopedia: The Western* (Woodstock, NY: Overlook, 1991).

Henry, Marilyn, and Ron DeSourdis. *The Films of Alan Ladd* (New York: Citadel, 1981).

Heston, Charlton, and Jean-Pierre Isbouts. *Charlton Heston's Hollywood: 50 Years in American Film* (New York: GT Publishing, 1998).

Hitt, Jim. *Words and Shadows: Literature on the Screen* (New York: Citadel, 1992).

Hoffmann, Henryk. *"A" Western Filmmakers: A Biographical Dictionary of Writers, Directors, Cinematographers, Composers, Actors and Actresses* (Jefferson, NC: McFarland, 2000).

Hyams, Jay. *The Life and Times of the Western Movie* (New York: Gallery Books, 1983).

Select Bibliography

Janis, Maria Cooper. *Gary Cooper Off Camera* (New York: Abrams, 1999).

Katz, Ephraim. *The Film Encyclopedia* (New York: Perigee, 1979; and New York: Harper-Perennial, 1998).

Kitses, John Demetrius. *Horizons West; Anthony Mann, Budd Boetticher, Sam Peckinpah: Studies of Authorship with the Western* (Bloomington: Indiana University Press, 1970).

Knight, Arthur, introd. *The New York Times Directory of the Film* (Salem, NH: Arno Press/New York: Random House, 1971).

Liandrat-Guigues, Suzanne. *BFI Classics: Red River* (London: BFI, 2000).

Lyons, Robert, ed. *My Darling Clementine: John Ford, Director* (New Brunswick, NJ: Rutgers University Press, 1984).

Marill, Alvin H. *The Films of Anthony Quinn* (New York: Citadel, 1975).

McBride, Joseph. *Hawks on Hawks* (Berkeley and Los Angeles: University of California Press, 1982).

McCarty, Clifford. *The Complete Films of Humphrey Bogart* (New York: Citadel, 1965).

Michael, Paul. *The Academy Awards: A Pictorial History* (New York: Crown, 1978).

Nash, Jay Robert, and Stanley Ralph Ross. *The Motion Picture Guide: Index* (Chicago: Cinebooks, 1987).

Parish, James Robert, and Gregory W. Mank. *The Hollywood Reliables* (Westport, CT: Arlington House, 1980).

Quirk, Lawrence J. *The Films of Paul Newman* (New York: Citadel, 1971).

_____. *The Films of Robert Taylor* (Secaucus, NJ: Citadel, 1975).

_____. *The Films of William Holden* (New York: Citadel, 1973).

Ricci, Mark, Boris Zmijewsky, and Steve Zmijewsky. *The Films of John Wayne* (New York: Citadel, 1970).

Sarris, Andrew. *The John Ford Movie Mystery* (London: Secker & Warburg and BFI, 1976).

Scott, C.H. *Whatever Happened to Randolph Scott?* (Madison, NC: Empire, 1994).

Sennett, Ted. *Great Hollywood Westerns* (New York: Abrams, 1990).

Simmons, Garner. *Peckinpah: A Portrait in Montage* (Austin: University of Texas Press, 1982).

Snodgrass, Mary Ellen. *Encyclopedia of Frontier Literature* (Oxford: Oxford University Press, 1997).

Springer, John. *The Fondas: The Films and Careers of Henry, Jane and Peter Fonda* (New York: Citadel, 1970).

Thomas, Tony. *The Films of Kirk Douglas* (New York: Citadel, 1972).

_____. *The Films of Marlon Brando* (New York: Citadel, 1973).

_____. *The West That Never Was* (New York: Citadel, 1989).

_____. *A Wonderful Life: The Films and Career of James Stewart* (New York: Citadel, 1988).

_____, Rudy Behlmer, and Clifford McCarty. *The Films of Errol Flynn* (New York: Citadel, 1969).

Tompkins, Jane. *West of Everything: The Inner Life of Westerns* (New York, Oxford University Press, 1992).

Tuska, Jon, ed. *Western Stories: A Chronological Anthology* (New York: Gramercy Books, 1995).

Vermilye, Jerry. *Burt Lancaster: A Pictorial Treasury of His Films* (New York: Falcon Enterprises, 1971).

Wills, Garry. *John Wayne's America: The Politics of Celebrity* (New York: Simon & Schuster, 1997).

Work, James C., ed. *Shane. Jack Schaefer: The Critical Edition* (Lincoln, London: University of Nebraska Press, 1984).

Zmijewsky, Boris, and Lee Pfeiffer. *The Films of Clint Eastwood* (New York: Citadel, 1996).

Index

Abbey, Edward 91
Abilene Town (1946) 46, 47
Acosta, Rodolfo 9, 114
Across the Wide Missouri 58, 59
Across the Wide Missouri (1951) 58, 59, 115
Adams, Claire 10, 119
Adams, Gerald Drayson 128
Adams, Julie (Julia) 16, 60
Adamson, Harold 73
Adamson, Stewart 28
Adobe Walls 63
Adorée, Renée 22
Advance to the Rear (1964) 91
The African Queen (1951) 115
Against All Odds (1924) 14
Agar, John 10, 53, 55
Ahern, Lloyd 135, 138
Aherne, Brian 35
Akins, Claude 8, 84, 137
The Alamo (1960) 81, 82, 83, 97, 119, 120, 124, 134
Albert, Marvin H. 14, 95, 96, 139
Albright, Lola 15, 97
Alcatraz 11, 12
Aldrich, Robert 8, 57, 66, 84, 85, 109, 11, 123, 124
Alexander, Dick 133
Alexander, Jane 107
Alexander, Jeff 76, 130
Alexander, Katherine 29
All the Pretty Horses 141
All the Pretty Horses (2000) 141
Almendros, Nestor 119
Along Came Jones (1945) 45, 46, 100
Along the Great Divide (1951) 58, 59
Alonzo, John 120
Altman, Robert 106, 108, 134
Alton, John 58, 139
Ambush 55
Ambush (1950) 55, 58
Ameche, Don 30

American Outlaws (2001) 142
Ames, Leon 135
Amfitheatrof, Daniele 94, 123
Amiel, Jon 136
Anderson, Gilbert M. "Broncho Billy" 4, 107
Anderson, James 10, 101
Anderson, John 11, 133
Anderson, Judith 49, 56, 104, 106, 133
Anderson, Linsay 70
Anderson, Roland 37
Anderson, Michael, Jr. 43
Andersson, Bibi 96
Andres, Luana 37, 139
Andrews, Dana 43, 44, 47, 48, 133, 135
Andrews, Del 16
Andrews, Robert D. 51
Andriot, Lucien 18, 22, 119
Angel and the Badman (1947) 41, 49, 50, 95, 97
Anhalt, Edward 97, 109, 110, 111
Ankrum, Morris 54, 55, 92, 131
Ann-Margret 95, 96, 114
Anne of the Thousand Days (1969) 102
Annie Oakley (1935) 28, 115
Another Man, Another Chance (1977) 118
Ansara, Michael 11
Antheil, George 29, 79
Anthony, Stuart 27, 40
Apache (1954) 66, 67, 111, 114, 124, 133, 138
The Apache Raider (1928) 19
Apache Rising 95, 96
Apache Territory (1958) 75
Apache Trail (1942) 41
Apfel, Oscar 3, 4
The Apostle of Vengeance (1916) 5, 6, 49
The Appaloosa 95
The Appaloosa (1966) 95

Archainbaud, George 43, 79
Ardrey, Robert 78
Arise, My Love (1940) 38
Arizona 37, 38
Arizona (1940) 37, 38, 72, 93, 121, 133
Arizona Bound (1927) 18
Arizona Days (1928) 19
Arizona Nights 18
Arizona Nights (1927) 18
The Arizona Wildcat (1926) 16, 17
The Arizonian (1935) 28
Arlen, Richard 19, 116
Armendariz, Pedro 54, 90
Armendariz, Pedro, Jr. 23
Armstrong, Paul 4
Armstrong, R.G. 7, 86, 89, 94, 112
Arness, James 12, 65
Arnold, Elliott 55, 120
Arnold, Jack 6, 133
Arouse and Beware 37
Arquette, Rosanna 124, 125
Arrow in the Dust 66
Arrow in the Dust (1954) 66
Arrow in the Sun 104, 105
Arrowhead (1953) 63, 118
Arthur, Jean 22, 29, 37, 38, 63, 64, 132, 133
The Aryan (1916) 5, 6
At Gunpoint (1955) 73, 115
Atterbury, Malcolm 133
Auer, Mischa 97
August, Joseph (H.) 5, 6, 7, 9, 10, 15, 16, 49
Aurthur, Robert Alan 78
The Authentic Death of Hendry Jones 84, 85, 143
Avalanche (1928) 19
Averback, Hy 101
Avil, Gordon 22
Awakenings (1990) 131
Axt, William 29
Aylesworth, Arthur 47

185

Index

Babe, Thomas 138
Bacall, Lauren 116, 117
Bacharach, Burt 100, 101
Backlash (1956) 69
Bacon, Lloyd 33, 68
Bad Bascomb (1946) 46
Bad Company (1972) 109, 110, 11, 121
Bad Day at Black Rock (1955) 69
Bad Girls (1993) 135, 136
The Bad Man 22
The Bad Man (1930) 22
The Bad Man of Brimstone (1938) 31
The Badlanders (1958) 76
Badman 97, 98
Baggot, King 15
Bailey, John 124
Baker, Carroll 24, 76, 77, 89, 91, 92
Baker, Graham 49
Baker, Joe Don 29
Baldwin, Stephen 135
Balin, Ina 85, 100
Ball, Suzan 26, 68
The Ballad of Cable Hogue (1970) 104, 105, 126, 142
The Ballad of Cat Ballou 93, 95
The Ballad of Josie (1968) 99
Ballard, Lucien 86, 89, 94, 95, 97, 99, 104, 128, 129
Ballin, Mabel 15
Balluck, Don 123
Balsam, Martin 9, 97, 139
Bancroft, Anne 24, 68
Bancroft, George 15, 18, 20, 34, 35, 41, 70
Banderas, Antonio 140
Bandolero! (1968) 138
The Bank Robber 113
Banks, Lionel 37
Banky, Vilma 16
Bar Nothin' (1921) 10
Barbarosa (1982) 122
Barcroft, Roy 101
Bardette, Trevor 119
Bardot, Brigitte 27
Barker, Lex 9, 112
Barker, Reginald 5
Barkin, Ellen 138
Barnes, George 16, 32, 37, 38, 64
Barrat, Robert (H.) 104
Barrett, James Lee 20, 94, 129
Barry, Don "Red" 120
Barry, Gene 75
Barry, John 26, 104, 105, 118, 130
Barry, Tom 19, 20
Barrymore, Drew 135, 136
Barrymore, Lionel 48, 66
Bartlett, Sy 75, 76
Barton, James 86
Basehart, Richard 3, 124
Basevi, James 37
Bassman, George 86
Bates, Florence 45, 66

Bates, Kathy 142
Bauchens, Anne 37
Baxter, Anne 12, 51, 53, 84, 125
Baxter, Warner 19, 20, 29, 30, 59, 134
Beach, Rex 3, 4, 12, 22, 23, 41, 42, 54, 69
Beauchamp, D.D. 67
Beaumont, Gerald 18
Beatty, Warren 107, 108
Beavers, Louise 27
Beck, Michael 124
Bedford, Barbara 15, 16
Bedoya, Alfonso 73
Beebe, Ford J. 19
Beecher, Janet 68
Beecroft, Jeffrey 130
Beery, Noah 14, 16, 47
Beery, Noah, Jr. 27, 73, 137
Beery, Wallace 22, 23, 28, 54
Beethoven, Ludwig van 118
Belasco, David 3, 4, 5, 14, 22, 24, 25
Bell, James 112
Bellah, James Warner 51, 53, 54, 55, 57, 81, 86, 116, 118
Bellamy, Earl 7
Bellamy, Madge 14
Belushi, John 119
Bend of the River (1952) 59, 60, 62, 99, 139
Bend of the Snake 60
Bennett, Joan 31, 32
Bentley, Irene 27
Benton, Bill W. 130, 135
Benton, Robert 109, 11
Berenger, Tom 119, 120
Bergen, Candice 47, 104, 105, 114, 115
Berger, Senat 94
Berger, Thomas 14, 104, 105, 106
Bergerman, Stanley 25
Bergman, Marilyn & Alan 109
Bergunker, Max 24
Bernstein, Elmer 11, 73, 81, 83, 85, 95, 97, 100, 101, 106, 116, 141
Bernstein, Isadore 25
Bernstein, Walter 81, 84
Berti, Sanh 121
Besier, Rudolf 14, 27
Best, James 16
Bettger, Lyle 5
Bevans, Clem 90
Beyfuss, Alex E. 4
Bezzerides, A.I. 66
Bickford, Charles 22, 23, 24, 25, 47, 51, 76, 97, 99
Biehn, Michael 135
Bierman, Emil 24
The Big Country 75, 77
The Big Country (1958) 75, 76, 77, 99, 114, 118, 121, 134, 139
"Big Hunt" 55
Big Jake (1971) 106, 107, 108, 109
The Big Knife (1955) 124

The Big Land (1957) 72
The Big Sky 60, 133
The Big Sky (1952) 59, 60, 62, 84, 118, 121, 133 139
The Big Trail (1930) 22, 23, 120
Big Tree, Chief 97
Billy the Kid (1930) 22, 23, 123
Billy the Kid (1941) 40
Bingham, Edfrid 15, 16
Binyon, Claude 37
Birch, Paul 101
Biroc, Joseph (F.) 73, 75, 109, 11, 139
Bishop, Julie 3
Bishop, William 7, 79
Bissell, Whit 139
Bisset, Jacqueline 111
Bite the Bullet (1975) 114, 115, 126, 135, 139
Black, Don 100, 101
Black, Lucas 141
Black Horse Canyon (1954) 66
Blackie-Goodine, Janice 133
Blake, Amanda 20, 130
Blake, Michael 45, 130, 131
Blake, Robert 26, 101
Blanchard, Mari 18, 72, 104
Blane, Sally 27, 139
Blankfort, Michael 40, 56, 69, 70, 122
Blazing Saddles (1974) 141
Blondell, Joan 119
Blood Brother 55
Blood on the Moon (1948) 51, 53, 139
Bloom, Claire 92, 93
Bloom, Harold, Jack 14, 63, 65, 140
Bloom, Verna 112
Bloomberg, Daniel J. 43
Blue, Monte 27, 90
Blue Blazes Rawden (1918) 7, 8
Blystone, John G. 15, 16, 31
Boehm, Sydney 130
Boetticher, Budd 6, 71, 71, 72, 75, 77, 81, 84, 142, 143
Bogart, Humphrey 33, 55, 73
Bogdanovich, Peter 109
Boles, John 101
Boleslawski, Richard 30
Boley, May 24
Bolton, Delle 109, 110
Bon Jovi, Jon 130, 132
Bond, Lillian 37
Bond, Ward 27, 44, 45, 51, 65, 70, 71, 82, 84
Bondi, Beulah 40, 66, 121
Boone, Richard 6, 75, 92, 121
Booth, Karin 9
Boothe, Powers 135
Borden, Olive 16, 18, 49
The Border Jumper 75, 77
The Border Legion 7, 14, 15, 22, 27
The Border Legion (1918) 7
The Border Legion (1924) 14, 15

Index

The Border Legion (1930) 22
Borgnine, Ernest 7, 72
Borsos, Phillip 122
Borzage, Frank 14, 26, 27
Bosworth, Hobart 4, 5, 43
Bottoms, Sam 68, 114
Bouchey, Willis 118
Bower, B.M. 3, 4, 9, 10, 16, 17, 18, 19, 22, 37, 38
Bowers, John 10, 15, 29, 30
Bowers, William 6, 55, 75, 77, 100, 127
Boyd, Russell 142
Boyd, Stephen 19, 77, 118
Boyd, William 18, 25, 110
Boyd, William "Stage" 23
Boyle, Charles (P.) 45, 46, 99
Boyle, Peter 112
Boyle, Robert F. 116
Brackett, Leigh 5, 78, 97, 119
Brady, Scott 14, 66, 125
Branagh, Kenneth 141
Brand, Max/Evans, Evan 10, 11, 12, 25, 26, 32, 43, 44, 45, 55, 58, 59, 67
Brand, Neville 10, 133
Branded (1951) 58, 59
Brando, Marlon 14, 61, 85, 117
Brandon, Henry 131
The Bravados 75, 77
The Bravados (1958) 75, 77, 123, 130
The Brave Cowboy 91
Breamer, Sylvia 12
Breed of Men (1919) 8, 9
Brendel, El 18, 92
Brennan, Walter 30, 31, 32, 37, 38, 39, 47, 51, 59, 68, 79, 80, 89, 98, 101, 114
Brent, George 31, 32, 41, 119
Brest, Martin 134
Brian, David 3, 112
Brian, Mary 19, 20, 21
"The Bride Comes to Yellow Sky" 60, 63
Bridges, Jeff 111, 120, 138
Bridges, Lloyd 60, 61, 62, 140
Brissac, Virginia 119
Britton, Barbara 9, 60, 63, 120
Broderick, Matthew 130
Brodie, Steve 9, 133
Broeckman, David 22
Broken Arrow (1950) 55, 56, 57, 86, 118, 121, 139
Broken Lance (1954) 66, 67, 100, 134
Broncho Apache 66, 67
Bronson, Charles 10, 78, 82, 83
Brooks, Jack 46, 107
Brooks, Mel 141
Brooks, Richard 70, 72, 95, 96, 114, 115, 133, 135, 139
The Brothers Karamazov 67
Broughton, Bruce 124, 135
Brower, Otto 19, 22, 24, 25, 47

Brown, Barry 111
Brown, Fayte 37
Brown, Harry 7, 58, 97, 127
Brown, Harry Joe 112
Brown, Helen 5, 137
Brown, James 9
Brown, Jim 28, 101
Brown, Johnny Mack 23, 114
Brown, Karl 12, 15, 131
Brown, Lew 20
Brown, Will C. 75, 77, 138
Brown, Winona 5
Browne, Porter Emerson 22
Browne, Roscoe Lee 109, 111
Brunette, Fritzi 11
Bryan, Alfred 20
Brynner, Yul 5, 81, 82, 125
Buchanan, Edgar 40, 41, 43, 44, 76, 86, 90, 119
Buchanan Rides Alone (1958) 75, 78
Buchholz, Horst 82
Buckner, Robert (H.) 32, 129
Buetel, Jack 6, 43, 44, 130
Buffalo Bill (1944) 44, 45, 89
Buffalo Grass 72
Bugles in the Afternoon 60, 63
Bugles in the Afternoon (1952) 60, 63
Bujold, Geneviève 118
A Bullet for the General (1966) 95, 96
Bumstead, Henry 133
Bunker, Robert 109, 110
Buñuel, Luis 71
Burgess, Dorothy 20
Burgess, Helen 29
Burks, Robert 63
Burnett, W.R. 25, 26, 37, 45, 51, 55, 63
Burnette, Smiley 97
The Burning Hills 69, 129
The Burning Hills (1956) 69, 70, 129
Burns, Bob 31, 70
Burns, Walter Noble 22, 23, 25, 29, 30, 40, 41
Burr, Raymond 7, 135
Burroughs, Jackie 122
Burt, Frank 67, 68
Burton, David 24, 25
Burton, Richard 95, 102
Busch, Niven 37, 38, 46, 48, 49, 50, 55, 78, 132, 133
Busey, Gary 122
Butch and Sundance: The Early Days (1979) 119, 120
Butch Cassidy and the Sundance Kid (1969) 100, 101, 102, 126, 134, 141
Butler, David 10, 45, 46, 119
Butler, Frank 97
Butler, Michael 124
Buttolph, David 37, 40, 44, 58, 123

Caan, James 33, 97, 98, 100, 118, 119
Caan, Scott 142
"The Caballero's Way" 19
Cabanne, Christy 30, 31
Cabot, Bruce 30, 31, 110
Cabot, Susan 18, 127
Cagney, James 33, 127
Cahn, Edward (L.) 25, 26, 90
Cain, Christopher 128, 129
Calhern, Louis 28
Calhoun, Rory 11, 140, 141
California (1946) 46
The Californio 101
Callaghan, Duke 99, 109, 110
Calleia, Joseph 29, 58, 115
Calvet, Corinne 15
Cameron, Rod 63, 123
Campbell, Colin 3, 4, 19
Campbell, David 137
Campbell, Glen 101
Campbell, Martin 140
Campeau, Frank 7, 10, 11, 22
Canada, Ron 139
Canterbury Tales 18
Canutt, Yakima 126, 127
Canyon Passage 46, 58
Canyon Passage (1946) 46, 47, 48, 115, 118, 135
Capshaw, Kate 132
Captain Buffalo 81
Captain Courtesy (1915) 4, 5
"The Captives" 72, 75
Carbonara, Gerard 43
Carder, Michael 72
Cardinale, Claudia 33, 95, 96
Carewe, Edwin 19, 23, 37
Carey, Harry 5, 6, 7, 8, 10, 11, 12, 26, 27, 28, 35, 40, 41, 49, 50
Carey, Harry, Jr. 10, 53, 54, 55, 56
Carey, Macdonald 55, 137
Carey, Olive 70, 129
Carmichael, Hoagy 46, 48
Carpenter, Chris 135
Carpenter, Edward Childs 4
Carpenter, Florence 9
The Carpetbaggers 96
Carr, Mary 18
Carradine, David 29, 120
Carradine, John 32, 34, 128
Carradine, Keith 120
Carradine, Robert 120
Carrillo, Leo 28
Carroll, John 75
Carson, Robert 40, 43, 119
Carson, Sunset 11, 131
Carter, Forrest 115, 116, 117
Carter, Helena 12, 63
Cash, Johnny 107, 108
Cassavetes, John 78
Castel, Lou 96
Castle, Peggie 16, 112
Castle, William 3, 118
Cat Ballou (1965) 93, 94, 95, 127, 134

Index

Cather, Willa 2, 49, 50
Catlow 106
Catlow (1971) 106
Cattle Annie and Little Britches 121
Cattle Annie and Little Britches (1991) 121
Cattle Queen of Montana (1954) 122, 131
Chadwick, Helene 15
Champion (1949) 117
Chan, Jackie 141
Chandler, George 125
Chandler, Jeff 8, 56, 57, 85, 86
Chandler, John (Davis) 31, 89, 94
Chandler, Lane 110
Chandler, Raymond 50
Chaney, Lon, Jr. 112
Chanslor, Roy 92, 94, 95
Chase, Borden 51, 56, 60, 62, 66, 67, 107, 109
Chernus, Sonya 115
Cheyenne Autumn 91, 92
Cheyenne Autumn (1964) 91, 92, 111, 114, 126, 139
Chip of the Flying U 3, 4, 9, 10, 16, 17, 38
Chip of the Flying U (1914) 3, 4
Chip of the Flying U (1926) 16, 17
The Chisholm Trail 51
Chisum (1970) 104
Chopin Frédéric 135
Christie, Julie 107, 108, 109
Christine, Virginia 10, 139
Churchill, Berton 34
Churchill, Marguerite 22, 23
Cilento, Diane 97
Cimarron 24, 81, 84, 100
Cimarron (1931) 24, 84, 100, 134
Cimarron (1960) 81, 82, 84, 100, 124
Cimino, Michael 120
Citizen Kane (1941) 33, 40
City Slickers (1991) 132
City Slickers 2: The Legend of Curly's Gold (1994) 133
Clark, Al 76
Clark, Cliff 64
Clark, Dan 15, 16, 18
Clark, Dennis Lynton 119
Clark, Frank 3
Clark, James B. 141
Clark, Matt 29
Clark, Roy 19
Clark, Susan 37, 100, 103, 107, 108, 109
Clark, Walter Van Tilburg 42, 43, 50, 66, 67, 107, 109, 143
Clarke, Charles G. 16, `123
Clarke, Mae 133
Clawson, Elliott J. 16
Claxton, William F. 72
Cleese, John 125
Clemets, Calvin 119

Clifford, Ruth 7
Clift, Montgomery 52, 53, 91
Clifton, Frank M. 19
Cline, Edward F. 15, 85
Cline, Wilfrid M. 115
Clothier, William (H.) 70, 75, 78, 81, 83, 85, 86, 89, 91, 92, 94, 95, 99, 106, 139
Cobb, Lee J. 77, 116
Coburn, James 19, 82, 83, 112, 117, 137
Cochran, Steve 7, 94
Cody, Iron Eyes 132
Cohen, Leonard 107, 108
Cole, Nat King 95
Collins, Joan 77
Collins, Ray 94
Colman, Ronald 16, 17
Colorado Territory (1949) 54, 55
Columbo, Russ 23
Comanche Moon 126
Comanche Station (1960) 81, 83, 84, 95, 127, 143
The Comancheros 84
The Comancheros (1961) 84, 85
Comes a Horseman (1978) 119
"Command" 55
Company of Cowards 91
Compson, Betty 15, 16, 114
Connor, Ralph 10
Connors, Chuck 10, 133
The Conquerors (1932) 25, 115
Conrad, William 9, 137
Conroy, Frank 43, 44
Conselman, William 27
Conte, Richard 3, 115
Conway, Jack 10, 11, 28, 60
Conway, Michael 122
Cooder, Ry 49
Cook, Will 11, 92, 95
Cook, Elisha, Jr. 138
Coolidge, Rita 124
Coon, Gene (L.) 14, 99
Cooper, Chris 139
Cooper, Courtney Ryley 37
Cooper, Dorree 137
Cooper, Gary 16, 17, 18, 20, 21, 23, 24, 25, 29, 30, 37, 38, 39, 45, 46, 49, 60, 61, 62, 66, 67, 76, 77, 78, 79, 80, 81, 85, 86, 117, 132
Cooper, Paul 121
Coppola, Francis Ford 131
Coquillon, John 111
Corbett, Glenn 27, 135
Corby, Ellen 63, 140
Cord, Alex 96
Corey, Jeff 3, 107, 119, 120
Corey, Wendell 3, 99
Cormack, Bartlett 22
Corman, Roger 16
Coroner Creek 51, 53
Coroner Creek (1948) 51, 53
Cortez, Ricardo 16
Cosmatos, George P. 135, 136

Costa, Don 99
Costner, Kevin 68, 125, 130, 131, 132, 134, 137, 138
Cotten, Joseph 48, 120, 137
The Count of Monte Cristo 26, 140
Courtright, William 19
Cousminer, A. 24
The Covered Wagon 12, 13
The Covered Wagon (1923) 12, 13, 14
Cowboy (1958) 75, 76, 77, 118
The Cowboys (1972) 109, 110, 111
Cox, Joel 133
Crabbe, Larry "Buster" 27, 123
Craig, James 125
Crain, Jeanne 15
Crane, Stephen 60, 63
Cravat, Nick 137, 138
Crawford, Broderick 127
Crawford, Joan 66, 118
Crawford, John 104
Crenna, Richard 16
"Cressy" 8
The Crimson Challenge 11
The Crimson Pirate (1952) 138
Crisp, Donald 6, 68, 114
Cristal, Linda 29, 85
Cromwell, John 23
Cronjager, Edward 19, 24, 25, 29, 40, 46, 48, 82
Crosby, Bing 96
Crosby, Floyd 60, 61, 125
Crow Killer 109, 110
Crowe, Russell 138
Crowley, Kathleen 24
Cruz, Penelope 141
Cruze, James 12, 16, 41
The Crying Game (1992) 134
Crystal Billy 132
Cukor, George 84
Cummings, Irving 19, 20, 79, 132
Cummings, Robert 31, 32, 131
Cunningham, Jack 12, 25, 26, 27, 40
Cunningham, John (M.) 5, 60, 61, 62, 63, 75
Curtis, Billy 112
Curtis, Ken 6, 132
Curtis, Tony 15
Curtiz, Michael 25, 31, 32, 35, 38, 84, 85, 86
Curwood, James Oliver 9, 10, 18, 24, 37
Cushman, Dan 142, 143
Custer of the West (1968) 99, 100

Dahl, Arlene 14
Dakota (1945) 45, 115
Dallas (1950) 56
Dalton, Dorothy 11
Dalton, Timothy 142
Damiani, Damiano 95, 96
Damita, Lily 24, 25
Damon, Matt 141
Dana, Leora 73, 74

Index

Dances with Wolves 130, 131
Dances with Wolves (1990) 118, 130, 131, 132, 134
Daniels, Bebe 11, 12, 108
Daniels, William (H.) 67, 89, 104
Dante, Michael 28
Danton, Ray 24, 133
Darby, Ken 60, 66, 68, 85, 89, 90, 133
Darby, Kim 101
The Dark Commad 37
Dark Command (1940) 37, 38, 120
Darnell, Linda 10, 44, 45, 47, 48, 94, 95
Darwell, Jane 3, 32, 43, 44, 47, 51, 97, 99
Davenport, Harry 44, 54
Daves, Delmer 56, 57, 69, 72, 73, 76, 77, 78, 80, 118
Davey, Allen M. 43
David, Christopher 137
David, Hal 10, 100, 101, 104
David, Mack 78, 81, 94, 97, 135
Davis, George W. 82, 90
Davis, Jim 5, 109, 121
Davis, Ossie 99
Daw, Marjorie 7, 11, 18, 119
Dawley, Searle 4
Day of the Bad Man (1958) 75
Day of the Outlaw (1959) 78, 139
Day, Shannon 11
Dead Man's Walk 126
The Deadly Companions (1961) 84, 85, 139
Deadwood 138
Dean, Faxon M. 11, 94
Dean, Jack 6
Dean, James 72
Dean, Lisa 130
Death of a Gunfighter 100, 101
Death of a Gunfighter (1969) 100, 101
De Carlo, Yvonne 11, 89
Decision at Sundown 72, 75
Decision at Sundown (1957) 72, 75
De Corsia, Ted 112
Dee, Frances 30, 31, 51
De Grasse, Robert 30, 44, 107
de Grasse, Sam 6
de Havilland, Olivia 6, 31, 32, 41, 42
Dehner, John 5, 78, 133
Dekker, Albert 99
De Kova, Frank 121
Delon, Alain 28
Del Rio, Dolores 19, 81, 92, 123
Demarest, William 45, 46, 123
De Mille, Cecil B. 3, 4, 5, 36, 61, 79, 81
De Mille, Katherine 138
Dennehy, Richard 124, 125, 140
Denning, Richard 3
The Deputy 123
Derek, John 16, 140

Dern, Bruce 29, 115
De Sade, Ana 124
De Santis, Joe 130
Desert Gold 8
Desert Gold (1919) 8
The Desert Pirate (1928) 19
The Desert's Price (1926) 16
The Desert's Toll (1926) 16
The Desire of the Moth 6, 7
The Desire of the Moth (1917) 6, 7
The Desperadoes (1943) 42, 43, 127, 142
Destry (1955) 67, 89
Destry Rides Again 25, 26, 32, 45, 67
Destry Rides Again (1932) 25, 26
Destry Rides Again (1939) 32, 35, 36, 91, 115, 139
DeSylva, B.G. 20
De Toth, Andre 49, 55, 59, 69
Deutsch, Adolph 49, 120
Devil's Doorway (1950) 55, 57, 58,
Devine, Andy 34, 45, 87, 89, 118
De Vinna, Clyde 31, 64
De Vol, Frank 89, 94, 140
De Voto, Bernard 58, 59
De Wese, Mohanndes 141
De Wilde, Brandon 41, 63, 64, 91, 110
De Witt, Jack 106
Dexter, Brad 82
Dexter, Pete 138
Dey, Tom 141
Diamonds (1999) 117
DiCaprio, Leonardo 138
Dickinson, Angie 24, 79, 101
Dierkes, John 115
Dietrich, Marlene 32, 36, 41, 42, 60, 63, 133
A Distant Trumpet 91, 92
A Distant Trumpet (1964) 91, 92
Dix, Beulah Marie 7, 11, 43
Dix, Richard 12, 14, 16, 24, 25, 27, 28, 54
Dmytryk, Edward 66, 67, 78, 80
Doc (1971) 106, 109
Dockendorf, Daniel 101
Doctorow, E.L. 97, 98
Dodge City (1939) 32, 35, 36, 38
Donahue, Troy 92
Doniger, Walter 58, 59
Donlevy, Brian 35, 41, 47, 48, 63, 110
Donnelly, Ruth 122
Doran, Ann 141
Dostoyefsky Fyodor 67
"A Double-Dyed Deceiver" 22
Doucette, John 10, 68, 137
Douglas, Gordon 76, 96, 135
Douglas, Kirk 6, 57, 60, 62, 68, 69, 73, 80, 85, 91, 98, 99, 108, 114, 115, 117, 138
Douglas, Melvyn 28, 50, 91, 121
Dove, Billie 15, 16, 139

Dowling, Joseph 6
Downs, Cathy 14, 47, 48, 116
Drago, Harry Sinclair 18
Drake, Charles 3, 137
Dreier, Hans 37
Dressler, Louise 12
Drew, Ellen 5, 59
Dru, Joanne 12, 51, 54, 55, 56, 59, 139
Drum Beat (1954) 66
DuBrey, Claire 8, 135
Duel at Diablo (1966) 95, 96
Duel in the Sun 46, 48, 133
Duel in the Sun (1946) 46, 47, 48, 123, 133
Duff, Howard 131
Duff, Warren 112
Dumas, Alexandre 26, 140
Dunaway, Faye 104, 105, 109
Dunham, "By" 89
Duning, George 54, 68, 73, 74, 141, 142
Dunlap, Paul 9
Dunn, Emma 23, 96
Dunne, Irene 24
Durham, Marilyn 111
Duryea, Dan 45, 46, 67, 99, 100
Duryea, George 22
Dutton, George 73
Duvall, Robert 24, 129, 135
Duvall, Shelley 107
Dvorak, Ann 119
Dwan, Allan 5, 6, 7, 22, 28, 48, 67, 73, 121, 131
Dwan, Dorothy 17, 121
Dylan, Bob 111, 112

Eastwood, Clint 23, 24, 64, 91, 92, 93, 106, 111, 112, 113, 115, 116, 117, 124, 125, 133, 134, 141
Edeson, Arthur 19, 22, 104
Edeson, Robert 5
Edington, May 14, 27
Edmundson, William 101
Edouart, Franciot 33
Edwards, Blake 11
Edwards, Sherman 81
Egan, Richard 10, 81, 118
El Dorado (1967) 80, 97, 98, 117, 118, 120, 139
Elam, Jack 6, 59
The Electric Horseman (1979) 120
Elliott, Sam 44, 135
Elliott, William ("Wild Bill") 94
Ellis, Edward 30
Ellison, James 29
Elmer, Billy 3, 5
Elwes, Cary 130
Emerson, Hope 82
Emhardt, Robert 3, 137
The Emigrants (1970) 114
Emmerick, Roland 141
Engel, Samuel G. 46, 47, 48
Enright, Ray 41, 42, 94
Erdman, Richard 15

Index

Erickson, Leif 16, 127
Erol, Jakub 125
Escape from Fort Bravo (1954) 66, 67
Essex, Harry 139
Estabrook, Howard 19, 24, 25, 119
Estevez, Emilio 128, 129, 132
Evans, Evan/Brand, Max 10, 11, 12, 25, 26, 32, 43, 45, 55, 58, 59, 67
Evans, Dale 140, 142
Evans, Gene 11, 40
Evans, Joan 27
Evans, Linda 120, 121
Evans, Ray 5, 76
Evanson, Edith 27
Evarts, Hal (G.) 15, 16, 27
Eyton, Bessie 3

Face of a Fugitive (1959) 78
Face to Face (1952) 60, 63
Fair, Elinor 18, 73
Fairbanks, Douglas 5, 6, 7, 8, 33, 36, 37
Faire, Virginia Browne 17
Fairfax, Marion 5
Faith, Russ 89
Fapp, Daniel (L.) 127
The Far Country (1955) 67, 68, 130, 133
Farnsworth, Richard 9, 119, 120, 122, 141
Farnum, Dustin 3, 4, 5, 8, 9, 20, 22
Farnum, William 3, 4, 8, 22, 25, 28, 64
Farr, Felicia 72, 74
Farrell, Colin 142
Farrow, John 63, 65, 90
The Fastest Gun Alive (1956) 69, 70
Father Murphy 121, 123
Fathers and Sons 138
Faust, Frederick Schiller 44
Fawcett, George 22
Faylen, Frank 125
Fellini, Federico 71
Fenton, Frank 66
Fenton, Leslie 54, 55, 119
Ferber, Edna 24, 81, 84, 99, 100
Ferguson, Frank 119
Fernandez, Emilio 127
Ferrari William 90
Ferrer, Jose 61
Ferrer, Mel 63
Ferry, April 137
A Few Good Men (1992) 134
Field, Betty 40
Field, Sally 97
Fielding, Jerry 11, 100, 116, 120
Fields, Joseph A. 28
Fighting Caravans 24, 25, 27
Fighting Caravans (1931) 24, 25, 99

Fighting Cressy (1919) 8
Fink, Harry Julian 94
Firecreek (1968) 99, 100
First Blood 63
Fisher, Clay/Henry, Will 67, 68, 69, 78, 99, 100, 101
Fisher, Frances 133
Fisher, Gerry 106
Fisher, Vardis 95, 99, 100, 109, 110
A Fistful of Dollars (1964) 91, 92, 93, 130
FitzSimons, Charles B. 85
Fix, Paul 44, 72, 123
The Flame and the Arrow (1950) 138
Flaming Lance 81
Flaming Star (1960) 81, 82, 84, 133
Fleischer, Richard 81, 113, 114
Fleischman, A.S. 84
Fleming, Rhonda 11, 73
Fleming, Victor 5, 7, 14, 19 20, 21, 22, 33, 54
Flippen, Jay C. 68, 107
Flying U Ranch 18, 38
Flying U Ranch (1927) 18
Flynn, Emmett (J.) 17, 31
Flynn, Errol 32, 35, 38, 41, 42, 45, 46, 79
Flynn, T.T. (Thomas) 67, 68, 119
Folsey, George (J.) 70, 128
Fonda, Henry 35, 36, 37, 38, 43, 44, 47, 48, 49, 51, 53, 73, 74, 79, 80, 91, 98, 100, 121, 122, 123
Fonda, Jane 31, 94, 95, 119, 120, 130
Fonda, Peter 33, 108
For a Few Dollars More (1965) 93, 94, 130
Foran, Dick 119
Forbes, Louis 68
Ford, Ernie 59
Ford, Francis 25, 64, 65
Ford, Glenn 6, 40, 41, 43, 54, 55, 72, 74, 76, 77, 84
Ford, Harrison 41
Ford, John (Jack) 8, 10, 11, 14, 16, 17, 18, 23, 32, 33, 34, 35, 46, 47, 48, 49, 50, 51, 53, 54, 55, 56, 57, 61, 70, 71, 81, 83, 84, 85, 86, 87, 88, 89, 91, 92, 112, 113, 118, 120, 132, 139
Ford, Wallace 72, 96
Foreman, Carl 3, 60, 124
Foreman, L.L. 60, 66
Forman, Tom 14, 16
Forrest, Steve 14, 84
Forsyth, Rosemary 95
Fort Apache (1948) 51, 53, 84, 95, 97, 123
Fort Dobbs (1958) 75
Fortune, Jan 37

Forty Guns (1957) 72, 73, 75
Foster, Dianne 19
Foster, Jodie 136
Foster, Lewis R. 114
Foster, Norman 116
Foster, Preston 26, 30, 31, 104
Four Faces West (1948) 28, 51, 53, 99
Fowler, Harry 10, 66
Fowler, Gene, Jr. 78
Fox, Finis 19
Fox, Norman 69, 72, 82
Fox, Wallace 28
Fraker, William A. 12, 104, 135
Franciosa, Anthony 101
Francis, Alec B. 19
Francis, Anne 23
Francis, Freddie 130
Frank, Harriet, Jr. 67, 91, 97, 109, 113
Franklin, Dave 68, 104
Franklin, Martha 20
Franks, Michael 113
Franz, Eduard 70
Frawley, James 112
Frederici, Blanche 23, 26
Fredricks, Ellsworth 67, 135
Freeman, Kathleen 9, 142
Freeman, Mona 16, 55
Freeman, Morgan 130, 133
Fregonese, Hugo 127
French, Valerie 24, 70, 72, 75, 131
Fresholtz, Les 114, 133
Freund, Karl 56
Friedhofer, Hugo 45, 56, 60, 63, 66, 85, 121
Friendly Persuasion (1956) 76
From Hell to Texas (1958) 75, 76, 77, 119, 126
Frontier Gal (1945) 45, 123
Frontier Marshal (1934) 27, 28
Frontier Marshal (1939) 28, 32, 58, 121
Frontiere, Dominic 24, 99
Fuller, Samuel 72, 75, 139
The Furies 55, 133
The Furies (1950) 55, 56, 78, 133
Furthman, Jules 43, 78, 79, 82, 84
Fusco, John 128, 132

Gable, Clark 25, 58, 59, 68, 69, 82, 91
Gabriel, John 97
The Gabriel Horn 67
The Galloping Devil (1920) 9
Gam, Rita 19
Gamet, Kenneth 58, 107
Gammon, James 138
Gandolfi, Alfred 3
Ganton, Douglas 137
Garden of Evil (1954) 66, 67, 115
Gardner, Ava 110
Garfield, Brian 33, 115, 117

Garmes, Lee 24, 46, 110
Garner, James 19, 96, 97, 98, 102, 103, 137, 141
Garrett, Grant 46
Garvarentz, George 123
Gates, Nancy 84
Gay, John 14
Gausman, Russell A. 41
Geer, Will 109, 119
Gentle Annie 44
Gentle Annie (1944) 44
George, Chief Dan 104, 116, 121
George, Christopher 20, 123
George, Maude 7
Geraghty, Gerard 30
Gere, Richard 136
Geronimo: An American Legend (1993) 135
Gershenson, Joseph 128
Gerstad, Harry 60
Gertsman, Maury 86, 140
Ghost (1990) 131
Giant (1956) 28, 72, 115
Gibson, Hoot 6, 17, 22, 28, 86
Gibson, Mel 141
Gielgud, Gwen Bagni 69
"The Gift of Cochise" 63, 65
Gilbert, Billy 108
Gilbert, Herschel Burke 8
Gilbert, L. Wolf 19
Gilchrist, Connie 125
Gilks, Alfred 14, 15
Gilkyson, Terry 6, 140
Gillis, Richard 104
Gilmore, Stuart 48, 82
Gilmore, Virginia 40
Gipson, Fred 89, 112
The Girl of the Golden West 4, 5, 12, 14, 22, 25
The Girl of the Golden West (1915) 4, 5
The Girl of the Golden West (1923) 12, 14
The Girl of the Golden West (1930) 22
The Girl Who Ran Wild (1922) 11
Gish, Lillian 47, 48, 81, 135
Glassberg, Irving 60
Glaum, Louise 6
Gleason, Adda 6
Gleason, James 79
Glenn, Scott 124, 125, 132
Glennon, Bert 12, 32, 45, 46, 56, 58
Glickman, Fred 56
Glory (1989) 130
Glover, Danny 125, 129
The Godfather Part III (1990) 131
Goin' South (1978) 118, 119
Gold, Ernest 10, 85
Gold Is Where You Find It (1938) 31, 32
Goldbeck, Willis 86, 119
Goldblum, Jeff 125
Golden, Olive 6

Goldman, William 24, 100, 101
Goldsmith, Jerry 20, 97, 104, 105, 135, 136
Goldstone, James 101
Gone to Texas 115, 116
Gone with the Wind (1939) 30, 33, 48
Gonzalez-Gonzalez, Pedro 16, 79
The Good Bad Man (1916) 5, 6, 36
Good Men and True 11, 12
Good Men and True (1922) 11, 12
The Good, the Bad and the Ugly (1966) 95, 96, 130
Goodboy, Joe 6
Goodbye, Mr. Chips (1969) 102
GoodFellas (1990) 131
Goodman, David Zelag 104
Goodman, John B. 41
Goodrich, Frances 124
Goodwin, Harold 11
Gordon, Dan 138
Gordon, Leo 11, 141
Goudal, Jetta 18
Grace, Henry 82, 90
Grahame, Gloria 14, 121
Grahame, Margot 28
Granger, Stewart 72, 135
Grant, James Edward 49, 50, 63, 65, 69, 75, 77, 83, 84, 89, 91, 96, 97
Grant, Kathryn 26
Grant, Rodney A. 131
Graves, Peter 15
Gray, Coleen 11, 51, 52, 53
The Gray Dawn 11
The Gray Dawn (1922) 11
The Great Bank Robbery 101
The Great Bank Robbery (1969) 101
The Great Escape (1963) 83
The Great K & A Train Robbery (1926) 16, 17, 38
The Great Man's Lady (1942) 41, 42, 45, 132
The Great Train Robbery (1903) 3
The Greatest Show on Earth (1952) 61
Green, Alfred E. 53, 82
Green, Faith 10
Green, Jack N. 133, 141
Green, John 95
Green, Walon 100, 101
Greene, Graham 130, 131
Greene, Lorne 5, 127
Greene, Mort 51
Greene, W. Howard 37, 40, 67, 70
Greenstreet, Sydney 41
Greenwood, Don, Jr. 90
Gregg, Virginia 6, 127
Gregory, James 92
Grey, Virginia 7
Grey, Zane 7, 8, 9, 10, 12, 14, 16, 17, 18, 22, 24, 25, 26, 27, 28, 31, 32, 33, 36, 37, 40, 45, 49, 67, 69
The Grey Fox (1982) 120, 122

Gries, Tom 99, 100, 101, 118
Griffith, D.W. 4
Griggs, Loyal 63, 64, 73, 75, 119
Grilikhes, Michael M. 95
Grimes, Gary 114
Gross, Larry 135
Gruber, Frank 43, 72, 101
Grusin, Dave 27, 107
Guffey, Burnett 14, 15, 63, 67, 123
Guinness, Alec 61
Gulick, Bill 6, 60, 62, 94
Gun Belt (1953) 142
Gun Down 115, 117
Gun for a Coward (1957) 72
Gun Fury (1953) 63
Gun the Man Down (1956) 70
A Gunfight (1971) 106, 107, 108, 130
Gunfight at the O.K. Corral (1957) 72, 73, 83, 98, 130, 134, 135, 138, 139, 140
The Gunfighter (1950) 55, 56, 65, 106, 123, 127
Gunfighters (1947) 49
Gunman's Chance 51, 53
The Guns of Fort Petticoat 72
The Guns of Fort Petticoat (1957) 72
Guns of North Texas 95
Guns of Paradise (1990) 132
Guns of Rio Conchos 91
Guns of the Timberland (1960) 81
Guns of the Timberlands 81
Gunsmoke 108
Guthrie, A.B., Jr. 58, 60, 62, 63, 64, 78, 81, 97, 98, 127, 132, 133
Guthrie, Carl (E.) 97

Hackett, Albert 138
Hackett, Joan 99, 100
Hackman, Gene 23, 24, 113, 114, 115, 133, 135, 138
Hageman, Richard 32, 51, 54, 56, 96, 97
Haines, William Wister 31
Hajos, Karl 24
Hale, Alan 14
Hale, Alan, Jr. 8, 131
Hale Barbara 10
Hale, Scott 115
Hale, William 100
The Half Breed (1916) 5, 6, 36
Hall, Conrad 16, 95, 100, 101, 102
Hall, Oakley 78
Hall, Porter 29, 64
The Hallelujah Trail (1965) 94
Hallelujah Train 94
Haller, Ernest 56, 75, 104
Halton, Charles 79
Hamill, Pete 106, 109
Hamilton, Donald 6, 67, 75, 76
Hamilton, George 33
Hamilton, James Shelley 14
Hand, Herman 24
Hands Across the Border (1926) 16

Index

Hang 'Em High (1968) 99, 100
"The Hanging Tree" 78
The Hanging Tree (1959) 78, 79, 80, 86, 118, 124
Hangman's Knot (1952) 60, 118
Hannah Lee (1953) 63
Hansen, Franklin 29
Harding, Ann 25
Harlan, Kenneth 12
Harlan, Russell 41, 43, 49, 51, 60, 70, 78, 114
Harline, Leigh 38, 51, 76, 101
Harling, W. Franke 32
Harper, Tess 132
Harris, Frank 75, 77
Harris, Joe 9, 64
Harris, Richard 23, 24, 94, 106, 107, 108, 116, 117, 133
Harrison, C. William 72
Hart, Dorothy 12
Hart, William S. 5, 6, 7, 8, 9, 10, 15, 16, 22, 47, 49
Harte, Bret 3, 4, 5, 6, 7, 8, 9, 11, 12, 14, 29, 30, 60, 67
Hartley, Mariette 86
Harvey, Lawrence 83, 93
Harvey, Paul 37
Haskin, Byron 124
Hathaway, Henry 26, 27, 40, 41, 58, 59, 75, 76, 77, 81, 90, 91, 95, 96, 100, 101, 103, 109, 115, 120, 125, 126
Hatton, Raymond 5, 6, 15, 22, 23, 25, 108
Hausen, Robert 104
Hawks, Howard 51, 53, 57, 60, 62, 78, 79, 80, 97, 98, 106, 114, 118, 120, 139
Hawks, J.G. 6, 8, 37
Haycox, Ernest 32, 35, 41, 46, 48, 56, 58, 59, 60, 63, 95, 96
Hayden, Russell 121
Hayden, Sterling 6, 67, 127
Hayes, George "Gabby" 45, 101, 140
Hayes, John Michael 95
Hayward, Lillie 119
Hayward, Susan 8, 47, 48, 58, 59, 115
Hayworth, Rita 81
Hazard, Lawrence 41
Head, Edith 86
Headin' South (1918) 7, 8, 36
Headrick, Richard 9
Heath, Hy 56
Heaven's Gate (1980) 120, 121
Heckart, Eileen 114
Heflin, Van 30, 31, 64, 73, 74, 81, 109, 109
Hehr, Addison 82, 90
Heilbron, Adelaide 12
Heindorf, Ray 45
Heinl, Bernd 132
Heisler, Stuart 45, 46, 119
The Hell Bent Kid 75, 77

Heller, Lukas 104
Heller in Pink Tights (1960) 81, 84, 129, 142
Heller with a Gun 81, 84
Hellman, Monte 96
Hellman, Sam 32, 37, 46, 48, 56, 58
Hell's Heroes (1930) 22, 23, 99
Hell's Hinges (1916) 5, 6, 49
Helton, Percy 108
Hemphill, Doug 135
Henabery, Joseph 7, 11, 12, 116
Hendrix, Wanda 19, 121
Henriksen, Lance 138
Henry, O. 19, 20, 22, 23
Henry, Will/Fisher, Clay 67, 68, 69, 78, 99, 100, 101
Hepburn, Audrey 81, 84
Hepburn, Katharine 49, 50, 114, 115
Herbert, F. Hugh 37
The Heritage of the Desert 14, 15, 25, 32, 36
The Heritage of the Desert (1924) 14, 15
Heritage of the Desert (1932) 25
Heritage of the Desert (1939) 32
Hershey, Barbara 116, 117
Hersholt, Jean 68
Heston, Charlton 12, 76, 94, 99, 100, 117, 118
Heydt, Louis Jean 82
Hibbs, Jesse 125
Hickman, Howard 10
Hickox, Sidney (Sid) 54, 55, 58, 122
Hicks, Russell 73
Higgin, Howard 25
High Noon (1952) 59, 60, 61, 62, 67, 73, 75, 79, 86, 89, 108, 112, 120, 124, 130, 134
High Plains Drifter (1973) 111, 112, 113, 117, 125
High Sierra (1941) 55
High Vermilion 58, 59
Hilb, Emil 24
Hill (Vidor), Elizabeth 29
Hill, George Roy 100, 102
Hill, Marianna 112
Hill, Walter 120, 135, 138
Hillyer, Lambert 8, 9, 10, 101
Hinds, Samuel S. 27, 32, 51
Hingle, Pat 12, 92, 99
The Hired Hand (1971) 106, 108
Hively, George 56
Hoch, Winton (C.) 51, 54, 55, 70, 86, 119, 120
Hodiak, John 3, 59
Hoffman, Dustin 102, 104, 105
Hoffman, Lee 99, 111
Hogan, James P. 31, 32, 43
Hogan, Michael 44
Holden, Jennifer 78
Holden, William 8, 37, 38, 40, 41, 55, 67, 81, 101, 102, 121

Hollander, Frederick 32
Hollenberger, Harry 37
Holliman, Earl 19
Holly, Helen 10
Holmes, Helen 6
Holt, Felix 67
Holt, Jack 11, 12, 14, 15, 19, 22, 59
Holt, Tim 34, 112
Hombre 97
Hombre (1967) 97, 118, 121, 126
Homeier, Skip 20
Homer 133
Hondo (1953) 63, 64, 65, 84, 95, 117, 129
Honky Tonk (1941) 40
Hoove, Marilyn & Joe 76
Hope, Gloria 8
Hopkins, Anthony 140
Hopkins, Bo 41, 114
Hopper, Dennis 29, 112
Horgan, Paul 91, 92
Horne, Lena 101
Horner, James 132, 137
The Horse Soldiers 78, 81
The Horse Soldiers (1959) 78, 81, 121, 139
The Horse Whisperer (1998) 140
Horseman, Pass By 91
Hough, Emerson 12, 13, 14, 31, 32
Hough, John 124
Hour of the Gun (1967) 97, 98, 113, 129, 142
Houser, Lionel 37
How the West Was Won 118, 119
How the West Was Won (1963) 89, 90, 91, 114, 130, 140
Howard, James Newton 137
Howard, John 138
Howard, Leslie 26, 27
Howard, Ron 64, 114, 116
Howard, Vechel (Howard Rigsby) 84, 85
Howard, William K. 15, 18, 66
Howards End (1992) 134
Howe, James Wong 49, 50, 91, 93, 97, 116, 118
Hud (1963) 91, 97
Huddleston, Floyd 99
Hudson, Rock 15, 72, 85, 125
Huffaker, Clair 19, 81, 84, 91, 97, 98, 99, 130
Huggins, Roy 60, 63
Hughes, Howard 43, 44
Hughes, Mary Beth 9, 43, 138
Hughes, Russell S. 69, 76
Hulette, Gladys 14
Hull, George C. 10
Hull, Henry 36, 37, 118
Humberstone, H. Bruce 124
Hunnicutt, Arthur 60, 73, 97, 98, 114, 119
Hunt, Hugh 82
Hunt, J. Roy 19, 28
Hunt, Linda 124, 125, 137

Hunter, Jeffrey 15, 70, 71, 83, 100, 101
Hunter, John 120, 122, 138
Hunter, Tab 24
Huppert, Isabelle 120
Hurst, Paul 64
Hurt, John 120
Huston, Anjelica 129
Huston, John 25, 54, 83, 91, 108, 111, 127
Huston, Walter 20, 21, 25, 26, 43, 48, 54, 56, 58
Hutchinson, Josephine 95, 140
Hyer, Martha 14, 95

Iliad 98
In Old Arizona (1929) 19, 20, 134
In Old Oklahoma (1943) 43
"In the Carquinez Woods" 5
Ince, Thomas H. 4
Independence (1987) 127
The Indian Fighter (1955) 67, 69
Ingraham, Lloyd 18, 19
Invitation to a Gunfighter (1964) 92
Ireland, Jill 29, 131
Ireland, John 3, 133
The Iron Horse (1924) 14, 113
The Iron Mistress 60
The Iron Mistress (1952) 60
Ivers, Julia Crawford 5
Ives, Burl 76, 138, 139
Ivory, James 134

Jaccard, Jacques 6
Jackson, Felix 32
Jackson, Frederick 30
Jackson, Helen Hunt 5, 6, 19, 29, 30
Jackson, Howard 96
Jackson, Jennie 86
Jaeckel, Richard 16, 73, 139
Jagger, Dean 40, 49, 50, 132
James, Will 41, 106, 109
Jarre, Kevin 135
Jarre, Maurice 14, 95, 109, 111, 114
Jarman, Claude, Jr. 57
Jennings, Gordon 33
Jennings, William Dale 7, 109, 111,
Jenson, Roy 28
Jeremiah Johnson (1972) 100, 109, 110, 111
"Jeremy Rodock" 69
Jerome, M.K. 45
Jesse James (1927) 18
Jesse James (1939) 32, 36, 99, 123, 127
Jewel, Betty 18
Jim the Conqueror 18
Jim the Conqueror (1927) 18
Johnny Guitar (1954) 66, 67, 72, 138
Johnson, Ben 8, 53, 56, 85, 109, 114, 132, 139

Johnson, Chubby 114
Johnson, Dorothy M. 78, 80, 86, 88, 104, 106, 117, 124
Johnson, Kay 22, 23
Johnson, Lamont 108, 109
Johnson, Nunnally 32, 45, 46, 81, 118
Johnson, Russell 14
Johnston, J.W. 3
Jones, Buck 41
Jones, Carolyn 20, 79, 80
Jones, Grover 19, 37, 40
Jones, Harmon 110
Jones, Henry 140
Jones, Jennifer 47, 48
Jones, L.Q. 18, 89, 94
Jones, Quincy 100
Jones, Shirley 27
Jones, Stan 56, 66, 70, 90
Jones, Tommy Lee 129, 141
Jordan, Neil 134
Jory, Victor 122
Journey to Shiloh 99, 100
Journey to Shiloh (1968) 99, 100
Jubal (1956) 69, 70, 118
Jubal Troop 69, 72
Julian, Rupert 7
June, Ray 26
Junior Bonner (1972) 132
Jurado, Katy 18, 60, 61, 62, 66, 76, 85, 112
Just Tony (1922) 11, 12

Kane, Joel 72, 75
Kane, Joseph (Joe) 63, 115
The Kansan (1943) 42, 43
Kantor, Mackinlay 37, 44, 63, 118
Kaper, Bronislau (Bronislaw) 63, 97, 123, 124
Kaplan, Jonathan 136
Kaplan, Sol 9, 58, 131
Karlin, Fred 29, 113
Karlson, Phil 125
Kasdan, Lawrence 124, 125, 137, 138
Kasdan, Mark 124
Katt, William 119, 120
Katterjohn, Monte M. 5
Kaufman, Philip 115
Kaye, Buddy 123
Kaye, Stubby 95
Kazan, Elia 49, 50
Keach, James 121
Keach, Stacy 40, 109, 121
Keel, Howard 7, 98
Keep the Change (1992) 134
Keith, Brian 10, 68, 75, 85, 95, 139
Keith, Robert 25, 96
Kelland, Clarence Budington 37, 38, 41, 58, 59, 92, 93
Keller, Harry 127
Kelley, DeForest 9, 140
Kelley, William 118
Kelly, Grace 60, 61, 62

Kelly, Helen 7
Kelly, Nancy 36
Kelton, Elmer 2, 129
Kemper, Charles 56
Kennedy, Arthur 3, 63, 68, 96, 131
Kennedy, Burt 11, 69, 71, 72, 78, 81, 97, 98, 101, 103 114
Kennedy, Douglas 5, 112
Kennedy, George 15, 94
The Kentuckian (1955) 67
Kenyon, Charles 14
Kenyon, John Russell 14
Kernochan, Sarah 136
Kerrigan, J. Warren 12, 13, 14, 49
Keyes, Evelyn 9, 43
Kibbee, Roland 3, 66, 106, 124
Kid Blue (1973) 111, 112
Kid Rodelo 95
Kid Rodelo (1966) 95
Kilian, Victor 119
The Killer (1921) 10
Kilmer, Val 135, 136
Kilvert, Lilly 137
King, Anita 5
King, Henry 16, 17, 32, 36, 56, 76, 106, 122, 123
King, Louis 27, 86
Kingston, Winifred 3, 4, 5, 6, 8, 97
Kirkwood, James 90
Kline, Kevin 124, 125, 141
Kline, Richard 125
Kline, Wally 41
Knapp, Evalyn 25
Knibbs, Henry Herbert 16
Knight, Fuzzy 27, 116
A Knight of the Range (1916) 5, 6
Knopf, Christopher 114
Knox, Alexander 58, 59, 138
Koenekamp, Fred (J.) 11, 114
Kohler, Fred 14, 23, 25, 27, 31
Kovacs, Laszlo 26, 119
Kramer, Cecile 44, 49
Kramer, Stanley 61, 62
Krasner, Milton 45, 58, 59, 89, 128
Kress, Harold F. 90
Krims, Milton 27
Kristofferson, Kris 29, 112, 120, 139
Kruger, Otto 114
Krumgold, Sigmund 24, 32
Kulp, Nancy 10, 132
Kurosawa, Akira 71, 93
Kutcher, Ashton 142
Kyne, Peter B. 4, 5, 8, 9, 11, 12, 18, 19, 22, 23, 29, 30, 31, 40, 50, 51, 54, 73, 75

Ladd, Alan 54, 63, 64, 92, 93
The Lady from Cheyenne (1941) 40
Lai, Francis 118
Laine, Frankie 74
Lake, Florence 120

Index

Lake, Stuart N. 27, 30, 37, 38, 46, 47, 48, 56, 58, 92, 93
Lake, Veronica 49, 50
Lamb, Harold 29
Lambert, Jack 9
L'Amour, Louis 63, 65, 67, 69, 72, 75, 81, 84, 91, 95, 99, 106, 111, 128, 129
Lancaster, Burt 57, 59, 66, 67, 73, 81, 83, 95, 96, 98, 99, 107, 108, 109, 111, 121, 137, 138
Landis, Cullen 8, 9
Landon, Joseph
Landon, Michael 121
Lane, Allan ("Rocky") 112
Lane, Charles 135
Lane, Diane 121, 129, 138
Lane, Nora 18, 19, 22, 51
Lane, Rosemary 33
Lang, Charles (B.), Jr. 40, 58, 73, 81, 84, 85, 89, 140
Lang, Fritz 37, 38, 40, 63, 116
Lange, Arthur 45
Lange, Johnny 56
Larch, John 11, 137
Larsen, Keith 15
Larter, Ali 142
LaRue, Jack 27
La Rue, Lash 7, 139
LaShelle, Joseph (Joe) 16, 89, 130
La Shelle, Kirk 20
Lasky, Jesse, Jr. 128
The Last Hard Men (1976) 115
The Last Hunt 69, 72
The Last Hunt (1956) 69, 70, 72, 115, 116, 117, 135
The Last of the Duanes (1924) 15
The Last Picture Show 109
The Last Picture Show (1971) 109
The Last Posse (1953) 63, 115
The Last Round-Up (1934) 27
Last Stand at Papago Wells 75
The Last Sunset (1961) 84, 85, 124, 139
The Last Trail 18
The Last Trail (1921) 10
The Last Trail (1927) 18
Last Train from Gun Hill (1959) 78, 79, 80, 83, 135, 139, 140, 142
The Last Wagon (1956) 69, 97, 130
Laszlo, Ernest 66, 124
Lathrop, Philip (H.) 6, 138
Laurani, Salvatore 95
Laven, Arnold 11
The Law and Jake Wade (1958) 75, 76
Law and Order (1932) 25, 26
Law and Order (1953) 122
A Lawless Street (1955) 68
Lawrence, Barbara 19
Lawrence, Vincent 49
Lawton, Harry 100, 101
Lawton, Charles, Jr. 73, 74, 84, 85, 94, 95

Lea, Tom 78, 80, 142, 143
Leahy, Agnes Brand 22, 24
Leavitt, Sam 94
Ledger, Heath 141
Lee, Peggy 66
The Left Handed Gun (1958) 75, 76, 78, 126
"Legends of the Fall" 137
Legends of the Fall (1994) 134, 137
Legrand, Michel 120
Lehman, Johnny 63
Leigh, Janet 18, 63
Leipold, John 24, 32
Lelouch, Claude 118
LeMay, Alan 45, 46, 55, 69, 70, 81, 84, 92, 93
Leonard, Elmore 15, 72, 74, 97, 98, 106, 107, 108
Leone, Sergio 10, 91, 93, 94, 95, 96, 117, 130, 133, 134
Lerner, Sam 40
Levis, Henry 120
Levy, Melvin 29
Lewis, Eugene B. 8
Lewis, Geoffrey 28
Lewis, Harold 58
Lewis, Joseph H. 141
Lewis, Vera 19
The Life and Times of Judge Roy Bean (1972) 109, 110, 111, 127
The Light of Western Stars 7, 8, 15, 22, 37
The Light of Western Stars (1918) 7, 8, 22
The Light of Western Stars (1925) 15
The Light of Western Stars (1930) 22
The Light of Western Stars (1940) 37
Lin McLean 7, 8
Lindon, Lionel 58, 107
Lindsay, Margaret 31, 41
Linford, Dee 67, 69, 100, 101
Lipman, William 46
Lipsitz, Harold B. 18
Lipstein, Harold 58, 114
Lister, "Tiny" 135
Litel, John 110
Little, Ann 7, 124
Little, Cleavon 141
Little Big Man 104, 105, 106
Little House on the Prairie 121
Littlefield, Lucien 16
Liu, Lucy 141
Livingston, Jay 5, 76, 142
Livingston, Jerry 78, 81, 94, 127
Lloyd, Christopher 31, 119
Lloyd, Frank 8, 30, 31, 82
Locke, Charles O. 75, 77, 118
Locke, Sandra 116
Lockhart, Gene 73
Loesser, Frank 32, 37
Logan, Jacqueline 12, 14, 123
London, Jack 6

London, Julie 16, 76, 77, 78, 81, 141
London, Tom 19, 90
Lone Cowboy: My Life Story 106, 109
Lone Star (1996) 139
Lonely Are the Brave (1962) 91, 139
Lonesome Dove 125, 127, 129, 143
Lonesome Dove (1989) 129
The Long Chance 4, 11
The Long Chance (1915) 4
The Long Chance (1922) 11
The Long Riders (1980) 120, 121
Lootens, C.L. 32
Lord, Robert 15, 16, 25
Loren, Sophia 81, 84
Loring, Ann 30
Lott, Milton 8, 69, 72
Love, Bessie 6, 127
Love Me Tender (1956) 130
Lovering, Itho 32
Low, Warren 73
"The Luck of the Roaring Camp" 8, 9, 30, 60, 63
The Lucky Horseshoe (1925) 15, 16, 38
Lund, John 133
Lupino, Ida 8, 54, 55, 132, 138
Lust for Gold (1949) 54, 55
Lyn, Dawn 107
Lynley, Carol 85
Lyon, William A. 76
Lyons, Chester 29

MacArthur, Charles 22
MacDonald, Ian 3, 119
MacDonald J. Farrell 8, 9, 14, 15, 18, 24, 51, 53, 60, 66
MacDonald, Joseph (P.) 46, 48, 91, 99, 100
MacDonald, Katherine 7, 8, 70
MacDonald, William Colt 28, 99
MacDowell, Andie 136
Macht, Gabriel 142
Mackay, John Victor 32, 37
Mackenna's Gold 100, 101
Mackenna's Gold (1969) 100, 101, 11
MacKenzie, Aeneas 41, 44
MacLaine, Shirley 76
MacLane, Barton 27, 40, 101
MacLeod, Robert 95, 101
MacMahon, Aline 68, 132
MacMurray, Fred 29, 30, 132
MacPherson, Jeanie 29
Macready, George 112
Maddow, Ben 51, 133
Madison, Guy 11, 68, 139
Magnificent Seven The (1960) 66, 81, 82, 83, 96, 88, 93, 130, 134, 140
Mahoney, Jock 9, 130
Main, Marjorie 37, 40, 115

Major Dundee (1965) 93, 94, 118, 123, 124, 139
Malden, Karl 79, 85, 96
Malone, Dorothy 15, 54, 55, 79
Malone, Molly 8, 60, 85
A Man Alone (1955) 67
A Man Called Gannon (1969) 100, 101
"A Man Called Horse" 104, 106, 124
A Man Called Horse (1970) 104, 106, 117, 124
The Man Called Noon 111
The Man Called Noon (1973) 111
The Man from Colorado (1948) 51, 142
The Man from Dakota (1940) 37
The Man from Laramie 67, 68
The Man from Laramie (1955) 67, 68, 99, 139, 140, 142
The Man from Painted Post (1917) 6, 7, 36
The Man from Wyoming (1924) 14
Man in the Saddle 58, 59
Man in the Saddle (1951) 58, 59
Man in the Wilderness (1971) 106, 107, 108
Man of Conquest (1939) 32
The Man of the Forest 10, 16, 17, 26
The Man of the Forest (1921) 10, 26
Man of the Forest (1926) 16, 17
Man of the West (1958) 75, 76, 77, 78, 86, 99, 130
Man to Man (1922) 11, 12
The Man Who Loved Cat Dancing 111
The Man Who Loved Cat Dancing (1973) 111
"The Man Who Shot Liberty Valance" 86, 88
The Man Who Shot Liberty Valance (1962) 42, 53, 86, 87, 88, 89, 120, 124, 130, 136, 139
Man with the Gun (1955) 126
Man Without a Star 67, 69, 100, 101
Man Without a Star (1955) 67, 69, 101, 121, 123, 139, 142
Mann, Anthony 56, 57, 60, 62, 63, 64, 67, 68, 71, 73, 74, 76, 84, 97, 99
Mannheimer, Albert 40
Mantley, John 119
March, Fredric 97
Marcucci, Robert P. 89
Margo 30
Marin, Edwin L. 44, 45, 59
Marion, Frances 7, 16, 26, 27
Maris, Mona 26
Marked Men (1919) 8, 9
Marley, (J.) Peverell 75, 92
Marlowe, Hugh 58, 59, 63, 66, 122
Marques, Maria Elena 58

Marsh, Mae 99
Marshall, Brenda 54
Marshall, George 26, 32, 40, 41, 42, 75, 77, 89, 91, 115
Marshall, Tully 18, 22, 23, 25, 43
Marta, Jack (A.) 45, 60
Martin, Chris-Pin 64
Martin, Dean 7, 79, 95, 98, 138
Martin, Strother 9, 101, 103, 120
Martinelli, Elsa 69
Marvin, Lee 14, 60, 70, 72, 85, 94, 96, 104, 105, 113, 114, 134
The Mask of Zorro (1998) 140
"Massacre" 51, 53
Massey, Paul 137
Massey, Raymond 123
Masterson, Mary Stuart 136
Mastroianni, Marcello 71
Maté, Rudolph 92
Mathews, Carole 78
Matthau, Walter 9, 69, 91, 141
Mature, Victor 5, 68, 47, 48, 135, 140
Maverick 108
Maverick (1994) 137
The Maverick Queen 69
The Maverick Queen (1956) 69, 70
Maxwell, Charles 45
May, Karl 93
Mayes, Wendell 9, 78
Mayfield, Les 142
Maynard, Ken 112
Maynard, Kermit (Tex) 108
Mayo, Virginia 10, 54, 55, 58, 59, 84
Mazurki, Mike 131
McBain, Diane 92
McCabe 106, 108
McCabe & Mrs. Miller (1971) 196, 107, 108
McCambridge, Mercedes 8, 66
McCampbell, B.H. 78, 79
McCarthy, Cormac 141
McClung, Hugh 9, 47
McClure, Doug 28, 138
McConaghy, Jack 45
McCord, Ted 58, 78
McCoy, Horace 40, 41, 68
McCoy, Tim 119
McCrea, Joel 22, 30, 31, 36, 44, 45, 49, 50, 54, 55, 86, 88, 89, 131, 132
McCulley, Johnson 140
McDermott, Dylan 142
McDermott, John 10
McDonald, Francis (J.) 99
McDonnell, Mary 130, 131
McDowall, Roddy 19, 140
McEveety, Vincent 100
McGann, William 118
McGowan, J.P. 6, 18
McGraw, Charles 3, 81, 120
McGuane, Thomas 33, 115
McGuinness, James Kevin 56

McIntire, John 66, 68, 81, 132, 133
McIntire, Tim 109, 112
McKay, Brian 106
McLaglen, Andrew V. 57, 89, 91, 94, 95, 98, 117
McLaglen, Victor 9, 53, 54, 55, 79
McLerie, Allyn Ann 104, 110
McLintock! (1963) 89, 90, 91, 97
McMurtry, Larry 2, 29, 91, 109, 125, 127, 129, 136, 143
McNally, Stephen 137
McQueen, Steve 23, 82, 83, 96, 120, 121, 132
McVeagh, Eve 9, 60, 139
Meehan, George 40, 43
Meek, Donald 34, 47
Meeker, Ralph 75
Meighan, Thomas 7
Melford, George 6, 7, 12, 14, 85
Mellor, William (C.) 41, 58, 63, 90
Meltzer, Lewis 40, 58, 59, 138
Melville, Herman 67
Mercer, Johnny 95
Meredith, Burgess 139
Merrill, Gary 5, 131
Metty, Russell 27, 68, 119
Meyer, Emile 127
Meyer, Nicholas 136
Michaels, Dolores 23, 79
Michelena, Beatriz 3, 4
Middleton, Robert 118
Midnight Cowboy (1969) 102
Mifune, Toshiro 71
Miglis, John 134
Milan, Lita 76, 78
Miles, Vera 20, 70, 71, 86, 87, 89, 109
Milius, John 44, 109, 110, 135
Milland, Ray 63
Millar, Stuart 114, 115
Miller, Arthur 91
Miller, Arthur (C.) 43, 56, 104, 106
Miller, Winston 46, 47, 48
Millhauser, Bertram 31
Millican, James 68
Mills, Jack 90
Milner, Victor 29, 32, 37, 56, 110
Milton, Franklin E. 90
The Mine with the Iron Door 14, 15, 29
The Mine with the Iron Door (1936) 14, 15, 29
Mineo, Sal 33, 116
Miner, Steve 142
The Misfits (1961) 91
"Mission with No Record" 55
The Missouri Breaks (1976) 115, 116, 117
Mr. Smith Goes to Washington (1939) 35
Mitchell, Cameron 8, 68, 137

Index

Mitchell, Donald O. 125
Mitchell, Millard 56, 63, 64, 65
Mitchell, Rhea 5
Mitchell, Thomas 32, 34, 35, 43, 44, 86, 89
Mitchum, Christopher 43, 106
Mitchum, John 9, 142
Mitchum, Robert 7, 49, 50, 67, 80, 97, 98, 101, 102, 139
Mix, Tom 10, 11, 12, 15, 16, 17, 18, 25, 26, 37, 38
"M'liss" 4, 7, 8, 11, 29
M'liss (1915) 4
M'liss (1918) 7, 8
M'liss (1936) 29
Mockridge, Cyril (J.) 43, 46, 66, 86, 119
Moffit, Jack 49
Mohr, Hal 32, 60, 63, 114
The Money Corral (1919) 8, 9
Monroe, Marilyn 16, 66, 86, 91
Montana (1950) 56
Montana Rides! 58, 59
Monte Walsh 18, 104, 105, 106, 133, 143
Monte Walsh (1970) 104, 105, 106, 121, 127, 133
Monteros, Rosenda 82
Montgomery, George 6, 141, 142
Montiel, Sarita 75
Moore, Colleen 10, 129
Moore, Richard 99
Moorehead, Agnes 114
Moorer, Allison 140
Moreau, Jeanne 104, 105
Moreno, Antonio 20, 97
Moreno, Rita 24
Morgan, Dennis 137
Morgan, Henry (Harry) 5, 68
Moriarty, Michael 124, 125
Moross, Jerome 75, 76, 78, 123
Morricone, Ennio 19, 91, 94, 95, 100, 104, 111
Morris, Chester 20, 30
Mostel, Zero 101
Mountain Man 95, 100, 109, 110
Mowbray, Alan 101, 135
Muir, Jean 30, 31
A Mule for the Marquesa 95, 96
Mulford, Clarence Edward 70
Mulligan, Richard 101
Mulroney, Dermot 128
Muni, Paul 20
Munson, Ona 45
Murphy, Audie 14, 74, 84, 108
Murphy, Mary 24
Murphy, Ralph 58
Murphy, Richard 66
Murray, Don 20, 77, 81
Murray, Ken 87
Musson, Bennet 10
My Darling Clementine (1946) 46, 47, 48, 58, 65, 80, 93, 95, 99, 100, 113, 123, 134, 135

My Heroes Have Always Been Cowboys (1991) 132
My Name Is Nobody (1973) 111
My Outlaw Brother (1951) 58, 59, 122
My Reminiscences as a Cowboy 75, 77
Myers, Henry 32
Myrow, Josef 70
The Mysterious Rider 10, 18, 31
The Mysterious Rider (1921) 10
The Mysterious Rider (1927) 18
The Mysterious Rider (1938) 31
The Mysterious Witness (1923) 12, 14

Naish, J, Carrol 29, 112
The Naked Spur (1953) 63, 64, 65, 113, 124
The Name's Buchanan 75, 78
Nan of Music Mountain 6, 7
Nan of Music Mountain (1917) 6, 7
Nash, Mary 31
Natteford, Jack 104
Natwick, Mildred 54
Naughton, Edmund 16, 106, 108
Nazarro, Ray 127
Neal, Patricia 91
Neider, Charles 5, 84, 85, 142, 143
Neilan, Marshall 8, 76
Neill, Sam 140
Neilson, James 68
Nelson, Charles 94
Nelson, Lori 26
Nelson, Ralph 6, 96, 105
Nelson, Ricky 79, 98
Nelson, Willie 122, 132
Neumann, Kurt 76
Nevada 18
Nevada (1927) 18
Nevada Smith (1966) 95, 96
The New Land (1972) 114
Newman, Alfred 29, 38, 51, 89, 104, 106
Newman, David 109, 111
Newman, Emil 63
Newman, Lionel 6, 58, 66, 130
Newman, Paul 15, 78, 91, 93, 97, 101, 102, 111, 126, 136
Newman, Randy 137
Newman, Walter 94
Nicholaus, John M., Jr. 75
Nichols, Dudley 26, 28, 32, 58, 60, 62, 72, 75, 81, 82, 84
Nicholson, Jack 31, 96, 117, 118, 119
Nicol, Alex 68
Niehaus, Lennie 124, 133, 141
Nielsen, Leslie 11, 76
The Night Horseman 10, 45
The Night Horseman (1921) 10, 38
Night Passage 72
Night Passage (1957) 68, 72, 74

Nilsson, Anna Q. 9, 10
Nolan, Jeanette 86, 89, 140
Nolan, Lloyd 29, 30, 125
Norman, Marc 113
North, Alex 91, 92, 114, 126, 132
North, Edmund H. 58, 130
North, Sheree 26, 116
North of the Rio Grande (1922) 11, 12
North of 36 14, 31, 32
North of 36 (1924) 14, 15
North to Alaska (1960) 81, 91, 120, 126, 130
North West Mounted Police (1940) 37, 38, 45, 134
Norton, William 19, 99
Novak, Eva 9, 10, 11, 129
Novak, Jane 8, 9, 131
Novak, Kim 101
Nugent, Frank (S.) 51, 53, 54, 69, 70, 94, 95
Nyby, Christian 51

Oakie, Jack 30, 119
Oakland, Vivian 16
Oates, Warren 19, 89, 94, 108, 112, 122, 123
O'Brian, Hugh 15, 116
O'Brien, Edmond 5, 86, 89, 125
O'Brien, George 14, 17, 26, 27, 125
O'Connell, Arthur 121
O'Connell, Kevin 125
Odd Man Out (1947) 55
Ogle, Charles 7, 11, 12, 14, 37
O'Hara, Maureen 10, 44, 45, 56, 85, 89, 90, 91, 95, 107, 108, 109
Okada, Daryn 142
Oklahoma! (1955) 69
The Oklahoma Kid (1939) 32, 33
Oklahoma Territory (1960) 81
Old Gringo (1989) 130
Old Surehand 93
Oliver, Edna may 24, 25, 41
Olivier, Laurence 95
Olsen, Moroni 28, 66
Olsen, Theodore V. 100, 101, 104, 105, 135
O'Malley of the Mounted (1921) 10, 11
On the Night Stage (1915) 4, 5
Once Upon a Time in the West (1969) 100, 123, 130, 136
One-Eyed Jacks (1961) 84, 85, 118, 124, 143
100 Rifles (1969) 101
O'Neill, Eugene 67
O'Neill, Henry 31, 85
Only the Valiant (1951) 58
Orloff, Lee 135
O'Rourke, Frank 6, 95, 96, 101
Orth, Marion 19
O'Sullivan, Maureen 26, 27, 73, 75, 140
O'Toole, Peter 102

"The Outcasts of Poker Flat" 8, 9, 30, 60, 63
The Outcasts of Poker Flat (1919) 8, 9
The Outcasts of Poker Flat (1937) 30, 31
The Outcasts of Poker Flat (1952) 60
The Outlaw (1943) 42, 43, 44, 54, 84, 89
The Outlaw Josey Wales (1976) 115, 116, 117
Outlaws of red River (1927) 18, 38
The Outrage (1964) 91, 92, 93, 97, 111, 118, 126
Overland Red (1920) 9, 10
Overton, Al, Jr. 114
Owen, Gwil 140
Owen, Reginald 27
Owen, Seena 8, 9, 96
Owens, Patricia 15
The Ox-Bow Incident 42, 43, 63, 109, 143
The Ox-Bow Incident (1943) 42, 43, 44, 65, 99, 109, 115, 123, 135, 142

Pacino, Al 134
Pacula, Joanna 135
Page, Geraldine 14, 63, 64, 127
Paget, Debra 26, 56, 57
Paige, Janis 11
The Painted Desert (1931) 24, 25
Paiva, Nestor 96
Pakula, Alan (J.) 119
Palance, Jack 9, 63, 64, 95, 96, 104, 105, 128, 129, 132
Pale Rider (1985) 64, 124, 125
Pallette, Eugene 16, 66
Palmer, Betsy 73, 74
Palmer, Ernest 56
Palmer, Patricia 9
Papas, Irene 70
Paramore, Edward E., Jr. 19, 24, 70
Parker, Arthur Jeph 116
Parker, Eleanor 11, 66, 69
Parker, Fess 15
Parker, Jean 29, 30, 56, 68
Parker, Willard 139
Parks, Van Dyke 138
Parrish, Robert 6, 76, 80, 138
"The Parson of Panamint" 5, 11, 12, 40
The Parson of Panamint (1916) 5, 6, 22
Pascal, Ernest 46
"Paso por Aqui" 28, 51, 53, 54
Pat Garrett and Billy the Kid (1973) 85, 111, 112, 113, 119, 124, 126, 142
Pate, Michael 9, 66
Patric, Jason 135
Patrick, Gail 120
The Patriot (1916) 5, 6

The Patriot (2000) 141
Patten, Lewis B. 5, 100, 101
Paxton, Bill 135
Payne, John 67, 130
Payton, Barbara 18, 97
Peace Marshal 42, 43
Peck, Gregory 6, 48, 51, 53, 56, 58, 59, 76, 77, 91, 99, 101, 102, 109, 130
Peckinpah, Sam 15, 84, 85, 86, 88, 89, 94, 100, 102, 103, 104, 105, 111, 112, 113, 123, 125, 126, 132, 133, 139
Peebles, Mario Van 135
Pegg, Vester 8, 59
Pellicer, Pina 85
Penn, Arthur 11, 76, 104, 105, 106, 117
Pennick, Jack 53, 93
Penny, Edmund 104
Peoples, David Webb 133, 134
Peppard, George 19, 91, 137
Percy, Eileen 7
Perkins, Anthony 74, 111, 133
Perkins, Jeffrey 130
Perkins, Kenneth 59
Perkins, Millie 96
Perrine, Valerie 120
Perry, Frank 109
Perry, Harry 11, 125
Perry, Paul 7, 90
Perry, Walter 7
Peters, House 5, 97
Peters, Jean 16, 141
Petersen, William 132
Peterson, Robert 37
Petrie, Howard 99
Pevney, Joseph 9
Phillips, Lou Diamond 86, 128, 129, 132
Piantodosi, Arthur 114
Picerni, Paul 11
Pickens, Slim 9, 112, 123, 124, 14
Pickford, Mary 7, 8, 26, 27
Pierson, Frank R. 94
Pillars of the Sky (1956) 69, 86
The Pioneer Scout (1928) 19
Pitts, ZaSu 25
Pizer, Larry 121
The Plainsman (1936) 28, 29, 81, 86, 99, 133, 142
Planck, Robert 27
Planer, Franz 75, 76, 81
Pleshette, Suzanne 31, 92
Plunkett, Walter 90
Pocket Money (1972) 126
Points West 19, 22, 38
Points West (1929) 19, 20, 22
Poitier, Sidney 96
Polito, Sol 12, 31, 32, 82
Pollack, Sydney 27, 95, 99, 109, 110, 120
Polonsky, Abraham 101
The Pony Express (1925) 15, 16
Poore, Vern 133

Porter, Edwin S. 3
Portis, Charles 26, 100, 101, 103, 115
Posse (1975) 114, 115
Posse (1993) 135, 136
Posse from Hell 84
Posse from Hell (1961) 84
Post, Ted 100
Potoker, Oscar 24
Powdersmoke Range (1935) 28
Powell, Paul 11
Powell, William 18, 124
Power, Tyrone 35, 36, 49, 58, 59
Powers, Stefanie 95
Powers, Tom 68
Preminger, Otto 67
Presley, Elvis 28, 84, 118
Preston, Robert 8, 54, 63, 68, 89, 127, 132
Previn, André 20
Previn, Charles
Price, Vincent 135
The Professionals (1966) 66, 95, 96, 113, 115, 127, 135, 136, 138
The Proud Ones (1956) 69, 70, 73, 113
Puenzo, Luis 130
Puig, Eva 99
Pullman, Bill 136
Purcell, Gertrude 32
Purcell, Lee 112
Pursued (1947) 49, 50, 78, 118
Pyle, Denver 9, 139

Quaid, Dennis 121, 138
Quaid, Randy 121
Qualen, John 89, 127
The Quick and the Dead (1995) 136, 138, 141
The Quiet Man (1952) 61, 91
Quinn, Anthony 5, 44, 80, 84, 142

Rackin, Martin 8, 116
"Raiders Die Hard" 75
Raimi, Sam 138
The Rainbow Trail 7, 8, 15, 16
The Rainbow Trail (1918) 7, 8
Rainbow Trail (1925) 15, 16
Raine, William MacLeod 66
Rainer, Ralph 31
Raines, Ella10, 44, 45, 63, 129
Rainey, For 74
Rains, Claude 32
Raksin, David 70, 99
Ralston, Esther 26, 27, 137
Ramona 5, 6, 19, 29, 30
Ramona (1916) 5, 6
Ramona (1928) 19
Ramona (1936) 28, 29, 30
Ramrod 49, 115
Ramrod (1947) 49
Rancho Notorious (1952) 59, 60, 63
Randall, Stuart 128

Index

The Rare Breed (1966) 95
Rashomon (1950) 93
Rath, Earl 106
Ravetch, Irving 9, 58, 67, 91, 97, 109, 113
Rawhide (1951) 58, 59, 115, 126
The Rawhide Years 69
The Rawhide Years (1956) 69
Ray, Nicholas 66, 67, 119
Rayfiel, David 106
Raymaker, Herman C. 19
Raymond, Usher 142
Reagan, Ronald 121, 122
Red River (1948) 32, 41, 50, 51, 52, 53, 55, 62, 79, 102, 109, 111, 114, 117, 118, 120
Red Sun (1971) 141
Redford, Robert 31, 101, 102, 109, 110, 111, 120, 140
Ree, Max 24
Reed, Carol 55
Reed, Donna 10
Reed, Pamela 120
Reed, Tom 22, 25, 41
Reid, Carl Benton 112
Reid, Wallace 7, 12
Remick, Lee 81
The Renegade 60
Rennahan, Ray 32, 46, 49, 51, 54, 67, 120
Rettig, Tommy 40
The Return of a Man Called Horse (1976) 115, 116, 117
The Return of Frank James (1940) 37, 38
The Return of Little Big Man 105
The Return of Martin Guerre (1982) 136
Return of the Seven (1966) 95, 96
Return to Lonesome Dove (1993) 136
The Revengers (1972) 115
Rey, Fernando 5, 71, 137
Reynolds, Ben (F.) 7, 11, 26, 27, 97
Reynolds, Burt 29, 101
Reynolds, Debbie 91
Reynolds, Lynn 9, 10, 15, 16, 18
Rhodes, Eugene Manlove 6, 7, 11, 12, 14, 27, 28, 51, 54
Rich, Irene 8, 51, 129
Rich, Lillian 16, 66
Richards, Robert L. 56
Richardson, Jack 9
Richardson, Joey 141
Richter, Conrad 49, 50, 99
Riddle, Nelson 10, 97, 125
Ride in the Whirlwind (1966) 95, 96
Ride Lonesome (1959) 78, 81, 143
Ride the High Country (1962) 84, 86, 88, 89, 112, 123, 126, 127, 129, 134
Ride the Man Down 60, 63, 115
Ride the Man Down (1952) 59, 60, 63, 115, 123

Ride, Vaquero! (1953) 124
Rider of Death Valley (1932) 25, 26
The Rider of the Ruby Hills 67
Riders of the Purple Sage 7, 8, 15, 16, 36
Riders of the Purple Sage (1918) 7, 8
Riders of the Purple Sage (1925) 15, 16
Riders of Vengeance (1919) 8, 9
Ridgeway, Fritzi 23
Ridin' the Wind (1925) 15, 15
Rigby, L.G. 18
Rio Bravo (1959) 78, 79, 80, 84, 97, 98, 114, 117, 118, 120, 124, 134, 138
Rio Conchos (1964) 91
Rio Grande (1950) 55, 56, 57, 58, 72, 91, 119, 139
Rio Lobo (1970) 80, 104, 106, 118, 120, 139
Ripley, Clements 44
Risdon, Elizabeth 44
Ritchie, William (Will) M. 11, 16, 18
Ritt, Martin 3, 91, 93, 97, 130
Ritter, Tex 114
Ritter, Thelma 89, 101
River of No Return (1954) 66, 67, 139, 141
Rivero, Jorge 106
The River's End 9, 10, 24, 25, 37
The River's End (1920) 9, 10
The River's End (1931) 24, 25
The River's End (1940) 37
Robards, Jason 11, 98, 104, 119, 141, 142
Robbers' Roost 26, 27, 67
Robbers' Roost (1933) 26, 27
Robbers' Roost (1955) 67, 142
Robbins, Harold 96
Roberts, Kenneth 73
Roberts, Marguerite 49, 100, 129
Roberts, Pernell 81
Roberts, Roy 115
Roberts, Theodore 8
Roberts, William 75, 77, 81, 82, 114, 139
Robertson, Dale 12
Robin, Leo 31
Robin Hood of El Dorado (1936) 28, 29, 30
The Robinhood of El Dorado 29, 30
Robinson, Edward G. 92, 93, 111, 112
Robinson, Edward R. 41
Robinson, George 22, 29, 45, 76
Rock, Philip 66
Rockwell, Norman 46
Rocky Mountain (1950) 55, 58
Rodriguez, Estelita 19, 79, 96
Roe, Vingie E. 12
Roemheld, Heinz 125

Rogell, Albert (S.) 19, 26, 127
Rogers, Roy 140
Roizman, Owen 29, 115, 137
Roland, Gilbert 92, 122, 137
Rolfe, Sam 63, 65
Roman, Ruth 14, 68, 140
Romance of the Rio Grande (1929) 19, 20
Romeo and Juliet 27
Romero, Cesar 137
Ronne, David 125
Rooney, Mickey 9, 122
Roosevelt, Buddy 28, 112
Rooster Cogburn (1975) 114, 115
Root, Wells 135
Rose, Jackson 25
Rose, Reginald 75
The Rose of the Rancho 3, 25
Rose of the Rancho (1914) 3, 5
Rosenberg, Stuart 132
Rosenthal, Laurence 16, 107, 114
Ross, Katharine 41, 95, 101, 103
Ross, Lillian Bos 113
Rossen, Robert 81
Rosson, Arthur 18, 22
Rosson, Harold (Hal) 18, 24, 40, 46, 97, 128
Rough Night in Jericho (1967) 97
Rouse, Russel 69
Rowland, Gena 91
Rowland, Roy 63, 138
Royle, Edwin Milton 3, 4, 7, 24, 41
Royle, Selena 58
Rozsa, Miklos 44, 70, 138
Rubens, Alma 6, 7
Rubinstein, John 109, 112
Ruggles, Wesley 24, 37, 38, 132
Rule, Janice 24
Run for Cover (1955) 67, 68
Run of the Arrow (1957) 72, 73, 75
Rush, Barbara 18, 97
Russell, Bo 58
Russell, Charles M. 17
Russell, Gail 14, 50, 70, 72, 85
Russell, Henry 99
Russell, J. Gordon 15
Russell, Jane 10, 43, 44, 68
Russell, John 10, 36, 53, 132
Russell, Kurt 135, 136
Ruthven, Ormond B. 40
Ruttenberg, Joseph 29
Ryan, Mitch 19
Ryan, Robert 68, 70, 06, 07, 98, 99, 100, 101, 103, 112, 113
Rydell, Mark 111
Ryder, Loren L. (L.L.) 31, 33, 37

Saddle the Wind (1958) 75, 76, 78, 118
The Saga of the Billy the Kid 40
Saint, Eva Marie 101, 103
Saint Johnson 25, 26
Sainte-Marie, Buffy 104

Index

Sakall, S.Z. 45
Sale, Richard 118
Salisbury, Monroe 6
Salomy Jane (1914) 3, 4
Salomy Jane (1923) 12, 14
"Salomy Jane's Kiss" 3, 4, 12, 14
Salter, Hans J. 60, 68, 137
San Antonio (1945) 45, 46
Sand (1920) 9, 10
Sande, Walter 108
Sandoz, Mari 91, 92, 96
Sands of Iwo Jima (1949) 102
Santa Fe Trail (1940) 37, 38, 122
Santell, Alfred 19
Santschi, Tom 16, 18, 24
Sarafian, Richard (C.) 106, 108
Sarazzin, Miachael 37, 100, 101
Saul, Oscar 94
The Savage (1952) 60
Savage, Les, Jr. 11, 66, 76
Savage Sam 89
Savage Sam (1963) 89
Savalas, Telly 14, 99, 137
Sawtell, Paul 104
Sawyer, Joseph (Joe) 122
Saxon, John 28, 101, 111
Sayles, John 139
Sayre, Joel 28
The Scalphunters (1968) 99, 100, 138
Scent of a Woman (1992) 134
Schaefer, Jack 63, 64, 69, 72, 91, 104, 105, 106, 132, 133, 143
Schallert, William 11
Scharf, Walter 43, 45
Schayer, (E.) Richard 10, 25
Schell, Maria 79, 80, 81, 84
Schepisi, Fred 122
Schnee, Charles 6, 51, 56, 90
Schoefield, Paul 30
Schoenbaum, C. Edgar 59
Schrock, Raymond 11
Scorsese, Martin 131
Scott, Brenda 99, 100
Scott, Lizabeth 67
Scott, Randolph 22, 26, 27, 31, 32, 36, 40, 47, 49, 59, 71, 75, 77, 81, 84, 86, 88, 89, 127
Scott, Timothy 31, 138
The Sea of Grass 49, 50
The Sea of Grass (1947) 49, 50
The Searchers 69, 70
The Searchers (1956) 45, 69, 70, 71, 84, 85, 93, 95, 102, 109, 113, 120, 134
Sears, Fred F. 73
Sebastian, Dorothy 17
Secrets 14, 26, 27
Secrets (1924) 14
Secrets (1933) 26, 27
Segall, Harry 30
Seiler, Lewis (Lew) 16, 17, 18, 27, 48, 90
Seitz, George B. 15, 16, 44
Seitz, John (F.) 119

Selander, Lester 119
Sellers, William 55
Selwynne, Clarissa 15
Selznick, David O. 48
Semler, Dean 43, 130, 132
"Sergeant Houck" 72
Sergeant Rutledge (1960) 81, 83, 99, 136
Serlig, Rod 75
Seven Angry Men (1955) 67
Seven Men from Now (1956) 69, 70, 71, 72, 81, 127, 143
Seven Samurai (1954) 93
Seven Ways from Sundown 81
Seven Ways from Sundown (1960) 81
Seymour, Dan 5, 135
Shalako 99
Shalako (1968) 99, 129
Shamroy, Leon 44, 58, 144
Shane 63, 64, 133
Shane (1953) 28, 63, 64, 65, 72, 75, 93, 109, 115, 125, 133, 134, 139
Shanghai Noon (2000) 141
Shannon, Harry 92
Sharif, Omar 101
Sharp, Alan 106, 109
Shaughnessy, Mickey 9
Shaw, Robert 100
Shayne, Robert 135
She Wore a Yellow Ribbon (1949) 54, 55, 65, 95, 97, 102, 120, 139
Sheen, Charlie 128, 129
The Sheepman (1958) 75, 76, 91, 115, 127
Shenandoah (1965) 93, 94, 139
The Shepherd of the Hills 9, 10, 19, 40, 41, 45
The Shepherd of the Hills (1920) 9, 10
The Shepherd of the Hills (1928) 19
The Shepherd of the Hills (1941) 40, 41, 120
Sher, Jack 63, 128
Sheridan, Ann 5, 32, 97
Sherin, Edwin 106, 107, 108
Sherman, George 198, 109, 132
Shields, Arthur 104
Shirreffs, Gordon (D.) 3
Shoot Out (1971) 106, 107, 109
The Shooting (1966) 96
The Shootist 115, 116, 134
The Shootist (1976) 80, 115, 116, 117, 122, 134, 139
Shorr, Lester 133
Short, Luke 49, 50, 51, 53, 55, 58, 60, 63, 115
Short Grass (1950) 123
Showdown at Boot Hill (1958) 75, 77
"Showdown Trail" 72
Shryack, Dennis 124
Shuken, Leo 32
Shumate, Harold 18, 27, 43, 123

Sickner, Roy N. 100, 101
Siegel, Donald (Don) 84, 101, 106, 115, 116, 117, 132, 133, 134
Siegel, Otto 82
Siemaszko, Casey 128, 129
Sills, Milton 23
Silva, Henry 19
Silver City (1951) 58, 59
Silver Dollar (1932) 111
Silver Lode (1954) 66, 67, 73, 75, 100, 121
Silver Queen (1942) 41
Silver Valley (1927) 18
The Silver Whip (1953) 63, 141
Silvera, Frank 3, 104, 107
Silverado (1985) 124, 125
Silverheels, Jay 9, 120
Silverstein, Elliot 95, 106, 117
Silvestri, Alan 130, 132, 138
Simmons, Jean 76, 97
Simmons, Russell 12, 22, 79
Sinatra, Frank 5, 140
Sinclair, Harold 78, 81
Singing Guns 45, 55
Singing Guns (1950) 55, 56
Siodmak, Robert 100
Six Black Horses (1962) 100
Skall, William (V.) 29, 37, 38, 40, 116
Skerritt, Tom 142
Skiles, Marlin 85, 121
Skinner, Frank 46, 99
The Sky Pilot (1921) 10, 30
The Sky Pilot: A Tale of the Foothills 10
Slater, Barney 12, 72, 75, 119
Slater, Christian 132
Sleeper, Martha 27
Sloane, Paul 31
Slocum, Tom 121
Sloman, Edward 110
Smith, Alexis 10, 45, 46, 135
Smith, C. Aubrey 26, 27
Smith, Clifford 5, 6, 17, 31
Smith, Kent 125
Smith, Leonard 40
Smith, Paul J. 38, 125
Smith, Ted 45
Smith, Will 141
Smithee, Allen 101
Smits, Jimmy 130
Smoky Valley 67
Snell, David 40
Snodgress, Carrie 124, 125
Snyder, William (E.) 124
Sokoloff, Vladimir 86
Soldier Blue (1970) 104, 105
Solinas, Franco 95
Sommersby (1993) 136
Sondergaard, Gale 116
Sonnenfeld, Barry 141
The Sons of Katie Elder (1965) 93, 94, 95, 120, 138
South of Rio Grande 58, 59
Space Cowboys (2000) 141

Index

Sparkuhl, Theodor 30, 31
Spearman, Frank H. 5, 6, 7, 16, 17, 31, 51, 54
Spencer, Dorothy 32
Spencer, Douglas 82
The Spikes Gang (1974) 113, 114
Spinotti, Dante 138
The Spoilers 3, 4, 12, 22, 23, 41, 69
The Spoilers (1914) 3, 4
The Spoilers (1923) 12
The Spoilers (1930) 22, 23
The, Spoilers (1942) 41, 42
The Spoilers (1956) 69, 86, 141
Springfield Rifle (1952) 60
Springsteen, R.G. 130
Sprotte, Bert 8, 10, 54
The Squaw Man 3, 4, 7, 24
The Squaw Man (1914) 3, 4, 22, 81
The Squaw Man (1918) 7, 81
The Squaw Man (1931) 24, 81
Stack, Robert 9
"Stage Station" 41
"Stage to Lordsburg" 32, 35, 95, 96
Stagecoach (1939) 32, 34, 35, 36, 49, 65, 84, 89, 96, 97, 113, 120, 134, 142
Stagecoach (1966) 95, 96, 97
Stagecoach to Fury (1956) 70, 72
Stairs of Sand (1929) 19, 22
The Stalking Moon 100, 101
The Stalking Moon (1969) 96, 100, 101
Stallings, Laurence 22, 54, 99
Stamp, Terence 129
Stand Up and Fight (1939) 32
Standing, Herbert 5
Standing, Jack 6
Stanton, Harry Dean 16
Stanwyck, Barbara 28, 32, 36, 41, 56, 68, 75, 121, 131, 132
The Stars in Their Courses 97, 98
Station West 51, 53
Station West (1948) 51, 53, 139
Stay Away, Joe 143
Steck, H. Tipton 8, 64
Steele, Bob 28, 128, 129
Steele, Karen 24, 75, 81, 84
Steele, Marjorie 63
Steenburgen, Mary 119
Steiger, Rod 15, 72, 75, 95, 121
Stein, Herman 125
Steiner, Max 24, 25, 31, 41, 45, 68, 70, 78, 91, 107, 109
Step on It! (1922) 11
The Stepsons of the Light 14
Sterling, Jan 12
Stern, Daniel 132
Stevens, Charles 92
Stevens, George 28, 63, 64, 72, 115, 132, 139
Stevens, Inger 104
Stevens, Louis 29, 90

Stevens, Stella 104, 105
Stewart, James 32, 35, 36, 56, 57, 60, 62, 65, 65, 68, 69, 71, 74, 85, 86, 89, 91, 94, 95, 99, 100, 116, 117, 124, 139
Stewart, Roy 26
Stoloff, Ben 26, 82
Stone, George (E.) 6, 24, 25, 28
Stone, John 15, 16, 18, 85
Stone, Lewis 9, 20
Stone, Milburn 120
Stone, N.B., Jr. 86
Stone, Sharon 138
Storm, Barry 54
Stothart, Herbert 54
Stout, Archie 25, 27, 46, 49, 51, 54, 63, 94, 95
Stowe, Madeleine 136
Stradling, Harry 49, 66
Stradling, Harry, Jr. 15, 114
Stradling, Walter 7
Strange, Glenn 112
The Stranger 113
The Stranger Wore a Gun (1953) 63
Strauss, Peter 105
Streets of Laredo 126
Streets of Laredo (1949) 54, 55
Strenge, Walter 70, 72, 81
Strode, Woody 3, 83, 96, 99, 136, 137
Studi, Wes 135
Sturges, John 57, 67, 69, 73, 76, 81, 82, 83, 93, 97, 98, 99, 133, 134
Sugarfoot 58, 59
Sugarfoot (1951) 58, 59
Sullivan, Barry 75, 137
Sullivan, C. Gardner 5, 15, 94
Sundown at Crazy Horse 84, 85
Sundown Jim 41
Sundown Jim (1942) 41
The Sundowners (1950) 55
Sunset Pass 19, 22
Sunset Pass (1929) 19, 22
Support Your Local Gunfighter (1971) 103
Support Your Local Sheriff (1969) 100, 101, 103, 127
Surtees, Bruce 31, 111, 115, 116, 124
Surtees, Robert (L.) 70, 75, 109, 111, 125
Sutherland, Donald 141
Sutherland, Kiefer 96, 128, 129, 132
Sutter's Gold (1936) 28, 29
Swarthout, Glendon 8, 78, 81, 115, 116, 133, 134
Swarthout, Miles Hood 115, 117
Swenson, Karl 119
Swerling, Jo 37, 38
Swickard, Charles 5, 6, 8, 20

Taggart 91
Taggart (1964) 91

Talbott, Gloria 24, 141
Taliaferro, Hal 119
Tall in the Saddle (1944) 44, 45, 84
The Tall Men 67, 68, 69
The Tall Men (1955) 67, 68, 69, 113
The Tall Stranger (1957) 72, 129
The Tall T (1957) 72, 73, 75, 81, 95, 97, 121, 127, 143
Talmadge, Norma 14, 27
Tamblyn, Russ 27
The Taming of the Shrew 91
Tamiroff, Akim 110
Taradash, Daniel 60, 63
Tashman, Lilyan 16
Taylor, Dub 137
Taylor, Elizabeth 72
Taylor, Estelle 24, 25
Taylor, Joan 20
Taylor, Robert 70, 72, 78, 101
Taylor, Rod 20
Teal, Ray 116, 118
Tell Them Willie Boy Is Here (1969) 100, 101
Tellegen, Lou 18
Temple, Shirley 19, 27
Tenant, Barbara 5
"Tennessee's Partner" 5, 6, 67
Tennessee's Partner (1916) 5, 6
Tennessee's Partner (1955) 67, 68, 122
Tension at Table Rock (1956) 70
Tessari, Duccio 91
The Testing Block (1920) 9, 10
The Texan (1930) 22, 23
The Texans (1938) 31, 32
Texas (1941) 40, 41, 77, 115, 142
Texas Rangers (2001) 142
The Texas Rangers (1936) 28, 29, 55
The Texas Rangers (1951) 142
The Texas Rangers: A Century of Frontier Defense 29, 30, 54, 55
Thaxter, Phyllis 10
Theby, Rosemary 12
Theiss, William 119
These Thousand Hills 78, 81, 133
These Thousand Hills (1959) 78, 81, 133
They Came to Cordura 78, 81, 134
They Came to Cordura (1959) 78, 81, 134
They Died with Their Boots On (1942) 41, 42, 92
Thomas, B.J. 102
Thomas, Henry 141
Thomas, Kristin Scott 140
Thomas, Nona 6
Thomas, William C. 67
Thomson, Fred 16, 18
Thompson, J. Lee 101
Thompson, Keene 19, 24, 31
Thornton, Billy Bob 141
Thorp, Raymond W. 109, 110

Index

Thorpe, Harry 7
Thorpe, Richard 59, 132
Three Bad Men (1926) 16, 17, 18
The Three Godfathers 5, 8, 9, 22, 23, 29, 50, 51, 54, 75
Three Godfathers (1916) 5
Three Godfathers (1936) 28, 29, 30
3 Godfathers (1948) 50, 51, 54, 120
Three Hours to Kill (1954) 115, 135
"Three-Ten to Yuma" 72, 74
3:10 to Yuma (1957) 72, 73, 74, 80, 95, 109, 118, 134, 142
Thunder God's Gold 54
Thunder in the Dust 55
Thunder Mountain 28
Thunder Mountain (1935) 28
Thunder Mountain (1947) 49
Thundercloud, Chief 68
The Thundering Herd 15, 26, 27
The Thundering Herd (1925) 15
The Thundering Herd (1933) 26, 27
Tide of Empire 19, 22
Tide of Empire (1929) 19, 22
Tidy, Frank 122
Tidyman, Ernest 111
Tierney, Gene 10, 37, 38, 132
Timberjack 143
The Time It Never Rained 129
Tin Pan Alley (1940) 38
"The Tin Star" 60, 62, 63
The Tin Star (1957) 72, 73, 74, 75, 80, 84, 99, 123, 133
Tiomkin, Dimitri 46, 48, 51, 60, 61, 73, 78, 80, 81, 82, 83, 97, 114, 119, 120
Tippette, Giles 113
To Follow a Flag 69
To the Last Man 12, 14, 26, 27, 36, 49
To the Last Man (1923) 12, 14
To the Last Man (1933) 26, 27
Tobey, Kenneth (Ken) 9
Todd, Thelma 18
Toland, Gregg 37, 38, 43, 51, 54
Toll, John 137
The Toll Gate (1920) 9, 10, 49
Toluboff, Alexander 32
Tom Horn (1980) 120, 121
Tombstone (1942) 41
Tombstone (1993) 135
Tombstone: An Iliad of the Southeast 41
Tony Runs Wild (1926) 16, 17
Toomey, Regis 132
Torrence, Ernest 12, 14, 15, 24, 25, 26
Totten, Robert 101
Tourneur, Jacques 46, 48, 67, 118
Tover, Leo 92
Towers, Constance 81, 83
The Track of the Cat 66, 67
The Track of the Cat (1954) 66, 67, 139
Tracy, Spencer 49, 50, 66, 67, 69, 97

Trail Street (1947) 49
Trail Town 46
The Train Robbers (1974) 114
The Tramplers (1966) 95
Traven, B. 54
Travis, Neil 130
The Treasure in Silver Lake 93
Treasure of the Ruby Hills (1955) 67
The Treasure of the Sierra Madre 54
The Treasure of the Sierra Madre (1948) 54
Trevor, Claire 32, 34, 36, 37, 40, 41, 43, 44, 68, 141, 142
Tribune to a Bad Man (1956) 69, 70
Triumphs of a Man Called Horse (1983) 123, 124
Troell, Jan 24, 113, 114
Trooper Hook (1957) 72, 96, 132
Trosper, Guy 84, 85, 90
Trotti, Lamar 43, 51, 53, 60, 63
Trouble Shooter 32
True Grit 100, 101, 115
True Grit (1969) 80, 100, 101, 102, 103, 115, 120, 126, 129, 134
The True Story of Jesse James (1957) 72
Trumbo, Dalton 84
Truthful Tulliver (1917) 6, 7, 49
Tuchock, Wanda 22
Tucker, Forrest 9, 63, 72, 127
Tully, Richard Walton 3, 25
Tully, Tom 122
Tumbleweeds 15, 16
Tumbleweeds (1925) 15, 16, 49
Tuska, Jon 143
Twelvetrees, Helen 25
Twin Sombreros 49
The Twinkle in God's Eye (1955) 122
Twist, John 27, 28, 30, 116
Two Flags West (1950) 55, 58
Two Mules for Sister Sara (1970) 104, 106
Two Rode Together (1961) 84, 85
Tyler, Richard 114
Tyler, Tom 18, 28, 66
Tyrrell, Susan 47

Ullman, Daniel (B.) 9
Ullmann, Liv 33, 113, 114
Ulzana's Raid (1972) 109, 110, 111, 124, 138
Under the Tonto Rim 19
Under the Tonto Rim (1928) 19
Unforgiven (1992) 24, 118, 133, 134
The Unforgiven 81, 84
The Unforgiven (1960) 81, 83, 84, 127, 138
Union Pacific (1939) 32, 33, 36, 81, 132, 142
Ure, Mary 100

Useless Cowboy 45
Utah Blaine 72
Utah Blaine (1957) 72

Val of Paradise 12
The Valdez Horses 99, 111
Valdez Is Coming 106, 108
Valdez Is Coming (1971) 196, 107, 108
Valdez, the Halfbreed (1973) 111
Vale, Vola 9, 10, 11, 104
Vallejo, Harry 10, 56
The Valley of the Giants 9, 9, 18, 31
The Valley of the Giants (1919) 8, 9
The Valley of the Giants (1927) 18
Valley of the Giants (1938) 31
The Valley of the Rising Sun 41
Valley of the Sun (1942) 41, 42
Van Buren, Mabel 5, 6, 11, 12, 49
Van Cleef, Lee 15, 94, 95, 96, 130
Van Der Beek, James 142
Van Dyke, W.S. (II) 43
Van Fleet, Jo 73
Van Trees, James 27
The Vanishing American 15, 16, 36, 67
The Vanishing American (1925) 15, 16
The Vanishing American (1955) 67
Varconi, Victor 116
Varsi, Diane 77
Vaughn, Alberta 22
Vaughn, Robert 82
Velez, Lupe 22, 24
Vengeance Valley 58, 59, 115
Vengeance Valley (1951) 58, 59
Vera Cruz (1954) 66, 67, 86, 114, 121, 124, 138
Vidor, Charles 28, 43
Vidor, King 10, 22, 23, 29, 55, 67, 69, 101, 122, 123
Vincenzoni, Luciano 95
The Violent Men (1955) 67, 68, 111
Virginia City (1940) 37, 38
The Virginian (1914) 3, 4, 5, 22, 81
The Virginian (1923) 12, 14
The Virginian (1929) 19, 20, 21, 22, 58, 86
The Virginian (1946) 46, 48
The Virginian: A Horseman of the Plains 3, 4, 12, 14, 19, 20, 21, 22, 32, 46, 48, 143
Viva Villa! (1934) 28
Vogel, Paul C. 115
Voight, Jon 102
Volonte, Gian Maria 26, 94, 137
Von Sydow, Max 20

Wagner, Robert 23
Wagon Master (1950) 55, 56, 97, 139
Wagon Wheels (1934) 27
Waite, Ric 120
Wales, Ethel 12
Wales, Wally 28, 119

Index

Walken Christopher 120
Walker, Clint 18, 101
Walker, Joseph 37
Walker, Robert 50, 59
Walker, Robert, Jr. 101
Wallace, Earl W. 119
Wallace, Irving 6, 63, 130
Wallach, Eli 5, 81, 96
Waller, Eddy 118
The Wallop (1921) 10, 11
Walsh, Brock 137
Walsh, David M. 104
Walsh, Raoul 19, 22, 23, 41, 42, 46, 49, 50, 54, 55, 57, 58, 59, 91, 92, 120
Walthall, Henry B. 11, 29
The Wanderer of the Wasteland 14, 15, 45
The Wanderer of the Wasteland (1924) 14, 15
The Wanderer of the Wasteland (1945) 45
War Paint (1953) 63
"War Part" 54, 55
The War Wagon (1967) 97, 98, 99, 120
Ward, Fannie 6
Ward, Jonas 75, 78
Ward, Robert 121
Warden, Jack 9
Ware, Helen 20
Warlock 78
Warlock (1959) 78, 79, 80, 100, 123, 142
Warner, David 104
Warner, H.B. 16
Warren, Charles Marquis 130
Washburn, Beverly 43
Washington, Denzel 130
Washington, Ned 38, 60, 61, 68, 70, 73, 78, 94, 97, 116
Waters, John 18, 94
Waterston, Sam 120
Watkins, Greg 130
Watson, Waldon O. 94
The Way West 58, 97, 127, 133
The Way West (1967) 97, 98, 124, 133, 139
Wayne, Aissa 91
Wayne, John 22, 23, 32, 34, 35, 41, 42, 44, 45, 51, 52, 53, 54, 55, 56, 57, 60, 63, 65, 70, 71, 79, 80, 83, 84, 85, 86, 87, 89, 90, 91, 95, 97, 101, 102, 103, 106, 109, 111, 114, 115, 116, 117, 119, 120, 134
Wayne, Mabel 19
Wayne, Patrick (Pat) 33, 91, 129
Wayne, Sid 81
Weaver, Dennis 14
Webb, James R. 66, 75, 76, 89, 90, 92, 114
Webb, Richard 5, 135
Webb, Robert D. 73, 130
Webb, Roy 44, 58, 122

Webb, Walter Preston 29, 30, 54, 55, 90
Webster, Paul Francis 78, 81, 124
Weidler, Virginia 31
Weiland, Paul 133
Welch, Raquel 37, 101
Welcome to Hart Times 97, 98
Welcome to Hart Times (1967) 97, 98
Weldon, Joan 26
Welles, Halsted 72, 74, 78
Welles, Orson 33, 54
Wellman, Paul I. 60, 66, 67, 69, 72, 84, 85, 96
Wellman, William (A.) 25, 29, 30, 43, 44, 45, 51, 53, 57, 58, 59, 63, 65, 115, 139
Wells, Robert 70, 99
Wells Fargo (1937) 30, 31, 72
Wenstrom, Harold 28
Werker, Alfred (L.) 16, 19, 73, 115
Werner, Oskar 95
West, Brian 113
West, Jessamyn 75, 76
West of the Pecos 27, 45
West of the Pecos (1934) 27
West of the Pecos (1945) 45
Westbound (1960) 84
Westcott, Helen 19, 140
Westerfield, James 108
Western Stories: A Chronological Anthology 143
Western Union 40
Western Union (1941) 40, 41, 127
The Westerner (1940) 37, 38, 39, 45, 54, 76, 86, 119, 121, 134
The Westerners 9, 10
The Westerners (1919) 9, 10
Westward the Women (1952) 60
Whelan, Arleen 6, 49, 135
Whelan, Tim 73
When a Man's a Man 14, 15, 28, 45
When a Man's a Man (1924) 14, 15, 30
When a Man's a Man (1935) 28
When the Daltons Rode (1940) 37
Where Men Are Men (1921) 10
While Satan Sleeps (1922) 11
Whispering Smith 5, 6, 16, 17, 31, 51, 54
Whispering Smith (1916) 5, 6
Whispering Smith (1926) 16, 17, 30
Whispering Smith (1948) 51, 54
White, Stewart Edward 9, 10, 11, 18, 47
The White Buffalo 118
The White Buffalo (1977) 118
White Gold (1927) 18
White Oak (1921) 10, 11
Whiting, Richard 20
Whitman, Stuart 16, 85
Whitmore, James 10, 120
Who Rides with Wyatt 100, 101

Wiard, William 121
Wichita (1955) 67, 68
Wicked Water 63
Widmark, Richard 3, 53, 57, 67, 80, 83, 85, 91, 92, 98, 101, 102
Wild Bill (1995) 138
The Wild Bunch (1969) 66, 100, 101, 102, 103, 112, 113, 121, 123, 126, 129, 139
The Wild Horse 66
Wild Horse Mesa 15, 25, 49
Wild Horse Mesa (1925) 15
Wild Horse Mesa (1932) 25
Wild Horse Mesa (1947) 49
Wild Wild West (1999) 141
Wilde, Cornel 5, 130
Wilder, Gene 141
Wilder, John 136
Wilder, Robert 75, 76
Wilke, Robert (J.) 107, 130
Will Penny (1968) 99, 100, 118, 129
Willat, Irvin 14, 15, 116
Willes, Jean 12, 69, 130
Williams, Bill 133
William, Elmo 60
Williams, Guinn ("Big Boy") 28, 86
Williams, John 109, 111, 116
Williams, Kathlyn 4
Williams, Rhys 101
Williams, Russell 130
Willie Boy 100, 101
Willingham, Calder 84, 85, 104
Wills, Chill 40, 77, 81, 82, 85, 89, 119
Wilson, Gertrude 10
Wilson, Lois 12, 14, 16, 25, 123
Wilson, Owen 141
Wilson, Stuart 140
Wincer, Simon 129
Winchester '73 (1950) 55, 56, 57, 65, 100
Windsor, Marie 11, 141
The Wings of Eagles (1957) 71
Winnetou 93
The Winning of Barbara Worth 16, 17, 45
The Winning of Barbara Worth (1926) 16, 17
Winninger, Charles 101
Winningham, Mare 137
Winters, Shelley 99
Wise, Robert 3
Wiseman, Joseph 8
Wister, Owen 3, 4, 7, 8, 12, 14, 19, 21, 31, 32, 40, 46, 48, 143
Withers, Grant 79
Witney, William 5
Wolf Song (1929) 19, 20, 22
Wolfe, Ian 133
Wolheim, Louis 22
The Woman of the Town (1944) 44
A Woman's Fool (1918) 7, 8
Wonder, Stevie 141

The Wonderful Country 78, 80, 143
The Wonderful Country (1959) 78, 80, 126, 139
Wood, Natalie 70, 71
Wood, Sam 15, 54
Woods, Harry 99
Wooley, Sheb 10
Woonston, Ellen 18
Worden, Hank 133
Wray, Fay 22, 23, 28
Wright, Harold Bell 9, 10, 14, 15, 17, 19, 28, 29, 40, 41, 44, 45
Wright, Teresa 8, 49
Wright, Will 86
Wrigley, Dewey 32
Wurlitzer, Rudolph 111
Wyatt, Jane 43
Wyatt Earp (1994) 137, 138
Wyatt Earp: Frontier Marshal 27, 28, 32, 46, 47, 48, 58

Wyckoff, Alvin 3, 4, 5, 73
Wyler, William 22, 23, 37, 38, 39, 54, 75, 76, 77, 121
Wymore, Patrice 16
Wynn, Keenan 6, 127
Wyoming 14
Wyoming (1947) 115

"Yankee Gold" 63
The Yankee Senor (1926) 16, 17
Yellow Sky (1948) 51, 53, 63, 100, 115
Yellowleg 84
Yellowstone Kelly 78
Yellowstone Kelly (1959) 78
Yojimbo (*The Bodyguard*, 1961) 93
Yordan, Philip 66, 67, 68, 75, 77
York, Jeff 138
Young, Carleton 108
Young, Loretta 30, 40, 45, 46, 141
Young, Rob 133

Young, Robert 40, 140
Young, Victor 30, 32, 37, 38, 41, 49, 54, 63, 66, 68, 70, 72, 73
Young, Waldemar 12, 29
Young Billy Young (1969) 100, 101
Young Guns (1988) 128, 129
Young Guns II (1990) 130, 132
The Young Land (1959) 78
Yowlachie, Chief 96

Zamparelli, Elsa 130
Zandy's Bride (1974) 113, 114
Zane, Billy 135
Zeliff, Seymour 14
Zerbe, Anthony 29, 114
Zeta-Jones, Catherine 140
Zinnemann, Fred 59, 60, 61, 62, 69, 74, 132, 139
Zsigmond, Vilmos 23, 120
Zuckerman, George 6, 139
Zwick, Edward 130

www.ingramcontent.com/pod-product-compliance
Lightning Source LLC
Chambersburg PA
CBHW081557300426
44116CB00015B/2915